Intersensory Perception and Sensory Integration

PERCEPTION AND PERCEPTUAL DEVELOPMENT

A Critical Review Series

Series Editors:
Herbert L. Pick, Jr.
University of Minnesota, Minneapolis, Minnesota
and
Richard D. Walk
George Washington University, Washington, D.C.

Volume 1   **Perception and Experience**
Edited by Richard D. Walk and Herbert L. Pick, Jr.

Volume 2   **Intersensory Perception and Sensory Integration**
Edited by Richard D. Walk and Herbert L. Pick, Jr.

A Continuation Order Plan is available for this series. A continuation order will bring delivery of each new volume immediately upon publication. Volumes are billed only upon actual shipment. For further information please contact the publisher.

Intersensory Perception and Sensory Integration

Edited by
RICHARD D. WALK
George Washington University
Washington, D.C.

and
HERBERT L. PICK, JR.
University of Minnesota
Minneapolis, Minnesota

PLENUM PRESS • **NEW YORK AND LONDON**

Library of Congress Cataloging in Publication Data

Main entry under title:

Intersensory perception and sensory integration.

   (Perception and perceptual development; v. 2)
   Includes bibliographical references and index.
   1. Perception. 2. Intersensory effects. I. Walk, Richard D. II. Pick, Herbert L. III. Series.
[DNLM: 1. Perception. 2. Sensation. W1 PE78GM v. 2/WL 705 I62]
BF311.I59   153.7   80-29204
ISBN 0-306-40610-1

© 1981 Plenum Press, New York
A Division of Plenum Publishing Corporation
227 West 17th Street, New York, N.Y. 10011

Printed in the United States of America

Contributors

Eugene Abravanel, Department of Psychology, George Washington University, Washington, D.C.

Emily W. Bushnell, Department of Psychology, Tufts University, Medford, Massachusetts

George Butterworth, Department of Psychology, University of Southampton, Southampton, England

Malcolm M. Cohen, Naval Air Development Center, Warminster, Pennsylvania

Bryant J. Cratty, Department of Kinesiology, University of California, Los Angeles, California

James E. Cutting, Department of Psychology, Cornell University, Ithaca, New York

Paul Fraisse, Centre H. Pieron, Université René Descartes, Paris, France

B. Hermelin, Medical Research Council (MRC), Developmental Psychology Unit, London, England

Bill Jones, Department of Psychology, Carleton University, Ottawa, Ontario, Canada

James R. Lackner, Department of Psychology, Brandeis University, Waltham, Massachusetts

Susanna Millar, Department of Experimental Psychology, University of Oxford, Oxford, England

N. O'Connor, Medical Research Center (MRC), Developmental Psychology Unit, London, England

Herbert L. Pick, Jr., Center for Research in Human Learning, University of Minnesota, Minneapolis, Minnesota

Dennis R. Proffitt, Department of Psychology, University of Virginia, Charlottesville, Virginia

Jacqueline M. F. Samuel, Department of Psychology, George Washington University, Washington, D.C.

Richard D. Walk, Department of Psychology, George Washington University, Washington, D.C.

Preface

This volume on intersensory perception and sensory integration is the second volume of the series, *Perception and Perceptual Development: A Critical Review Series*. The topic of the volume is timely, for in recent years, many investigators have noted that information about any natural event is obtained by a perceiver from a variety of sources. Such an observation immediately leads to the question of how this information is synthesized and organized. Of course, the implication that there are several discrete input channels that must be processed has come under immediate attack by researchers such as the Gibsons. They find it extremely artificial to regard natural information as being cut up and requiring cementing. Nevertheless, the possibility that during ontogenesis, perception involves the integration of separate information has attracted the attention of scholars concerned with both normal and abnormal development. In the case of normal development, a lively controversy has arisen between those who believe perceptual development goes from integration toward differentiation and those who hold the opposite view. In the case of abnormal psychological development such as learning disabilities, many workers have suggested that perceptual integration is at fault.

In thinking about the issues raised in this volume, we are particularly indebted to our former teachers and colleagues: Eleanor and James Gibson, T. A. Ryan, Robert B. MacLeod, and Jerome Bruner.

We are pleased to acknowledge the secretarial help of Karen Weeks in the preparation of this volume. Preparation of the book was supported in part by a Program Project Grant from the National Institute of Child Health and Human Development (HD–05027) to the Institute of Child Development, by the Center for Research in Human Learning of the University of Minnesota, and by a National Institutes of Health Biomedical Research Support Grant (2–S07–RR07019–14) to George Washington University.

HERBERT L. PICK, JR.
RICHARD D. WALK

Introduction

This book is concerned with the interrelation of sense modalities. How does stimulation of one modality—vision, for example—interact with that of another—audition, for example? The book's primary focus is on the perceptual aspects of intermodal relations in contrast with sensory aspects. Thus none of the contributions addresses such questions as whether stimulation of one sense modality changes the threshold for detection of stimulation in another. Rather, the chapters address such questions as whether a tactual and visual shape are the same, or whether a visual and auditory spatial locus are perceived as the same place.

It seems patently obvious that the way to understand perception is to analyze how sensory stimulation is processed by the different sense modalities. In fact, it sometimes appears that there is no other alternative. This pervasive view is perhaps a tribute to the success of Johanes Müller's doctrine of Specific Nerve Energies. According to this doctrine the different qualities of our sensory experience were based on the nerve energies which the different nerves carried from receptor organ to brain, or on the particular loci of the brain at which these nerves ended. Müller's doctrine was based on the anatomical and physiological evidence of the time and on a philosophical tradition which argued that we could not know anything of the external world, only the state of our nerves. Müller's doctrine led in turn to the structuralist psychology of Wundt and Titchener, in which our mental experience was analyzed in terms of a set of attributes such as quality, intensity, protensity, attensity, etc. Any given percept could be broken down into sensations of vision, audition, taste, etc., of a particular intensity, duration, clarity and size, or combinations of these attributes. Although the extreme mentalism of this approach is now gone, its heritage is still reflected in our emphasis on the processing of stimulation by the specific sense modalities. Consider, for example, the typical courses in a psychology department on vision and audition. (There are usually no courses for the other sense modalities simply because there is not as big a knowledge base for how these work.) And consider the listing in psychological abstracts of the main topics for audition, vision, and the lower senses.

Our current commonsense view of how to understand perception has not always been so one-track. Although the concept of separate sense modalities can be traced back to Aristotle, he also had the concept of *sensus comunis,* which referred to a capacity for awareness of properties which were common to the various sense modalities. These resembled the attributes of the structural psychologists, and included, for example, magnitude, number, form, unity, and motion. (See Marks, 1978 for a review and analysis of this concept.) Focus on this aspect of perception draws our attention away from the separate sense modalities and permits us to consider the common information that we gain about the world. Although the attributes of Aristotle's *sensus comunis* are fairly abstract, thinking about these common attributes permits one to take seriously an alternative way of understanding perception. This alternative, following Gibson (1966), involves analyzing the way stimulation provides information about the real world as we believe it exists. The implications of such an approach for intermodal aspects of perception are that instead of an analysis of separate sense modalities perception is analyzed in terms of the information which is acquired about important aspects of the world, or for various specific purposes whether through one or several of the traditional sense modalities. This is a very functional approach to perception and is brought out in this book most explicitly in Cohen's chapter on visual-proprioceptive interactions.

Both of these approaches to intermodal perception and sensory integration generate their own problems and questions, many of which are the topics of chapters in this volume. The classic sense-modality approach is both anatomically and phenomenologically based. Each sense modality has its own receptor organ and nerve system and creates particular qualities of experience. But this immediately leads to the question of specifying the sense modalities. This is easy for audition, vision, odor, and taste, which have obvious receptor organs. But what of touch, proprioception, and kinesthesis? What are the receptor organs? For touch, the skin? But what of deep pressure and somatic perception? For proprioception, are joints, muscle spindles, and tendon organs all to be considered part of the receptor organ? These are the anatomical questions. Phenomenologically, there also seem to be problems of specification. For kinesthesis we sense ourselves being moved when the vestibular apparatus is stimulated in an appropriate way. But we get the same perception from visual stimulation, and in fact in some conflict situations the visual kinesthesis is stronger (Lee & Lishman, 1975). Butterworth's chapter in the present volume describes some similar experiments with children.

Perhaps these questions of specifying sense modalities can be solved. We also want to know how the information of the different sense modalities gets integrated. The first aspect of this question is whether the integration is built into the organism or whether it develops as a function of experience. This nativism–empiricism issue was one of the earliest to interest philosophers and psychologists, and many of the chapters in this volume address it in one way or another.

The next aspect of the question how information gets integrated concerns what, specifically, the integration is like. One might consider three scenarios. In the first, each sense modality has an equal status, and stimulation via any particular modality is encoded in a modality-specific form. When it is to be integrated for use with other modality-specific information it is translated by some sort of correspondence rules; yet the information never really loses its modality-specific identity. In the second scenario, there is a hierarchical order of sense modalities for any particular type of information. Irrespective of the modality through which the information is acquired, it gets translated and recorded in a form which is relevant to a particular modality. For example, Pick (1974) made such an analysis with respect to spatial information. The argument was that spatial information was encoded in a visually relevant form no matter what the input modality. See Freides (1974) for an extension of this line of reasoning. In the present volume, Samuel applies this sort of analysis in making predictions about individual differences in intermodal relations. Finally, according to the third scenario, information going through any particular modality is translated into an amodal form and is equally available to relate to new information originating in any modality. If the classic sense-modality approach is accepted, it seems possible, in principle, at least to distinguish experimentally among these different scenarios.

The last scenario of amodal encoding may bring us close to the second general functional approach discussed above. The main difference would seem to be that in the functional approach the amodal representation of information is taken directly from original stimulation. There is no intermediate modality encoding at all. The functional approach poses its own problems, partially overlapping with those of the classical modality approach. First we have to decide what kinds of information can be and are abstracted amodally from the stimulation. For example, information can be extracted from the optic array for self-movement. This is normally redundant with classical kinesthetic information about self-movement. It is difficult from this point of view to know how the separate sense modalities contribute to a variable of self-movement. From the classical modality point of view the separate modalities can be isolated or placed in conflict. But from the functional point of view such procedures are artificial and may not result in normal information processing. Secondly, the functional approach does not avoid the anatomical issue. The question of by what mechanism stimulation is transduced from the environment must be solved sometime. Receptors and receptor organs are important at some level. It is possible that the functional approach will direct the attention of those investigating receptor mechanisms to somewhat different or additional questions, but the basic questions are still there. Finally, the nativism–empiricism question still remains. Its form is somewhat different. No longer is it asked whether the integrating of information from the separate sense modalities is built into the organism or whether it is built up from experience. But a new question is posed as to whether the extraction of amodal variables from various sources and combinations of sources of stimulation occurs as a function of maturation or experience.

The functional orientation toward intermodal processing of information emphasizes perception in the service of some purpose. Very often this purpose is action. Action is an important locus for the study of intermodal processes because it is always accompanied by stimulation via a number of the classical modalities. In most ordinary acts we receive visual, proprioceptive, tactual, and kinesthetic feedback stimulation, and of course have knowledge of efferent innervation. How is all of this integrated? A number of chapters in this volume address issues relevant to this question.

The reader will find the issues raised in the foregoing analysis implicit in many of the chapters even when they are not made explicit. The book is divided into three sections. In the first section intermodal relations are analyzed with a focus on perceptual development. (Bushnell and Butterworth are concerned primarily with infants, and Jones and Abravanel with older children.) The nativism–empiricism issue is a central one in the chapters in this section, and the reader will note that there is still a lively controversy as to whether intermodal relations are best thought of as going from a primitive unity to differentiated modalities or whether they are better understood as starting from separate and distinct modalities, being integrated as a function of development. The second section includes chapters on intermodal relations in adults. It is heavily oriented toward intermodal relations in sensorimotor activities but also includes intermodal aspects of rhythm perception (Fraisse). The final section focuses on intermodal relations with respect to special populations. The research discussed in these chapters contributes toward a general understanding of intermodal relations and at the same time helps in explaining the behavior of those particular groups: the blind (O'Connor & Hermelin; Millar), deaf and retarded children (O'Connor & Hermelin), and various types of athletes (Samuel). Motor aspects of intermodal relations are also included in this section in Cratty's analysis of the motor-training programs for children with learning difficulties.

References

Friedes, D. Human information processing and sensory modality: Cross-modal functions, information complexity, memory, and deficit. *Psychological Bulletin,* 1974, *81,* 284–310.

Gibson, J.J. *The senses considered as perceptual systems.* New York: Houghton Mifflin, 1966.

Lee, D.N., & Lishman, J.R. Visual proprioceptive control of stance. *Journal of Human Movement Studies,* 1975, *1,* 87–95.

Marks, L.E. The unity of the senses: Interrelations among the modalities. New York: Academic Press, 1978.

Pick, H.L., Jr. The visual coding of non-visual spatial information. In R.B. MacLeod & H.L. Pick, Jr. (Eds.), *Perception: Essays in honor of James J. Gibson.* Ithaca: Cornell University Press, 1974.

Contents

3 • **Integrating the Information from Eyes and Hands: A Developmental
     Account**
     Eugene Abravanel

4 • **The Developmental Significance of Cross-Modal Matching**
     Bill Jones

7 · Multisensory Aspects of Rhythm
Paul Fraisse

10 · Coding Strategies of Normal and Handicapped Children
N. O'Connor and B. Hermelin

11 · Sensory-Motor and Perceptual-Motor Theories and Practices: An Overview and Evaluation
Bryant J. Cratty

12 · Individual Differences in the Interaction of Vision and Proprioception
Jacqueline M. F. Samuel

Intersensory Perception and Sensory Integration in Children

Introduction

The first section of the present volume carefully analyzes the development of intermodal relations in normal children. Bushnell and Butterworth both examine this development in infants while Abravanel and Jones concentrate on children of preschool age and above. The point of departure for all these chapters is the originally philosophical issue of whether intersensory coordination develops as a function of experience or whether it is in some sense innate. However, the authors all stress somewhat different aspects of this issue. Bushnell, while concentrating empirically on the relation between visual and tactual perception, begins with the contrast between Bower's view of the neonatal organism as possessing a primitive unity of the senses and Piaget's more empiricist view that the equivalence of sensory inputs from different modalities is a function of experience. Butterworth also contrasts the concept of this primitive unity with an empiricist view in his focus on the relation between visual and auditory perception. Later in his chapter, when he considers visual kinesthesis, Butterworth moves to the issue of object–self differentiation in perceptual development. The issue of visual kinesthesis (our perception of our own movement via visual stimulation) becomes important in relation to the question of whether the proximal sensory modalities—touch, proprioception, kinesthesis—provide meaning for or calibrate the distal modalities—vision and audition—by an associative mechanism. To the extent that visual kinesthesis is present in very young babies, such a simple empiricist hypothesis seems untenable. Both Bushnell and Butterworth suggest that the contrast as typically posed is somewhat simplistic. Their common alternative solution is to suggest that there is not an innate equivalence of sense-modality information but rather an innate mechanism for helping the infant find those modality-specific types of information which are equivalent. For example, Bushnell suggests that behaviors like the rooting and tonic neck reflexes create conditions for the infant to realize the environmentally highly probable connection between tactual stimulation and a visual source of such stimulation. At the same time, Butterworth cites facts such as that neonates turn their eyes in response to auditory stimuli as evidence for an inherent connection between the auditory and visual systems. He points out that such reflexive connections do not in any sense imply reflective knowledge. However, they may be the basis for subsequent development of reflective knowledge.

Butterworth also reiterates another distinction made by Bower; namely, that an innate association between two or more sense modalities might occur with or without modality differentiation. That is, one may perceive a single object or event on the basis of simultaneous auditory and visual stimulation but still not be aware that the two pathways of information are different or even, for that matter, that there are two pathways. Alternatively, one could be aware that the pathways are different and in fact know which is which while still perceiving a single object. Actually, it is difficult to imagine how one would be aware that simultaneous information from two modalities specified the same object unless there were some more general correspondence of information between the two modalities. For example, simple simultaneous stimulation over two sense modalities should not generally specify the same object, since we are always being stimulated via several modalities and in general the sources of stimulation are not the same. A baby may very well be looking at a mobile hanging over her head while hearing her father's voice. To further specify identity of information source over two sensory modalities would probably require mapping of spatial location between two modalities or an identity of temporal patterning in the stimulation from two modalities. Butterworth does review a number of studies which illustrate the young infant's sensitivity to intermodal congruence of temporal patterning.

In their analysis of development of intermodal relations in children older than infants, both Abravanel and Jones also begin with a philosophical analysis of the issues. Jones points out that, theoretically, it may be no more puzzling that two things are perceived as equivalent when information is derived from two sensory modalities than that two things are perceived as equivalent when the information is derived from a single sense modality. However, few regard the latter as a particularly knotty problem. Because they are dealing with older children, Abravanel and Jones stress the question as to whether performance on intramodal tasks improves faster with age than performance on intermodal tasks. In this connection, they both are critical of the widely cited work of Birch and Lefford for not experimentally determining whether intramodal improvements were responsible for the intermodal improvement they observed. Both Abravanel and Jones are particularly concerned with the way information is analyzed in the different sense modalities. In Abravanel's analysis, research is examined with a focus on the perceptual activity in which the subjects actually engage during intermodal tasks. Jones, on the other hand, pays more attention to the methodology and design of the studies of intra- and intermodal research and in the patterning of results from such investigations.

The Ontogeny of Intermodal Relations: Vision and Touch in Infancy

EMILY W. BUSHNELL

1. Introduction

The ontogeny of intermodal functioning and knowledge has long been considered by philosophers and psychologists. The question of the origin and development of cross-modal knowledge was raised in the seventeenth century, when Molyneux wrote his famous letter to Locke inquiring about the abilities of a blind man hypothetically restored to sight (cited in Gregory, 1966). The answer to this monumental query is still a matter for debate.

> How does the human organism arrive at the position where the perceptual systems are coordinated with each other so that, for example, stimulation to one modality gives rise to expectancies for stimulation to another? (McGurk, Turnure, & Creighton, 1977, p. 138)

Some argue that intersensory liaisons are inborn. Bower (1974, 1977), for instance, believes that the senses are coordinated at birth. He claims that even for newborns, visible variables specify tactual consequences, auditory stimulation specifies something to see and to touch, and tactual stimulation specifies something to see. In fact, according to Bower, the senses at birth are not at all differentiated from one another;

EMILY W. BUSHNELL • Department of Psychology, Paige Hall, Tufts University, Medford, Massachusetts 02155.

a "primitive unity" of the senses exists and the infant's perception is "supramodal." "It seems that a very young baby may not know whether he is hearing something or seeing something" (Bower, 1977, p. 78). Development is seen by Bower as a process of differentiation, which is determined by maturational increases in information-processing capacities and environmental reinforcement contingencies. The infant becomes increasingly sensitive to which modality registers each input and also dissociates the senses, understanding, for example, that something visible need not be graspable nor must something which can be heard be visible.

Opposing the innateness view represented by Bower are those who maintain that during the early stages of infancy the various perceptual systems are independent. Development is thus a process of integration. This integration is accomplished via various means according to different theorists. The empiricists, such as Berkeley and Helmholtz (discussed in E. J. Gibson, 1969), as well as the developmental psychologist Jean Piaget (Piaget, 1952) believe that experience is responsible for the coordination of the senses. The world contains lawful stimulus correlations, and by simply interacting with the world, the infant discovers these correlations. For example, a particular shape always produces a distinct visual impression and also a distinct tactual impression. Through simultaneously looking at and touching such a shape, the child notes the repeated co-occurrence of the unique visual and tactual impressions. The two sensory impressions become associated, equivalent, substitutes for one another, or as Piaget says, "reciprocally assimilated."

I do not believe that these two views are incompatible. Intermodal development is not a matter of integration *or* differentiation. Rather, if the rich variety of relations which are possible between inputs from two senses is acknowledged, it is apparent that *both* of these processes must occur before one's understanding of reality is congruent with that reality. In this chapter I present a speculative outline of cross-modal development. The outline covers only the period of infancy, since I believe the most basic and universal aspects of cross-modal functioning develop during this period. Except for an initial example, the discussion is also limited to relations between the two senses, vision and touch. The analysis of this pair will sufficiently illustrate a developmental sequence and developmental processes which I believe apply to relations between all pairs of senses. I should also state at the outset that J.J. Gibson's conceptualization of the senses as systems for obtaining information (Gibson, 1962, 1966) has been adopted here. The senses are thought of as active instruments which seek and explore, not as passive recipients. Thus throughout this chapter, when touching or the tactual sense is spoken of, actions such as reaching toward objects and manual search are included. Although these certainly may be considered motor behaviors, here they are considered perceptual activities, just as ocular scanning is perceptual. A flow chart (see Figure 1) of the developmental sequence to be presented is offered at the end of the chapter. It might be useful to study that figure briefly before going on to read the outline in detail.

2. The Neonate

It is my contention that the neonate possesses little if any cross-modal knowledge of any kind. There is certainly no logical imperative that the infant begin life with any such knowledge. Quite to the contrary, reason would seem to favor the view that cross-modal correspondences may generally be acquired through experience. Spelke and Owsley (1977) have demonstrated that infants just 4 months old will look toward the one of their parents whose voice is played on a neutrally located tape recorder. This intermodal behavior must have been acquired, since faces and voices are related in an arbitrary rather than a systematic fashion. Two persons with quite similar faces may have very dissimilar voices, and two persons with quite different faces may have similar voices. One can predict what the face will look like from the sound of a voice only if one is acquainted with the person to whom the face and the voice belong. If idiosyncratic intersensory coordinations such as those between faces and voices can be detected by very young infants as Spelke and Owsley showed, then it is entirely possible that more systematic ones such as those between visual and tactual shapes or visual and tactual locations become known via experience as well. It is indeed rather plausible, given the countless exposures which occur during each day to objects and events which exemplify such systematic intersensory coordinations. Furthermore, adults are able to adapt to artificially induced changes in the "calibrations" of visual and tactual "scales" for various perceptual properties, such as the changes in size, location, and shape effected by magnifying and minifying lenses, wedge prisms, and telestereoscopes (cf. E.J. Gibson, 1969; Held, 1965). That they do so is evidence that these calibrations are not fixed at birth.

In addition, there is no unequivocal evidence that the neonate possesses visual-tactual knowledge of any kind. One behavior which has been studied extensively and which is related to intersensory functioning is reaching. An extension of the hand toward a seen target may indicate that for the reacher, visual and tactual locations are equivalent, that something visible indexes something palpable at the same spot. Bower, Broughton, and Moore (1970a) reported that they observed directed reaching in neonate humans. They presented five 6- to 11-day-old infants with a small sphere in five different positions, and they observed that 70% of all arm extensions by the infants were within 5° of the object at their zeniths. Bower later reported that these infants actually contacted the sphere on 40% of their arm extensions (Bower, 1974).

However, there are a number of methodological problems in the Bower *et al.* research. Notable among these are the lack of any objective criteria for classifying an arm movement as an extension and the failure to include a control period during which no visual object is present but the infant's hand and arm movements are nevertheless carefully observed. Two groups of researchers conducted studies similar to Bower's but with improved procedures (Dodwell, Muir, & DiFranco, 1976; Ruff & Halton, 1977). Neither group was able to validate Bower's report of reaching by newborns. Each concluded that their subjects' arm movements in the presence of visual stimuli were neither directed nor intentional, and each observed considerably less contact than Bower reported.

A number of psychologists have observed infants longitudinally and in natural circumstances; none of these have seen any reaching during the newborn period. The infants studied by Piaget (1952) and by White, Castle, and Held (1964), for example, reportedly engaged in both visual and manual activities during the first weeks after birth, but these were unrelated. The infants were not observed to follow with their eyes the movements of their hands, to reach toward objects they saw, or to look toward objects clutched in their hands.

Bower's report of reaching by neonates (Bower *et al.*, 1970a) is thus at odds with the results of more explicit, adequately controlled laboratory studies and naturalistic, longitudinal studies. It seems fair to conclude that neonates do not try to touch what is seen. The converse of reaching, turning the eyes toward what is touched or felt, may also indicate that visual and tactual space are coordinated or equivalent for the organism at some level. All researchers, including Bower, agree that newborns do not look toward their hands if they are contacted by something or someone or if something is placed in them (Bower, Broughton, & Moore, 1970b; Piaget, 1952).

Another behavior indicative of visual-tactual space coordination is recognition of the discrepancy posed by a virtual object. A virtual object is an optically created visual image of an object which appears tangible, but is not. Adults react to such violations of nature with verbalizations, smiling and laughter, and inspection of the optical device to see how the trick is accomplished. Were infants to show any sort of analogous reactions, then they too must have expected that something would be contacted at the visual image's location. Bower *et al.* (1970a) presented a virtual object created by a stereoscopic shadow-caster to 11 infants aged 8–31 days. The virtual object was moved in toward the infant until reaching for it began and was left in front of the infant as long as reaching persisted or until the infant became upset. "The results were that all the virtual object infants cried, with a latency after the first reach of 15–75 seconds" (p. 680). Bower *et al.* (1970b) concluded that "from the very beginning the infant is aware of the conflict between visual and tactual that is posed by the virtual object" (p. 53).

As with Bower's neonatal-reaching study, the virtual-object study is subject to a number of criticisms. The choice of crying as the critical response is perhaps the most serious flaw. There were a number of other factors in Bower's experiment which may have provoked crying, including two potentially upsetting but purely visual properties of the stereoscopic display (see Gordon & Yonas, 1976) and the fact that the virtual-object infants (but not the control infants) had to wear goggles and sit in the dark. Furthermore, other researchers who have presented virtual objects to infants have not observed distress as one of the responses to the situation (Bushnell, 1979b; Field, 1977; Gordon & Yonas, 1976; Lamson, 1976). It seems quite likely that the crying Bower observed was indicative of something other than visual-tactual coordination.

Thus of those researchers observing newborn infants, only Bower claims to have evidence for visual-tactual coordination. "However, such evidence has been called into question on methodological grounds, and, pending replication, these studies should not be taken as a challenge" (Ramsay & Campos, 1978, pp. 84–85) to the empiricist viewpoint adopted here and otherwise uncontested by the literature. Intersensory development takes off from birth, at which point vision and touch are not integrated. However, they are not then necessarily differentiated; integration and differentiation are by no means the only relations possible nor are they mutually exclusive. The newborn does not know that visual and tactual inputs have implications for one another, nor does he know that vision and touch are distinct modalities. Rather, I propose he knows nothing concerning the relations between vision and touch. Each of these senses provides stimulation to which the newborn responds, but he does not behave in accord with any beliefs about the two senses' bearings on one another, either positive or negative, any more than he behaves in accord with notions about the possible relations between two inputs from the same sensory channel.

From this lowly starting point, how does the development of visual-tactual knowledge proceed? Although the neonate has no intersensory knowledge, he does have a number of behaviors which ensure the discovery of the visual-tactual relations which exist in our world. First, the newborn has localization abilities in the two senses being discussed, namely, vision and touch. Researchers using a variety of techniques have observed that the newborn can and does aim the eye at visual stimuli located in space (cf. Brazelton, 1969; Bronson, 1974; Harris & Macfarlane, 1974; Salapatek & Kessen, 1966). Similarly, the newborn responds to tactual stimulation with directionally appropriate movements of particular body parts (cf. Brazelton, 1969; Twitchell, 1970). These newborn within-mode localization behaviors are sensorimotor reflexes and do not represent any real conceptual knowledge of space. However, even they are something more than exists for cross-modal knowledge. While newborns reflexively aim their eyes at visual stimuli, they do not similarly aim their eyes at tactual stimuli. Although they respond reflexively with hand movements to tactual stimulation to their hands, they do not move their hands in response to visual stimulation. At birth, visual space and tactual space exist, but they are not related to one another.

The neonate also possesses at least two reflexes which are ideally suited for effecting the equivalence of visual and tactual locations which is absent at birth. These are the rooting reflex and the tonic neck reflex (TNR). The rooting reflex obviously evolved for reasons having to do with feeding and not for reasons having to do with the coordination of vision and touch. However, since both eyes and mouth are located in the same head, when the infant turns the mouth toward the stroking nipple, the eyes also turn toward it. If the infant's eyes are open and if feeding is not initiated in the dark, the infant will "accidentally" see the stimulus which elicited rooting. This coincidental (so far as the infant is concerned) pairing of visual and tactual stimulation in time and space occurs repeatedly in the early days of life.

The tonic neck reflex similarly provides the infant with countless instances of visual and tactual stimulation coincident in time and space. According to Brazelton (1969), this postural reflex probably exists since it facilitates the baby's delivery from the uterus, and it influences behavior for several months after birth. Note that a baby in the TNR position is pointing with the arm and gazing with the eyes toward the same direction. If the baby happened to contact anything manually, that contact would be "accidentally" observed visually.

The TNR may be involved in the question of relations between vision and touch in infancy in another way, too. It seems possible that the "reaches" or "extensions" observed by Bower et al. (1970a), Dodwell et al. (1976), and Ruff and Halton (1977) were artifacts introduced by postural tendencies of the neonate such as the TNR. When an infant turns the head to look at a visual stimulus presented off-midline, the TNR is set off. The consequent arm extension may appear to be an attempt to contact the visual stimulus. The arm extension may even result in contact some of the time, given that the stimulus is of reasonable

size and placed within arm's length. Yet the apparent reaching and occasional contact are entirely fortuitous and due to the TNR rather than to any intention or cross-modal knowledge on the infant's part.

3. Equivalence of Location

According to the view proposed here, the first intersensory knowledge to fill the neonatal void asserted above is the knowledge that visual space and tactual space are equivalent. The establishment in infancy of the equivalence of visual and tactual space follows a pattern which I believe is common in intersensory development and in human intellectual development generally. Developmentally, *performing* knowledge precedes *conscious* knowledge. Performing knowledge refers to intersensory behaviors which are unaccompanied by cognitive activities concerning sensory inputs. The organism behaves appropriately so far as the inputs from two sensory channels are concerned, but these behaviors are "unanalyzed routines," acquired and controlled by mechanical means, such as sensorimotor reflex chains, conditioning, or mimicry. Initially, knowledge of this performing sort is acquired and applied to just a few specific situations. Once some critical number of specific and individually learned instances which all operate alike is accumulated, the commonality among them is noted. A "rule" is abstracted, an invariant detected, etc. This performance rule is then applied generally to novel situations as well as to the familiar ones which engendered it. It is in fact overapplied, employed in situations for which it is not appropriate. This overgeneralization is unequivocal evidence that a general rule has been abstracted, though the rule does not yet represent conscious knowledge as it is not yet amenable to reflection by the organism behaving in accord with it. After the rule has been abstracted and applied for some time and the pertinent behaviors have attained a certain level of fluidity, the behavioral routines are internally analyzed and knowledge is elevated to the conscious level. Conscious knowledge entails that intersensory behaviors are supported by some sort of conceptual awareness or intelligent thinking about sensory inputs, and they may be accompanied by cognitive activities, such as expectancy, surprise, evaluation, and correction. At this point (and not before), violations of and exceptions to the rule can be noted, mistakes of the overgeneralization sort can be recognized. Finally, specific rules or ways to cope with the exceptions to the general rule can be learned. This general pattern of development, moving from scattered appropriate behavior to understanding a natural or man-made system and its exceptions, is clearly illustrated by aspects of language acquisition (for instance, cf. Brown, 1973; Cazden, 1968; and

Clark, 1974). Let me next describe in detail how, it seems to me, the development of knowledge about the relations between visual and tactual space fits this pattern.

Recall that for the neonate visual and tactual space are not integrated. Newborns neither reach out to touch what they see nor turn to see what they feel touching them. The first advance beyond this state of affairs is that infants learn for a few particular items that where they see the objects they are also touchable and where they touch the objects they are also visible. This initial specific-item learning is probably just a matter of discriminative operant conditioning or, as Piaget more elegantly phrases it, attempts "destined to make interesting sights last." The ecology of the young infant's world along with the rooting reflex and the TNR guarantee that the baseline operant level of seeing and touching the same location simultaneously is high. Such accidental instances are apt to be reinforced. Chance contacts with objects while watching them often have as their results the swinging of the objects, pleasurable tactual consequences, or interesting auditory effects. For behaviors which occur and are reinforced frequently in the presence of a certain discriminative stimulus, the operant "rate of emission" increases whenever that stimulus is again confronted—the infant reliably strikes out at a particular mobile, for instance. Such accurate, fisted "swiping" toward particular objects has usually been observed first when infants are about 2 months old (cf. Brazelton, 1969; White *et al.,* 1964). At this point, the infant has performing knowledge of the equivalence of visual and tactual space, but only in those few specific situations in which intermodal behavior has occurred and been reinforced frequently and consistently.

Support for the suggestion that visually stimulated reaching is initially item-specific is primarily anecdotal. Piaget's child Laurent reached for and grasped his father's hand upon seeing it before he attempted to grasp other visually presented objects (Piaget, 1952). Mothers frequently report that their infants strike out at their crib gyms or other particular toys before they reach for any and every object seen. For many children the first "object" localized visually and then reached for is their own hand. Consider, for example, Piaget's observation 73, which also points out the initial fortuitousness of simultaneous looking and touching:

> In effect, through clasping of the hands which necessarily takes place in front of the face in a reclining child, Laurent eventually studied them by looking at them attentively. This regular connection, although its cause is fortuitous, results quite naturally in leading to the influence of the glance on the movement of the hand. Thus at 0;2 (24) Laurent rubs his hands, 5 to 10 cm. from his mouth, without sucking them. He separates them and then grasps them again at least twenty times in succession while looking at them. It would appear, in such an instance, that visual pleasure alone were the cause of the repetition of the phenomenon. (1952, p. 104)

White *et al.* (1964) also observed infants visually monitoring their hands' approach and interplay as they clasped them at midline before the same infants reliably reached for objects offered to them. There is also some evidence that differences in the amount of opportunity for fortuitous visual-tactual behavior and consequent reinforcement are related to differences in the age at which intentional reaching is first exhibited (cf. Bower, 1977; Piaget, 1952; White & Held, 1966). Such a relation supports the suggested role of a process like operant conditioning in the initial equating of visual and tactual locations.

Thus, by the age of around 3 months, infants have equated visual and tactual space with regard to a few particular items. They consistently reach out to touch the sight of their own hands, their dangling toys, etc. Shortly after this, when visual and tactual locations have been individually equated for several specific items, this performing knowledge generalizes. A "rule" is abstracted from experience with a limited number of objects and is applied to all objects. Thus, just 2 days after he first reliably reached out only for his father's hand, Laurent reached out for all manner of objects (Piaget, 1952). This abstraction and application of a general rule seems to be something beyond stimulus generalization of the learning-theory sort. It is more akin to the "induction of latent structure" which occurs during language acquisition (Brown & Bellugi, 1964). The behavioral rule "What I can see in a place I can also touch in that same place" is suddenly employed for all sorts of objects and locations, even those very different from the two or three for which location equivalence was initially slowly and mechanically established. There is nothing like a generalization gradient. Rather, visual space and tactual space are truly "mapped onto one another." A number of researchers have reported that reliable reaching for any and all seen objects is first observed when infants are between 3 and 6 months of age (e.g., Frankel, 1974; Halverson, 1931; Piaget, 1952; White *et al.,* 1964). Bower *et al.* (1970b) and Piaget (1952) are the only researchers to have investigated at what age infants turn their heads to look toward a tactual stimulus. They reported that this behavior also is first observed when infants are between 3 and 6 months of age. To illustrate, Piaget (1952) noted:

> with regard to looking at everything that is grasped, it is remarkable that this tendency appears precisely at the same time as the complementary tendency. Observations 85 and 89 show that Jacqueline at 0;6(3) and Lucienne at 0;5(1) bring to their eyes that which they grasp, on the very date when they begin to grasp systematically what they see. The same day they also tend to look at their hand when it is held outside the visual field. (p. 119)

At this time, vision and touch are coordinated or integrated, insofar as location is concerned.

For the next several months infants *over*apply this equivalence of vision and touch—they overgeneralize the abstracted rule or detected invariant. They try to touch visible things and to see things which are felt even when such efforts are inappropriate. Vision and touch are integrated for space, which they were not at birth, but they are not yet differentiated. Infants at this stage are not yet aware that vision and touch, though often redundant, are in fact distinct modalities and their inputs are not always or necessarily related. Several erroneous behaviors and constraints exhibited during the third quarter of the first year reveal this incomplete state of infants' knowledge concerning the relations between vision and touch. For example, infants have problems with glass, a surface one can see through but not reach through. Eight-month-olds typically pick and scratch at the surface of transparent barriers, trying to reach directly through the glass to obtain the objects seen on the far side (Bruner, 1970; Bushnell, 1979b). They persist in this behavior even after confronting the barrier once, and even after one demonstrates how to detour around or under the glass to obtain the object. Infants between 6 and 10 months of age also repeatedly grasp at substances such as smoke or water running from a tap, substances which are visible but not graspable. They have troubles, too, with mirrors, which consist of a surface which causes objects to be visually located in a place other than where they are tactually located. Brazelton (1969) describes an 8-month-old who "patted the image [of herself] with her hand and tried to kiss it. She put her forehead up against the mirror and blinked hard as she did in games with her parents" (p. 195). Berthenthal and Fischer (1978) observed the behaviors of 6- to 20-month-old infants in several different situations involving a mirror. The 6-month-olds and some of the 8-month-olds characteristically looked at and touched some part of their mirror images when placed in front of a mirror. These same 6- and 8-month-old infants also failed on several other mirror tasks requiring that they find an object or a location on their own bodies upon seeing the mirror's reflection of that object or body location. Finally, Millar and Schaffer (1972) found that 6-month-olds failed to acquire a touching response when the auditory and visual consequences of touching were spatially displaced 60° from the manipulandum, although they acquired the response readily when the reinforcement and manipulandum were located in the same spot.

In all of these instances—glass, smoke, mirrors, etc.—the usually applicable rule of spatial contiguity between visual and tactual "events" is violated. Infants who have discovered that rule only recently cannot deal with or even recognize such violations. They behave only in accord with the notion that visual space and tactual space are equivalent. If applying that rule does not lead to attainment of the object, the infant persists and reapplies that same rule. If applying that rule does not lead to interesting consequences at that locus, the infant assumes there are no interesting consequences and his attention recedes. That the object cannot be obtained or that it must be obtained via another route or in another location or that the situation is one of "remote control" are possibilities the infant cannot entertain at this point. Knowledge is still only performing knowledge. It is more genuinely motor behavior or stimulus–response knowledge and not really intersensory knowledge at all. I have discussed its acquisition at great length because such performing knowledge apparently precedes and then gives rise to true sensory–sensory knowledge which I have called *conscious intermodal knowledge*, in the course of normal development.

The most dramatic conflict situation concerning visual and tactual locus is the virtual object, defined above. A number of researchers have presented a virtual object to infants in the middle of their first year and observed their behaviors as they reached for and contacted the object locus (Bower *et al.*, 1970b; Bushnell, 1979b; Field, 1977; Gordon & Yonas, 1976; Lamson, 1976). With the exception of Bower *et al.*, who reported that 5- and 6-month-olds showed marked surprise upon encountering the virtual object, these researchers found that 5- to 11-month-old infants did not react strongly to the discrepancy between visual and tactual existence at a location. Generally, the infants either engaged in a variety of prehensile activities at the object's locus (pinching, poking, adding a second hand, etc.) or simply gave up and stopped attending. They did not react as adults typically do, with dramatic surprise followed by amusement and problem solving. The infants' behavior clearly suggests that they believe they should be able to touch what they see where they see it, but the point to be stressed is that infants seem to *go on believing that* even after getting their hands to the object's locus and feeling nothing. Infants younger than a year of age do not seem to realize that there is something exceptional going on, something that is to be dealt with and understood in an other-than-usual manner. They simply keep trying to get ahold of the object, as an adult might when wearing gloves and trying to pick up a thin dime. Infants offered a virtual object behave as they do with glass and smoke, persisting in reaching to loci seen, automatically applying their one, usually reliable, behavioral rule, unable to recognize and deal with its failures.

From this state of overapplied, performing knowledge of the equivalence of visual and tactual space, intermodal development, at about 7 months of age, begins to progress on several fronts. These involve not only intersensory knowledge relevant to location, but also relevant to object features such as size, shape, and texture, and even to implied actions. I shall continue describing the development of knowledge concerning space and then return to these other equally important developments.

Further development of cross-modal spatial knowledge beyond the overapplied, performing level is dependent on two things. First, knowledge must become conscious rather than performing, as those terms have been defined. According to the analyses of Bruner (1970) and Schaeffer (1975), in order for this change of level to occur, the actual skills involved in applying cross-modal knowledge must be routinized or "modularized." That is, infants must become adept at reaching to spots localized visually and looking to spots localized tactually. They must become expert enough at these behaviors so that they need not attend to carrying them out, so that they can perform them efficiently, "without thinking about them." Only then can infants devote their attentions to *why* they are doing something rather than to *how* they do it. They can then anticipate the sensory consequences of their acts rather than having to utilize all their mental energies just to motorically execute those acts. The most essential element for such skill modularization is practice, that is, executing the behavior over and over. There is no doubt that 6- to 9-month-old infants engage in such practice. They do grasp at all they see and they do turn to see what is touching them or what they are holding. Such frequent use of cross-modal behaviors leads to their refinement as skills and allows them to be analyzed, enabling intelligent bases for them to arise.

Once knowledge concerning the equivalence of visual and tactual space is conscious, infants can hold genuine expectations in accord with that knowledge about events, and they can be surprised, upset, or amused when those expectations are violated. They can recognize violations of the rule about the spatial contiguity of visual and tactual events and then learn how to cope with such exceptions as glass, mirrors, etc. Thus Brazelton (1969) describes an 11-month-old child who

> spotted a favorite toy reflected in the mirror. As if she had forgotten, she reached for it in the mirror. When she banged her hand on the mirror, she laughed out loud—suddenly brought to the realization that she had made a mistake. (p. 149)

Confronting such exceptions to visual-tactual equivalence is in fact the second thing (in addition to the practice required to enable knowledge to become conscious) necessary for cross-modal development beyond the overgeneralizing state of the 6- to 9-month-old. Once the rule concerning visual and tactual space is conscious, the infant need only encounter some exceptions to it to know that there *are* exceptions to it. The rule can then be "pulled back" and applied only to its appropriate range. Special rules applying to the extraordinary situations can be acquired.

Thus 1-year-olds immediately or after a single unsuccessful contact reach around or under glass barriers to grab the objects they see (Bruner,

1970; Bushnell, 1979b). They do not persist in pushing against the clear surface to follow their line of sight with their hands, as 8-month-olds do. They have learned that with this special surface one cannot touch an object by reaching directly to where it is seen. At around 9 months of age children also begin to understand mirrors. Berthenthal and Fischer (1978) found that some 8-month-olds and most 10-month-olds could locate a hat suspended above their heads and moving with their bodies after observing the hat's image in a mirror. These infants were not able to find a toy behind them from observing its reflection, however. Unlike the hat, the toy was not connected to the infant's body, so its movements were independent of the infant's movements. Twelve-month-olds could find the toy reflected in the mirror but actually located behind them. However, when they saw their reflection in a mirror, they did not touch or remark upon their own noses to which a dot of rouge had been applied. Eighteen-month-olds understood mirrors thoroughly enough that they did touch or remark upon their rouged noses after looking in a mirror. These infants have learned that for this special surface, objects are not where they look to be, but may be tactually found if the translation rule of reflection is combined with their visual locations. Children over a year old no longer try to pick up smoke curls or running water, though they may enjoy running their hands through these substances. They have learned that not all visual objects are tangible, just as not all tangible objects are visible (glass). At this point in development, vision and touch are differentiated as well as integrated, so far as space is concerned. The child knows that things *usually* can be touched where they are seen and seen where they are touched, but not always or necessarily.

Specific rules to augment the general one of visual-tactual equivalence (such as how to deal with transparent surfaces and how mirrors work) can of course be acquired only if the pertinent specific situations are encountered. Thus when and in what order children learn to cope with extraordinary substances like glass, mirrors, and smoke will depend on when and in what order they encounter such substances after they possess the equivalence rule consciously. According to the view presented here, individuals who have never encountered transparent or reflective surfaces would not have differentiated the senses of vision and touch, just as individuals living in a world full of virtual objects would not even have integrated the two senses. However, assuming a normal, modern-day existence, infants' cross-modal knowledge concerning space is essentially complete by the middle of the second year. They will have integrated visual space and tactual space, become aware of that integration, and then differentiated them. Now what of cross-modal knowledge concerning aspects of the world other than location?

4. Equivalence of Perceptual Features

There is no acceptable evidence that visual and manual scales for perceptual features such as size, shape, and texture are calibrated at birth. Bower (1972) reported that newborns differentially adjusted their hands as they reached for objects of different sizes. However, whether Bower's young subjects were actually reaching has already been questioned. Additionally, only one camera angle was used, making hand–object contact and hand positioning difficult to assess objectively, and Bower's scorers could see which object was being presented. The measures were taken from film frames selected by working backward from the time of contact, so that even a very basic operational rule on the part of the infant, such as "keep closing the hand until the object is grasped," would result in differential hand positions prior to contact with objects of different sizes. These characteristic methodological and interpretational flaws cause us to question Bower's report of anticipatory hand-shaping by neonates. Bruner and Koslowski (1972) also reported manual sensitivity to visual size in prereaching infants. The nativist implications of their results that visual perceptual features such as size, shape, and texture are equated with their tactual correlates at birth must also be questioned. First, their infants were by no means newborn—the youngest age tested was 10 weeks. Second, the small object was presented only at midline whereas the large object necessarily extended into the periphery. This location difference might have produced artifactual effects caused by the nature of postural proclivities (such as the TNR) of young infants.

In fact, the existence of within-mode sensitivity to relational perceptual features in neonates is questionable. For instance, newborns cannot discriminate visual stimuli differing in shape if confounding factors such as brightness and contour density are controlled (Bronson, 1974). Moreover, size, shape, and texture calibration could not easily occur (and these calibrations must occur after birth—they cannot be fixed at birth, given the adult flexibility referred to earlier) and certainly cannot easily be tested until infants have equated visual and tactual space at about 5 months of age. Only then do infants simultaneously look at and touch objects frequently enough for calibration. Hence, I propose that intermodal development relevant to perceptual features does not really begin until infants attain the stage of overapplied, performing knowledge of the equivalence of visual and tactual space described above. At that point, it will be recalled, infants try to obtain manually all that they see and to obtain visually all that they feel.[1]

---

[1] Just as this chapter was sent to the editors, at the March 15–18, 1979, meetings of the Society for Research in Child Development, Meltzoff and Borton presented data indicating

The consistent reaching of 5- to 6-month-olds for seen objects then enables intermodal knowledge concerning object properties to be acquired at the performing level. This performing knowledge is evidenced by anticipatory hand-shaping. Just as reaching in the appropriate direction is behavior in accordance with the equivalence of visual and tactual location, differentially adjusting the hand's position upon seeing and prior to grasping objects of different sizes, shapes, or textures is behavior in accordance with the equivalence of visual and tactual perceptual features.

The acquisition of anticipatory hand-shaping can reasonably be attributed to the reinforcement contingencies of infants' early attempts to reach, obtain, and retain objects. Infants, after coordinating visual and tactual space, initially reach for objects of all sizes, shapes, and textures with a characteristic, from-above, wide-open hand approach. Twitchell (1970), discussing both visually and tactually elicited prehension, noted that at 6 months "dexterous prehension is still impossible. A small object is particularly difficult for the infant to handle. He attempts to sweep it into the palm, all the fingers flex together" (p. 330). Halverson (1931) observed that infants from 16 to 28 weeks usually approached an object (any object) with the hand held high, and then came down upon it, "raking it in." This single approach style is not efficient for all objects. Such a palmar grasp is particularly unsuitable for small objects, objects with small parts, and long, thin objects. The use of such a grasp in reaches for these sorts of objects is often unsuccessful, resulting either in the infant's failing to obtain the goal object altogether or in the infant's ending up just barely clutching the object and not retaining it for long before it drops.

Over the first few months of reaching experience, as motor control

---

that 1-month-old infants are capable of recognizing shapes cross-modally. They used Gottfried's oral-familiarization and visual-fixation test procedure and found that a significant proportion of the infants fixated the visual shape which matched the tactual (oral) stimulus longer than they fixated the nonmatching shape. These results are extremely interesting, and if they withstand the scrutiny to which the scientific community is sure to subject them, they will force certain revisions in several theories of infant perceptual development, including ideas in this chapter. The revisions potentially demanded are not all that drastic, however. Even though Meltzoff and Borton interpret their data as evidence that infants have an innate capacity to make intermodal matches, the possibility that the visual-tactual correspondences demonstrated may have been learned has not been ruled out. One-month-olds have certainly had considerable opportunity to see objects they have just mouthed and to mouth objects they have just seen. Further, Meltzoff and Borton's results do not necessarily have implications for the time course of the development of visual-tactual (manual) correspondences discussed in this chapter. It is quite plausible that a developmental *décalage* exists between visual-tactual (oral) knowledge and visual-tactual (manual) knowledge, since clearly the mouth is used in an active, exploratory manner several months before the hands are used in such a manner.

matures and the palmar grasping style is differentially extinguished for various sorts of objects, differential hand-shaping emerges. Twitchell (1970) reported that the thumb–finger opposition required to pick up small objects appears during the second half-year of life, when the grasp reflex can be fractionated. Halverson (1931) and Brazelton (1969) similarly observed that the superior-forefinger or pincer grasp emerged when infants were 8 or 9 months old. This grasp is then employed to pick up those previously difficult small objects, objects with small parts such as knobs and handles, and long, thin objects resting on surfaces. Eight-month-olds, unlike beginning reachers, also appropriately use a bimanual spreading grasp for large objects such as beach balls, and they rotate the forearm in order to approach vertically oriented sticklike objects from the side rather than from above. They slap at or smear a puddle of liquid or a glob of applesauce rather than attempting to pick it up. At this point infants have become skilled at obtaining objects, and they possess performing-level cross-modal knowledge about object features.

Conscious-level cross-modal knowledge concerning object features arises not so much from the repetition of performing-level behaviors as from the activity which typically follows an infant's obtaining an object, whether that obtaining was clumsy or skilled. Upon succeeding at a particular endeavor to grasp a seen object or see a grasped object, the 6- to 7-month-old infant engages in a characteristic sort of play with the object (Fenson, Kagan, Kearsley, & Zelazo, 1976; Schofield & Uzgiris, 1969). This sort of play has been called "examining behavior" by Schofield and Uzgiris (1969), and it is distinct from other sorts of object play engaged in by older infants. In examining behavior, the infant's

> visual attention to an object is combined with extensive manipulation of the object in the context of exploring it. In examining, the infant turns the object around, pokes at it, feels its surface, moves its parts, while attentively observing his manipulations. The infant's interest appears to be focused on the object itself rather than on the activity to which the object contributes. (Schofield & Uzgiris, 1969, p. 3)

This intense, multisensory interaction with single objects seems to have two important and very much related derivatives. One of these is the Piagetian object concept (cf. Schofield & Uzgiris, 1969), which will not be discussed in this chapter. The other is the conscious calibration of visual and tactual scales for object dimensions, such as size, shape, and texture. By repeatedly looking at and feeling objects at the same time, and by doing so with a variety of objects, infants are able to detect or discover the nature-given correlations between visual size and tactual size, visual shape and tactual shape, visual texture and tactual texture. They integrate vision and touch for perceptual features, as they have already integrated them for location. The limited empirical evidence which exists regarding the coordination of vision and touch for object features in infancy supports this argument that somewhat after they exhibit visually guided reaching, infants partially complete the process of equating vision and touch for perceptual dimensions, such as size, shape, and texture.

Bryant, Jones, Claxton, and Perkins (1972) employed a third sensory mode, audition, to study recognition of shapes across vision and touch by infants. Their subjects ranged in age from 6 to 11½ months, with a mean age of 8½ months. The procedure consisted of three successive phases. First, two objects different in shape were visually presented to the infant. The two objects used were either a complete and an incomplete ellipsoid or a complete and an incomplete cuboid. The second phase was a tactual presentation of one of the two objects seen in the initial phase. The experimenter placed one of the objects in the infant's hand in such a manner that neither the infant nor the mother saw which object it was. While the infant's hand was on the object, the experimenter made it produce a noise, an event presumed to enhance the attractiveness of the object being held. Finally, both objects were again visually presented, and after both had been looked at, the infant was allowed to reach toward or "choose" one of them. Which object the infant chose was recorded.

Twenty-three of the 30 infants offered the complete and incomplete ellipsoids reached for the one of the pair which they had previously touched. This number is significantly greater than could be expected by chance, and both confirms that noise-producing objects are attractive to infants and demonstrates that infants can, under some circumstances, recognize objects cross-modally. Only by recognizing which of the two objects they were looking at was the nice, noisy one which they had felt could the infants have so consistently selected it. With the second pair of objects, the complete and incomplete cuboids, the infants chose randomly. The authors suggest that the failure with the cuboids might have been because "both objects in this pair had only straight contours, and that a straight-straight discrimination is a very difficult one either tactually or cross-modally" (p. 304). Apparently, not all shapes are equally recognizable cross-modally for infants in the second half-year of life. That is, cross-modal recognition abilities are still developing; complete calibration is a protracted process.

Bryant et al. (1972) used infants of a rather wide age range in their study, and they reported only their overall results. It would be interesting to know for both the easy ellipsoid pair and the difficult cuboid pair whether the infants who did not select the felt object were on the average younger than those who did. It would also be interesting to know whether a given infant would either pass or fail with both pairs or whether some might pass with the ellipsoids but not with the cuboids. Bryant *et al.* did not use a within-subjects design, however, so this question must also remain unanswered. Very generally, the Bryant *et al.* study shows that infants younger than 12 months "can transmit some information about shape across modalities without the benefit of words" (p. 304).

Gottfried, Rose, and Bridger (1977) also found evidence for cross-modal shape recognition by infants. They used a familiarization technique similar to that used in studies of infant visual memory. Six pairs of stimuli were used, one each for three cross-modal tasks and three intramodal tasks. The first phase of the procedure was a 30-sec familiarization interval. For one of the cross-modal tasks, the oral task, either a small cube or a small sphere was inserted into the infant's mouth without the infant's seeing the object and left there for 30 sec. For the other two cross-modal tasks, the tactual tasks, one of the pertinent pair of objects was placed in the child's hand, again surreptitiously, and the subject was encouraged to palpate it for 30 sec. The object pairs for these two tasks were (a) a barrel-shaped object and a cross and (b) a cylinder and a ridged dowel similar to a decorative staircase strut or chair leg. For the three intramodal tasks one of each pair of objects was visually shown to the infant for 30 sec. The familiarization interval was followed by a 20-sec visual-recognition memory interval. For each task the familiar stimulus and its novel pair partner were simultaneously visually presented out of the infant's reach. The amount of time spent looking at each of the objects was recorded. Finally, the pair of objects was moved to within reach, and the infant was permitted to reach for one of them.

For each task, including all the cross-modal tasks, the 1-year-old subjects looked significantly longer at and reached significantly more often toward the novel stimulus than at and toward the familiar stimulus. Such differential behavior upon seeing the objects would not have been possible if the infants had not recognized visually which of the pair was the one they had explored orally or tactually. The authors concluded that 1-year-olds "can gain knowledge about the shape of an object by feeling it, and by mouthing it, and they can make this information available to the visual system" (Rose, Gottfried, & Bridger, 1977, p. 3). It should be noted that each of the cross-modal object pairs used by Gottfried *et al.* contrasted an object with straight contours and an object with curved contours. The pairs were thus comparable to the "easy" pair used by Bryant *et al.*, the complete and incomplete ellipsoids.

Ruff and Kohler (1978) used a procedure identical to that employed by Gottfried *et al.* to study cross-modal recognition by 6-month-olds. The infants were tactually familiarized with either a cube or a sphere and then were visually presented with both shapes in the final phase of the procedure. The infants did not look significantly longer at the novel shape, as Gottfried's older subjects did, nor did they significantly select the familiar shape over the novel one, as Bryant's subjects did. However, the prior tactual experience did bias the infants' spontaneous preference for one of the shapes. In general the infants looked more at the sphere than at the cube on test trials, but the infants who had previously felt the sphere looked significantly more at it than the infants who had felt the cube. The tactual experience therefore seemed to lead to a relatively weak tendency to prefer the familiar stimulus. Thus, 6-month-olds relate visual shape and tactual shape, at least when two maximally distinguishable forms are contrasted. However, their cross-modal knowledge is not reflected in the same straightforward manner as is that of older infants, suggesting that it is just nascent.

The present author (Bushnell, 1979a) used the violation-of-expectancy or surprise paradigm to investigate cross-modal object recognition by 8-, 9½-, and 11-month-olds. A mirror arrangement allowed one object to be seen in a particular spot, while a second, sometimes different object was actually located there. Thus, if one reached into the apparatus and grasped the object, the expectancy formed from looking at it might be violated. Infants' reactions to such discrepancies were observed. The objects used were a fur-covered cylinder and a smooth plastic object with several knobs or projections, so the objects differed in both shape and texture. Each of the 16 infants in each age group participated in four trials, representing the four possible arrangements of these two objects. The trials were presented in pairs, each pair consisting of a control trial, in which the seen and felt objects were identical, and a trick trial, in which the seen and felt objects were different. On each trial the infants were encouraged to reach for, grasp, and manipulate the object they were looking at, and the infants' manual and visual behaviors as they contacted the object and during the following 20 sec were videotaped.

The data tapes for each infant were scored for several attentional measures. The 8-month-olds did not differentially respond to trick and control trials, but both the 9½-month-olds and the 11-month-olds looked significantly longer at the object on trick trials than on control trials. Two naive observers also watched the tapes and for each trick-control pair of trials made a forced-choice judgment as to whether the trick or the control trial was first. The judgments were based on a variety of behavioral clues, such as the infant's facial expressions, the accuracy and confidence with which the objects were grasped, whether or not the infant attempted to look under the apparatus at the object touched, and whether or not the hand groped or searched around the area of the object after contacting it. The observers were unable to order accurately the trials for the 8-month-old subjects, were moderately accurate for the 9½-month-olds, and were extremely accurate for the 11-month-olds. Thus, the 9½- and 11-month-old infants recognized the visual-tactual discrepancies of shape and texture and responded to them with a variety of problem-solving behaviors, but the 8-month-olds failed to provide similar evidence of conscious cross-modal knowledge.

In an earlier study (Bushnell, 1978), a similar procedure was used to investigate the abilities of 15-month-olds to recognize visual-tactual discrepancies. The trick trials in this study employed pairs of objects differing only in shape (a cross and a cube), only in size (a large cube and a small cube), and only in texture (a fur-covered cylinder and a cylinder filled with water), as well as a pair of objects different in all three of these dimensions (a fur-covered cylinder and a small cube). For the size, texture, and all-three-dimensions tricks, the infants touched the object for shorter amounts of time and visually monitored their touching more closely on trick trials than on the appropriate control trials. The infants did not differentially attend to shape trick and control trials. Forced-choice judgments based on the infants' manual behaviors on each trial were significantly accurate for all except the shape-relevant trials. Finally, the infants engaged in manual search more frequently on size, texture, and all-three-dimensions trick trials than on the appropriate control trials. For the shape trials, manual search was equally infrequent on the trick and control trials. These results indicate that by 15 months of age infants have equated vision and touch for some aspects of size and texture. They also support the finding by Bryant *et al.* that infants may be unable to cross-modally discriminate certain, perhaps subtly differing shapes even when they are capable of other cross-modal discriminations.

The literature concerning infants' visual-tactual knowledge of perceptual features clearly could and should be augmented in several ways. Convergent results from studies following a variety of procedures, studying a wider range of ages, and using objects differing in more precisely defined ways are necessary before it can be established at what age and in what sequence such knowledge is acquired. Nonetheless, the evidence which has been reviewed is compatible with the hypothesis that during the third quarter-year of life, infants begin calibrating vision and touch for perceptual dimensions, such as size, shape, and texture. Evidence of cross-modal knowledge for these properties has not been reported at all in infants younger than 6 months, and for infants between 6 and 9 months, whether or not such evidence has been found varies with the procedures and particular stimuli used. Evidence of conscious cross-modal knowledge of size, shape, and texture has been reported by several researchers studying infants 9 months of age or older, though it is also clear that the knowledge of such infants is not yet complete. Calibration begins when the infant can get hold of objects and engages in examining behavior at 6–7 months, but it is not accomplished entirely in the next couple of months. Subtle, albeit systematic visual-tactual relationships may not be attended to even well after other, more salient ones are dealt with competently.

In addition, as with location, there are "exceptions" to these visual-tactual correlations relevant to perceptual features and discovered during object play. There are objects which do not feel as they look like they should or look like they feel they should. Most pointed objects feel sharp and painful if touched, as needles, nails, and thorns do. However, pointed objects made of rubber, such as the massager on the end of a toothbrush, do not feel painful when touched. Certain paint finishes and plastic fabrics look wet, but do not feel wet. Such unique objects must be individually confronted before they are recognized as exceptions and coped with adequately, so no general age norms or sequences can be outlined as can for more "normal" objects. It is interesting to note that when initially faced with exceptional objects bearing ambiguous or unexpected perceptual features, children and even adults "revert" to examining behavior. The idiosyncratic relationships of the visual and tactual images of such objects must be explored and discovered via simultaneous looking and touching, just as the more general relationships applying to most objects were. When considering these exceptional objects, it becomes apparent that cross-modal knowledge is indistinct from cognitive or worldly knowledge.

5. Equivalence of "Actions"

Through the last quarter of the first year, examining behavior is superseded as the predominant style of play with objects by what may be called *functional play*. In functional play, infants' attention and exploration centers on what a particular object does or what one can do with it, rather than on what the object is. Infants engage in "relational" acts, such as touching one object with another or putting one object inside another. Imitation of others' actions toward or with particular objects is a common form of functional play. In their study of the developmental progression of play, Fenson et al. (1976) found that functional play commences at around 9 months of age, and by 13 months it has replaced examining behavior as the characteristic style of object play. Observations made by Piaget (1952) also stress the predominance of functional play at around a year of age. His fifth sensorimotor stage is, in fact, characterized by the "tertiary circular reaction," a behavior pattern by which the child deliberately investigates relations between actions and their effects.

Functional play has consequences for cross-modal development, just as examining behavior had slightly earlier in development. Through functional play infants add "action" components or "affordances" (cf. Gibson, 1979; von Fieandt, 1974) to their understandings of particular objects and various perceptual features. For instance, "rollability" may be added to infants' notions of balls or round things generally. Such advances pertain to cross-modal knowledge in that these action components may involve perceptual behaviors and features from several senses. For example, when an object is recognized via one sensory mode, exploratory action in a second sensory mode may be implied, as a seen flower implies "smell me." Similarly, when an action is perceived via one sensory mode, knowledge about the involved objects' properties in other sensory modes may be entailed. When one sees something sliced through with a knife, for instance, one knows that the substance must feel soft and malleable like butter or clay. It is this sort of cross-modal knowledge that is, I think, engendered by functional play.

There is very little evidence concerning this aspect of cross-modal knowledge, the visual-tactual "equivalence of actions." The few studies which are relevant deal with very basic perceptual actions which may be implied by any and all objects. As such, the coordinations of these actions with one another and with perceptual features are among the first of their kind to be established, and their development overlaps considerably with the development of cross-modal knowledge about perceptual features.

One group of studies deals with the concordance of visual and tactual exploratory behaviors. Schaffer and Parry (1969, 1970) found that infants 8 months and older gave evidence of both differential visual behavior and differential manipulative behavior toward a second object presented following repeated or lengthy presentations of a nonsense object. For example, they both touched and looked at the novel object longer than the familiar object. Six-month-olds, however, showed differential visual behavior toward the novel object but manipulated the familiar and novel objects equally. Schaffer and Parry concluded that though younger infants perceive selectively according to whether a stimulus is familiar or not, they do not concordantly act selectively.

Rubenstein (1974) and Ruff (1976) also studied the concordance of visual and manipulative responses to novelty, and they each found that 6-month-olds did respond differentially in both the visual and manipulative modes. However, whereas in Schaffer and Parry's studies the novel objects differed from the familiar ones only visually (in color), in both the Rubenstein and the Ruff studies the novel objects differed from the familiar ones visually and tactually (in shape). Thus, manipulation of the novel object after reaching could have been maintained either by contin-

ued visual inspection or by tactual information about novelty. In either case, perceptual information would be guiding action, but only if manipulation were maintained by visual inspection could the behavior be considered cross-modal.

Steele and Pederson (1977) also investigated 6-month-olds' visual and manipulative exploration, specifically varying how the novel and familiar objects differed. One object was presented on seven familiarization trials, and then, on the eighth and ninth trials, a novel object was presented. For some infants the novel object differed from the familiar one only in color, that is, only visually. For others the novel object was different in shape and/or texture, that is, both visually and tactually. For all infants, visual fixation per trial decreased with repeated exposures to the first object and increased upon presentation of the novel object. However, increased manipulation of the novel object occurred only for the shape- and/or texture-change groups, who experienced new information tactually as well as visually. For the color-change groups, who experienced only new visual information, manipulation continued to decrease over the dishabituation trials. Steele and Pederson concluded that for 6-month-old infants "new tactile cues are needed to control manipulative exploration of novel objects (p. 105). . . . To respond to a novel stimulus in both response systems (visual and manipulative), the object must present novel visual and tactual information to the infant" (p. 110). What Rubenstein (1974) and Ruff (1976) considered to be concordance was simply two distinct systems, one visual and one tactual, each responding to novelty in a single location in a similar fashion.

The results of the several studies discussed above fit together nicely if, as Steele and Pederson (1977) suggested, the nature of the novelty presented is taken into account, and if cross-modal development is considered. In those instances when the test object was novel only visually, infants younger than 8 months did not exhibit concordant looking and manipulating responses, whereas infants older than 8 months did behave concordantly. Infants of all ages behaved concordantly when the test stimuli were novel both visually and tactually. These data may be taken as evidence that for younger infants the activities of visual exploration and tactual exploration are not equivalent. Visual exploration is controlled only by visual perceptual features and events (such as novelty) and tactual exploration by tactual features and events. For older infants, who perceive objects and events as units rather than in terms of their several separate components, visual exploration and tactual exploration are equivalent. They are both appropriate ways to deal with a novel object, regardless of how that novelty is defined. If something is different visually, it is different wholly for older infants and is worthy of exploration or differential responding in all modes.

Another rather pervasive action implied by perceptual events and about which there is evidence is search. One can see or feel something disappear, and one can then search for it visually or manually. Harris (1971) studied the search behavior of infants 7–9½ months old and 11–13½ months old. An object was presented on a platform in front of the infants. For half of the infants, the platform was covered with Plexiglas so that they could only see the object. The other half of the subjects could both see and touch the object. After the infants had examined the object, it disappeared, receding into a box. The duration of time each infant reached into the box and searched for the object was recorded. Harris found that the younger subjects searched just as long as the older ones did only when they had both seen and touched the object prior to its disappearance. If they had only seen the object, the younger subjects did not search for it persistently. The older subjects searched persistently both when they had seen and touched the object prior to its disappearance and when they had only seen it.

Just as with the exploration data, these findings can be interpreted in terms of cross-modal knowledge of objects and actions. Suppose that in order for younger infants to search manually for something, it and its disappearance must be manually experienced. With older infants, even an object only visually experienced and seen to disappear will be searched for manually. Older infants have equated visual search and manual search as reasonable means to relocate something with which perceptual contact of any kind has been lost. The object and ways to deal with it are all part of a unitary concept, the component parts of which all bear implications for one another.

Some work by Gratch (1972) can be considered in this light, too. Gratch presented 6½-month-olds with a number of Piagetian object–concept tasks, including one in which an object was covered with an opaque cloth after the child had reached for and grasped it. Whether or not each infant removed the cloth was noted. Exactly half of the infants failed in this situation—that is, they removed the cloth on no more than one of three trials. One interpretation of this result is that the object had disappeared only visually and hence was searched for only visually. The infants did frequently look down at their covered, toy-holding hand. Since the object had not disappeared tactually, it was not searched for tactually by these young infants, whose visual and tactual "perceptual-action" systems were not yet coordinated.

Presumably, 6-month-olds would tactually search for an object which disappeared tactually, as it would if one were to pull the object out of an infant's hand. This variation has not been systematically studied, however. In fact, studies of cross-modal knowledge and behavior have generally been "unidirectional." Researchers have questioned whether visual information can be recognized or dealt with tactually and whether tactual information can be recognized or dealt with visually, but usually they have not investigated both issues within the same experimental framework. Yet to the extent that cross-modal knowledge truly involves equivalence or mutual, reciprocal assimilation, then with respect to any aspect of knowledge, vision should be to touch as touch is to vision. Any asymmetries would be interesting to know about, since they would have to be accounted for with some sort of "performance" (as opposed to "competence") factors.

Action components more specifically associated with particular object features have, unfortunately, not been investigated. Cross-modal knowledge of these would presumably be acquired somewhat later than the knowledge about actions applicable to objects in general discussed above. This more particular cross-modal knowledge is thought to arise from infants' functional play experiences with objects bearing the particular features. Thus, "rollability" is coordinated with visual and tactual roundness as babies observe others playing with balls, marbles, and wheels and then play with these objects themselves. "Pourability" is coordinated with the visual and tactual features specifying liquids and particulate matters, such as sand and sugar, as infants experiment in their play with these substances. It is not impossible to investigate empirically at what age infants possess such cross-modal action knowledge or "event perception." One might easily use the violation-of-expectancy paradigm or the preferential-looking (toward things and events that belong together) paradigm to study infants' notions about perceived actions or events and their implications for either the course of other events or for the perceptual features of the objects involved.

As with the equivalence of location and perceptual features, infants of a certain age make mistakes akin to overgeneralizations with respect to what I have called the equivalence of actions. Exceptions to the usual rules of what actions go with what perceptual features must be met and studied. Things which are round but also sticky may not roll! For example, by their first birthday, infants have learned that objects which look new and interesting should be explored tactually, as they are likely to feel new and interesting, too. Yet at their first birthday party, many infants meet with two exceptions to this rule—candle flames hurt when touched and soap bubbles disappear when grasped. It is more pleasant only to look at these special substances.

Another example of cross-modal action errors infants make is their behavior on a visual cliff. A visual cliff is a table apparatus constructed of glass and textured material such that there appears to be a drop-off or cliff to one side. Tangibly and actually, of course, that side is perfectly solid and safe to walk on. Walk and Gibson (1961) placed infants between the ages of 6½ and 14 months on a board centered between the "shallow" side and the "deep" side of such a cliff. Each infant's mother then encouraged her baby to crawl to her across the shallow side and across the deep side. All but three of the 36 infants refused to crawl over the deep side. Walk and Gibson concluded that by the time infants can independently locomote, they perceive a visually cued drop-off. What is interesting is that locomotion for infants is controlled or "afforded" so exclusively by visual information. The infants in Walk and Gibson's study rubbed the glass on the deep side and tested the surface with their hands and even their mouths, yet they would not crawl across it. For them, a surface had to look safe for locomotion, not just feel solid. The rule that a surface which does not look solid is not to be crawled across is overgeneralized by infants of this age and is followed even when it is inappropriate. The conflicting visual and tactual implications of transparent surfaces such as glass for the actions of safely crawling or walking have not been properly sorted out yet. It would be interesting to ascertain at what age children would trust the tactual indications of solidity, ignore the misleading lack of visual support (as adults do when they place cocktails and snack trays on Plexiglas tables), and crawl or walk over the deep side of a visual cliff.

6. Differentiation

Establishing the equivalences discussed above is only part of cross-modal development. In addition to learning that the senses of vision and touch often provide the same information, human infants must also learn that they do not always provide the same information. They must become aware that vision and touch are in fact two distinct senses, each with particular strengths and weaknesses so far as the perception of reality is concerned. They must learn to deal competently with situations in which information from the two senses is discrepant, as it is with glass, mirrors, or "wet-look" paint; or even unrelated, as an object's color is unrelated to how one handles it and an object's temperature is unrelated to how one optically scans it. In short, what Bower has called differentiation must occur in addition to integration, if one's cross-modal knowledge is to be complete.

There has been very little empirical investigation concerning the differentiation of the senses in infancy. Most of the investigation that has been done deals with infants' knowledge about special surfaces, such as mirrors or glass. This literature was discussed in Section 3, which also included some comments on the process of differentiation that I shall briefly review.

Before differentiation can occur, integration, it seems to me, must have occurred. Before a relationship can be analyzed or teased apart, it must have been synthesized or constructed. A state of differentiation is not the same as a state of independence, such as has been proposed to exist between vision and touch at birth. Differentiation entails knowledge that the senses are related, but also knowledge that they are not identical. Furthermore, not only must vision and touch be integrated before differentiation can occur, but also the integration must become conscious knowledge. Many lower animals have extremely adequate performing knowledge of some visual-tactual equivalences, but because their knowledge is never elevated to the conscious level, they are incapable of differentiating the senses in even the most rudimentary meaning of the term. Frogs, for instance, cannot learn to inhibit snapping at prey behind glass barriers (Maier & Schneirla, 1964), whereas human infants ultimately do learn not to reach directly toward objects behind or under transparent surfaces. Only if the knowledge of visual-tactual equivalence is conscious can the disruptive events which force differentiation be experienced as such. Once knowledge of the equivalence of vision and touch has become conscious, then when infants encounter some unusual surfaces, objects, or situations, they are able to recognize the unusualness and are forced to admit that vision and touch are not entirely isomorphic. To their equivalence rules they must add little corollaries which outline the exceptions to those rules. Most likely differentiation occurs first with respect to location, since the conscious visual-tactual equivalence of location precedes the other equivalences and since counterexamples for those equivalence rules (glass, mirrors, etc.) are pervasive in the environment of a Western-society middle-class child. Once differentiation has occurred for one aspect of cross-modal functioning, differentiation for other aspects may be facilitated. That is, knowing that vision and touch do not always provide equivalent information about an object's location may make it easier to believe that they also do not always provide equivalent information about an object's perceptual features or about what actions are appropriate. For differentiation in these later aspects of cross-modal knowledge, perhaps fewer counterexamples need to be encountered, since the lessons of those which forced the first instance of differentiation carry over.

It has been noted that differentiation regarding visual and tactual space begins to occur at around 9 months of age, when infants show evidence of partially understanding transparent surfaces and mirrors. There are absolutely no data concerning other aspects of cross-modal differentiation. However, the results of the present author's cross-modal recognition study (Bushnell, 1978) may be relevant. Recall that 15-month-old infants were presented a visual object that did (control trials) or did not (trick trials) match its tactual impression. In addition to the results already discussed, it was found that although in all other respects they did not respond differentially to trick and control shape trials, on one type of shape trick trial the infants peeked under the apparatus considerably more frequently than on any other trial. On the size, texture, and all-three-dimensions trick trials, the infants did not engage in such visual search very often, though they did grope around the apparatus with their hands. These differences, if reliable, may indicate that 15-month-olds believe that for the dimension of shape, vision is more precise than touch and should be used to double-check things in cases of conflict or ambiguity, whereas for the dimension of texture, touch is more veridical. They also apparently know that small items may be difficult to get hold of, and one may have to persist and grope around for them. These bits of knowledge are the sort that one who had differentiated vision and touch would possess.

One can think of a number of ways to investigate cross-modal differentiation further. At what age would a child proclaim the experimenter crazy for asking the color of something that the child held in the dark or for asking whether a liquid only seen and not touched was hot or cold? At what age would children viewing a blurred object or even a virtual object through goggles assume that something was funny about their eyes and inspect or remove the goggles? At what age would they remove heavy gloves and feel a novel substance before judging whether it was sticky or slippery? Such research possibilities are reminiscent of work on "metamemory" (Kreutzer, Leonard, & Flavell, 1975; Wellman, 1978) and "metalanguage" (Gleitman, Gleitman, & Shipley, 1972). It would be amusing and revealing to study children's "metamodal" knowledge, which might be termed the last frontier of cross-modal knowledge.

7. Summary

I have proposed a flow chart (see Figure 1 below) summarizing the ontogeny of relations between vision and touch in infancy. The boxed-in entries describe the state of infants' cross-modal knowledge at the various approximate ages listed on the left. Arrows between boxes depict sequential or "epigenetic" relations, and the entries along the arrows between pairs of boxes indicate the events on which change from one knowledge state to the next is contingent. Note in the figure that both Piaget's process of integration—the establishment of the several equivalences—and Bower's process of differentiation are part of cross-modal development. Although Bower's time course seems to me to be radically wrong in that he believes visual-tactual integration to be present at birth,

I do believe he is correct in noting that infants must learn that the senses are distinct and do not always or necessarily bear upon one another. Note too that a variety of mechanisms are involved in effecting cross-modal development at various points, ranging from operant conditioning in the early months to higher-level processes such as the hypothesis testing, inference, and deduction implicated in the later phases of development. I would also stress my conviction that cross-modal development, often conceived of as purely perceptual, is intertwined via the child's play with cognitive development, albeit to a greater extent at some points in its time course than others. With such conclusions as these, the matter of cross-modal development has certainly not been simplified. Rather, I have tried to establish that the ontogeny of inter-modal relations is not a simple, unitary process but is instead a many-faceted one, the development of which is gradual, complex, and inter-dependent with experiences and with developments on other fronts.

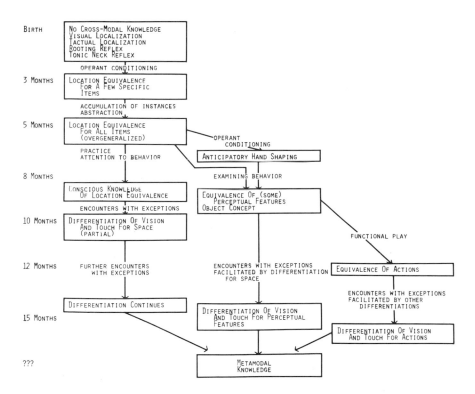

Fig. 1. A flow chart summarizing the proposed ontogeny of relations between vision and touch during infancy.

8. References

Berthenthal, B.I., & Fischer, K.W. Development of self-recognition in the infant. *Developmental Psychology*, 1978, *14*, 44–50.

Bower, T.G.R. Object perception in infants. *Perception*, 1972, *1*, 15–30.

Bower, T.G.R. *Development in infancy*. San Francisco: W.H. Freeman, 1974.

Bower, T.G.R. *A primer of infant development*. San Francisco: W.H. Freeman, 1977.

Bower, T.G.R., Broughton, J.M. & Moore, M.K. Demonstration of intention in the reaching behavior of neonate humans. *Nature*, 1970, *228*, 679–681. (a)

Bower, T.G.R., Broughton, J.M., & Moore, M.K. The coordination of visual and tactual input in infants. *Perception and Psychophysics*, 1970, *8*, 51–53. (b)

Brazelton, T.B. *Infants and mothers*. New York: Dell, 1969.

Bronson, G. The postnatal growth of visual capacity. *Child Development*, 1974, *45*, 873–890.

Brown, R. *A first language: The early stages*. Cambridge: Harvard University Press, 1973.

Brown, R., and Bellugi, U. Three processes in the child's acquisition of syntax. *Harvard Educational Review*, 1964, *34*, 133–151.

Bruner, J.S. The growth and structure of skill. In K. Connolly (Ed.), *Mechanisms of motor skill development*. New York: Academic Press, 1970.

Bruner, J.S., & Koslowski, B. Visually preadapted constituents of manipulating action. *Perception*, 1972, *1*, 3–14.

Bryant, P.E., Jones, P., Claxton, V. & Perkins, G.M. Recognition of shapes across modalities by infants. *Nature*, 1972, *240*, 303–304.

Bushnell, E.W. *Cross-modal object recognition in infancy*. Paper presented at the annual meeting of the American Psychological Association, Toronto, 1978.

Bushnell, E.W. *Infants' reactions to cross-modal discrepancies*. Paper presented at the annual meeting of the Midwestern Psychological Association, Chicago, 1979. (a)

Bushnell, E.W. *Visual-tactual knowledge in infancy*. Unpublished dissertation, University of Minnesota, 1979. (b)

Cazden, C. The acquisition of noun and verb inflections. *Child Development*, 1968, *39*, 433–438.

Clark, R. Performing without competence. *Journal of Child Language*, 1974, *1*, 1–10.

Dodwell, P.C., Muir, D., & DiFranco, D. Responses of infants to visually presented objects. *Science*, 1976, *194*, 209–211.

Fenson, L., Kagan, J., Kearsley, R.B., & Zelazo, P.R. The developmental progression of manipulative play in the first two years. *Child Development*, 1976, *47*, 232–236.

Field, J. Coordination of vision and prehension in young infants. *Child Development*, 1977, *48*, 97–103.

Frankel, D.G. *Coordinating a reach in visual space*. Unpublished doctoral dissertation, University of Minnesota, 1974.

Gibson, E.J. *Principles of perceptual learning and development*. New York: Meredith, 1969.

Gibson, J.J. Observations on active touch. *Psychological Review*, 1962, *69*, 477–491.

Gibson, J.J. *The senses considered as perceptual systems*. Boston: Houghton Mifflin, 1966.

Gibson, J.J. *The ecological approach to visual perception*. Boston: Houghton Mifflin, 1979.

Gleitman, L.R., Gleitman, H., & Shipley, E.F. The emergence of the child as grammarian. *Cognition*, 1972, *1*, 137–164.

Gordon, F.R., & Yonas, A. Sensitivity to binocular depth information in infants. *Journal of Experimental Child Psychology*, 1976, *22*, 413–422.

Gottfried, A.W., Rose, S.A., & Bridger, W.H. Cross-modal transfer in human infants. *Child Development*, 1977, *48*, 118–123.

Gratch, G. A study of the relative dominance of vision and touch in six-month-old infants. *Child Development*, 1972, *43*, 615–623.

Gregory, R.L. *Eye and brain*. New York: McGraw-Hill, 1966.

Halverson, H.M. An experimental study of prehension in infants by means of systematic cinema records. *Genetic Psychology Monographs*, 1931, *10*, 107–286.

Harris, P.L. Examination and search in infants. *British Journal of Psychology*, 1971, *62*, 469–473.

Harris, P., and Macfarlane, A. The growth of the effective visual field from birth to seven weeks. *Journal of Experimental Child Psychology*, 1974, *18*, 340–348.

Held, R. Plasticity in sensory–motor systems. *Scientific American*, 1965, *213*, 84–94.

Kreutzer, M.A., Leonard, C., & Flavell, J.H. An interview study of children's knowledge about memory. *Monographs of the Society for Research in Child Development*, 1975, *40* (1, Serial No. 159).

Lamson, G.L. *The development of accuracy in human infants' reaches to a visually specified three-dimensional object*. Unpublished manuscript, University of Minnesota, 1976.

Maier, N.R.F., and Schneirla, T.C. *Principles of animal behavior*. New York: Dover Publications, 1964.

McGurk, H., Turnure, C., and Creighton, S.J. Auditory-visual coordination in neonates. *Child Development*, 1977, *48*, 138–143.

Millar, W.S., & Schaffer, H.R. The influence of spatially displaced feedback on infant operant conditioning. *Journal of Experimental Child Psychology*, 1972, *14*, 442–453.

Piaget, J. *The origins of intelligence in children*. New York: W.W. Norton, 1952.

Ramsay, D.S., & Campos, J.J. The onset of representation and entry into stage 6 of object permanence development. *Developmental Psychology*, 1978, *14*, 79–86.

Rose, S.A., Gottfried, A., & Bridger, W.H. *Cross-modal transfer in fullterm and preterm infants*. Paper presented at the annual meeting of the American Psychological Association, San Francisco, 1977.

Rubenstein, J. A concordance of visual and manipulative responsiveness to novel and familiar stimuli in six-month-old infants. *Child Development*, 1974, *45*, 194–195.

Ruff, H.A. The coordination of manipulation and visual fixation: A response to Schaffer (1975). *Child Development*, 1976, *47*, 868–871.

Ruff, H.A., & Halton, A. *Is there directed reaching in the human neonate?* Paper presented at the biennial meeting of the Society for Research in Child Development, New Orleans, 1977.

Ruff, H.A., & Kohler, C.J. Tactual-visual transfer in six-month-old infants. *Infant Behavior and Development*, 1978, *1*, 259–264.

Salapatek, P., & Kesson, W. Visual scanning of triangles by the human newborn. *Journal of Experimental Child Psychology*, 1966, *3*, 155–167.

Schaeffer, B. Skill integration during cognitive development. In R.A. Kennedy & A. Wilkes (Eds.), *Studies in long term memory*. New York: Wiley, 1975.

Schaffer, H.R., and Parry, M.H. Perceptual–motor behavior in infancy as a function of age and stimulus familiarity. *British Journal of Psychology*, 1969, *60*, 1–9.

Schaffer, H.R., and Parry, M.H. The effects of short-term familiarization on infants' perceptual-motor coordination in a simultaneous discrimination situation. *British Journal of Psychology*, 1970, *61*, 559–569.

Schofield, L., and Uzgiris, I.C. *Examining behavior and the development of the concept of object*. Paper presented at the biennial meeting of the Society for Research in Child Development, Santa Monica, 1969.

Spelke, E.S., and Owsley, C.J. *Intermodal exploration and perceptual knowledge in infancy.* Paper presented at the biennial meeting of the Society for Research in Child Development, New Orleans, 1977.

Steele, D., and Pederson, D.R. Stimulus variables which affect the concordance of visual and manipulative exploration in six-month-old infants. *Child Development, 1977, 48,* 104–111.

Twitchell, T.E. Reflex mechanisms and the development of prehension. In K. Connolly (Ed.), *Mechanisms of motor skill development.* New York: Academic Press, 1970.

von Fieandt, K. Some psychological constituents and aspects of object perception. In R.B. MacLeod and H.L. Pick, Jr. (Eds.), *Perception: Essays in honor of James J. Gibson.* Ithaca: Cornell University Press, 1974.

Walk, R.D., & Gibson, E.J. A comparative and analytical study of visual depth perception. *Psychological Monographs, 1961, 75* (No. 15).

Wellman, H.M. Knowledge of the interaction of memory variables: A developmental study of metamemory. *Developmental Psychology, 1978, 14,* 24–29.

White, B.L., Castle, P., & Held, R. Observations on the development of visually-directed reaching. *Child Development, 1964, 35,* 349–364.

White, B., & Held, R. Plasticity of sensorimotor development in the human infant. In J. Rosenblith and W. Allinsmith (Eds.), *The causes of behavior.* Boston: Allyn and Bacon, Inc., 1966.

2

The Origins of Auditory-Visual Perception and Visual Proprioception in Human Development

GEORGE BUTTERWORTH

1. Introduction: The Genetic Method

Human development offers a distinctive type of inquiry within contemporary scientific psychology. James Mark Baldwin (1894) was the first psychologist to set out the advantages of the developmental approach to psychology.

> The study of children is generally the only means of testing the truth of our mental analyses. If we decide that a certain complex product is due to a union of simpler elements, then we may appeal to the proper period of child life to see the union taking place . . . there is hardly a question of analysis now under debate which may not be tested by this method. (p. 5)

Thus developmental psychology as method, "the genetic method" as Baldwin called it, unravels psychological processes by focusing on their ontogeny. Inevitably, the genetic method raises questions about the origins of cognitive processes and about the assumptions on which theories of development are based. This chapter is concerned with auditory-visual perception and with the role of vision in motor control. Although there is much to be learned on these topics from the study of older children (e.g., Birch & Lefford, 1967) or from the study of the

GEORGE BUTTERWORTH • Department of Psychology, University of Southampton, Southampton S09 5NH, England.

blind (O'Connor & Hermelin, 1978), our discussion will concentrate on
early infancy because questions of the origins of human knowledge
ultimately lead to the study of infants. Questions about origins reveal
that theories of intersensory and sensorimotor development rest on
certain basic assumptions concerning the perception of visual space.
These assumptions will be considered briefly in order to set the specific
topics of the chapter in their broader context.

2. Some Theoretical and Evolutionary Considerations

The classic problem in the psychology of visual perception is how
a two-dimensional retinal image can yield the experience of a three-
dimensional extended space. The resolution of this problem sets the
stage for theories of intersensory and sensorimotor development.

Berkeley (1709/1963) argued that "touch tutors vision" in development because he considered geometrical optics inadequate as a *theory* of
space perception, even though it may constitute a perfectly valid mathematical way of describing space:

> But those lines and angles by means whereof some men pretend to explain
> the perception of distance are themselves not at all perceived, nor are they
> in truth even thought of by those unskilful in optics. . . . In vain shall any
> man tell me that I perceive certain lines and angles which introduce into my
> mind various ideas of distance. (cited in Fraser, 1899, p. 179)

Berkeley did not entertain an alternative to a geometrical analysis of
visual space but tried to deal with its limitations by invoking a construc-
tionist theory. His solution to the problem of visual space perception
was to argue that it is learned by association between retinal, motor, and
tactual cues. Convergence of the eyes and the muscular effort involved
in active locomotion provide a spatial metric to give structure to the
two-dimensional retinal array. Similarly, properties of substantiality
thought to be peculiar to the sense of touch are attributed to visual
objects by a gradual process of learning by association. Starting from
these assumptions, the developmental problem becomes one of explaining how separate sensory and motor processes become coordinated in
development. Since muscular kinesthesis forms a primary space, development proceeds from proximal to distal spatial sensitivity, and audition
and vision must become associated with each other during development
through their common links with the kinesthetic modality.

Contrary to Berkeley, J.J. Gibson (1950, 1966) argues that to kick a
stone is no better guarantee of its presence than to see it. His is an

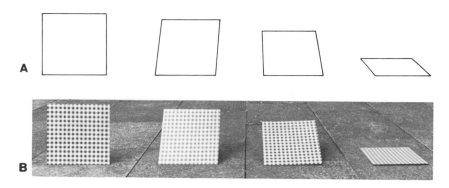

Fig. 1. Spatial information available in two-dimensional visual array. (A) Information in a geometric projection. (B) Information in a structured two-dimensional visual array.[1] Photo courtesy of A. Costall and T. Wright.

information-based theory of perception, in which no sensory system is necessarily more trustworthy than another. Gibson substitutes "ecological optics" for the physical optics to which Berkeley objected and, in doing so, he offers an alternative approach to the problem of intersensory coordination. For Gibson, space is not an empty container but is given by textured surfaces and objects that rest on surfaces. Reflected light, the "ambient array" available to an observer at a station point, preserves surface texture and the relative positions of objects in the retinal image. Invariant relations within the two-dimensional retinal array are sufficient to specify three-dimensional space directly to the perceiver. Figure 1 provides such an example. (See Braunstein, 1978, for an extended discussion of Gibson's theory of space perception and Costall, 1981, for a discussion of the more general implications of theories of "direct perception" for developmental psychology.)

One consequence of Gibson's alternative description of the information available in the retinal array is that flatness of the image need no longer bedevil theories of space perception, so that vision need not be tutored by touch in development. This fact, in turn, has implications for theories of intersensory functioning, particularly since Gibson's emphasis on the senses as information-seeking systems draws attention to their

[1] The geometric analysis of visual perception emphasizes the ambiguity of the two-dimensional retinal image. The same pattern at the eye could arise from an infinite number of objects. However, most objects are textured and set upon a textured ground. According to Gibson (1966) structural information within the two-dimensional retinal array is sufficient to specify a three-dimensional space directly.

potential equivalence in specifying object properties. In fact, Gibson argues that vision can specify substantiality directly. For example, a rigid object, when rotating, undergoes regular perspectival transformations of its external boundary, while internal texture relationships remain constant. A nonrigid object undergoes regular transformation both in its external boundary and in its internal structure, and since these properties are uniquely related to rigidity and elasticity, they are sufficient to specify them directly (see Section 5.2).

Theories of intersensory development have also been influenced by speculations about the evolution of sensory systems, perhaps through the temptation to assume that ontogeny recapitulates phylogeny. Gregory (1968) argues that eyes may have evolved from a primitive photosensitivity apparent in the surface membrane of single-celled organisms. He speculates that vision may have evolved from such a primarily tactile system because it has the advantage, over touch, of giving information about distant events. Similar speculations (but with an alternative interpretation) have been advanced on the origins of audition in mechanical receptors such as the lateral line organs of the fish (von Hornbostel, 1938). These speculations reinforce the notion that ontogeny (and evolution) proceed from proximal to distal sensitivity.

An alternative interpretation of much the same evolutionary data emphasizes the "unity of the senses" (Bower, 1974a,b; Marks, 1978; von Hornbostel, 1938). Separate modalities are thought to have evolved from an undifferentiated "supramodal" sensory system on which patterned stimulation in a variety of energy spectra has equivalent effects. The effective stimuli can be described in terms of energy transitions or abrupt discontinuities in intensity that activate the same behaviors whether the energy is mechanically, radiantly, or chemically transmitted. Of course, specialized receptors which appear as separate sensory systems become differentiated in evolution, but even among higher mammals, the senses retain some supramodal functional characteristics. Bower (1974b) has argued that if a developmental psychologist were forced to choose between extreme theories, it would be better to assume that the infant begins from a state of unity of the senses than from unrelated sensory systems, since the former is the more primitive state in evolution. It should be noted, however, that the question at issue is not whether *coordination* or *differentiation* of sensory modalities is the primary developmental process. The fundamental question is whether there exists a spatial relationship between the senses or between sensory and motor systems from birth. Coordination and differentiation can coexist as developmental processes even in the embryo, as Coghill (1929) pointed out long ago.

A third evolutionary scenario is that vision may form a primary spatial sense on which other senses have become modeled in the course of phylogenesis. Jerison (1973) argues that hearing and olfaction became important as distance senses in the evolutionary transition from reptiles to mammals. To avoid predatory reptiles, the mammals evolved in a nocturnal ecological niche. Selection pressures operated to integrate temporal information in a manner analogous to the spatial array typical of vision and for which appropriate brain structures were already available. One successful solution is demonstrated by echolocation in the bat, an auditory spatial process that provides precise distance information. With the appearance of diurnal mammals, such as the primates, vision became reemphasized as the primary spatial sense.

One extrapolation from this evolutionary scenario to developmental psychology is that distal sensitivity may precede proximal sensitivity; that is, the infant may be more sensitive to the spatial structure of the environment than to the spatial properties of the body (see Section 5.4). Another implication is that vision may have primacy among the senses, although no theory as yet adopts this as a guiding principle. It seems appropriate at this point to examine the developmental evidence, first with respect to auditory-visual coordination and later (Section 5 onward) with respect to visual-motor coordination.

3. The Origins of Auditory-Visual Perception

The literature on auditory-visual coordination in infancy is undoubtedly riddled with theoretical assumptions and conceptual confusion. In this section, we will begin by outlining Piaget's theory to bring out his emphasis on qualitative changes in the relationship between the senses that arise with development. However, Piaget's account is based on a number of assumptions that are questioned by contemporary research on oculomotor responses to sound in human neonates. This literature is surveyed because it bears on Piaget's theory and also because it relates to an alternative set of assumptions about the origins of development, the "primitive unity" theory. Following this discussion of the neonatal literature, we will examine the relationship between *detection* of intermodal equivalence and *anticipation* of information in one modality given information in another. This distinction has been further confounded with the question whether spatial colocation is a necessary condition for intersensory processing. The review of auditory-visual coordination in early infancy ends by making a distinction between functional connections linking audition and vision that are available from birth, and sensory coordination based on knowledge of intermodal equivalence. It is necessary to take into account both qualitative and quantitative changes in development to arrive at an understanding of the process of auditory-visual coordination.

3.1. Piaget's Theory

There is little doubt that responses to auditory and visual stimuli occur from birth in humans (see, e.g., Haith & Campos, 1977), but experimental research on intermodal functioning is of relatively recent origin, with perhaps the most influential theory being that of Piaget (1953, 1954). Piaget shares some of Berkeley's assumptions on the development of space perception, arguing that awareness of an extended space is slowly constructed as the infant acts on objects and becomes mobile. At birth, audition and vision encompass self-contained and unrelated spaces. In this theory, coordination is achieved over the first three postnatal months by a process of "reciprocal assimilation" of the motor programs guiding looking and listening. At the same time, a separate coordination is being established between visual and tactile spaces. Then, from 3 to 6 months, auditory-visual and visual-tactile spaces unite as the infant manipulates noisy objects in his visual field, fianlly to yield multimodal percepts of particular objects.

Very young infants may give the impression that there is coordination between seeing and hearing, but Piaget argues that they are merely attempting to see and hear at the same time. For example, at 1 month, 8 days, Piaget's son Laurent appears to be trying to localize a sound visually, but Piaget doubts whether this constitutes sensory coordination:

> His head oscillates slightly from right to left without yet finding the right location and his glance . . . also searches . . . but it is impossible to say whether the child tries to see the source of the sound or whether his looking simply accompanies pure auditory accommodation. (1953, p. 81)

Piaget argues that the child is not yet trying to see what he is hearing or hear what he is seeing but merely carrying out both activities simultaneously. Nevertheless, simultaneous activation of looking and listening provides the necessary conditions for their interpenetration. It is not until the third month that Piaget feels certain that coordination exists:

> At 2 months and 14 days Laurent observes one meter away, my pipe while I knock lightly on wood. He stops looking at the place of contact when the sound stops and immediately finds it again when I resume. (1953, p. 83)

The previously separate activities are now unified. This motor coordination heralds a new level of functioning in the child's cognitive development: recognition of "a sign charged with meaning." The infant

anticipates visual properties on the basis of auditory information and vice versa. Such behavior is more than learning by passive association, since the infant actively searches for correlations between sounds and visual images. As Piaget says, the child will try to "listen to faces and look at voices" (1953, p. 87). But even this activity remains primarily a spatial coordination of the sensory apparatus itself. It is not until the child develops prehension, between 3 and 6 months, that auditory and visual information unite with touch so that sensory stimulation is perceived as a property of objects.

Thus, in Piaget's theory, evidence for auditory-visual coordination is given by the development of expectancies that translate across modalities. Insofar as expectancies require familiarity with specific objects, the process may well depend on experience to occur. However, Piaget may have overlooked evidence of preadaptation for such learning in the response repertoire of the neonate.

3.2. Oculomotor Responses to Sound in the Neonate

Clinicians screening infants for deafness have long made use of eye movements, among other behavioral indices of auditory acuity (Bench, Collyer, Langford, & Wilson, 1976; Chun, Pawsat, & Forster, 1960; Ewing & Ewing, 1944, Froeschels, 1946). Since these investigations were not directly concerned with the question of auditory-visual coordination, information on the spatial relation between eye movements and sound tends not to be reported systematically. Recently, attention has turned to the study of oculomotor responses as a possible indicator of intermodal functioning.

In a single case study, Wertheimer (1961) found that a baby only 3 minutes old would reliably turn her eyes in the direction of a toy "cricket," clicked randomly at either ear. On the first trial, the baby made an ipsilateral eye movement, and the majority of all sound-contingent eye movements (18 out of 22 responses) were in the ipsilateral direction. Wertheimer concluded that a rough coordination between auditory and visual-motor space can be observed in the neonate.

A number of studies have since confirmed that neonates can make eye movements that are spatially coordinated with the locus of a sound. However, infants do not respond on every trial and consistent spatially coordinated responses, when they occur, depend on a multiplicity of factors including infant state, and intensity and duration of the stimulus. Thus, Butterworth and Castillo (1976) obtained evidence for predominantly contralateral eye movements to a fairly intense auditory stimulus

(an 85-dB tone of 500 msec duration), whereas Mendelson and Haith (1976) found evidence for predominantly ipsilateral sound-contingent eye movements to a tape recording of a male voice. Turkewitz, Birch, Moreau, Levy, & Cornwell (1966) found that the direction of the oculomotor response to sound depends on a complex interaction among infant state, the absolute intensity of the sound, and the ear of stimulation. High "effective" intensities produce predominantly contralateral eye movements, whereas moderate intensities produce ipsilateral eye movements. Finally, McGurk, Turnure, & Creighton (1977) found some evidence for contralateral eye movements in a replication of the Wertheimer study, again using a toy "cricket" as the auditory stimulus.

Taken as a whole, the evidence indicates that auditory and oculomotor systems are not completely independent at birth. Furthermore, the fact that the systems function in spatial relationship to each other suggests that the coordination observed is not simply a matter of separate sensory channels being activated simultaneously. It is true that auditory stimulation can lead to a general increase in arousal including activation of eye movements (Turkewitz, Moreau, Birch, & Davis, 1971), but an explanation based on arousal alone would not require spatial coordination. Nor are the data compatible with a simple associationistic hypothesis. Appropriate spatial responses often occur from the first trial in infants too young to have had any extensive experience through which the oculomotor response could have been learned (e.g., Wertheimer's subject was only 10 minutes old at the end of the experiment!).

A simple interpretation of the neonatal data is that oculomotor responses to sound are reflexive. Such an explanation has been offered by Jones and Kabanoff (1975) and Butterworth and Castillo (1976), who argued that eye movements may help stabilize auditory memory for position. However, a more complex explanation may be required, as Mendelson and Haith (1976) found that neonates showed spatial orientation to a sound played at the midline for periods up to 30 sec after stimulus onset. Infants were also observed to make systematic scanning movements of the eyes, even when the sounds were played in the dark. Since visual orientation exceeded the temporal boundaries of reflexive responding, Mendelson and Haith suggest that sound triggers an endogenous scanning program. They emphasize the active, exploratory nature of perception even in the neonate.

Although the evidence was not obtained developmentally, neuroanatomical studies also support the behavioral data. Harrison and Irving (1966) suggest that the medial olivary nucleus, located in the brain stem, is implicated in directing head and eyes toward a sound in diurnal

mammals with well-developed eyes. Evidence also exists for bimodal sensory processing in the visual cortex of monkeys (Morrel, 1972). Some cells in the *visual* cortex respond to *auditory* stimulation, particularly when auditory and visual stimuli are colocated in space. It seems possible that oculomotor responses to sound in the neonate may be subcortically mediated, with cortical representation developing later. (Detailed evidence is not available at present, but see Bronson, 1974, for an account of the relationship between subcortical and cortical processes in visual development.)

In summary, there is evidence for spatially organized connections between oculomotor and auditory systems in human neonates, and it is possible that this coordination goes beyond reflexive responding. However, it would be rash to conclude that neonates *expect* a sight to accompany a sound. A functional connection may merely help to ensure that under ecologically valid conditions, a sight will usually accompany a sound.

3.3.   The Primitive-Unity Hypothesis

Demonstrations of auditory oculomotor coordination in neonates are compatible with "primitive unity" as the starting point for development. Bower (1974b) has suggested two versions of this hypothesis, although most experiments have not distinguished between them. Bower points out that development could start from primitive unity either with or without modality differentiation. With modality differentiation, there is spatial coordination between the senses at birth, and the infant can discriminate auditory and visual information. Without modality differentiation, there is spatial coordination, but the infant cannot tell whether he is looking or listening to something. Thus, intersensory-conflict experiments with neonates should yield different outcomes depending on the particular relationship between the senses that exists at birth.

Bower argues that if there is no sensory unity, then the infant should not be aware of any discordance between separate auditory and visual loci, since sight and sound are not related by a common spatial framework. Presumably, the infant would respond either to the auditory or the visual locus, or alternate between them. If there is perfect unity without modality differentiation, then the infant can only compromise between two simultaneous sources of stimulation. Since the baby would lack any sensory basis on which to choose other than intensity or relative salience, there should be no evidence of conflict. Only in the case of perceptual unity with modality differentiation could the infant show signs of conflict, perhaps by response suppression or some other indicator. These alternatives are summarized in Table 1.

Castillo and Butterworth (1980) carried out an experiment to distinguish between the alternatives shown in Table 1. Newborn infants were presented with either conflicting or congruent auditory and visual stimuli and their eye movements were videotaped. The auditory stimulus was a 62-dB sine wave "tone" of 450 Hz and 1-sec duration presented in blocks of ten trials over one of two loudspeakers subtending 30° on either side of the infant's midline. The baby was seated, facing a white cloth enclosure that completely filled the visual field. The loudspeakers were placed behind the cloth screen. Three groups of infants were tested (N = 8 per group). For one group, the sounds were presented in the unstructured visual field (sound-only group). For a second group, a visual target consisting of a pair of small red circles drawn on a card was suspended in front of the active loudspeaker so that auditory and visual loci were always congruent. For the third group, the visual target was mounted in front of the inactive loudspeaker so that it was always diametrically opposite the auditory locus. The sounds were presented when the infants' eyes were oriented to the midline, and the videotapes were later scored "blind" by two observers who noted the direction of the infants' sound-contingent eye movements. The results are shown in Figure 2.

As the graph shows, there was evidence for consistent spatial coordination between the oculomotor response and the auditory locus only in the two conditions where a visual target was available. In the congruent condition a significant proportion of all sound-contingent eye movements was in the direction of the sound, although the proportion declined toward chance level at the end of the series of trials. In the incongruent condition, a significant proportion of all eye movements was contralateral to the sound and toward the visual target. The proportion

Table 1. Intersensory Spatial Conflict and Neonate Sensory Organization (Bower, 1974b)

Sensory organization	Effect of conflicting auditory and visual loci
No spatial relation between the senses at birth	No conflict perceived by infant
Sensory unity without differentiation of modalities	No conflict perceived by infant
Sensory unity with modality differentiation	Conflict perceived by infant

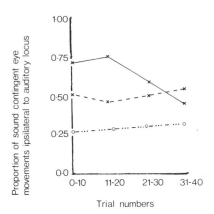

Trial numbers

Fig. 2. Auditory-oculomotor coordination in neonates (Castillo & Butterworth, 1980): (×—×) congruent auditory and visual loci; (×--×) sound only; (○····○) incongruent auditory and visual loci (chance level: 0.50).

of eye movements to the visual target remained constant throughout the series. In the sound-only condition, there was no evidence for consistent spatial coordination.

At first sight, the results might be thought to support the hypothesis that development starts from unrelated auditory and visual spaces, since there is no coordination in a blank visual field, and the infant consistently looks toward the visual target when one is available. However, close inspection of the data reveals that infants did experience a conflict, since the proportion of spatially coordinated sound-contingent eye movements in the incongruent condition was significantly greater than in the congruent condition. It is possible that spatially coordinated, ipsilateral, sound-contingent eye movements may depend on the presence of structure in the visual field, and most studies have not controlled for this. However, Mendelson and Haith report accurate spatial orientation in neonates to sounds presented at the midline in the dark. Thus, lack of visual structure may not explain the lack of coordination under sound-only conditions. Turkewitz, Birch, & Cooper (1972a,b) suggest that pure tones are not very effective directional stimuli, so an alternative explanation for lack of consistent coordination under sound-only conditions may lie in the type of stimulus used by Castillo and Butterworth. Nevertheless, the results do show that presence of the visual target enhanced the spatial coordination of the sound-contingent eye movements. More importantly, however, infants were significantly more likely to look toward the visual target when auditory and visual loci conflicted than when they were congruent. This observation suggests that infants were not attending to the visual modality only but were localizing the sound with respect to the visual target. Visual dominance over auditory localization is also found in adults (Howard & Templeton, 1966), so the attainment of this result with neonates may reflect a basic mechanism in auditory localization.

A number of explanations for visual dominance have been offered in the past (see Posner, Nissen, & Klein, 1976), but in the present context, a spatial-localization hypothesis seems sufficient. Von Hornbostel (1938) pointed out that vision and audition differ in their spatial properties: "For there is one real contrast between the eye and the ear. No sound is ever so much an object as is a fixed, visible thing" (p. 215). The continuous availability of the visible target may provide the clue to the dominance of vision over audition. Auditory localization is thought to depend mainly on binaural differences in time, phase, and intensity of auditory stimulation. However, such a system places a load on memory since the perceiver must somehow hold the locus in mind after the sound has stopped. Jones and Kabanoff (1975) have suggested that auditory-position memory in adults may be stabilized by monitoring spatially correlated command signals for eye movements. However, even this system would have the disadvantage that the stored command signal would be in error the moment a new head or eye movement occurred. Stability of auditory memory would be greatly enhanced if the sound were localized with respect to an object in visual space. A stable visual locus provides a distinctive "allocentric" spatial referent that remains invariant with changes in the position of the observer. Since, under normal conditions, auditorily elicited eye movements will generally result in afferent visual information, it is conceivable that the systems may have evolved to be mutually supportive in auditory localization. Under conditions of spatial conflict, the stable allocentric visual-location code may take precedence over unstable auditory memory for position.

This hypothesis has the advantage that the neonate need not be attributed innate ideas to explain why auditory and visual information interact from birth. It remains unnecessary to argue that the infant "anticipates" visual consequences on an auditory stimulus. The hypothesis of mutually supportive spatial-location systems may also explain why infants at 3 months prefer to look at whichever of two identical visual displays is spatially congruent with an auditory stimulus (McGurk & MacDonald, 1978). As Spelke (1976) has pointed out, it would be of doubtful adaptive significance for the infant to be born with a set of well-defined beliefs about the information available to audition and vision. Nature, with more economy, might provide a set of flexible strategies for discovering the particular combinations of auditory and visual information that occur in the world. A spatial interaction between audition and vision that tends toward spatial colocation of patterned auditory and visual information might be one example of an adaptive mechanism that lends coherence to, but is independent of, the content of any particular experience.

3.4. Detection of Intermodal Equivalence

Many investigations of intersensory perception in slightly older babies tend not to distinguish between several aspects of coordinated functioning. One distinction, often ignored, is between *detection* of cross-modal equivalence and *anticipation* across modalities when the infant is given information in one modality. Detection may not depend on memory, since perception of equivalence may occur in real time. Anticipation, however, may depend on the ability to store information over time. It is difficult to demonstrate habituation to visual stimuli, a process of information storage implicit in recognition memory before about 3 months (Cohen & Gelber, 1975). Hence, it should be equally difficult to demonstrate cross-modal *anticipation* if recognition is involved. However, this would not mean that infants are unable to *detect* cross-modal equivalence earlier in development. Most studies do not make it clear whether detection or anticipation is being studied.

A second source of confusion concerns the spatial relation between patterned information obtained through audition or vision. Does the infant *expect* spatial colocation from the outset, or do these expectations, if they exist, depend on an initial capacity to detect colocation? The discussion of oculomotor responses to sound in neonates in Sections 3.2 and 3.3 suggests that detection would be the more parsimonious hypothesis, but again the distinction between detection and anticipation is usually not strictly adhered to. A number of studies have made use of a spatial-dislocation paradigm, in which auditory and visual information are placed in conflict, without disentangling these issues.

Aronson and Rosenbloom (1971) carried out an experiment said to demonstrate that infants as young as 30 days expect the sight of the mother's face to be spatially congruent with the sound of her voice. Infants were separated from the mother by a glass screen and her voice was relayed stereophonically over loudspeakers so that it appeared to come from straight ahead, coincident with the mother. After fairly prolonged experience of congruent stimulation (2 or 5 min), the balance between the loudspeakers was altered so that the mother's voice came from 90° to one side. The infants became emotionally disturbed and they would refuse to look at the mother even after spatial congruity was restored. The authors concluded that infants were upset by the violation of the unity of their perceptual world.

McGurk and Lewis (1974) and Condry, Haltom, and Neisser (1977) failed to replicate Aronson and Rosenbloom's study. They found no evidence of emotional disturbance under conditions of spatial dislocation of the mother's face and voice. However, in the first of these replications, the congruent episode was only 30 sec long and in the second, 60 sec long. That is, infants did not have as extensive experience of congruent auditory and visual information as in the original study. It is possible that emotional disturbance may depend on intraexperimental experience, and these replication studies failed to take this into account. However, these studies do suggest that upset may have nothing to do with innate expectancies about perceptual unity. There is, on the other hand, some evidence for early cross-modal perception, since Carpenter (1974) reports visual avoidance in 3-week-old infants who observed a stranger miming to a tape recording of the mother's voice and, reciprocally, visual avoidance of the mother miming to a tape recording of the stranger's voice. Bergman, Haith, and Mann (1971) also showed that infants of 7 weeks are sensitive to some aspects of the face–voice combination. They found that after the mother starts speaking to the infant, the infant's visual scanning becomes localized around the region of the mother's eyes. Nevertheless, the face–voice paradigm has not been notably successful in demonstrating intersensory coordination in young infants.

In part, the problem may lie in confusion of spatial correspondence of bimodal information with those aspects of patterned auditory and visual information that might be equivalent. The intramodal literature suggests one hypothesis which may be worth considering briefly. There is reasonable evidence that by 1 month, infants recognize their mother's voice (Mehler, Bertoncini, Barriere, & Gerschenfeld, 1978; Mills & Melhuish, 1974). Mehler and colleagues suggest that recognition may be based on the characteristic pattern of intonation, since infants showed no recognition when the mother spoke in a monotone. Cues for facial perception have not been widely studied in young infants, although configurational properties of the face defined by hairline, hair length, and hair color may be important (Dirks & Gibson, 1977). Since infants look at the area around the eyes when the mother is speaking (Bergman *et al.*

1971), it is possible that one basis for detection of intermodal equivalence may lie in the common emotional properties expressed by the mobility of the face and the intonation of the voice (see Hamlyn, 1978, for a discussion of the philosophical basis of this hypothesis).

A more direct equivalence between auditory and visual aspects of language is suggested by recent studies of auditory-visual correspondence of phonetic categories. McGurk and MacDonald (1976) showed that children from 3 years experience an auditory illusion when they observe a film showing an adult speaking in temporal coordination with a noncorresponding sound track. For example, if the adult says "ba ba" but the accompanying sound track is "ga ga," the observer hears "da da." Immediately the observer looks away from the film, and the true sound is heard; immediately upon looking back, the illusion reappears. The authors suggest that the illusion depends on intersensory equivalence. Lip movements bear an invariant relation to phonetic features, such as place of articulation, that are in turn related to certain features of the acoustic waveform. Hence the visual configuration of the mouth can specify to some degree the phonetic feature that will be heard. The incompatibility or compatibility of the auditory and visual information for phonetic features results in fusion to form a completely new sound (or combinations of sounds, in some cases). Given the sensitivity of the human infant to the phonetic aspects of speech (Eimas, 1975), extension of this line of research into infancy may produce extremely interesting data on the significance of intermodal perception for language acquisition.

To return to the available evidence on intermodal equivalence: Clearer results have been obtained with inanimate objects. Lyons-Ruth (1977) familiarized 4-month-old infants over repeated trials with a sounding toy presented in the visual field. On test trials, babies were presented either with the same toy–sound combination or with a novel toy paired with a familiar sound. Infants looked away from the mismatched toy–sound pair but not from the familiar pair. It is not certain whether looking away reflected disappointment due to disconfirmation of an expectation or whether the baby was searching for the original object. However, the results are consistent with the hypothesis that infants perceive sound as an attribute of a specific object by about 4 months, since they relate knowledge obtained in the auditory mode to information obtained in the visual mode.

In another study, Lyons-Ruth (1974) presented infants of 14, 17, and 22 weeks with an object moving to the left of the visual field, in temporal synchrony with a sound. Infants observed the movement under two conditions, either with the sound spatially congruent with the visual object or with the sound coming from a location diametrically opposite. Infants showed more behavioral arousal, as evidenced by limb and body movements, during the incongruent episode than during the congruent episode. The author argues that bimodal inputs which covary temporally are assumed by the infant to also covary spatially. Such an assumption would allow the infant to distinguish between bimodal information relating to a single object and bimodal information that is merely concurrent.

This explanation has the advantage of specifying the stimulus parameters to which the infant may be attending, but it is again couched in terms of what the baby "expects." Closer examination of the data suggests an alternative interpretation. Only the older infants looked toward the dislocated sound, which demonstrates that they were aware that it was merely concurrent with the moving visual stimulus. The younger infants registered a conflict between auditory and visual loci, as evidenced by behavioral arousal, but they fixated the visual stimulus even more strongly than under the congruent condition. McGurk (McGurk et al., 1977) performed a similar experiment with neonates. These infants also continued to track a moving visual stimulus under conditions of auditory-visual conflict. Rather than argue that covariation is expected by young infants, it may be more parsimonious to explain their behavior as visual capture under conditions of intermodal conflict (much as in the study by Castillo and Butterworth [1980] reported in Section 3.3).

Perhaps the best evidence that infants can detect equivalence and predict across modalities (at least from the fourth month) comes from recent studies by Spelke. In one experiment (Spelke, 1978), infants were shown two films simultaneously in which a toy animal moved up and down in a regular rhythm. In one film the animal "bounced" once every 2 sec, and in the adjacent film twice a sec. A separate sound track located between the films was played, in which a percussion sound accompanied each impact for one of the moving toys but not the other. Infants preferred to look at whichever film moved in synchrony with the sound track. Spelke argues that infants may have detected the common rhythm of auditory and visual stimulation. More interestingly, the sight of an impact may be intermodally equivalent to its sound. Discovery of this common property of auditory and visual stimulation could not have been based on previous experience in real life, since the sounds made by the toys were arbitrary and artificial. Nor could it have been learned by association during the experiment, since both films were simultaneously contiguous with the sound. Spelke argues that detection of equivalence did not depend on a common spatial direction for sight and sound. However, the sound was ambiguously located with respect to both films, being between them, so common properties of patterning may have led the infant to perceive the films as colocated. Before it can be concluded that some degree of spatial colocation is not necessary for *detection* of intersensory equivalence, it would seem necessary to perform control experiments in which the sound track is located well away from the visual stimuli.

However, colocation seems not to be necessary for *anticipation* across modalities. Spelke and Owsley (1977) demonstrated cross-modal anticipation in infants between 3.5 and 7.5 months. The infants were seated in front of their mother and father, who sat quietly, without moving their mouths, while a tape recording with sequences of both their voices was played. The sound was located randomly with respect to either parent; yet infants looked toward the parent whose voice they heard significantly more frequently than would be expected by chance. Since visual orientation to the appropriate parent cannot have been based on the spatial location of the sound, it appears that visual search can be independent of spatial correspondence once it is based on knowledge of intermodal equivalence.

Bower (1977) has studied space perception in a congenitally blind infant equipped with an electronic echo-locating device. The aim of the study was to establish whether spatial information obtained through hearing in the blind infant might be equivalent to space perception through visual information in the sighted. The electronic device was worn on the infant's head from 4 months. It continuously irradiates the environment with ultrasound and converts the sonic reflections into an audible tone. Echoes from distant objects produce a high-pitched sound and those from nearer objects a lower-pitched sound. The amplitude of the sound signals the size of the reflecting object (loud is large and soft small), and the clarity of the signal gives information for texture (soft surfaces produce a "fuzzy" signal and hard surfaces a "sharp" signal). The audible signal is stereophonic so that direction of the reflecting surface is signaled by differences in time of arrival at the ears. At 4 months the infant, on first wearing the device, showed convergence of the eyes to an approaching object and divergence to a receding object. By about 6 months the infant began to reach for an auditorily specified object, and at 9 months he showed the placing response—extension of the arms as if to break a fall—when lowered toward an auditorilly specified surface. Although this investigation was more exploratory than experimental, it does suggest that hearing can specify spatial properties of the environment in blind human infants. Replications and detailed longitudinal studies of congenitally blind infants equipped with echo-locating devices could produce very powerful evidence for detection of auditory-visual equivalence in infancy.

4. Summary and Conclusions: Auditory-Visual Coordination

This chapter began by presenting the genetic method as a means of disentangling complex theories of intersensory functioning. Evidence was reviewed for a spatially organized, functional relation between the auditory and oculomotor systems from birth. This coordination may be enhanced by intrinsic spatial properties of the visual system that act to ensure auditory and visual colocation. Such a functional relation might in turn facilitate the detection of intermodal equivalence, since sounds are usually accompanied by sights. This is not the same as an ability to *anticipate* visual consequences on auditory stimulation. Anticipation may depend on experience and perhaps on the development of cortical functions. Nevertheless, there is evidence that by 4 months infants can anticipate across modalities, and that this ability is independent of spatial correspondence. It seems possible that such a developmental achievement may have its roots in a built-in spatial relation between the senses.

Thus, although Piaget was probably mistaken in assuming development to begin from discrete sensory modalities (and in emphasizing touch as the final arbiter of objectivity—see Sections 5.2 and 5.3), his theory is sufficiently subtle to emphasize qualitative changes in the relationships between modalities which occur with development. Only spatial connections are required to turn in the direction of a sound, whereas when the infant looks in the direction of a specific object or person given only patterned auditory information, the action is based on knowledge of equivalence. Now perception functions across modalities on the basis of *stored* information, and this is a qualitative change in the relationship between the senses.

The tendency for the literature to be polarized into "innate" vs. "acquired" has perhaps caused researchers to overlook the possibility of an innate functional relationship between audition and vision that provides a unitary spatial framework in relation to which patterned information can be detected. If the hypotheses advanced above are correct, the spatial organization of the senses at birth should ensure that where cross-modally equivalent information is available in the infant's world, it will be rapidly detected.

5. Visual Proprioception

The remainder of this chapter reviews several topics related to the development of visual-motor coordination. It may seem strange to juxtapose research on sensorimotor processes with research on intersensory functioning, since these are often considered watertight psychological compartments. However, as was pointed out in Section 2, these problems are linked through assumptions concerning the perception of visual space and through assumptions about the role of touch in tutoring vision. This section begins by considering sources of information available for specifying movement of the self. Traditionally, kinesthesis was considered a separate sensory modality, given by information from the muscles and joints. J.J. Gibson (1966) breaks with this tradition and argues that information for self-movement is better considered an amodal, intersensory aspect of stimulation. In particular, vision provides direct evidence for self-movement in a stable environment. Before considering Gibson's hypothesis of "visual proprioception," the traditional theory of sensorimotor coordination is outlined. There follows a discussion of the relation between vision and touch in development as evidenced by infants' responses to visually solid but tactually impalpable objects, and by their reactions to patterns of visual information that specify an impending collision. The final section considers patterns of visual information that specify movement of self. This discussion raises further epistemological issues in relation to Piaget's theory of infant–environment adualism. Piaget argues that infants cannot distinguish between "self" and "not self" until they conceive of self as an object. The evidence is reviewed and an attempt is made to reconcile Gibson's direct and Piaget's mediated theories of self-perception.

5.1. Theories of Visual-Motor Coordination

J.J. Gibson (1966) coined the term "visual proprioception" to draw attention to the role of vision in providing information for movement of self over and above proprioceptive cues given by the mechanical-vestibular system. He argues that kinesthesis is not a unitary sensory modality but an *amodal,* intersensory property of stimulation that is equivalent in specifying movement of self whether it arises as feedback from the vestibular, skeletal, or visual systems. Visual proprioception specifies movement of self by perspective transformations of the retinal image arising from movements of an observer through a stable space. Total motion of a structured visual array outward from a stationary central point specifies movement of the observer in a particular direction, given by the focus of optical motion. Such a flow pattern is thought sufficient to allow the observer to make the distinction between movement of self and movement of the world since the stimulus information has an objective and a subjective pole built in.

Once again, Gibson's description of the information available in the flow of visual information at the retina touches on developmental questions. In the traditional empiricist account, the information for movement of self is given by motor kinesthesis—proprioceptive input from the muscles and joints. Motor kinesthesis constitutes a primary space, and visual-motor coordination develops by association between motor commands signaling specific patterns of movement and contingent changes in the retinal image. The early work of Held and his associates (e.g., Held & Hein, 1963) on the role of active movement in the development of visual-motor skills seems to have been based on this assumption. More recently, however, a consensus that a neonativist theory may be more appropriate has developed, following extensive research with animal and human subjects (Ganz, 1975). Briefly, there is evidence for preadapted patterns of activity based on a molar coordination between radial directions in visual and motor space. For example, an action such as limb extension in the general direction of an object may be based on just such a preexisting coordination (Hein, 1974). In this revised view, the role of active movement in development is to refine the innate coordination by establishing feedback control. That is, the developmental problem is to convert visually *elicited* into visually *guided* actions and hence make the transition from unskilled to skilled performance. This revision of the theory has the advantage that an innate relation between visual and motor space can be flexibly recalibrated with growth.

Nevertheless, the question of how patterns of sensory information acquire their significance in relation to motor acts remains open. Piaget (1953) retains the assumption of empiricist theories that sensory input becomes progressively structured by action. It is not until the infant acquires the "object concept" (a belief in the permanence and spatiotemporal identity of objects) at around 18 months that sensory input is perceived according to its objective properties. Reciprocally, the infant acquires knowledge of self as an object and thus becomes able to distinguish between events contingent on his own actions and events independent of action. For Piaget, objectivity is not "built in" to sensation. The adualism of infant experience cannot be overcome until objective, conceptual knowledge is acquired.

To summarize the major alternatives, Piaget maintains that sensory structure arises with the infant's developing capacity to act, just as intersensory coordination is said to occur when the infant can simultaneously see, hear, and touch an object. J.J. Gibson, on the other hand, emphasizes the information available in the stimulus array, with respect to both intersensory coordination and ego motion. His is not a developmental theory, although he maintains that structure need only be discovered and not constructed. In the remaining sections of this chapter the aim is to establish whether structure in stimulation arises with the infant's developing capacity to act (in which case Gibson's epistemology describes the inverse side of the equation to Piaget's), or whether structure is inherent in the functioning of perceptual systems and hence has primacy in development.

5.2. Reaching for Virtual Objects

Bower has applied the genetic method to the developmental relation between vision and touch. These studies often depend on precocious reaching in infants under 3 months of age as an integral aspect of their methodology (Bower, 1972; Bower, Broughton, & Moore, 1970a, 1970b). Bower argues that reaching and grasping are at first visually elicited and that vision can specify tactual consequences. For example, in some studies infants view an illusory "virtual object" that appears to be solid and suspended in front of them. Infants become emotionally disturbed when the hand passes through the object for which they are reaching. Bower maintains that vision dominates touch early in development, hence it is unlikely that touch can tutor vision. Later, reaching becomes differentiated into two components—a visually elicited arm extension followed by visual guidance of the hand onto the object, and a tactually elicited grasp. Thus, his general account of a transition from visually elicited to visually guided reaching and grasping is consistent with the animal literature (Ganz, 1975).

There have been some failures to replicate Bower's observations (Dodwell, Muir, & DiFranco, 1976; Ruff & Halton, 1977), but in these studies the experimenters did not even obtain any directed arm movements in young infants. Other studies confirm a progression from visually elicited to visually guided reaching in development (Alt, 1968; Lasky, 1977; McDonnel, 1975). It is generally found that infants under 5 months do not correct for error in reaching induced by viewing the visual target through prisms. From about 5 months onward infants begin to correct misreaching as the hand and the prismatically displaced object simultaneously come into the field of view. Thus, there is evidence that infants can at least get their hands into the vicinity of an object, even though this is not proof that vision also specifies tactual consequences.

From informal observations made by the author, there appear to be a number of critical conditions to be met before reaching can be observed in infants of about 1 month. Reaching and grasping were observed when the infant was alert, seated with support and with arms free. Reaching and grasping followed intent visual fixation on a black-and-white-striped stick suspended within the infant's reach. Infants appeared to bend from the waist toward the object, starting with arm and elbow well away from the body and with the hand open. Then the hand was rapidly directed toward the stick so that the fingers closed on it as the reach terminated. Although these observations were informal, it is difficult to explain even a limited number of such cases as occurring by chance. It seems likely that further experiments which pay careful attention to detailed aspects of method will resolve this controversy.

Similarly, there have been failures to replicate Bower's observations on reaching for virtual objects. Field (1977) claims that infants even up to 7 months are not surprised when their hand reaches a virtual object and passes through it. Yet naturalistic observation suggests that one can observe surprise in younger infants when an apparently solid object turns out not to be palpable. One has only to observe an infant reaching for a column of water squeezed from a sponge at bath-time. The author's daughter showed great surprise at 4 months when her hand passed through the water as she was attempting to grasp it. However, it is not the intention here to make a case by anecdotal evidence; nor need such anecdotes indicate innate visual specification of tactual properties. The aim is to make the point that laboratory investigations involving prisms, polarizing goggles, and virtual objects may not obtain positive results simply because their methodology is so complicated.

An alternative approach has recently been taken by E.J. Gibson, Owsley, and Johnston (1978). They have shown that infants differentiate visually between "rigid" and "elastic" motions of an object. Infants were first habituated to three types of rigid, rotating motions of a sponge. The display was then changed either to another rigid motion, or to an elastic motion induced by squeezing the sponge in a cyclical rhythm to produce a rippling motion on its surface. Infants showed recovery from habituation following the elastic motion but not following the rigid motion. The authors conclude that by 5 months infants are able to visually differentiate these properties of substance. In Piaget's theory, perception of rigidity follows experience of objects being displaced manually in the infant's visual field. E.J. Gibson (Gibson *et al.*, 1978) points out that the "motor scheme" common to all four rigid motions, necessary for a Piagetian explanation, would be extremely hard to identify. The results do not support Piaget's (1954) claim that object movements corresponding to rigidity "are surely not perceived as such by the child before 9 or 10 months" (p. 97).

Although perception of substantiality in early infancy is a somewhat untidy area of research at the moment, evidence is beginning to emerge that certain properties of substance may be directly specified in perception. It should be noted, however, that even if the infant does directly perceive substantiality, tactual exploration may still be a necessary aspect of conceptual development. Specific knowledge about particular objects, such as the nonsolidity of water, remains something for the infant to discover.

5.3. Neonatal Responses to Looming

Looming is accelerated optical expansion of a delimited portion of the visual field (J.J. Gibson, 1950). Many organisms show innate avoidance to looming objects (Schiff, Caviness, & Gibson, 1962), and it is argued that this pattern of visual information specifies an imminent collision. Since the visual information specifies tactual consequences, this can be considered another example of intersensory correspondence.

Bower, Broughton, and Moore (1970c) found that 2-week-old human infants respond to looming. They withdraw their heads and raise their arms as if defending themselves, whether the stimulus is an approaching real object or its optical equivalent, a symmetrically expanding shadow. Ball and Tronick (1971) extended these results to demonstrate that avoidance is specific to optical-expansion patterns on a "collision" course with the infant. An asymmetrical expanding shadow, on the "miss" path, results in visual tracking with no obvious defensive behaviors. These results therefore suggest that the human infant, like many other organisms, responds innately by avoiding patterns of optical information with possible harmful consequences.

It has been suggested that head withdrawal in very young infants may not be a response to looming (Yonas, Bechtold, Frankel, Gordon, McRoberts, Norcia, & Sternfels, 1977). Yonas (Yonas *et al.,* 1977) argues that infants may merely be visually tracking the rising contour at the top of the expanding shadow. Yonas (personal communication) favors the theory that responses to looming first appear at around 3 months and depend on neural maturation. Avoidance responses of the head become fully consolidated with other behaviors, such as blinking and manual defensive movements, at around 8 months.

While it is clear that fully integrated defensive behaviors appear only after a long period of development, there is now sufficient evidence to suggest that infants do respond to looming from birth. Bower (1977) presented neonates with a projected shadow of a rotating trapezoid, so that information for an impending collision with the infant's nose occurred only when the top edge of the shadow was moving downward. Infants pushed their heads against the back of the seat with greater force when the contour was falling than when it was rising. Ball (1979) has shown that postural adjustments of the head in 1- to 2-month-old subjects are specific to expansion of the visual field. In this experiment the expanding shadow only moved sideways or downward. Ball and Vurpillot (1976) showed that defensive responses do not depend on motion of a single contour since an expansion pattern comprised of over 800 circles also elicited avoidance reactions in infants 3–6 weeks of age. Finally, Cicchetti and Sroufe (1978) found that optical expansion also elicits avoidance in Down's syndrome infants at least as early as the second month of life. These infants are notably late in neuromuscular maturation, which might be taken as evidence against a maturationist hypothesis.

The results as a whole suggest that infants respond to structural properties of visual stimulation before the advent of independent locomotion and before extensive tactile-kinesthetic experience. Further research is required to isolate the critical parameters of stimulation, although Ball (1979) has suggested that simultaneous expansion in two dimensions about a stationary central point may be necessary to perceive movement in depth. It is interesting to note that the infant's avoidance response occurs at the moment when the symmetrically expanding shadow occludes most of the stationary background. In real life, a similar sequence of optical events would only occur at the moment preceding impact of a projectile directed toward the eyes. The objective information is directly specified in the pattern of optical expansion (see Section 5.4.1). The adaptive significance of such an avoidance response should therefore be obvious.

5.4. Visual Proprioception and Posture

Lee and Aronson (1974) showed that infants use visual information to monitor their posture when they first learn to stand unsupported. This fact was demonstrated by putting mechanical-vestibular cues that specify a stable posture into conflict with visual information specifying instability. The infants stood on a stable floor, inside a "movable room" comprising three walls and a ceiling, facing the interior end wall of the room. The whole room moved backward or forward so that the resulting flow of visual information corresponded to that ordinarily contingent on body sway. The infants compensated for a nonexistent loss of balance so that they swayed, staggered, or fell in the direction opposite the plane of instability specified by the misleading visual information. When the end wall moved toward the infant, the infant fell backward, while if the end wall receded, the infant fell forward. Lee and Aronson argue that infants monitor the stability of their posture through "visual proprioception."

This study raises a number of questions about the origins of the proprioceptive function of vision, and about its role in the acquisition of motor control, that are very similar to the issues raised in the discussion of visual-motor coordination in Section 5.1. Does vision acquire its proprioceptive function as a consequence of motor activity, perhaps as the infant learns to stand? Butterworth and Hicks (1977) studied the stability of the seated posture under conditions of discrepant visual feedback using the "moving room method." Infants who could sit or stand unsupported were compared with infants who could sit but who could not stand. Even though the latter group were several months younger, their response to discrepant visual feedback when sitting was at least as great as that of infants who could sit or stand without support. Thus, vision does not acquire its proprioceptive function as a result of the upright stance.

In a later study, Butterworth and Cicchetti (1978) examined the role of motor experience on the proprioceptive effects of vision, again using the "moving room" technique. In this study, normal infants who could either sit or sit and stand without support were compared with Down's syndrome infants who had similar experience of the postures. Down's syndrome infants (mongoloids) are severely hypotonic. Their muscles are extremely flaccid, which makes it difficult for them to support their own weight, and their postural development is usually severely retarded—by approximately 6 months for sitting and a further 10 months for standing. The reason for comparing these two groups was to establish whether the motor-retarded infants differed from the normal infants in their response to discrepant visual feedback.

The results are summarized in Figure 3. On the average, the intensity of compensation is greater for the standing posture than for the sitting posture in both groups. In normal infants, the effect of discrepant visual feedback declines with experience of standing and of sitting, and the

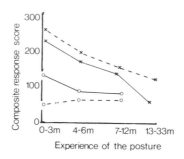

Fig. 3. Postural compensation made by normal and Down's syndrome infants to movement of the visual surrounds (Butterworth & Cicchetti, 1978): (×) standing unsupported; (○) sitting unsupported (infants unable to stand); (---) Down's syndrome infants; (——) normal infants. The composite score shows the average intensity of response to movement of the visual surround (300 = fall; 200 = stagger; 100 = sway; 0 = no noticeable postural compensation.) (Reproduced with permission of *Perception*. Copyright 1978, Pion Publications.)

developmental course runs parallel for the two postures. Although the average intensity of compensation is less for sitting, complete loss of stability resulting in a fall can nevertheless be observed in normal infants in the first 3 months after the sitting posture is acquired. Furthermore, sitting infants respond to discrepant visual feedback before they have acquired independent mobility, so response to the movement of the whole surround is not a consequence of active locomotion.

The Down's syndrome infants presented paradoxical results. Down's infants who had recently learned to sit unsupported were significantly *less* responsive to movements of the surround than normal infants of similar experience, whereas Down's infants who had recently learned to stand unsupported were somewhat more responsive to movement of the surround than normal babies (Figure 3). Their lack of responsiveness when sitting, however, was not due to any inability to perceive discrepant visual information. When the seated Down's infants were retested standing supported by an adult, they became as responsive as the normal infants to movements of the surround. This fact suggests that the magnitude of response to the discrepant visual information is a function of the particular posture. Down's infants do not differ from normals in their ability to perceive optic flow patterns, but they do differ in the way they make use of the information depending on whether they are sitting or standing. One simple interpretation of these results is to suppose Down's infants to differ from normals in their level of "sensoritonic equilibrium" (Wapner & Werner, 1957). They seem to require a higher level of mechanical-vestibular stimulation before they compensate for the discrepancy generated by movement of the surround.

In the standing posture, the intensity of response declines with experience for both the Down's and normal infants, so that eventually postural stability becomes relatively independent of the stability of the surround (see Figure 3). At the same time, cognitive indicators emerge that suggest the infant knows he is stable and the room is moving. For example, in the first 3 months after acquiring the upright posture, if infants expressed any emotion when the room moved, they would fall over and cry. After 12 months experience of standing they might sway slightly and the emotion was always laughter, as if movement of the room was an incongruous event independent of self.

Thus, to maintain their balance the infants were almost completely dependent on the stability of the surround during the first 3 months after acquiring the upright posture, and the effect gradually declined thereafter. It is interesting to note that adults also become completely dependent on the stability of the surround when in an unfamiliar posture, such as balancing on a narrow beam (Lee & Lishman, 1975). Early in the acquisition of postural control, balance seems to depend critically on congruence between visual and mechanical-vestibular indices of postural stability. With experience, control of the posture gradually shifts in favor of the mechanical-vestibular system and the infant becomes progressively able to overrule the visually specified instability. Thus, the function of visual proprioception may be to calibrate, or "fine tune," the mechanical-vestibular system against the stable surround, so that the infant gains autonomous motor control (Lee & Aronson, 1974).

5.4.1. Structural Properties of Looming and Movement of the Whole Surround. It has not yet been demonstrated that postures acquired even earlier in development, such as control over the head, are monitored with respect to the surround, although the general pattern of results for sitting and standing suggests that this might be the case. Nor is it known whether gaining head control gives rise to meaningfully structured visual flow patterns or whether response to movement of the whole surround is innate. The evidence on looming suggests that infants do respond innately to optical-expansion patterns, so it is likely that response to movement of the whole surround may also be built-in.

There are a number of reasons to suppose that the infant perceives looming and the optic flow pattern of the "moving room" as two distinct classes of visually specified events. For example, the response to looming occurs when the optical-expansion pattern nears a maximum and occludes most of the background, whereas infants respond immediately to movements of the whole surround. Defensive responses to looming are not accompanied by equal and opposite responses to optical contraction, whereas postural adjustments are appropriate to forward, backward, and lateral movements of the whole surround (Butterworth & Hicks, 1977). Recent research with adults suggests that the internal relations among parts of the optic flow pattern specify two distinct classes of events — movement of an object toward an observer, and movement of an observer in a stationary environment (Brandt, Wist, & Dichgans, 1975; Johansson, 1977; Lee & Lishman, 1975). The relationship between optic flow pattern in the peripheral and foveal parts of the retina is critical. For instance, Johansson (1977) showed that a visual flow pattern over a very small area of the extreme periphery of the retina was sufficient to induce an illusion of self-movement in adult subjects, despite the simultaneous availability of optical information for a stationary environment over the rest of the retina. Looming, on the other hand, seems to depend on the relationship between an expanding textured flow pattern in focal vision (Trevarthen, 1968) and visual information for a stationary background in the periphery. When the former almost occludes the latter, an impact is imminent.

Thus, self-motion is perceived when the retinal periphery registers a symmetrical optic flow pattern, even if the center of the visual field is stationary. Under ecologically valid conditions, this is the only possible interpretation of such a flow pattern, since the background must be considered stable. Object motion will be perceived when a bounded area of the visual field is in motion relative to a stationary background registered in peripheral vision, as in looming. Again, this is the only possible interpretation of such a sequence of events at the retina. Finally, movement of an observer relative to a moving object will be specified by an expanding (or contracting) flow pattern in central vision relative to an optic flow pattern in peripheral vision. All of this depends on a built-in specification that the background registered in peripheral vision is stable and external to self.

5.4.2. *Visual Proprioception and the "Adualism" Hypothesis.* If it is assumed, for the moment, that responses to movement of the whole surround are innate, then this assumption has interesting implications for Piaget's hypothesis of infant adualism. First, it would imply that over evolutionary time, the perceptual system has come to "recognize" the feedback or visual flow pattern that would be contingent on self-movement, before the organism has acquired mobility. The relationship between the organism and the structured visual environment constitutes a kind of feedback-control loop in which movement of the body is directly specified in the contingent visual flow pattern. Thus, even under conditions of passive movement the organism would make the distinction between movement of self and movement of the environment, since the internal structure of the optic flow pattern (i.e., of the peripheral field relative to the central field) can specify only such a sequence of events. However, the distinction is imposed on the perceiver by the natural ecology, since, even though self-movement may be *specified,* it is clear that it is not *objectively known.* The infant betrays dependence on what is specified under the ecologically invalid conditions of the "moving room." Early in the acquisition of postural control, the infant compensates for *nonexistent* loss of balance, even though he is objectively stable. Only after some experience of the posture does the infant become able to overrule what is specified in favor of what is objectively the case. This process involves more than merely attending to mechanical-vestibular cues rather than visual cues. It heralds a new level of functioning in which self-knowledge can mediate and to some extent overrule what is visually specified. Thus, it would appear that J.J. Gibson may be correct when he argues that visual flow patterns have an objective and a subjective pole built-in, but Piaget is also correct to emphasize the qualitatively different status in development of objective knowledge of the self. One intriguing possibility is that objective knowledge may have its developmental origins in prestructured feedback, such as visual proprioception. Active movement with respect to a stable surround not only adds mechanical-vestibular information for self-movement, but will also generate optic flow patterns at the retina which are perfect spatiotemporal analogues of the movement. The invariant properties of the flow pattern may be perceived by the developing infant and internalized as a representation of self—the body image.

6. General Conclusions

Research on auditory-visual coordination and on aspects of visual-motor coordination in infancy suggests that the time for posing developmental questions in extreme form (innate vs. acquired, maturation vs. learning) has long since passed. A degree of relationship between the senses may be necessary for any kind of development to take place, just as motor acts may necessarily first occur with respect to a stable and external environment. These functional properties of intersensory and sensorimotor organization may form the basis for detecting multimodal properties of objects for the acquisition of motor control, and may indeed form part of the underpinning for such cognitive constructs as the "self-concept."

The strength of both the Gibsonian and Piagetian approaches is their concern for epistemological issues. Gibson's description of the structural properties of stimulation leads to questions about the significance of perception for the developing child. Piaget's major emphasis is on the structure of objective knowledge and how this is related to action. It is tempting to conclude that actions do not give rise to perceptual structures de novo, since in so many instances perceptual structures seem to have significance for the infant before any extensive motor experience could have occurred. Thus, perception may have primacy in development. However, these perceptual structures clearly do not have the same epistemological status as objective knowledge; "to perceive" is not synonymous with "to know." Although information may be innately detected in perception, it can eventually be overruled by objective knowledge. The time has come for students of infant cognition to move away from sterile controversies arising from overgeneral models, and to move toward more subtle analyses that take into account qualitative changes with epistemological significance for cognitive growth.

7. References

Alt, J. *The use of vision in early reaching*. Unpublished honors thesis, Harvard University, 1968.

Aronson, E., & Rosenbloom, S. Space perception in early infancy: Perception within a common auditory-visual space. *Science,* 1971, *172*, 1161–1163.

Baldwin, J.M. *Mental development in the child and the race*. New York: Macmillan, 1894.

Ball, W. *Infant responses to optical expansion: Avoidance not tracking*. Unpublished manuscript, Department of Psychology, Swarthmore College, PA 19081, 1979.

Ball, W., & Tronick, E. Infant responses to impending collision: Optical and real. *Science,* 1971, *171*, 818–820.

Ball, W., & Vurpillot, E. La perception du movement en profondeur chez le nourisson. *L'Annee psychologique,* 1976, *76*, 383–399.

Bench, J., Collyer, Y., Langford, C., & Wilson, I. Studies in infant behavioural audiometry, I, II, III. *Audiology,* 1976, *15*, 85–105, 302–314, 384–394.

Bergman, T., Haith, M.M., & Mann, L. *Development of eye contact and facial scanning in infants*. Paper presented at a meeting of the Society for Research in Child Development, Minneapolis, March 1971.

Berkeley, G. *A new theory of vision*. London: Dent & Sons, 1963 (Originally published, 1709.)

Birch, H.G., & Lefford, A. Visual differentiation, intersensory integration and voluntary motor control. *Monographs of the Society for Research in Child Development,* 1967, *32* (2), 1–87.

Bower, T.G.R. Object perception in infants. *Perception,* 1972, *1,* 15–30.

Bower, T.G.R. *Development in infancy.* San Francisco: W.H. Freeman, 1974. (a)

Bower, T.G.R. The evolution of sensory systems. In R. B. MacLeod & H. L. Pick, Jr. (Eds.), *Perception: Essays in honor of James J. Gibson.* Ithaca: Cornell University Press, 1974, pp. 141–165. (b)

Bower, T.G.R. Comment on Yonas et al. Development of sensitivity to information for impending collision. *Perception and Psychophysics,* 1977, *19,* 193–196.

Bower, T.G.R., Broughton, J.M., & Moore, M.K. The coordination of visual and tactual input in infants. *Perception and Psychophysics,* 1970, *8,* 51–53. (a)

Bower, T.G.R., Broughton, J.M., & Moore, M.K. Demonstration of intention in the reaching behaviour of neonate humans. *Nature,* 1970, *228,* 679–680. (b)

Bower, T.G.R., Broughton, J.M., & Moore, M.K. Infant responses to approaching objects: An indicator of response to distal variables. *Perception and Psychophysics,* 1970, *9,* 193–195. (c)

Brandt, T., Wist, E.R., & Dichgans, J. Foreground and background in dynamic spatial orientation. *Perception and Psychophysics,* 1975, *17,* 497–503.

Braunstein, M.L. *Depth perception through motion.* New York: Academic Press, 1978.

Bronson, G. The post-natal growth of visual capacity. *Child Development,* 1974, *45,* 873–890.

Butterworth, G.E., & Castillo, M. Coordination of auditory and visual space in newborn human infants. *Perception,* 1976, *5,* 155–160.

Butterworth, G.E., & Cicchetti, D. Visual calibration of posture in normal and motor retarded Down's syndrome infants. *Perception,* 1978, *7,* 513–525.

Butterworth, G.E., & Hicks, L. Visual proprioception and postural stability in infancy: A developmental study. *Perception,* 1977, *6,* 255–262.

Carpenter, G. Mother's face and the newborn. *New Scientist,* 1974, *61,* 742–744.

Castillo, M., & Butterworth, G.E. *Neonatal localization of a sound in visual space.* Unpublished manuscript, University of Southampton, 1980.

Chun, R.W.M., Pawsat, R., & Forster, F.M. Sound localization in infancy. *Journal of Nervous and Mental Disorders,* 1960, *130,* 472–476.

Cicchetti, D., & Sroufe, L.A. An organizational view of affect: Illustrations from the study of Down's syndrome infants. In M. Lewis & I. Rosenblum (Eds.), *The development of affect.* New York: Plenum Press, 1978.

Coghill, G.E., *Anatomy and the problem of behavior.* London: Cambridge University Press, 1929.

Cohen, L., & Gelber, E.R. Infant visual memory. In L.B. Cohen & P. Salapatek (Eds.), *Infant perception from sensation to cognition.* Vol. 1 New York: Academic Press, 1975, pp. 347–399.

Condry, S.M., Haltom, M., & Neisser, U. Infant sensitivity to audio-visual discrepancy: A failure to replicate. *Bulletin of the Psychonomic Society,* 1977, *9* (6), 431–432.

Costall, A. Theories of direct perception and their developmental implications. In G.E. Butterworth (Ed.), *Infancy and epistemology.* Sussex:Harvester Press, 1981.

Dirks, J., & Gibson, E. Infants' perception of similarity between live people and their photographs. *Child Development,* 1977, *48,* 124–130.

Dodwell, P.C., Muir, D., & DiFranco, D. Responses of infants to visually presented objects. *Science,* 1976, *194,* 209–211.

Eimas, P.D. Speech perception in early infancy. In L.B. Cohen & P. Salapatek (Eds.), *Infant perception from sensation to cognition.* Vol. 2. New York: Academic Press, 1975, pp. 193–231.

Ewing, I.R., & Ewing, A.W.C. The ascertainment of deafness in infancy and early childhood. *The Journal of Laryngology and Otology,* 1944, 309–333.

Field, J. Coordination of vision and prehension in young infants. *Child Development,* 1977, *48,* 97–103.

Fraser, A.G. *Selections from Berkeley.* Oxford: Clarendon Press, 1899, p. 179.

Froeschels, E. Testing the hearing of young children. *Archives of Otolaryngology,* 1964, *43,* 93–98.

Ganz, L. Orientation in visual space by neonates and its modification by visual deprivation. In A.H. Riesen (Ed.), *The developmental neuropsychology of sensory deprivation.* New York: Academic Press, 1975, pp. 169–210.

Gibson, E.J., Owsley, C.J., & Johnston, J. Perception of invariants by 5 month old infants: Differentiation of two types of motion. *Developmental Psychology,* 1978, *14,* 407–415.

Gibson, J.J. *The perception of the visual world.* Boston: Houghton Mifflin, 1950.

Gibson, J.J. *The senses considered as perceptual systems.* Boston: Houghton Mifflin, 1966.

Gregory, R.L. The evolution of eyes and brains, a hen and egg problem. In S.J. Freedman (Ed.), *The neuro-psychology of spatially oriented behaviour.* Ontario: Dorsey Press, 1968, pp. 7–17.

Haith, M.M., & Campos, J.J. Human infancy. *Annual Review of Psychology,* 1977, *28,* 251–293.

Hamlyn, D.W. *Experience and the growth of understanding.* London: Routledge & Kegan Paul, 1978.

Harrison, J.M., & Irving, R. Visual and non-visual auditory systems in mammals. *Science,* 1966, *154,* 738–743.

Hein, A. Prerequisite for development of visually guided reaching in the kitten. *Brain Research,* 1974, *71,* 259–263.

Held, R., & Hein, A. Movement produced stimulation in the development of visually guided behaviour. *Journal of Comparative and Physiological Psychology,* 1963, *56,* 872–876.

Howard, I.P., & Templeton, W.B. *Human spatial orientation.* London: Wiley, 1966.

Jerison, H.J. *Evolution of the brain and intelligence.* New York: Academic Press, 1973.

Johansson, G. Studies on visual perception of locomotion. *Perception,* 1977, *6,* 365–376.

Jones, B., & Kabanoff, B. Eye movements in auditory space perception. *Perception and Psychophysics,* 1975, *17* (3), 241–245.

Lasky, R.E. The effect of visual feedback of the hand on the reaching and retrieval behaviour of young infants. *Child Development.* 1977, *48,* 112–117.

Lee, D.N., & Aronson, E. Visual proprioceptive control of standing in human infants. *Perception and Psychophysics,* 1974, *15,* 529–532.

Lee, D.N., & Lishman, J.R. Visual proprioceptive control of stance. *Journal of Human Movement Studies,* 1975, *1,* 87–95.

Lyons-Ruth, K. *Integration of auditory and visual spatial information during early infancy.* Unpublished paper, Harvard University, 1974.

Lyons-Ruth, K. Bimodal perception in infancy: Response to auditory-visual incongruity. *Child Development,* 1977, *48,* 820–827.

Marks, L.E. *The unity of the senses: Interrelations among the modalities.* New York: Academic Press, 1978.

McDonnel, P.M. The development of visually guided reaching. *Perception and Psychophysics,* 1975, *18,* 181–185.

McGurk, H., & Lewis, M.M. Space perception in early infancy: Perception within a common auditory-visual space? *Science,* 1974, *186,* 649–650.

McGurk, H., & MacDonald, J. Hearing lips and seeing voices. *Nature,* 1976, *264,* 746–748.

McGurk, H., & MacDonald, J. Auditory-visual coordination in the first year of life. *International Journal of Behavioural Development,* 1978, *1,* 229–240.

McGurk, H., Turnure, C., & Creighton, S.J. Auditory-visual coordination in neonates. *Child Development,* 1977, *48,* 138–143.

Mehler, J., Bertoncini, J., Barriere, M., & Gerschenfeld, D.J. Infant recognition of mother's voice. *Perception,* 1978, *7* (5), 489–614.

Mendelson, M.J., & Haith, M. The relation between audition and vision in the human newborn. *Monographs of the Society for Research in Child Development,* 1976, *41* (4), Serial No. 167.

Mills, M., & Melhuish, E. Recognition of mother's voice in early infancy. *Nature,* 1974, *252,* 123–124.

Morrell, F. Visual systems view of acoustic space. *Nature,* 1972, *238,* 44–46.

O'Connor, N., & Hermelin, B. *Seeing and hearing and space and time.* New York: Academic Press, 1978.

Piaget, J. *The origin of intelligence in the child.* London: Routledge & Kegan Paul, 1953.

Piaget, J. *The construction of reality in the child.* New York: Basic Books, 1954.

Posner, M.I., Nissen, M.J., & Klein, R.M. Visual dominance: An information processing account of its origin and significance. *Psychological Review,* 1976, *84,* 137–171.

Ruff, H., & Halton, A. *Is there directed reaching in the human neonate?* Paper presented at the biennial meeting of the Society for Research in Child Development, New Orleans, March 1977.

Schiff, W., Caviness, J.A., & Gibson, J.J. Persistent fear responses in rhesus monkeys to the optical structures of "looming." *Science,* 1962, *136,* 982–983.

Spelke, E.S. Infants' intermodal perception of events. *Cognitive Psychology,* 1976, *8,* 553–560.

Spelke, E.S. *Acquiring intermodal knowledge.* Paper presented at the International Conference on Infant Studies, Providence, Rhode Island, March 1978.

Spelke, E.S., & Owsley, C.J. *Intermodal exploration and perceptual knowledge in infancy.* Paper presented at the biennial meeting of the Society for Research in Child Development, New Orleans, March 1977.

Trevarthen, C. Two visual systems in primates. *Psychologische Forschung,* 1968, *31,* 299–377.

Turkewitz, G., Birch, H.G., Moreau, T., Levy, L., & Cornwell, A.C. Effect of intensity of auditory stimulation on directional eye movements in the human neonate. *Animal Behavior,* 1966, *14,* 93–101.

Turkewitz, G., Moreau, T., Birch, H.G., and Davis, L. Relationships among responses in the human newborn: The non-association and non-equivalence among different indicators of responsiveness. *Psychophysiology,* 1971, *7* (2), 233–247.

Turkewitz, G., Birch, H.G., & Cooper, K.K. Responsiveness to simple and complex auditory stimuli in the newborn. *Developmental Psychobiology,* 1972, *5* (1), 7–19. (a)

Turkewitz, G., Birch, H.G., & Cooper, K.K. Patterns of response to different auditory stimuli in the human newborn. *Developmental Medicine and Child Neurology,* 1972, *14,* 487–491. (b)

von Hornbostel, E.M. The unity of the senses. In W. D. Ellis (Ed.), *A source book of Gestalt psychology.* London: Routledge & Kegan Paul, 1938, pp. 211–216.

Wapner, S., & Werner, H. *Perceptual development*. Worcester, Mass.: Clark University Press, 1957.

Wertheimer, M. Psychomotor coordination of auditory and visual space at birth. *Science,* 1961, *134,* 1692.

Yonas, A., Bechtold, A.G., Frankel, D., Gordon, F.R., McRoberts, G., Norcia, A., & Sternfels, S. Development of sensitivity to information for impending collision. *Perception and Psychophysics,* 1977, *21,* 97–104.

3

Integrating the Information from Eyes and Hands: A Developmental Account

EUGENE ABRAVANEL

1. Introduction

Questions about the relations among the senses have historic roots (Aristotle, 1941; Brentano, 1977). To understand the mechanisms by which perceptual information is equated or transferred between two or more perceptual subsystems (see J.J. Gibson, 1966) is to arrive at the fundamental questions of attention, perception, and learning. The scope of the problem may account for why theorists have, off and on, taken up the problem since the time of ancient Greece (see Boring, 1942). Here, my aims will be less ambitious. I will restrict myself to a few topics that deal with the relation between vision and haptics (active grasping and touching) from a developmental perspective. I intend to examine what we know about intersensory abilities during infancy and early childhood, because many of the issues quite naturally point us in that direction.

In order to find out how and by what means the perceptual subsystems are linked, we must know something about the early state of coordination, or lack thereof, and how development proceeds from there. Next, I would like to examine the roles that attention, exploration, and perceptual activity might play in both the early and later development of visual and haptic information gathering. To get a bit ahead of myself, I should say here that from a psychological (as contrasted with a neuro-

---

EUGENE ABRAVANEL • Department of Psychology, George Washington University, Washington, D.C. 20006.

physiological) approach to the question, developments in information handling and discrimination may prove to be the key factors that enable and limit the integration of visual and haptic subsystems.

An anecdotal event might set the stage for thinking about how the perceptual subsystems or modalities are related to each other. My case is that of a young child who has seen moths and butterflies on the wing or perched here and there. On a dark night while ascending the steps to her house she reaches for the banister and coincidentally wraps her hand around a stationary moth. The moth does not remain immobile for long, and begins to flutter inside the child's hand. Let us assume that before releasing the insect the curious youngster held the moth prey just long enough to identify it. How was she capable of knowing what it was that she held captive in her hand, given that she had never held one before? And, what does this achievement imply about the organization of perceptual subsystems?

There are at least two principal approaches to understanding our subject's performance. The first approach depends on the assumption that information acquired through one modality is not stored exclusively in a modality-specific form or "place." Instead, information that is retained by the nervous system is made "supramodal"; that is, it is transformed into a configuration or state that is not specific to the characteristics of any single subsystem. Essential properties and configural relations in the information are extracted, schematized, and held in a schematic or abstract form. In this way, an information-handling "mechanism" is hypothesized to explain two major accomplishments: (1) the equation of two objects or events where the acquisition of information was exclusively by eyes in the past, and exclusively by hand in the present instance, and (2) the recognition that two or more objects or events perceived via one subsystem are similar but not identical.

Only some characteristics of objects can be encoded and stored in a supramodal form. Shape, texture, area, length are properties that may be so encoded, just as movement and time are capable of being encoded and retained in supramodal storage. By contrast, some properties of experience—hue, odor, weight—are modality-specific. Perception has evolved in such a way that the subsystems provide overlapping information regarding some environmental attributes, but also specific and distinctive information for which each subsystem is specialized. Aristotle maintained that the distinctive or proper sensitivity of each subsystem defined it and qualified it as a sense.

The second major approach to the problem of explaining how our curious youngster was able to know on that dark night that it was a moth she held in her hand appeals to one or another variant of symbolic-linguistic coding. The argument runs as follows: Once the child begins to acquire conventional language—or, potentially, a private symbolism—she names or labels information that is acquired perceptually. These stored symbols are activated whenever an object is perceived by sight or by hand, and serve to link the otherwise different and disparate forms of information. The assumption is that the sight of a moth is qualitatively different from the haptically acquired "feel" of the moth, and that the two kinds of information are not directly comparable. Therefore, a symbolic mediator is needed to serve in the role of a *tertium quid*.

The difficulty with this explanation of the case of the child and the moth is that it begs the question. If the child who has never before handled a moth but only seen it is to make use of language to assist her, something in the haptic perceptual pickup must activate the appropriate linguistic symbol. That is, the object must be discriminated and identified before it can be labeled "moth." Given that discrimination and identification are prior conditions for labeling, it would seem that words cannot provide the necessary basis for the intersensory linkage. It is important, therefore, that our child had never before gotten hold of such a creature in daytime; if she had on some previous occasion, then haptic recognition could have resulted from a prior connection between sight and feel. Much of our experience is of the latter form, and involves joint or correlated information acquisition between two or more perceptual subsystems.

Although our example of the child and the moth is common enough, in actuality it is difficult to be certain of the outcome. Can she actually recognize the moth exclusively by haptic pickup having had only visual commerce with moths on prior occasions? As we will see, this is a question that investigators have attempted to answer in the laboratory under conditions that partially overlap the naturally occurring case.

The role of prior experience raises a central point. One cannot appeal to prior associations between visual and haptic information to explain the recognition process for objects or events that have not been jointly investigated (note the classical problem of object recognition after restoration of sight to a blind person: Gregory, 1966; Hebb, 1949; von Senden, 1932). Yet, it is likely that on the many occasions when objects are looked at and handled (or, looked at and listened to, etc.), joint information pickup results in the storage of multisensory information. The sight, smell, and feel of a rose provide several forms of information, some of which are perceptually specific and others supramodal. Concomitant pickup of this information may be highly significant for attending to intersensory similarities and functionally equating the separate configurations. It is a common experience to be able to identify or match a flower with its fragrance or felt shape and texture. There is every reason to believe that simultaneous multisensory inspection has made the process by which it happens especially efficient.

If the current analysis is sound, we have two principal problems before us. The first is to explain intersensory recognition and transfer where an object or event has been experienced through only one subsystem in the prior life of the person. The next is to understand the development of perceptual processing such that a person who normally uses his or her perceptual subsystems jointly and complementarily may be capable of perceiving accurately with less than what is usually given to the perceiving organism. We typically search for our car keys by using a combination of visual, haptic, and auditory information, but if we are capable of detecting them among many other objects—door keys, etc.— on a moonless night, we must be working with less information than we usually possess. Does this impair performance? If so, to what degree, and under what conditions?

2. Undifferentiated Perception and the Unity of the Senses

Several lines of thinking have come down to us as attempts to explain the ontogenetic relations among the perceptual subsystems or senses. One hypothesis has argued for a primitive unity of the senses at the time of birth, and perhaps even during the fetal period. Both ontogenetic and phylogenetic (see Ryan, 1940) evidence are adduced to favor the argument for a primitive unity. Werner (1934) spoke for this formulation some time ago, saying that early in infancy there exists a subjective synesthesic matrix which differentiates into the several perceptual subsystems with growth. He maintained that the initial unity is of an undifferentiated sort, a global sensorium that may be excited by visual, tactile, auditory, or kinesthetic stimulation. Although purely speculatively, he suggested that the phenomenal aspect of stimulation is likely to be similar irrespective of the particular sensory pathways through which stimulation has been transmitted. Werner even suggested that early in ontogenesis the color blue is not perceived as a hue, but in terms of such sensory characteristics as intense or dull, sharp or blunt, clear or obscure, heavy or light, penetrating or resisting. Thus, stimulation of two perceptual subsystems such as the auditory and visual might produce similar organismic reactions, perhaps having to do with intensity and clarity, and a relationship is established on the basis of the similarity. In this way, one might hope to account for synesthetic effects later in life, and for the fact that we can speak of a *bright* sound or color, a *dull* edge or taste. This form of the argument for a unity among the senses at

birth does not require perfect integration or full ability to equate information between two subsystems. However, it appears to be generally
compatible with recent evidence for intersensory facilitation (Mendelson
& Haith, 1976) during early infancy.

The most important feature of the foregoing hypothetical view of
perceptual unification during early life is that a progression is postulated:
initial unity of a subjective-synesthetic type, followed by differentiation
of subsystems such that specialization of information gathering is possible
(but with an underlying unity still present), and then the progressive
coordination of information derived from each subsystem so that correspondences and equivalences of a refined nature are possible. An
advantage of this formulation is that a primitive unity is postulated from
the start rather than having to be explained via learning. Yet full weight
is given to improvements in intersensory development that result from
progressive differentiation and coordination of information. In its main
outline the formulation seems compatible with the stand taken by von
Hornbostel (1938) and by J.J. Gibson (1966).

Contrasting with the formulation of a primitive unity among the
senses is the belief in separate senses, each with its own tracts to the
brain, and each with its own phenomenal qualities. Leibniz (see Cassirer,
1951) argued for this conceptualization, believing that for the infant space
known via sight, touch, hearing, or smell has its own unique structure,
and that connections among the sensory experiences of space are forged
only by dint of joint occurrence. This is a variant of the formulation of
intersensory liaison based on experienced associations. But for Leibniz,
as for Piaget (1952; 1954) in our own time, associations are neither
random nor arbitrary; they depend on active efforts of meaningful
coordination. Thus, the two positions are different with respect to
whether they view the initial state of the senses as unified or separate.
They both, however, acknowledge the role of learning for improving
intersensory coordination.

3. Studies for Intersensory Coordination during Infancy

There are few studies with young infants that directly address issues
of intersensory coordination, despite the fact that they are the subjects
of choice for examining the ontogenesis of intersensory liaison, and for
dealing with an issue such as the "unity of the senses." As is often the
case, research relies on procedures that are usable with adults and older
children first, and only later do intrepid investigators find the combination
of methods that make it possible to study infants as well. We shall
examine three sets of studies with infants that are clearly relevant for

understanding intersensory development. The first deals with the infant's response to impending collision, while the second examines recent evidence for intersensory transfer and matching by infants. The last set deals with imitation during infancy, and its relation to intersensory processing.

3.1. Looming

As a large object rapidly approaches the face, an optical-expansion pattern is produced with the rate of expansion proportional to the speed of the object's advance. The typical adult reaction is defensive, with a drawing back of the head and a lowering of the chin if the object approaches in the frontal-parallel plane (see Schiff, 1965). Rather than speak of this adjustment by the viewer as *reflexive* (which has a way of detaching it from interesting ontogenetic problems), it can be said, following Bower (1974), that the adult reacts to the visual looming of an object as if it predicted tactual consequences. But an adult has experienced many occasions when a rapidly approaching object made a tactile impact on the face, as falling leaves do on a windy day. Therefore, his or her prediction might result from such prior coordinations of visual and tactual events. How might a young infant, who presumably has lived too short a time to have had such experiences, behave in a model experimental situation?

In an experiment with infants less than 2 weeks postpartum, Bower, Broughton, and Moore (1970a) attempted to answer this question. Infants were presented with a moving object that slowly approached the face while supported in a semiupright position. The following defensive reactions were reported as the object approached: head retraction, widening of the eyes, and raising of the hands to the face. Before concluding that a visual expansion pattern elicited adjustments to a forthcoming tactile impact, we must consider that the moving object displaced air toward the infant's face as well as presenting a looming image. The displacement of air is a tactile stimulus pattern that might have been sufficient for producing defensive reactions. Unfortunately, the response of infants to visual stimulation alone was not investigated. The findings of a replication by Ball and Tronick (1971) generally support those of the experiment by Bower *et al.* (1970a), but the role of air pressure was once again uncontrolled—which makes it impossible to attribute head withdrawal to perception of a visual expansion pattern. In recent work (Yonas, 1979; Yonas, Bechtold, Franke, Gordon, McRoberts, Norcia, & Sternfels, 1977) it has been proposed that backward head movements may result from an effort by the infant to track the upper contour of a looming figure. Using shadow displays that avoid the problem of air-pressure changes, Yonas and collaborators present evidence that head retraction is the infant's way of *visually* tracking an upward-expanding contour rather than avoiding an impending collision. Consequently, we must conclude at this time that "looming" studies with young infants do not permit the interpretation of visual-tactile coordination, as was originally believed.

3.2. Haptic-Visual Transfer and Matching of Shape by Infants

In a highly original study, Bryant, Jones, Claxton, and Perkins (1972) demonstrated a method for studying haptic-to-visual transfer of a shape discrimination during infancy. To my knowledge, this was the first investigation to provide evidence for intersensory transfer of shape information to infants under 1 year. Prior to this study, researchers were unable to investigate transfer or matching with children under 3 or 4. The procedure cleverly took advantage of the appealing character of sounds for infants around 9 months old. First, it was established that the infants would preferentially reach for a sound-producing object. Next, with a new group of subjects, the sound-producing object was placed in the infant's hand for haptic inspection without visual regard. While the infant was inspecting the object by hand, the experimenter tilted it so that it would emit its fetching sounds. Last, the object was placed in full view alongside the comparison object which had not been handled. With a particular pair of shapes, 23 of 30 infants reached for the object that had been handled previously, although only 19 of 30 infants reached for the handled object in the case of another pair of shapes. In a replication, very similar findings were obtained. Thus, at least for one pair of shapes Bryant *et al.* (1972) present evidence for haptic-to-visual transfer of shape information. The object that was presumably interesting under haptic inspection because it produced a sound was visually identified even when out of reach.

The difference in findings for the two pairs of shapes might be informative about the capacity for shape differentiation when perception is either haptic or visual. Intersensory transfer was better with the pair of objects that were both oval, and in which one member of the pair had a rectilinear wedge removed from an end. The infants may have picked up the distinction between an all-curved object and one that has straight lines as well. The objects in the second pair were cubelike, so that the rectilinear wedge in one member of the pair would not have been distinctively different from the other contours of the shape. Thus, during infancy, as well as at older ages, the capacity for intersensory transfer or matching is limited by the difficulty of intrasensory discrimination through one perceptual subsystem.

The sensory surface of the human visual system is restricted to the ocular region, whereas the haptic system of active grasping, holding, and palping of surfaces can function at many different regions of the body. Its organs are multiple. The hand is the most familiar haptic organ, but the mouth is as effective for some purposes (McDonald & Aungst, 1967), and is probably more sensitive to many textures. The feet, especially the toes, can be used for exploration, for determining the solidity of a surface (as when we stick a toe in the mud), and for perceiving texture or shape. Other parts of the body may be pressed into service for haptic perception where the need arises (see J.J. Gibson, 1966; Revesz, 1950).

Infants characteristically mouth a great variety of objects from the age that they begin active prehension until nearly the end of their first year. We suspect that this is not solely pleasure-seeking activity, but also a form of epistemic behavior that leads to knowledge about shapes and textures of things—as well as their edibility. It has not been easy to determine an infant's knowledge about a shape that he haptically mouths but does not see. But a recent investigation by Gottfried, Rose, and Bridger (1977) has made some headway, and has contributed much-needed information about intersensory recognition between haptics and vision. The principal aim of the study was to determine whether infants (1-year-olds) would demonstrate intersensory transfer of a shape discrimination between haptic and visual subsystems. One of the tests involved oral haptics and the other manual haptics. The essential method chosen by the investigators was the now-familiar habituation method, in which a subject shows decreased interest in viewing an item or pattern that has become familiar as a result of prolonged inspection (Fagan, 1970). With this paradigm, intersensory transfer of shape perception might be inferred if infants who have mouthed a shape for a period of time are less responsive to that shape than to a new one when it is later presented visually.

Results of the investigation indicated that intersensory transfer of shape recognition had occurred. Infants who received oral-haptic standard shapes to perceive, later looked significantly longer at novel shapes than at the familiar standard ones. Also, infants reached more for novel than for familiar shapes that were offered visually following oral-haptic perception. A similar pattern of results was found when standard objects were placed in the infant's hand for manual-haptic exploration followed by the test of visual recognition (as inferred from visual fixation and reaching preferences). Although not lacking in some procedural difficulties, especially with respect to ensuring inspection of standard shapes by the infants, the investigation by Gottfried et al. (1977) confirms the earlier finding of intersensory shape recognition among infants of about the same age by Bryant et al. (1972). Moreover, it demonstrates that the results of oral-haptic perception may be transferred to visual comparisons as readily as those of manual-haptic perception.

The habituation paradigm provides an indirect method for determining whether discrimination has occurred in an infant too young to follow instructions. Therefore, we can expect to see the paradigm used increasingly for studying intersensory integration during the early period of infancy. (For additional relevant research see Allen, Walker, Symonds, & Marcell, 1977; Rose, Gottfried, & Bridger, 1978.)

These few studies of intersensory processing during infancy lead us to conclude that by 12 months—and perhaps sometime earlier—infants are capable of haptically and visually tuning in their attention to common or invariant properties of objects. Seeking out visual and haptic equivalences or analogues is highly adaptive, and could be one of the active mechanisms that the infant employs as he coordinates vision and reaching, seeks to grasp the object that is seen, and turns to look at the object that he touches or mouths. Being alert to the invariants of objects and events as they are explored multimodally enables the infant to achieve several ends: (a) a reduction of overall information load, because it is the same object that is seen and mouthed rather than two separate ones; (b) substitution of mode of perception, because the object may be handled or visually inspected; and (c) the possibility of a division of labor between the actions performed visually and haptically, now that some equivalences of properties are perceivable.

In his ontogenetic theory, Piaget (1952) has highlighted the importance of the search for intersensorally equivalent or analogous information by Stage 3 of sensorimotor development. From Piaget's perspective, it would not be remiss to expect that the infant of 8–12 months is at work searching for multisensory information. As yet, we lack sufficient observational data that might demonstrate such behavioral organization on a day-to-day basis, but the infant is looking increasingly like an organism that is at least tuned into the activity of attending to and integrating intersensory information.

3.3. Evidence from Early Imitation

Imitation and observational learning are complex but fundamental ways in which human beings, and many other animal species, acquire new knowledge. Imitation also serves a broad set of social functions by creating the conditions for the sharing of actions, attitudes, and values among people. Psychologists and social thinkers have been puzzling over the nature and dynamics of imitation for a long time (Baldwin, 1895; Bandura, 1971; Guillaume, 1926/1971; McDougall, 1908).

Most students of the subject agree that imitative ability and interest begin sometime during infancy, although it remains problematic at what point reliable evidence of its presence becomes manifest (Abravanel, Levan-Goldschmidt, & Stevenson, 1976; Guillaume, 1926/1971; Piaget, 1951; Uzgiris & Hunt, 1975). The approximate chronological age when various imitative achievements become possible is important, but even more important are the underlying capacities that they imply. When a 9-month-old sees an adult lift a spoon to stir the sugar in his teacup, he may attempt to imitate the action. If the action is a familiar one, then the sight of an adult stirring his tea with a spoon may facilitate a similar action—one that the infant has been capable of producing previously. No new acquisition need have taken place, only the reinstatement of a familiar act.

However, if stirring in a cup is a novel action that has not been present in the infant's behavioral repertoire to this point, there is the possibility that learning of a new action via observation may begin. Assuming that the child has never stirred with a spoon, several links in a behavioral chain must be coordinated. He must note the objects or body parts involved—hand, spoon, cup—and properly interrelate them. Even a partially successful reproduction of the action must be quite an accomplishment, one which is typically too much for the average infant of under 9 months (see Abravanel *et al.*, 1976; Bayley, 1969).

Yet between 8 and 12 months infants can acquire the novel sequence via observation. The infant is capable of visually guiding his hand to spoon and cup in a way that resembles his visually derived perception or memory of what the adult is doing (or has just done). In this case, all objects and components of the action as observed and imitated could be said to have been under visual guidance. What if the observed action had nothing to do with teaspoons and cups, but involved a gesture—let us say a facial gesture? In this case, the observed action would be visible to the child, but his own reproduction of it would have to rely on proprioceptive regulation. Thus, imitation of an eye blink, a tongue protrusion, or a tap on one's own cheek depends on an intersensory linkage—which is my reason for considering the origins of imitation in this paper. The facial gesture of the model is visually perceived by the child, but he cannot visually monitor his own facial reproduction. For successful imitation to occur, visual and proprioceptive information must be equated. We are tempted to conclude, therefore, that at an age when nonvisible facial gestures are imitated, we have evidence that intersensory patterning of a complex nature is occurring.

The fact of the matter is that systematic study of the origins of nonvisible facial imitation is in progress at this time, and it should not be too long before we have a decent body of descriptive data with which to think about the problem. At present, we are lacking the descriptive base that will be needed to support theoretical propositions about early imitation. In his studies of several decades ago on the origins of intelligent action in the child, Piaget (1951) outlined a developmental progression of imitative ability. He argued on theoretical grounds, but with only limited empirical evidence, that true imitation of nonvisible gestures is observable late in infancy or during the second postpartum year. Piaget maintained that the ability to make the intersensory coordination between visual and proprioceptive-kinesthetic information is a Stage 4 sensorimotor accomplishment—in his conceptualization of growth—of considerable significance for the organization of complex actions in general, and for imitation specifically. Piaget goes to considerable lengths to support his view that the imitation of nonvisible actions during this stage (approximately 8–12 months in this society) is true, purposive imitation, rather than a conditioned response that simply happens to resemble one made by the model. Similarity between the infant's action and that of the model conceivably could occur by means of operant conditioning. Piaget wishes to distinguish between behavioral similarity that might result from shaping and reinforcement, and similarity that relies on active efforts to accommodate to what is seen and to organize an action along the lines of that which has been perceived. If we accept this distinction between conditioning and true imitation, we have another source of data that argues for the presence of a sophisticated type of intersensory equivalence during the first year of life. Some recent investigations have questioned whether Piaget dated the origins of the ability to imitate nonvisible gestures later than is actually the case. Because this achievement is so significant as an early manifestation of intersensory-equivalence formation, it is important to determine how early in the first year infants are capable of it. In our study (Abravanel et al., 1976) of normal, reasonably privileged infants, we reported that 31% of 6-month-olds and 50% of 9-month-olds made imitative tongue protrusions after having seen a model present the action. However, only 25% of 9-month-olds imitated lip-smacking movements. And, for some gestures that contained nonvisible components—such as touching the top of the head with a hand—not a single infant within the first 12 months imitated the model. Thus, some infants demonstrated the ability to reproduce imitatively certain nonvisible gestures by 6, 9, and 12 months of age, but this was never the case for more than 50% of the samples prior to 15 months of age. These results, then, are reasonably consistent with Piaget's rough age placements for the imitation of nonvisible gestures. However, two possibilities need to be considered: first, that individual variation in the development of imitative competence may be considerable, and second, that one might have to study infants under 6 months in order to observe imitative competence relatively unalloyed with complex motivational forces. The second possibility has been taken seriously by a few farsighted investigators, and has already led to some research.

In an exploratory study with a single 6-week-old infant, Gardner and Gardner (1970) modeled four actions for the infant over a period of days. Two of the actions were nonvisible facial gestures (tongue protrusions and mouth opening and closing), and both of these were imitated in at least two-thirds of the modeled instances. By contrast, two visible gestures (finger extension and hand opening and closing) were imitated in fewer than one-half of the modeled instances. Meltzoff and Moore (1977) have been eager to find the youngest age at which imitation of facial gestures such as lip curling, mouth opening, and tongue protrusion is observable. They have reported the presence of imitative tongue protrusions and mouth openings in infants as young as 16–21 days postpartum. As might be expected, the Meltzoff and Moore results have stimulated considerable controversy, and it will be a while before the evidence from their research, as well as from other attempts at replication of these findings (see Anisfeld, Masters, Jacobson, & Kagan, 1979), can be sifted and evaluated. There are particularly pernicious problems of control and observation (to say nothing of the infant's state and endurance) in seeking to do rigorous research on early imitation. In addition, there are problems of just how to interpret an infant's reaction that follows on the heels of an examiner's modeled action. The possibilities, but also difficulties, of interpretation are nicely summarized by Gardner and Gardner (1970):

> When an action of [the model] precedes a similar activity by an infant, and no efforts have been made to train the response, at least four possible explanations can be offered: (1) the child may simply have been aroused and so responded with one of his limited repertoire of behaviors; (2) the child may match the general rhythm or shape, merely because his attempts to assimilate the spectacle necessarily involve certain behaviors with similar properties; (3) the child may note the general vectorial or modal characteristics (shape, direction, rhythm) and match these properties, yet not at the specific zone in which they have occurred; (4) the child may note both the modal properties of the behavior and the particular zone in which it occurred, imitating the behavior directly. (p. 1209)

Recognizing that these and other difficulties at this time prevent a simple statement about the ages at which imitation of nonvisible gestures can be said to be evident, we are led to spell out at least two clear alternatives: (1) that infants may possess the ability to organize a small set of intersensory equivalences during the first weeks after birth, and (2) that the capacity for organizing the intersensory equivalences implied by the imitation of nonvisible gestures undergoes a slow, and perhaps uneven growth, but that it is present during the first year of infancy. The second interpretation would support the evidence that we have examined earlier for haptic-visual shape-matching ability at around 12 months. In any case, acceptance of either alternative would lead us to focus on infancy as the period when intersensory coordinations become evident. As contrasted with the situation of just a few years ago, we now have a better sense of how we might go about studying processes and outcomes during the earliest formative period.

4. Postinfancy Developmental Research

The chronology of the research effort on the development of inter-sensory equivalence and transfer did not begin neatly with the infant studies that we have examined, but with a group of cross-sectional investigations of children. In examining the results of this research I will be selective, concentrating on principal issues and findings, and using studies illustratively. I have chosen to deal only with those investigations that inquire into the ability to equate and translate information between visual and haptic or kinesthetic subsystems. (For a review of the extensive work on auditory integration, see Fraisse, this volume.)

Most studies of intersensory matching have followed the procedure of presenting information (e.g., a shape) for inspection via one subsystem, and matching to sample in the complementary subsystem with one or more comparisons. Where a single comparison object is judged in relation to the standard object, the procedure calls for a sameness–difference decision. Early studies frequently compared performance only under intersensory treatments (visual-haptic or haptic-visual), whereas later research has made use of the full complement of two intersensory and two intrasensory conditions. Intrasensory controls are important, because without them it may be impossible to argue that intersensory matching or transfer are limiting performance; intrasensory accuracy could be responsible for any limitation of successful performance.

In studies where transfer of training, rather than matching, was the method employed, subjects were required to learn either a difficult discrimination or an associate such as a nonsense syllable for each of several objects. Transfer across subsystems could then be estimated in terms of the number of trials to relearning in the second subsystem. (See Freides, 1974, and Pick, Pick, & Klein, 1967, for more detailed reviews of this literature.)

The highly influential research of Birch and Lefford (1963, 1967) set the stage for much of the later work, and served as a point of departure for theoretical controversy. In their first monograph, Birch and Lefford (1963) presented growth curves of improvements in intersensory shape matching as evidence for the development of intersensory integration during childhood. Likewise, the data from a number of other investigations clearly point to improvements with age in both matching and transfer of information between vision and haptic or between vision and kinesthesis. What are we to conclude from these findings?

It is tempting to infer that changes in the central nervous system are responsible for bringing together the separate information of vision and haptics. As cortical maturation proceeds, more effective integration of primary projection areas of the brain takes place. Sherrington (1906) has been cited in support of this position, and from a psychological standpoint it simplifies matters—if only by shunting the problem over to the neurophysiologist. There are potentially, however, more psychological approaches to the problem. One approach is to ask about similarities between visual and haptic information handling, and whether such similarities change with growth. The other is to raise the question, as some have, of whether the curves that allegedly chart the progression of intersensory liaison during childhood are really dealing with an intersensory linkage rather than with intrasensory perceptual ability. I will begin a consideration of the first alternative to cortical maturation here, and will expand on it in a later section dealing with perceptual exploration and activity. Then, I will turn briefly to the reasons for skepticism toward the notion that the original Birch and Lefford growth curves reflect intersensory integration at all.

It is reasonable to believe that the anatomical and physiological differences between vision and haptics are such that processes specifically connected with transforming information from one subsystem to another (much the way that one must translate between the code of one language to that of another, or from pictures to words) are brought into play when matching or transfer take place between these two subsystems of perception. The pickup and encoding mechanisms of vision and haptics are not likely to be identical, so that—at minimum—translation mechanisms from one code to the other would have to be acquired and perfected. And, where modes of transformation (reduction, compression, schematization) are different in important respects between subsystems, more than simple translation might be involved. This argument emphasizes the importance of information-handling mechanisms that enable homomorphic constructions across subsystems such that equivalences may be perceived and difficult distinctions made. Accordingly, if there are deficiencies in the intersensory linkage mechanisms that are overcome with development, these are to be understood as information-handling deficiencies and not the result of topographical central-nervous-system separations. Thus, progress in intersensory matching or transfer need not force the conclusion that the cortex is more effectively closing the gap between separate channels of perception. Instead, development may rely more on learning to perceive homomorphically by either subsystem, and acquiring specific transformational algorithms.

The above analysis is consistent with the Birch and Lefford position in one important respect. It strongly implies the possibility that information-handling strategies (both intra- and intersensorally), translation rules, and bridging mechanisms of a psychological nature may have to be *acquired* to produce effective intersensory liaison. However, acquisition is not in any direct way reducible to cortical maturation.

A more direct challenge to the cortical-integration position comes from the argument that intersensory processing is in many instances no more difficult than intrasensory processing (see Bryant, 1968; Rudel & Teuber, 1964). A deficiency in intersensory matching might be the result of relatively poor intrasensory pickup or recognition. To draw a crude analogy with a (literal) pipeline, fluid may fail to move from one end of a pipeline to the other because of obstructions at one end, not because of any transmission limitations of the pipe. The recent research literature attests to the debate over whether intersensory or intrasensory improvements are, therefore, the responsible agents for growth curves of alleged intersensory integration. In order to resolve at least this issue, one might hope to find a relatively clear pattern of performance when comparing four visual and haptic matching conditions: intrasensory visual (visual-visual), intrasensory haptic (haptic-haptic), matching visual standard against haptic comparisons (visual-haptic), and matching haptic standard against visual comparisons (haptic-visual). Unfortunately, the pattern of results has been anything but clear. A diverse collection of studies has produced certain consistent results, but others that appear contradictory. I shall consider some representative studies without seeking to be exhaustive. (See Jones, this volume, for a fuller treatment.)

4.1. Processing Shape versus Length

Most research, either with young children, older children, or adults, achieves the greatest success when standard and comparison items are processed fully visually (visual-visual). This result has held true for a wide variety of shapes and lengths (and even some textures). By contrast, the remaining three comparisons have yielded less consistent results.

In an early investigation to include all four comparisons, Rudel and Teuber (1964) found haptic-haptic matching of shape the most difficult condition. However, the method of presentation in that condition was successive, whereas in the other conditions it was simultaneous, making a comparison problematic.

Under simultaneous shape matching with children as subjects, Milner and Bryant (1970) reported that haptic-haptic matching was the most difficult of the four conditions. But when delays were introduced between presentation of standard and comparisons, haptic-haptic matching was equal in difficulty with haptic-visual and visual-haptic performance. One cannot conclude that intersensory processing is the more difficult from this set of findings.

Studying children aged 5 and 10 years, Goodnow (1971) failed to replicate the results of Hermelin and O'Connor (1961), who in an early study found no differences among the four conditions with a shape-matching task. Goodnow, instead, indicated that for her subjects the haptic-visual match was the poorest of the four, and the visual-visual the best.

With children as young as 3 years, Rose, Blank, and Bridger (1972) reported equal levels of accuracy for matching shapes under the four conditions when all objects were simultaneously available. However, with the introduction of a 15-sec delay between standard and comparisons, the three conditions including a haptic component were hampered about equally. Related evidence with 4-year-olds is presented by Millar (1971), who found that visual-haptic, haptic-visual, and haptic-haptic recognition of shape equivalences were not significantly different in difficulty.

The findings of these investigations and others strongly raise the possibility that haptic processing may be as detrimental to fully accurate shape discrimination as any requirement for bringing together information between two perceptual subsystems. But, as we have seen, the results do not permit an unalloyed statement that haptic perception is the limiting factor in intersensory functioning. In fact, if one chooses to compare variances as a measure of intertask difficulty, as Björkman (1967) and Davidon and Mather (1966) have done, the finding has been that variance is the greatest in the intersensory conditions even though the number of incorrect discriminations may be no higher than in the haptic-haptic condition.

Working with the dimension of length rather than with shape, Connolly and Jones (1970) reported that intersensory matches were more difficult than intrasensory matches, including the usually difficult haptic-haptic match. Likewise, Freides (1975) noted that length adjustments were poorer under intersensory than under intrasensory conditions, with haptic-haptic accuracy second only to visual-visual accuracy. By contrast, the rank order for matching of shape as opposed to length adjustment was visual-visual, visual-haptic, haptic-haptic, and haptic-visual.

Thus, there is more than a hint in the findings of these diverse studies that the pattern of performance may be different for shape and a spatial dimension such as length. It appears that when discriminating or equating length information, intersensory processing poses the greater difficulties. But when the shape of objects is the type of information to be handled, intrasensory haptic matching sometimes presents the greatest difficulty. In this vein, some research indicates that any condition involving haptic perception, or recall of information derived haptically (cf. Goodnow, 1971), appears to depress accuracy to about the same extent.

Bryant (1968) has attempted to make sense of the pattern of discrepant findings for the properties of shape and length by maintaining that length is coded in absolute terms (e.g., centimeters, inches, etc.), whereas shape is coded in relational terms (e.g., a square is four-sided and rectilinear), and that absolute coding is more difficult under intersensory matching or adjustment conditions. This is a plausible hypothesis that might account for some of the divergent findings regarding shape and length discrimination measured inter- and intrasensorally. Yet, in an investigation with adults that involved the perceptual synthesis of two lengths presented either inter- or intrasensorally, no significant differences emerged for the following combinations: visual-visual, haptic-haptic, or haptic-visual (Abravanel, 1971). Although these results are not what one would predict from Bryant's conceptualization, it may be that the act of synthesizing or combining disparate lengths should not be expected to result in the same pattern of relative performance as simply producing an intersensory judgment of a kinesthetically perceived length—as in the research of Connolly and Jones, of Millar, and of Freides. Success at synthesizing two lengths might depend more heavily on quantitative knowledge and on ability to compose lengths than is the case in attempting to perceive the magnitude of a single length.

At the present time, then, there is reason to believe that the comparative study of inter- and intrasensory coordination for different properties of objects —especially for continua such as length and area— might be profitable, and that Bryant's formulation provides a useful theoretical underpinning for this type of inquiry.

5. Perceptual Activity and Exploration

One heuristic way of approaching the development and articulation of intersensory integration is to consider that, in a fundamental sense, the problems are essentially those of understanding perceptual learning and development. The previously considered research on intersensory liaison during infancy tells us that integration exists from very early in life, but that it must be perfected. The changes and improvements that occur with age, with familiarization, and with practice, build on earlier achievements. And, although the course of development may be influenced by neurological growth, there is no current evidence to convince us that changes in brain organization are contributing specifically to intersensory processing rather than to general developments in perception and cognition.

If, as J.J. Gibson (1966) has stressed, and Werner (1934) and von Hornbostel (1938) have also argued, a perceptual system is the large entity, with each modality a specialized subsystem of perception, then important changes in perception might best account for growth in the efficiency and effectiveness of intersensory processing. It is for this reason that studies demonstrating the importance of intramodal perceptual discrimination and memory have been so valuable (see Abravanel, 1972; Bryant, 1968; Freides, 1974; Goodnow, 1971). In the mature individual, the effectiveness and scope of intersensory processing might be seen as a complex result of (a) earlier perceptual development, (b) learning to use the organs of each perceptual system in ways that facilitate particular performances (such as perceiving shape or texture), and (c) acquiring the perceptual activities that enable homomorphic constructions of potential information by eye and by hand (to concentrate on these subsystems).

In this section, our primary interest is in examining the ideas and evidence for changes, during growth, of the ways in which the visual and haptic subsystems are deployed for gathering information. If the two subsystems operate in similar ways, we may assume that they are both under some larger, supramodal (or cognitive) control. By contrast, if they are deployed differently, it is likely that they would detect different "kinds" of information, and that intersensory integration would be difficult. Perceptual development might then depend on learning to use the organ systems in ways that provide homomorphic information. The central idea is nicely summarized in a quotation from Rudel and Teuber (1964) in which they speculate on the necessary underpinnings of intersensory matching and transfer:

> There is some common aspect of perceptual activity which permits one to utilize information from within a sensory channel or from several channels in such a way that invariant properties of objects are extracted. (p.6)

As we shall see, research during the past two decades has added substance to this hypothesis.

If one were to examine the gross anatomy of the eyes, hands, and mouth–tongue organs, which comprise the visual and principal organs of haptic perception, there would seem to be little reason to expect similarity of function. Yet, the eyes and the hands especially are deployable in analogous fashion. The perceiver can scan large areas by sweeps of the eyes or the hands across a surface; he can follow a contour, or fixate small details, with either set of organs. Visual scanning may proceed along horizontal, vertical, or oblique axes; haptic scanning may proceed similarly. Moreover, fixations and scans may be interlaced in many different orders, may have different points of departure, and may proceed at different rates of speed; and these characteristics belong to haptics as much as to vision. Given these, and many more, gross similarities in the ways that eyes and hands are deployable for detecting surfaces, contours, and features, there appear to be few—if any—inherent limitations that would prevent the construction of equivalent percepts by the two subsystems. However, the organ differences between vision and haptics preclude complete isomorphisms of the activities used for information gathering. Where equivalent information is needed for purposes of intersensory matching or recognition, an active process of constructing homomorphisms may be necessary. For example, the eyes move conjugately, whereas the two hands may be differentially deployed simultaneously or successively. Even fingers engaged in examining a sculptured shape, or reading braille, may be assigned individually distinctive scanning roles. This cannot be done visually. Therefore, where systematic biases exist in information handling by the eyes and by the hands, there might be impediments to acquiring homomorphic information, and to the achievement of intersensory equivalents that rely on such information. Possible biases for these two subsystems might arise from a number of conditions:

(a) Differential visual and haptic orienting and attending to object characteristics, such that texture, solidity, or even orientation may be more salient when perceiving via one subsystem than via the other (Abravanel, 1970; Gliner, Pick, Pick, & Hales, 1969; Goodnow, 1971). Likewise, subsystem-specific qualities, such as color or brightness, might affect visual orientation and attention in a biasing manner, especially for the young or inexperienced perceiver.

(b) Difficulty in differentiating the perceptual and performatory functions of the hands might, once again, pose some problems for younger children. Since only haptics can accomplish the two aims, a unique separation of functions may have to be accomplished for effective haptic perception that would not be necessary for visual perception.

(c) Relative difficulty of coordinating specific pickup from the two hands and from the ten fingers as they contact different surfaces of an object or layout; a potential problem for which there exists no visual counterpart.

(d) Ease of visually or haptically constructing a unified percept of an object or surface. Here, differences in speed of scanning may play an important role, especially for complex objects or surfaces.

The partial overlap or similarity of pickup and processing modes that exists between haptics and vision suggests a basis for intersensory integration, but also points to reasons why it is likely to be imperfect. This is where learning and development are likely to play their parts. A small, but growing, research literature has begun to examine perceptual activity by eyes and by hands in children and adults. These studies can assist us by indicating whether perceptual exploration changes in significant ways with growth, what the nature of the changes might be, and whether corresponding changes might occur for both visual and haptic subsystems. Finally, the extent to which improvements in intra- and intersensory processing can be linked to changes in modes of exploration would be particularly important.

5.1.   Perceptual Activity When Perceiving Object Shape

A group of Soviet investigators at the University of Moscow have made an important early contribution to the study of whether and how perceptual exploration changes during growth (see reviews by Pick, 1964; Zaporozhets, 1961; 1965). The general aim of these investigations has been to demonstrate that the modes of perceptual exploration and information gathering are not fixed at birth or shortly thereafter—they are not, in short, the manifestation of an innate organization—but that they develop over a period of years. The conceptual framework that guides and buttresses the research enterprise is a form of "realism" which assumes the presence of a structured environment existing independently of the perceiver. The perceiver's task is to acquire internal models or simulacra that properly reflect the structural arrangements inherent in objects and events in the world. The argument is made that the things and happenings of the world are more accurately perceived and better known as the perceiver learns to "model" or "trace" the form of objects and events by means of his actions vis-à-vis these external objects and happenings. Simply opening one's eyes and fixating, or allowing environmental stimuli to march through the sensory channels, is not sufficient for developing internal models that reflect external structures and conditions.

In line with this conceptual framework, perception is construed as the active process of detection, search, and comparison that leads to the formation of efference copies which "depict" the environment. As such, the theory, or better metatheory, appears to be a variant of a motor-copy theory of perception. The argument presented is that knowledge of the environment becomes more veridical as the perceiver accurately learns to model the properties of things by means of his actions. Perceptual learning and development result from the accommodation of exploratory movements to the demands of object and event structure.

In addition, with growth the perceptual learner acquires the means to make more adequate comparisons between his internal models and the environmental object in order to correct and perfect the models. Clearly, this is an approach to the question of how perceptual learning and development proceed. The emphasis on learning to orient to potential sources of information, and to actively explore objects, pictures, and surfaces is a welcome counterpoint to a research predisposition that examines perception under conditions of minimal perceptual activity (e.g., the visual-fixation method of preventing vitiating eye movements), or as if information of all sorts simply fills the channels of sensation of the sentient animal.

The foregoing theoretical framework leads in a fairly straightforward fashion to investigation of how children explore objects and surfaces visually and haptically—the two subsystems that are most obviously involved in scanning and search. The results of only a few representative studies are summarized in this section. Usually, children are observed or filmed while engaged in visual inspection of a large shape pinned to a screen, or while haptically exploring an object of unfamiliar shape with vision occluded. In research by Zinchenko and Ruzskaya (1960), haptic exploratory movements of children engaged in shape matching were monitored. Between 3 and 6 years exploratory movements are reported to have changed significantly. At 3 and 4 years exploration seemed to be more attuned to manipulation of objects than to perceiving their shapes. By 5 and 6 years, however, manipulatory acts were apparently replaced by more clearly perceptual acts. Careful outlining of contours, systematic tracing with fingers, and simultaneous grasping of the shape as a whole by the outstretched hand were common tactics among 6-year-olds. Age-related changes in the quality of exploration were accompanied by improvements in accuracy of shape matching.

The development of visual perceptual activity was the subject of a later investigation by Zinchenko, Van Chzhi-tsin, and Tarakanov (1963). By filming eye-movement trajectories as children perceived novel, free-form shapes of the type used for studying haptic perception, it was possible to identify a set of age-related changes for the visual subsystem. Frame-by-frame analyses of eye-movement paths were used to reconstruct tbe sequence of scanning, and to produce a composite "portrait" of a child's visual activity (see Figure 1). The most significant scanning changes between ages involved the total number of saccades, the regions of the shape that were explored, and the completeness of visual exploration. Whereas 3-year-olds tended to fixate a single section of a shape for long periods, this tendency decreased with age. On average, the frequency of saccades increased with age. At 3 and 4 years eye-movement scans were chiefly within the boundaries of the shape, whereas at 5 and

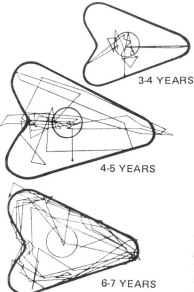

3-4 YEARS

4-5 YEARS

6-7 YEARS

Fig. 1. Eye-movement scanpaths of shapes typical at three ages. (From Zaporozhets, 1965, Figures 1, 2, and 3, pp. 86, 87, 88. Copyright 1965 by the Society for Research in Child Development, Inc. Reprinted by permission.)

6 years, inspection increasingly took place along the contours. Finally, a common finding was that the younger children overlooked substantial portions of a shape during visual inspection; by contrast, the older subjects gave evidence of having at least briefly inspected all parts.

Zinchenko *et al.* are quick to point out that their findings need not—and, in fact, do not—describe the way 3- and 4-year-olds visually scan familiar pictures of the sort one might encounter in a child's storybook. This means that for any eye-movement record there may be a substantial effect related to whether the visual material is familiar or novel. Clearly, the focus of this research was on the formation of new percepts where perceptual pickup strategies will be most critically important. One rather obvious methodological difficulty in this early series of studies involved positioning the camera lens so that it was always situated at the center of each shape. It is very possible that the lens was itself a compelling stimulus—especially for the younger children—and might have interfered with any disposition to explore more informative regions of the shape.

A second phase of the research by Zinchenko *et al.* may be particularly relevant to issues of intersensory matching and equivalence. In addition to filming the eye movements of children inspecting the standard figure, eye-movement records were also made for another group of children during the matching or recognition phase of the task. A general effect for all ages studied was that when inspecting the matching figures, children scanned more rapidly and fixated particular regions less than when exploring the standard shape. The matching figures "called for" examination and comparison in a way that perceiving an isolated standard had not. It is also probable that the comparison figures clarified the nature of the task and made exploration more purposeful. Notwithstanding these improvements in perceptual activity, the authors report that in other ways exploration of the matching figures continued to be poorly adapted to figural perception—especially at the younger ages.

Returning to the question of intersensory equivalence matching, the evidence from the innovative group of studies regarding the role of perceptual activity is only suggestive. In general, the evidence tells us that when young children of 3 or 4 years (and, by implication, prior to this age) perceive an unfamiliar shape or figure either visually or haptically, there are characteristics of the exploration that are transmodal. That is, perceptual pickup is guided by salient features, and is relatively restricted to some regions of the figure. With development over the next few years, exploration becomes more strategic in that it appears to be guided by more effective plans or search schemes. Comparing one novel figure with another requires a series of sequential steps: (a) awareness that the task requires shape perception (not performance), (b) a generic identification of the principal form characteristics, and (c) strategic exploration of features and relations leading to an integrated percept such that gross or fine comparisons may be made. The general outlines of the process seem to appear for either visual or haptic perception. With age, the matching phase of an equivalence task seems to profit increasingly from a schematization of the initial standard shape.

Additional descriptive data on the developmental course of haptic scanning are presented in a recent study by Kleinman (unpublished). The haptic exploration of children and adults was recorded while engaging in intramodal matching of complex geometric shapes. Kleinman reports that two trends correlated significantly with greater age: first, an increase in haptic orienting to details or features of the shapes; and second, greater attention to homologous features on the standard and comparisons. Despite growth in awareness of the importance of corresponding sections for making a proper match, between 6 and 10 years it was common to find children comparing mirror-image sections of the standard and comparison shapes. Adults occasionally made mirror-image comparisons, but the dominant perceptual strategy for most of them involved congruent tracing of corresponding contours. Moreover, with age, scanning strategies were more often adjusted to the discriminability of the shapes, providing evidence for the flexibility and adaptability of perceptual search to meet the difficulty level of the task. Correlating scanning strategies with accuracy of intrasensory matching proved significant in a number of respects even when the effects of age were controlled. Thoroughness of scanning, contour tracing, and feature comparison proved to have the highest correlations with accuracy of matching independently of age.

5.2. Perceptual Activity When Perceiving Length

Although ubiquitous, shape is only one of the several properties of objects that are perceivable visually or haptically. We will now consider length, which is a spatial property. Study of the perceptual activities involved when a subject perceives length, area, or circumference has some advantages over the study of shape perception by the two systems. In the first place, these spatial properties of objects are simpler than the multidimensional properties of many free-form or complex shapes. It is important to determine whether perceptual activities are the same when scanning for simpler attributes of objects as when exploring shape properties. Even more significant is whether the eyes and the hands scan in a homomorphic way when attempting, let us say, to gather information about the length of an object. At present, I do not know of any research that has monitored eye movements while a subject was engaged in perceiving the lengths of objects.

A second advantage to studying a quantitative dimension such as length is that one has more procedures from which to choose. Intra- or intersensory shape matching demands either a sameness–difference or match-to-sample procedure. Unless a delay is introduced between standard and comparisons, the subject explores the standard shape while the comparisons are present. By contrast, when dealing with a quantitative dimension such as length, it is possible to use the method of adjustment to good advantage. With the adjustment method, we can discern how a subject engages in exploration in the absence of comparisons that might guide him. Therefore, this method might come closer to assessing a subject's internal plans and strategies for perceiving.

As part of a descriptive study of haptic perceptual exploration in children between 3 and 14 years, Abravanel (1968) chose to observe and record the perceptual activities involved when children perceived length and circumference. Several spatial stimulus conditions were studied: haptic estimation of the lengths of wooden bars, haptic-kinesthetic estimation of lengths grooved into a board, circumferential magnitude, etc. For each condition of haptic pickup, an intersensory visual adjustment was made (except in the case of circumference where matching was the method) by means of a variable-length device. As a prerequisite for participation in the study, even the youngest children were required to demonstrate accurate intramodal visual adjustments to a visual standard. This ensured understanding of the proposition "making something (the variable line) as long as something else."

Most of the major changes in exploratory activity were found between 3 and 7 years. The exploratory activity of a majority of 3-year-olds and one-third of the 4-year-olds while engaged in perceiving the lengths of wooden bars was similar in a number of respects to the object identification and familiarization methods for comparable ages reported by Zinchenko and Ruzskaya (1960) when children were faced with a task of shape recognition. *Clutching, rotating,* and *global palping* of the standard bars were the most frequent perceptual activities at 3 years. The other commonly observed activity at 3 and 4 years was *passive holding of the ends of the bars* between the palms, with fingers loosely cupped around the sides. From these descriptive data, we concluded that at 3 and 4 years haptic exploration for length appeared to be little differentiated from haptic perception of solidity, area, and even weight. Manipulatory and performatory movements seemed to dominate the activity. By 5 years, on the other hand, performatory types of activities were noted in only a few cases, and by 7 years, they were no longer to be found. However, two other activities—*holding the ends of the bar between the hands,* and *sliding the fingers or hands from ends to center of the bar*—were observed in some 4-year-olds, and a majority of 5-year-olds. The trend begun at the younger ages increased by 7 and 8 years. Moreover, between 7 and 9 years, perceiving length by holding the ends of a bar between the fingers of both hands began to entail another activity: *active pressing of the ends of the bar.* This refinement of haptic length estimation is of particular interest, because by actively exerting pressure on the ends of a bar, length is perceivable as a distance between the two hands. Proprioceptive information through the hands, wrists, and arms provides spatial information of the distance, or length, occupied by a rigid object. Given the increases in accuracy of haptic length perception that accompanied these perceptual activities, we have reason to believe that the age-related changes in the manner of exploration are examples of perceptual development.

Another method that bypasses linear tracing of length, and relies on the proprioceptive information produced by a rigid, stationary application of the hand, is *spanning* the bar between the fingers of one hand with considerable pressure exerted on the ends of the bar. The method of spanning was present in roughly one-third of trials between 7 and 9 years; it increased in frequency of occurrence at still older ages.

In addition to the haptic exploratory methods deployed by the subjects in this investigation, the parts or sections of the hand used for exploration varied with age. The subjects of 3 and 4 years typically explored with the entire hand, and there was considerable palmar movement. This was true even for relatively short objects. With age, the fingers increasingly became the organs of perception, such that by 9 years children rarely used the palms for haptic perception. This finding is similar to that reported by Zinchenko and Ruzskaya (1960) for children engaged in haptic shape perception, and, therefore, would seem to indicate a general characteristic of how young children use their hands for perceiving.

A second stimulus condition in the Abravanel (1968) investigation supports the above results, and begins to add emphasis to trends already noted. With this condition, referred to as haptic/kinesthetic length perception, greater constraints on the expected range of perceptual activities were built into the task. Subjects were required to haptically perceive lengths grooved into Masonite boards, and to make visually equivalent length adjustments. In a situation of this sort, moving fingers along the length of the groove strikes us intuitively as a useful way to perceptually scan a line in order to compose its length. Between 3 and 5 years, children adopted this strategy increasingly; it appeared in roughly 33% of cases at 3 years, and in 62% at 5 years. However, at these younger ages, many children restricted their actions to a single movement along the grooved length. Others failed to explore or traverse the entire length. They scanned only a portion of it, often centering on a single section for a prolonged period. Incomplete scanning of the grooved lengths occurred in roughly 38% of cases at 3 years and 26% at 4 years, but in only 7% at 5 years. The main exploratory trend with age involved active engagement of the entire length. Principally, this was achieved by one of two methods, the first mobile, the second stationary. The mobile method involved repetitive tracing of the entire grooved length, whereas the stationary method relied on the use of spanning strategies. Extending the hand and fingers the length of the groove enabled the subject to span the length. Once again, we see evidence for the replacement, or supplementation, of a mobile perceptual method with a stationary one that offers a unified percept.

We can offer only some provisional hunches as to why older subjects elect spanning strategies for perceiving length. Spanning enables the perceiver to apply a known hand length to an unknown length in much the way that a meter stick might be applied to the task of measurement. In addition, this method replaces a sequential scanning strategy with a method of simultaneous information pickup (cf. J.J. Gibson, 1966; Revesz, 1950).

The formation of a unified percept or "image" may be an important contributor to effective haptic pickup and, indirectly, to intersensory-equivalence construction. The difficulty of achieving a unified percept of large objects is probably one of the distinctive limitations of haptic as opposed to visual information gathering. Until recently, unified gestalten have been assumed to be a property of the visual field. However, except for very small objects, or for those fixated at a distance great enough to produce a small retinal image, visual forms are probably unified by rapid, successive, sweeping eye scans (Noton & Stark, 1971; Yarbus, 1967). We now have good reason to suspect that, in haptic perception, spanning, gripping, or stationary "clamping" (as when length is perceived by pressing an object between the index fingers—see Teghtsoonian & Teghtsoonian, 1965) are modes of information pickup that are highly serviceable for effectively overcoming the relative slowness of haptic integration (Revesz, 1950).

In studying haptic perception among the blind, Hatwell (1966) and later Davidson (1972) have indicated that the blind—who clearly must rely more heavily on haptic perception than the sighted—often explore in ways that are likely to create unified percepts. Hatwell found that the blind, more than the sighted, perceived the area of an object by means of a unified simultaneous-grasping pattern. The sighted relied more on tracing the contour of an object with a single finger. Similarly, Davidson reported a difference in how the blind and the sighted explore an edge when determining whether it is straight or curved. The blind typically pressed all of the fingers of a hand against the edge, and in this way probably achieved a relatively simultaneous and unified impression of straightness or curvature. The sighted, however, more often employed a tracing strategy in which one or more fingers were moved along the edge. As for accuracy, the blind subjects proved to be more accurate with their method than were the sighted using their perceptual strategy.

These findings with the blind also lead us to wonder whether the greater reliance that the sighted place on sequential haptic movements in picking up certain types of information (e.g., form, area, or curvature) results from a tendency to transfer visually appropriate strategies to haptic forms of pickup. Since conjugate eye movements usually involve sequential scanning, the transferral of a perceptual pickup strategy from vision to haptics during development may be responsible for the deployment of sequential forms of information gathering in places where unified, simultaneous methods would yield more veridical information.

5.3. Perceptual Activity When Perceiving Complex Visual Displays

When two or more varied and complex surfaces or events are compared for similarity/dissimilarity, the perceiver must rely on a scanning strategy that is complete and systematic. Completeness, of course, is most important for determining similarity or full equivalence, whereas dissimilarity may be determined by noting a single difference—at which point scanning may reasonably end. The research examined thus far has shown that children under 5 years often explore an object or surface incompletely. Yet systematic search also includes such activities as following a spatial progression with eyes or hands (e.g., scanning progressively around a contour, straight across a row, from top to bottom, and so forth), and creating correspondence between a standard and one or more comparisons.

In a well-known study of how children visually search complex pictorial displays, Vurpillot (1968) demonstrated changes with age in the degree to which search was complete and systematic. Children between 4 and 9 years were presented with the task of determining whether pairs of pictured houses were identical in all respects (see Figure 2). The houses were similar in a global fashion in that each house contained six windows arranged symmetrically in two columns of three windows each. Some pairs of houses were identical, whereas others contained differences in the form of different household objects displayed in corresponding windows. Therefore, it is safe to say that where differences objectively existed between corresponding windows (thereby making the houses nonidentical), they were differences of detail. Accordingly, age-related findings are to be understood in terms of how effectively children scan for detailed information in a large display containing more overall pattern similarity than difference. Records of visual scanning were made using the corneal-reflection method (developed by Mackworth, 1968).

If we assume that the most effective scanning strategy for determining similarity and detecting differences between pairs of houses is to isolate homologous windows and to compare them in sets, we have an ideal standard against which to judge the actual patterns that were recorded. At ages 4 and 5, very few scanning sequences indicated that homologous windows were isolated and directly compared. However, by 6½, direct comparison of homologous windows was frequent; it was even more frequent at 9. Moreover, by 6½, the number of direct comparisons was greater for house pairs that had fewer differences between windows, and, therefore, would require more thorough scanning in order to detect the differences. Not only did perceptual activity change with age in a way that we would judge to be adaptive for the problem at hand, but accuracy levels increased correspondingly, with the greatest gains made between 5 and 6½ years. Notwithstanding this interesting pattern of results, a single caveat would seem to be in order. Vurpillot's subjects were instructed to determine whether "the two houses were the same all over." This could have been interpreted as an instruction to scan for global similarity (overall size, shape, and layout of windows). If so, we would expect many erroneous identity judgments where differ-

Fig. 2. Complex forms used by Vurpillot (1968) in her study of perceptual activity while perceiving form. (From Vurpillot, 1968, Figure 1, p.634. Reprinted by permission of the author and Academic Press, Inc.)

ences should have been reported. This was precisely what was found at the younger ages.

A useful follow-up study by Day and Bissell (1978) supports Vurpillot's findings, and further probes the way in which young children organize the task of comparing visual displays for similarity. Once again, children were asked to view house displays for sameness–difference determinations, but without accompanying eye-movement recording. A basic finding that essentially supports Vurpillot's was that two-thirds of the children (4-year-olds) did not exhaustively compare homologous windows in the pairs of houses in order to be certain that they were identical; nor did they search until a difference had been found in order to justify a judgment of nonidentity. By having subjects explain and justify their judgments, additional processing information was elicited that helps us to better understand the exploratory activities of the young child. First, many children made comparisons of windows on the same row when viewing a pair of houses, but frequently they were windows in nonhomologous positions (e.g., the two "mirror image" windows that would result from comparing the inner adjacent windows or the lateral outside windows). This type of comparison demonstrates a broad definition of "same" based on some rough topological criteria rather than on Euclidean homologues. Secondly, asking children to justify their judgments—as opposed to simply voicing them—led to a significantly more reflective processing style. Some children corrected originally wrong judgments, indicating that the young child is likely to suffer from an impulsive, nonreflective style. Anything that slows the rate of scanning and focuses the process of comparison making is likely to increase accuracy. Even having to justify your judgment to an adult fosters a more deliberate orientation than simply making a judgment. It is certainly true that adult interventions often serve to regulate and modulate the more impulsive judgments of young children (see Luria, 1961, for an expression and elaboration of this viewpoint).

The finding of Day and Bissell and of Kleinman (unpublished) that young children do not always subjectively define spatial location or orientation in the way that adults commonly do (or in a way that these children themselves will in a few years) is imporant for understanding age changes in judgments based on the perception of location and orientation, either intra- or intermodally assessed (cf. Abravanel, 1968; Bryant, 1974; Piaget & Inhelder, 1956). In a series of shape-matching studies of letterlike forms presented visually (Gibson, Gibson, Pick, & Osser, 1962), changes in orientation of a comparison shape were not sufficient to lead children to make difference judgments. We might say that a change of orientation was less salient than the constancy of shape. By contrast, haptically matching the identical shapes resulted in more attention to orientation and a higher incidence of difference judgments for differentially oriented standard and comparison shapes (Pick & Pick, 1966).

The discrepancy for the two subsystems might be understandable in terms of the ease of creating a total-shape gestalt in the visual and haptic conditions, and is of interest in its own right. Here, I would simply like to view these results as further indication that differences in the Euclidean or projective properties of shapes and displays that adults and older children isolate may not always be salient dimensions of difference for young children making spontaneous judgments. And, consistency or inconsistency of judgments with age may vary with the subsystem through which perception takes place. Of course, the results of E.J. Gibson et al. (1962) do not guarantee that differences in visual orientation are not perceived; they only assert that such differences may not be of the type that elicit spontaneous judgments of "difference." Much more research should be done on the problem of both visual and haptic determining of the bases for similarity.

A final study of eye-movement activity during visual discrimination or figural matching will be considered. Visual scanning was recorded by Mackworth and Bruner (1970) as children of 6 years and adults inspected either a blurred picture of a fire hydrant that was progressively focused at 10-sec intervals, or the same picture sharply focused. Children, more than adults, tended to concentrate their gaze on limited regions of either the blurred or focused pictures. In the sharp-picture situation, children concentrated on details and spent less time than the adults searching the other regions of the scene. Mackworth and Bruner were led to conclude that the children "could not examine details centrally and simultaneously monitor their peripheral fields for stimuli" that might be useful for closer inspection. It may be that this inferred difficulty of combining central and peripheral vision was responsible for the fact that children showed nearly twice as many very short visual movements as adults. Another notable point that distinguished visual activity at the two ages was the greater tendency of some children to fixate sharp edges—something the adults rarely did. The findings, as a whole, support the contention that even by 6 years scanning has not reached the adult form in significant respects. The children's strategies seem to be more one-track, with perceptual analysis and synthesis less effectively sequenced.

5.4. Summary

Our aim in this section has been to seriously consider the role of perceptual activities and exploratory strategies in perceptual development. The assumption that sustains this effort is that in order to understand effective intersensory development one must consider whether and how strategies of information gathering change during ontogenesis. Secondarily, it is useful to inquire whether scanning strategies for two perceptual subsystems such as vision and haptics are homomorphic and share many processing characteristics. To the extent that information is gathered visually and haptically in similar ways, we might have a nonverbal tertium quid to help explain the progress or limitations of intersensory patterning. Characteristics of perceptual activity and exploration are, of course, only the external manifestation of central planning and executive processes that direct the perceptual organs and integrate information obtained from them—all of which take place in relation to presenting stimulus or environmental conditions.

The results of all the scanning studies that we have reviewed are consistent in a number of respects. First, they demonstrate age-related changes in the way that objects and pictures are explored for purposes of identification, matching, or reconstruction. Secondly, at least in terms of group correlations, changes in perceptual activity do accompany important developments in the effectiveness of perception and judgment. Moreover, in a number of important respects perceptual exploration that proceeds visually or haptically has common characteristics. By 3 years, children are rather good perceivers, but they have some distance to go in cases where difficult discriminations are required, where they must be systematic and consistent, or where information-pickup strategies that depend on knowledge and expectancies about the world have not developed sufficiently. Therefore, it is important to reemphasize that the perceptual "style" of the young child confronted with novel perceptual information often is limited by being too global and incomplete for the task at hand, or by centrating on a few salient features. Especially in the case of haptic perception, the young child seems to be limited by a relative lack of differentiation between the perceptual and performatory roles of one and the same set of organs—the hands. With growth, scanning strategies change: they result in more complete information gathering and in what can be best described as a better capacity to integrate and unify parts of a perceptual field.

It was not possible to cite research in which both visual and haptic exploration were recorded simultaneously while a subject was engaged in intersensory matching. It would be useful to have research evidence of that kind, since it is most critical for determining the degree to which perceptual activities by hand and by eye overlap when engaged in a common task.

6. Conclusions

The weight of the evidence that we have considered leads me to conclude that at least a crude form of intersensory integration is present from early infancy—just how cannot presently be said with assurance. This conclusion generally supports the theoretical idea that the senses are unified—at least in some global way—from the beginning. However, more careful research on haptic-visual transfer during the neonatal period (perhaps along the lines suggested in the studies of Gottfried *et al.,* 1977), on early imitation of facial gestures, and on the coordination of visual orienting with auditory information will be needed to draw firm conclusions about very early competences.

In a similar vein, further investigation of the coordination of perceptual subsystems during the period roughly bracketed by 6 to 24 months will be needed. There is still a relative dearth of systematic data on process and achievement of intersensory patterning at these ages. Yet the little research that we have provides us with good reasons to believe that intersensory transfer and equation of information between vision and haptics is well under way during the latter half of the first year. The demonstrations of successful imitation of facial gestures, of oral/haptic-to-visual transfer of shape, and of haptic-to-visual transfer of shape discrimination, all strongly support the conclusion that intersensory accomplishments are being made during infancy.

How are we to account for the improvements with age in intersensory matching and transfer of the kind reported by a number of investigators? That performance improves is readily documented, but, as always, it has proven far more difficult to explain the changes that appear with age. My own judgment leads me to conclude that much of the improvement in intersensory processing with age results from general developments in perception and knowledge that are supramodal. In large measure, perceptual development consists of learning to attend to the most relevant features and relations of objects and events; of learning how to explore in order to canvass global information and to pick up more precise data. As these functions of perception develop, the organism becomes a more precise, astute, and specialized perceiver who is capable of making more differentiated and accurate judgments. The processing behind these age-related achievements is not modality specific; instead, it appears to be truly supramodal. This is not to deny the likelihood of a growing division of labor among the perceptual subsystems such that vision is greatly relied on for complex figural and spatial information, haptics for texture and hardness, audition for vibratory information. Such specialization surely might increase with age and experience, but the capacity for intersensory patterning of information in one subsystem along the lines of pickup in another subsystem probably depends for the most part on supramodal developments in perception and cognition. In laboratory investigations where intersensory processes are studied, the older subjects have a number of advantages over their younger counterparts: they know how to explore more effectively; their informational expectancies are likely to be better predictors of external-stimulus information than are those of the younger subjects; and their ability to restrict attention and search to relevant aspects of stimulation is significantly better than it was at an earlier age. These accomplishments are all translatable into better intersensory matching and transfer where information is either unfamiliar or complex.

Moreover, there is a great deal of evidence that demonstrates significant development of memory and representational systems during the ages of roughly 3–8 years. Strategies of information encoding and retrieval that develop during this period can be especially important for aiding the process of intersensory transfer, or for contending with multiple comparisons in a visual-to-haptic matching situation. The role of imagery as a linking mechanism during intersensory matching has been difficult to assess. Phenomenological reports indicate that subjects have visual images of haptically inspected surfaces and objects. Some subjects claim to rely heavily on such imagery. Just as imagery seems to play a significant role in the retrieval of many kinds of information—especially figural and spatial types—it may also serve as an important bridging mechanism for translating haptically acquired information into a form that we rely on most heavily—that is, a visual or implicitly visual-imaginal form. If imagery develops with age, as some theorists contend, then imagery could be a significant bridging mechanism that enables the older child or adult to perform more effectively in situations involving haptic-to-visual translations.

Yet another general development in perceptual functioning is the overcoming of field effects that lead to distortion and illusion. Perceivers of all ages are susceptible to certain classes of illusion, but young children are more prone to some of them (Pollack, 1972). Likewise, younger children have greater difficulty in using interoceptive or proprioceptive information to counteract the dominant effect of visual information in certain situations. Confronted with the rod-and-frame task (Witkin & Asch, 1948), where the subject must overcome a powerful visual pull by utilizing nonvisual information, children between 5 and 10 years make large frame-dependent (or visually determined) errors (Abravanel & Gingold, 1977; Vernon, 1972). Thus, learning to counteract the powerful effects of the visual field, and the not infrequent distorting effects of visual perception, is an important developmental achievement where it occurs. In intersensory situations where the perceiver is exposed to distorting field effects, successful adjustments and compensations may depend on the developmental status of the perceiver.

In the last analysis, our success in ontogenetically understanding the integration of the senses will depend on the progress that is made in understanding perceptual and cognitive growth. Most of the fundamental questions about intersensory processing are subspecies of larger-order questions about the functioning of perceptual subsystems and the informational coordinating mechanisms of the mind/brain. Our knowledge of intersensory processing will advance only to the degree that we are capable of linking it to more general knowledge about information handling.

7. References

Abravanel, E. The development of intersensory patterning with regard to selected spatial dimensions. *Monographs of the Society for Research in Child Development,* 1968, *32* (2), Serial No. 118.

Abravanel, E. Choice for shape vs. textural matching in young children. *Perceptual and Motor Skills,* 1970, *31,* 527–533.

Abravanel, E. The synthesis of length within and between perceptual systems. *Perception and Psychophysics,* 1971, *9,* 327–328.

Abravanel, E. Short-term memory for shape information processed intra- and intermodally at three ages. *Perceptual and Motor Skills,* 1972, *35,* 419–425.

Abravanel, E., & Gingold, H. Perceiving and representing orientation: Effects of the spatial framework. *Merrill-Palmer Quarterly,* 1977, *23,* 265–278.

Abravanel, E., Levan-Goldschmidt, E., & Stevenson, M.B. Action imitation: The early phase of infancy. *Child Development,* 1976, *47,* 1032–1044.

Allen, T.W., Walker, K., Symonds, L., & Marcell, M. Intrasensory and intersensory perception of temporal sequences during infancy. *Developmental Psychology,* 1977, *13,* 225–229.

Anisfeld, M., Masters, J.C., Jacobson, S.W., & Kagan, J. Interpreting "imitative" responses in early infancy. *Science,* 1979, *205,* 214–219.

Aristotle. *De Anima.* In R. McKeon (Ed.), *The basic works of Aristotle.* New York: Random House, 1941.

Baldwin, J.M. *Mental development in the child and the race: Methods and processes.* New York: Macmillan, 1895.

Ball, W., & Tronick, E. Infant responses to impending collision: Optical and real. *Science,* 1971, *171,* 818–820.

Bandura, A. Analysis of modeling processes. In A. Bandura (Ed.), *Psychological modeling: Conflicting theories.* Chicago: Aldine, 1971.

Bayley, N. *Bayley Scales of Infant Development.* New York: Psychological Corporation, 1969.

Birch, H.G., & Lefford, A. Intersensory development in children. *Monographs of the Society for Research in Child Development,* 1963, *28* (5), Serial No. 89.

Birch, H.G., & Lefford, A. Visual differentiation, intersensory integration and voluntary motor control. *Monographs of the Society for Research in Child Development,* 1967, *32,* Serial No. 110.

Björkman, M. Relations between intramodal and crossmodal matching. *Scandinavian Journal of Psychology,* 1967, *8,* 65–76.

Boring, E.G. *Sensation and perception in the history of experimental psychology.* New York: Appleton-Century, 1942.

Bower, T.G.R. Object perception in infants. *Perception,* 1972, *1,* 15–30.

Bower, T.G.R. *Development in infancy.* San Francisco: W.H. Freeman, 1974.

Bower, T.G.R. *A primer of infant development.* San Francisco: W.H. Freeman, 1977.

Bower, T.G.R., Broughton, J.M., & Moore, M.K. Infant responses to approaching objects: An indicator of response to distal variables. *Perception and Psychophysics,* 1970, *9,* 193–196. (a)

Bower, T.G.R., Broughton, J.M., & Moore, M.K. Demonstration of intention in the reaching behavior of neonate humans. *Nature,* 1970, *228,* 679–681. (b)

Brentano, F. *The psychology of Aristotle.* Berkeley: University of California Press, 1977.

Bryant, P.E. Comments on the design of developmental studies of cross-modal matching and cross-modal transfer. *Cortex,* 1968, *4,* 127–137.

Bryant, P.E. *Perception and understanding in young children.* New York: Basic Books, 1974.

Bryant, P.E., Jones, P., Claxton, V., & Perkins, G.M. Recognition of shapes across modalities by infants. *Nature,* 1972, *240,* 303–304.

Cassirer, E. *The philosophy of the enlightenment.* Princeton: Princeton University Press, 1951.

Connolly, K., & Jones, B. A developmental study of afferent-reafferent integration. *British Journal of Psychology,* 1970, *61,* 259–266.

Davidon, R.S., & Mather, J.H. Cross-modal judgments of length. *American Journal of Psychology,* 1966, *79,* 409–418.

Davidson, P.W. Haptic judgments of curvature by blind and sighted humans. *Journal of Experimental Psychology,* 1972, *93,* 43–55.

Day, M.C., & Bissell, J.S. Criteria for same and different judgments and visual comparison strategies of four-year-olds. *Child Development,* 1978, *49,* 353–361.

Fagan, J.F. Memory in the infant. *Journal of Experimental Child Psychology,* 1970, *9,* 217–226.

Freides, D. Human information processing and sensory modality: Cross-modal functions, information complexity, memory, and deficit. *Psychological Bulletin,* 1974, *81,* 284–310.

Freides, D. Information complexity and cross-modal functions. *British Journal of Psychology,* 1975, *66,* 283–287.

Gardner, J., & Gardner, H. A note on selective imitation by a six-week-old infant. *Child Development,* 1970, *41,* 1209–1213.

Gesell, A. *The embryology of behavior.* New York: Harper, 1945.

Gibson, E.J., Gibson, J.J., Pick, A.D., & Osser, H. A developmental study of letter-like forms. *Journal of Comparative and Physiological Psychology,* 1962, *55,* 897–906.

Gibson, J.J. *The senses considered as perceptual systems.* Boston: Houghton Mifflin, 1966.

Gliner, C.R., Pick, A.D., Pick, H.L., & Hales, J.J. A developmental investigation of visual and haptic preferences for shape and texture. *Monographs of the Society for Research in Child Development,* 1969, *34* (6), Serial No. 130.

Goodnow, J.J. Eye and hand: Differential memory and its effect on matching. *Neuropsychologia,* 1971, *9,* 89–95.

Gottfried, A.W., Rose, S.A., & Bridger, W.H. Cross-modal transfer in human infants. *Child Development,* 1977, *48,* 118–123.

Gregory, R.L. *Eye and brain.* New York: McGraw-Hill, 1966.

Guillaume, P. *Imitation in children.* Chicago: University of Chicago Press, 1971. (Originally published, 1926)

Hatwell, Y. *Privation Sensorielle et Intelligence.* Paris: Presses Univ. de France, 1966.

Hebb, D.O. *The organization of behavior.* New York: Wiley, 1949.

Hermelin, B., & O'Connor, N. Recognition of shape by normal and subnormal children. *British Journal of Psychology,* 1961, *52,* 281–284.

Kleinman, J.M. *Developmental changes in haptic exploration and matching accuracy.* Unpublished manuscript.

Luria, A.R. *The role of speech in the regulation of normal and abnormal behavior.* New York: Pergamon, 1961.

Mackworth, N.H. The wide angle reflection camera for visual choice and pupil size. *Perception and Psychophysics,* 1968, *3,* 32–34.

Mackworth, N.H., & Bruner, J.S. How adults and children search and recognize pictures. *Human Development,* 1970, *13,* 149–177.

McDonald, E.T., & Aungst, L.F. Studies in oral sensorimotor function. In J.F. Bosma (Ed.), *Symposium on oral sensation and perception*. Springfield, Ill.: C. Thomas, 1967, 202–220.

McDougall, W. *Introduction to social psychology*. London: Methuen, 1908.

Meltzoff, A.N., & Moore, M.K. Imitation of facial and manual gestures by human neonates. *Science*, 1977, *198*, 75–78.

Mendelson, M.J., & Haith, M.M. The relation between audition and vision in the human newborn. *Monographs of the Society for Research in Child Development*, 1976, *41* (4), Serial No. 167.

Millar, S. Visual and haptic cue utilization by preschool children: The recognition of visual and haptic stimuli presented separately and together. *Journal of Experimental Child Psychology*, 1971, *12*, 88–94.

Milner, A.D., & Bryant, P.E. Cross-modal matching by young children. *Journal of Comparative and Physiological Psychology*, 1970, *71*, 453–458.

Noton, D., & Stark, L. Scanpaths in saccadic eye movements while viewing and recognizing patterns. *Vision Research*, 1971, *11*, 929–942.

Piaget, J. *Play, dreams, and imitation in childhood*. New York: W.W. Norton, 1951.

Piaget, J. *The origins of intelligence in children*. New York: International Universities Press, 1952.

Piaget, J. *The construction of reality in the child*. New York: Basic Books, 1954.

Piaget, J., & Inhelder, B. *The child's conception of space*. London: Routledge, 1956.

Pick, A.D., & Pick, H.L., Jr. A developmental study of tactual discrimination in blind and sighted children and adults. *Psychonomic Science*, 1966, *6*, 367–368.

Pick, H.L. Perception in Soviet psychology. *Psychological Bulletin*, 1964, *62*, 21–35.

Pick, H.L., Pick, A.D., & Klein, R.E. Perceptual integration in children. In. L.P. Lipsitt & C.C. Spiker (Eds.), *Advances in child development and behavior*. Vol. 3. New York: Academic Press, 1967.

Pollack, R. Perceptual development: A progress report. In S. Farnham-Diggory (Ed.), *Information processing in children*. New York: Academic Press, 1972, Ch. 2.

Revesz, G. *The psychology and art of the blind*. 2nd ed. London: Longmans, Green 1950.

Rose, S.A., Blank, M.S., & Bridger, W.H. Intermodal and intramodal retention of visual and tactual information in the young child. *Developmental Psychology*, 1972, *6*, 482–486.

Rose, S.A., Gottfried, A.W., & Bridger, W.H. Cross-model transfer in infants: Relationship to prematurity and socioeconomic background. *Developmental Psychology*, 1978, *14*, 643–652.

Rudel, R.G., & Teuber, H.L. Cross-modal transfer of shape discrimination by children. *Neuropsychologia*, 1964, *2*, 1–8.

Ryan, T.A. Interrelations of the sensory systems in perception. *Psychological Bulletin*, 1940, *37*, 659–698.

Schiff, W. Perception of impending collision: A study of visually directed avoidant behavior. *Psychological Monographs*, 1965, *79*, Whole No. 604.

Sherrington, C. *The integrative action of the nervous system*. New York: Cambridge University Press, 1906.

Spelke, E. Infants' intermodal perception of events. *Cognitive Psychology*, 1976, *8*, 553–560.

Teghtsoonian, M., & Teghtsoonian, R. Seen and felt length. *Psychonomic Science*, 1965, *3*, 465–466.

Uzgiris, I.C., & Hunt, J.M. *Assessment in infancy*. Urbana: University of Illinois Press, 1975.

Vernon, P.E. The distinctiveness of field dependence. *Journal of Personality,* 1972, *40,* 366–391.

von Hornbostel, E.M. The unity of the senses. In W.D. Ellis (Ed.), *A sourcebook of Gestalt psychology.* New York: Harcourt Brace, 1938.

von Senden, M. *Raum- und Gestaltauffassung bei operierten Blindgeborenen vor und hach der Operation.* Leipzig: Barth, 1932.

Vurpillot, E. The development of scanning strategies and their relation to visual differentiation. *Journal of Experimental Child Psychology,* 1968, *6,* 632–650.

Vurpillot, E. *The visual world of the child.* New York: International Universities Press, 1976.

Werner, H. L'Unité des Sens. *Journal de Psychologie,* 1934, *31,* 190–205.

Witkin, H.A., & Asch, S.E. Studies in space orientation IV. *Journal of Experimental Psychology,* 1948, *38,* 762–782.

Yonas, A., & Petterson, L. Sensitivity in newborns to optical information for collision. Paper presented at the Meeting of the Association for Research in Vision and Opthalmology, May, 1978, Sarasota, Florida.

Yonas, A., Bechtold, A.G., Frankel, D., Gordon, F.R., McRoberts, G., Norcia, A., & Sternfels, S. Development of sensitivity to information for impending collision. *Perception and Psychophysics,* 1977, *21* (2), 97–104.

Yarbus, A.L. *Eye movements and vision.* New York: Plenum Press, 1967.

Zaporozhets, A.V. The origin and development of the conscious control of movements in man. In N. O'Connor (Ed.), *Recent soviet psychology.* New York: Liveright, 1961.

Zaporozhets, A.V. The development of perception in the preschool child. *Monographs of the Society for Research in Child Development,* 1965, *30* (2), Serial No. 100.

Zinchenko, V.P., & Ruzskaya, A.G. Comparative analysis of touch and vision: Communication VII. *Doklady Akademike Ped. Nauk RSFSR,* 1960, *4,* 85–88.

Zinchenko, V.P., Van Chzhi-tsin, B., & Tarakanov, V.V. The formation and development of perceptual activity. *Soviet Psychology and Psychiatry,* 1963, *2,* 3–12.

4

The Developmental Significance of Cross-Modal Matching

BILL JONES

1. Introduction

Philosophers and psychologists have sometimes argued that traditional distinctions between the spatial senses and, for that matter, between afferent sensory perception and efferent motor control are arbitrary and unhelpful (e.g., Börnstein, 1936; Freedman, 1968; von Hornbostel, 1927). Conceptual and experimental isolation of visual, auditory, and somesthetic processes (ultimately based upon Muller's so-called "law of specific nervous energies") led, undoubtedly, to a tremendous increase in knowledge of peripheral sensory physiology and to more or less detailed descriptions of sensory pathways to the central nervous system. Yet such work seemed to imply that human beings and other creatures see, hear, feel, and so on as isolated independent acts, as though individuals could only be known to each other as distinct independent visual, auditory, and sentient persons. Moreover ordinary language does not make the distinctions between modality dimensions which any treatment of, say, sight, hearing, and touch as isolated and distinct ways of knowing the world would seem to require. (Ordinary language is in fact shot through with synesthetic comparisons. See, e.g., Marks, 1975, for a recent discussion of synesthesia.) Of course, knowledge is perceptually based, but it is not obvious that it is visually based or (pace Berkeley)

BILL JONES • Department of Psychology, Carleton University, Ottawa, Ontario, Canada.

tactually based. By the 1960s these and other considerations had sparked a revival of interest in intersensory phenomena, which came to be seen not as marginally interesting effects but as central to any complete theory of perception (e.g., Freedman, 1968). Among developmental psychologists interest centered upon cross-modal matching, or tasks in which a person uses information derived from one modality as a standard, to make equivalence judgments about information from a second. For example, we might be asked to manually explore an object which is hidden from view and then to judge whether or not a second object, in the field of view but out of reach, is the same as the first.

I shall argue here that the theoretical basis for developmental studies of cross-modal matching has not always been clear, and I shall try to show that cross-modal matching is explicable on the same basis as within-modal matching. Equivalence judgments of two or more things require that each thing has been adequately perceived, no matter whether one thing is seen, another felt, and so on. No special problem of cross-modal matching need arise, any more than there need be a special problem in explaining why we can say that two things which we can see are or are not equivalent.

From the point of view of neurophysiology it is a mistake to think that perception is or can be limited to what can be said of the functioning of peripheral receptors and of their pathways to the cortex. Modern neurophysiology has made it clear that sensory systems have diffuse rather than segregated projections, and the concept of the cerebral cortex as the termination of independent modality-specific systems is more than ever becoming a pointless abstraction (see, e.g., Buser, Borenstein, & Bruner, 1959; Drager & Hubel, 1975; Fishman & Michael, 1973; Jung, 1961; Wickelgren, 1971). To take one example, the work of Wickelgren has shown that the superior colliculus, an organ implicated in sound localization and in the initiation of eye movements, receives visual, auditory, and somesthetic inputs. In other words, at higher levels of the nervous system space is represented by overlapping integrated inputs from a number of different modalities rather than by independent visual, auditory, and somesthetic spaces. In considering the problem of the sequential control of behavior Lashley (1951), in his still classic paper, reached much the same conclusion.

> The alternative to the isolated-path theory of the space co-ordinates is that the various impulses which modify postural tones are poured into a continuous network of neurons where their summated action results in a sort of polarization of the entire system . . . Their influence [i.e. of systems of space coordinates] pervade the motor system so that every gross movement of limbs or body is made with reference to the space system. The perceptions from

the distance receptors, vision, hearing and touch are also constantly modified
and referred to the same space co-ordinates. (p. 126)

We can take cross-modal matching for granted, therefore, in the
sense that we could only describe in terms of brain damage the perceptions of an individual who could not judge something he had seen to be
equivalent to something he had heard or felt. For developmental psychologists the interesting questions are, among others: What is the
significance of developmental changes in cross-modal matching? What
do failures in cross-modal matching indicate? Does cross-modal matching
operate differently and hence have a different significance at different
age levels?

2.   Birch and Lefford's Account of Cross-Modal Development

Birch and Lefford's influential monograph of 1963 provides a useful
starting point for examination of these questions. Essentially Birch and
Lefford argued for a general framework for perceptual (and perceptual-
motor) development in which the level of cross-modal matching efficiency
at a given age level indicates the degree of intersensory organization at
that level. They referred with approval to Sherrington's (1941) remark
that evolutionary developments had brought about more efficient connections between the senses and, repeating the old saw that ontogeny
parallels phylogeny,[1] they suggested that perceptual development is
characterized by a shift away from reliance on proximal stimulation
("tactual" dominance) to reliance upon teleoreception ("visual" dominance) accompanied by increasing intersensory liaison. Though Birch
and Lefford are not explicit, many other theorists hold that linguistic or

---

[1] Birch and Lefford's "phylogenetic" example is unfortunately quite unconvincing. In a
number of places they refer to Abbott's (1882) description of a frog which continues to
strike at a fly surrounded by sharp stakes even though it receives presumably painful cuts
in the process. The example suggested to Birch and Lefford that amphibians cannot
adequately integrate information deriving from vision (the sight of the fly) with that
deriving from touch (painful stimulation of the tongue), though there seems no reason not
to take Abbott's observations as an exemplification of *inhibitory* intersensory liaison.

Birch and Lefford go on to argue that a frog which does not strike at a quinine-coated
fly after one attempt must be able to integrate visual and gustatory stimuli. One could
equally argue that the striking response is inhibited solely by the taste of quinine. The
creature's initial response is visually guided, and subsequent nonresponding is determined
solely by taste and not by integration of sight and taste.

other (perhaps imagistic) mediation is necessary to bring together functionally independent modalities (e.g., Bridger, 1970; Ettlinger, 1967).[2]

In their own study Birch and Lefford (1963) used geometrical forms from the Seguin Form Board test as stimuli. Subjects aged 5 to 11 years simultaneously perceived two forms and made a same-different judgment. There were three conditions, what Birch and Lefford called visual-kinesthetic (VK), haptic-kinesthetic (HK), and visualhaptic (VH). Haptic conditions allowed the child to actively manipulate the forms, whereas in kinesthetic conditions the child gripped a stylus which was passively moved around the outline of the form. Matching errors decreased more or less linearly with age for all three conditions. Birch and Lefford concluded, since relations between the different sensory systems developed in an orderly fashion at different rates, that their results indicated a developmental increase in the child's ability to integrate intersensory information.

Yet just what may we conclude from the facts that there was improvement with age for all three conditions and that rates of improve-

---

[2] No one has clearly explained how linguistic mediation between modalities is supposed to work. One might imagine that a person learns to associate a name with a seen object and then learns to associate the same name with the same felt object. Since the names are the same the person indirectly associates the seen and the felt object. Some such associationist theory is clearly behind Berkeley's (1925) otherwise puzzling assertion that "we never see and feel one and the same object. That which is seen is one thing and that which is felt is another." Berkeley went on to say that "the combinations of visible ideas hath constantly the same name and the combination of tangible ideas wherewith it is connected. . . . "

It has never been clear on this basis how individuals can make cross-modal matches of objects which they cannot name, nor how animals (e.g., Wilson, 1965) and preverbal infants (e.g., Bryant, Jones, Claxton, & Perkins, 1972) could have cross-modal abilities. It is also implausible to think that an individual in normal conditions typically has quite independent experiences through vision and through touch of the same object. One might suggest that the individual learns to associate a name with an object which he both sees and feels at the same time, but this solves nothing. How is the individual to know that the name refers to both (or either) the visible and tangible aspects of an object if we hold that the two are logically distinct—that, as Berkeley would have it, there are in fact two objects? Of course human beings generally reflect perceptual discriminations in the language, and linguistic mediation might mean only that discrimination is facilitated by naming (cf. Koen, 1971). This is a long way from suggesting that the existence of language is a necessary or a sufficient condition for cross- or within-modal matching.

A similar comment might be made about imagistic mediation, which often seems to mean little more than that we remember what we see. Blank (1974) argues that visual-tactual transfer "could not occur unless the child were carrying over some visual representation" (p. 233). On one interpretation this is pure tautology. In order to remember what we have seen we must remember what we have seen. Conceivably Blank takes "visual representation" to be equivalent to "visual image," but she gives no reasons for thinking that remembering what we have seen necessarily requires imagery.

ment differed between conditions? It is certainly not obvious on this basis alone that relations between different sensory systems must develop at different rates. Birch and Lefford's data showed, in fact, a near perfect negative correlation between intercepts and slopes of the functions for the three conditions;[3] that is, their data may simply exemplify the "developmental rule" that with increasing age those tasks which are originally the more difficult tend to develop at a faster rate. In this particular case we can learn nothing about processes responsible for development since, as Birch and Lefford noted themselves, developmental increases in cross-modal matching abilities might arise either because intersensory liaison becomes more efficient or because children become increasingly able to make equivalence judgments about standard and comparison items presented in the same modality. Graphs for Birch and Lefford's three conditions were certainly not parallel, but since no within-modal control conditions were included it is quite possible that improvements in the cross-modal conditions were dependent upon developmental gains in the child's ability to pick up haptic and kinesthetic information.

This point was argued at length by Bryant (1968), who noted that when within- and cross-modal conditions are compared across age groups an age–conditions interaction could indicate developmental improvements in intersensory organization independent of expected improvements in intrasensory processing. However, Millar (1972a) and Milner and Bryant (1968), for example, have reported age changes in visual and tactual within- and cross-modal matching which fail to demonstrate independent improvements in cross-modal abilities (see also Jones & Robinson, 1973).[4] Thus there appears to be little evidence for the hypothesis that intersensory organization develops either at a different rate from or independently of intrasensory development. Moreover, despite its antiquity there is surprisingly little evidence for the view that touch is dominant in early life (which would enable us to speak of infancy as characterized by a "tactual" space).[5] The work of Fantz (1958),

---

[3] From Birch and Lefford's graphs I have calculated least-squares linear fits as follows: VK, $y = 9.53 - .69x$ ($r^2 = .93$), KH, $y = 6.80 - .53x$ ($r^2 = .97$), and VH, $y = 4.50 - .35x$ ($r^2 - .87$).

[4] One study of auditory-visual cross-modal matching by Alexander (1977) did result in a significant age–conditions interaction. I shall discuss this study in some detail below.

[5] It has traditionally been thought that only touch, of the spatial senses, can give a sense of reality. Partly for this reason, Berkeley (1925) argued that visual space is parasitic upon tactual space. However, Berkeley assumed that tactual judgments are logically prior to visual judgments and not that tactual space is necessarily developmentally or temporally prior to visual space. We may note that some contemporary philosophers, such as Armstrong (1962), have argued that a person without a sense of touch could not be taught the concept of a material object.

Hershenson (1967), Bower (1966) and others has shown that neonates incapable of independent locomotion can make quite sophisticated visual discriminations including judgments of depth by means of the same binocular parallax cues as adults (Bower, 1966). Furthermore, tactile perception is very inefficient in infants and young children. Gottfried, Rose, and Bridger (1978), using a preference technique, found no evidence that children younger than 12 months could remember tactually perceived forms. With somewhat older children (up to about 5½) there is general agreement from studies which have compared shape matching by vision and by touch that visual matching is relatively skilled whereas tactual matching is often at no more than a chance level (e.g., De Leon, Raskin, & Gruen, 1970; Goodnow, 1971a; Millar, 1971). Only one study (Rose, Blank, & Bridger, 1972) has shown asymptotic tactual matching by children as young as 3. Nearly all other studies serve to confirm Goodnow's apt comment that "a sharp division appears, somewhere around 5:6 . . . between chaos and relative accuracy in matching complex shapes by hand" (Goodnow, 1971a, p. 91). Tactual perception does not seem to be a "spontaneous" skill in young children in that 4- and 5-year-olds ordinarily will not manually explore objects which they can also see (Abravanel, 1972a; Cronin, 1973).[6] All in all there is little evidence to suggest that early development is characterized by tactual dominance. On the contrary, young children appear to acquire tactual matching skills only with difficulty over the course of development (see also Millar, 1972a; Milner & Bryant, 1968).

Nothing I have said implies that we should think of space as being primarily visual in young children, as Warren, for example, (1970) has suggested. In fact further evidence against Birch and Lefford's assumptions has been found in demonstrations that infants are capable of intersensory judgments. Aronson and Rosenbloom (1971) found that 30-day-old neonates show signs of distress when they see their mother in one position and hear her voice coming from another (see also Lyons-Ruth, 1977), and Bower, Broughton, and Moore (1970) have shown that neonates can also coordinate visual and tactual data to control guided reaching movements. Most interestingly a number of workers (Allen, Walker, Symonds, & Marcell, 1977; Bryant, Jones, Claxton, & Perkins,

---

[6] Active tactual exploration of form in combination with visual information may conceivably result in greater efficiency. Experimenters who have claimed that bisensory visual and tactual information is ineffective have also typically found that visual matching is nearly errorless (e.g., De Leon *et al.*, 1970; Millar, 1971). Studies in which visual matching was less than perfect have shown that combined visual and tactual stimulation may result in increased accuracy (e.g., Denner & Cashdan, 1967), though perhaps because of increased motor activity rather than tactile pickup per se (see also Goodnow, 1969).

1972; Gottfried, Rose, & Bridger, 1977) have indirectly demonstrated cross-modal processing on the part of infants less than 12 months old. Bryant *et al.* found that infants between 6 and 11 months were significantly more likely to reach for a visually presented object which they had previously touched but not seen than for one which they had not touched or seen. Allen *et al.* examined habituation of heart rate and skin potential in infants whose average age was 6 months, and found significantly greater recovery for both responses when a different temporal sequence was presented in visual and auditory cross- and within-modal conditions. In short, there is little evidence for the proposition that early development is characterized by proximal tactual dominance and there is quite strong evidence that neonates are capable of perceptual judgments based upon intersensory integration (Allen *et al.*, 1977; Aronson & Rosenbloom, 1971; Bower *et al.*, 1970; Gottfried *et al.*, 1977).

Although Birch and Lefford's work had considerable interest, the theory that changes in cross-modal matching indicate changes in intersensory organization is open to criticism on conceptual and empirical grounds. I have no objection to Birch and Leffords's argument that integration of information deriving from all sense modalities is one of the major functions of the cerebral cortex. Nevertheless, one can still reasonably suggest that age differences in cross-modal matching can best be explained in terms of age differences in within-modal matching. I shall now try to show by a more detailed review of visual-tactual, visual-kinesthetic, and visual-auditory matching experiments that the development of cross-modal matching can, in general, be accounted for on the basis of pickup of information within modalities.

3. Visual-Tactual Cross-Modal Matching

Obviously, information pickup in the visual and tactual modalities is different. If vision may be said to be holistic, tactual perception is traditionally described as successive in that we must infer what an object is from a sequence of distinct impressions. There is considerable evidence, some of which I shall review here, that tactual perception is less efficient than visual perception. I shall further argue that developmental data on cross-modal matching, both of form and of texture, can be explained on the basis of relative visual efficiency combined with differences in the ways in which visual and tactual information has been presented. First it will be useful to clear up or at least consider some important methodological problems.

3.1. Methodological Considerations

In any cross-modal matching experiment the subject is asked to compare one or more standard items with one or more comparison items, so that cross-modal matching is an example of the matching-to-sample paradigm. Basically there are four ways in which standard and comparison items may be presented: (1) Both a standard and a set of one or more comparison items can be presented together ("simultaneous" presentation); (2) the standard and the comparison items are presented simultaneously and each item in the comparison set is presented separately ("simultaneous-sequential" presentation); (3) the standard and comparison items are presented successively and all items in the comparison set are presented together ("successive" presentation); (4) the standard and the comparison items are presented individually in sequence ("sequential" presentation). Typically experimenters have required subjects to match one standard to one or more comparisons, though Hermelin and O'Connor (1961) and Goodnow (1971a) had subjects compare several standards with a number of possible matches.

Standard and comparison items may be presented in either modality giving four conditions: visual standard with visual comparison (VV), tactual standard with tactual comparison (TT), visual standard with tactual comparison (VT), and tactual standard with visual comparison (TV). Very few studies have attempted even a partial comparison of presentation methods and modality conditions (see, e.g., Cronin, 1973; Jones & Robinson, 1973; Rose *et al.*, 1972), though presentation methods may account for much of the variance between studies.

There are many other possible sources of variance in visual-tactual matching experiments, including whether forms are familiar or unfamiliar, two-dimensional or three-dimensional, and how vision is occluded for tactual pick up. Familiar geometric forms probably allow relatively more efficient classification at least by older children and adults, which could lessen differences between visual and tactual processing (see Koen, 1971). The majority of studies have, however, made use of arbitrary "nonsense" forms constructed according to a variety of methods (e.g., Brown & Owen, 1967). In a sense all forms presented tactually will be three-dimensional and have depth; yet the relatively flat cutouts used in a number of studies effectively restrict manual exploration to tracing the outline. Three-dimensional objects may in theory allow more efficient tactual pickup since a wider range of manual exploratory strategies are possible.

It is also conceivable that the method of occluding vision for tactual presentation may influence performance. If the subject has his eyes open and the form is shielded, visual interference is possible (e.g., Abravanel,

1971b). On the other hand, one could argue that with eyes shut it is more difficult for subjects to form a visual representation of the tactually perceived form (cf. Warren, 1970). Abravanel (1971) did in fact find differences between eyes-open and a method using light-occluding goggles, with some advantage accruing to the latter method. Apparently no other studies have controlled this factor.

One final methodological point is worth mentioning. With a few exceptions (e.g., Garvill & Molander, 1973; Hermelin & O'Connor, 1961; Koen, 1971), within- and cross-modal matching efficiency of both children and adults has been assessed in terms of error rates. When the subject is required to make a same-different judgment of two forms, the error rate confounds discrimination accuracy with some bias to respond same or different. An increase in bias will in general increase error rates whether or not there has been a change in accuracy. One might reasonably expect subjects to be biased to say that the comparison form is different when they have less information about the standard (typically when the standard is perceived through touch). This supposition was confirmed by Garvill and Molander (1973) with adult subjects. To the best of my knowledge no studies of shape matching with children have broken down error rates so as to indicate bias differences between conditions. The problem is, of course, partly logistic. Tactual perception is very time consuming and it is often difficult, particularly if the subjects are children, to carry out sufficient trials to allow stable estimates of response bias.

Several studies have made use of a forced-choice procedure which requires the subject to select the correct match for the standard from a set of at least two comparison items. In principle, the proportion correct from a forced-choice experiment is an estimate of accuracy unconfounded with response bias (see, e.g., Green & Swets, 1966). However, in requiring the subject to scan a set of comparison items, the procedure itself is likely to result in more errors of tactual matching than of visual matching. If all comparisons are present simultaneously then manual exploration will still be sequential. If comparison items are presented in sequence we need assume that retention of information is equivalent whether it is derived from vision or from touch. There is some evidence against this assumption (e.g., Goodnow, 1971a; Rose et al., 1972). Moreover, the use of proportion-correct assumes that the subject does not show positional biases (say to the first item in the comparison set). There is no reason a priori to expect children not to show such biases nor, perhaps, for the bias to be more pronounced when comparison items are tactually perceived. For present purposes I shall leave the problem of dependent measures as it stands and assess efficiency largely in terms of error rates for the different conditions.

3.2. A Theory of Visual-Tactual Matching

Perhaps the simplest theory of cross-modal matching between vision and touch is that performance depends upon processing in the modality which is the more efficient of the two for a given task. If pickup of information is more efficient when presentation is visual, one may hypothesize about the effects of presentation conditions on cross-modal matching. If the standard and the comparison items are presented successively or sequentially, the subject in the VT task should have adequate information about the standard so as to be able to control manual exploration of comparison items with reasonable efficiency. TV matching, on the other hand, should be relatively inefficient since the subject would not have sufficient information about the standard from tactual pickup and literally would not know what to look for in the comparison set. In TT matching pickup of information about both standards and comparisons will be inefficient. One should expect, therefore, the typical ordering of modality conditions given successive or sequential presentation to be VV > VT > TV > TT. When presentation is simultaneous, VT and TV conditions differ only in that normally there will be only one standard item and more than one comparison item. The subject has visual data available to guide manual exploration, and since there are typically fewer items to be tactually perceived in the TV condition one should expect the ordering TV > VT or possibly TV = VT if the subject has sufficient time to adequately explore all tactual alternatives. As tactual perception becomes more efficient over the course of development, differences between presentation methods and between the three conditions involving tactual processing should become less pronounced and ultimately the ordering should become VV > TT = VT = TV.

3.3. Visual-Tactual Matching of Form

There is little doubt that discrimination of form is more efficient when standards and comparisons are presented visually. Visual matching is superior to tactual matching for normal adults (e.g., Abravanel, 1971; Cashdan, 1968; Freides, 1975; Garvill & Molander, 1973; Goodnow, 1971a; Owen & Brown, 1970), adolescents (e.g., Lobb, 1965), and children (e.g., Bryant & Raz, 1975; Goodnow, 1971a; Jackson, 1973; Jones & Robinson, 1973; Millar, 1972a; Milner & Bryant, 1968; Rudel & Teuber, 1964, 1971), as well as for brain-damaged children (Rudel & Teuber, 1971) and retarded children and adults (Jones & Robinson, 1973; Zung, 1971). Only two exceptions seem to have been published. Rose *et al.* (1972) found error-free performance for all four within- and cross-modal matching conditions in a group of 3-year-olds. This study is difficult to evaluate because of ceiling effects. In the most difficult conditions of the experiment, in which a 15-sec delay was interposed between presentation of a standard and of two comparison items, modal error rates, to judge from reported means and standard deviations, were probably zero. The second exception is Hermelin and O'Connor's (1961) paper. Like Rose *et al.*, they found no significant differences between the four conditions (though performance was nonoptional) for normal children from 4 to 7 years. Imbeciles were superior in purely tactual matching. However, an exact replication with normal children (Goodnow, 1971a) failed to confirm Hermelin and O'Connor's finding that visual and tactual matching do not differ.

Studies of cross-modal transfer of form, in which the subject is trained to some criterion to make discriminations when information is presented through one modality, and then retrained with information derived from a second modality, have also shown in general that performance is more efficient when information is derived visually. Both adults (e.g., Garvill & Molander, 1971) and children (e.g., Pick, Pick, & Thomas, 1966) require more trials to criterion for tactual than for visual learning. Especially revealing is a comment by Pick (Pick *et al.*, 1966) that 30% of first-graders had to be dropped from a study of visual-tactual cross-modal transfer because they found tactual training so difficult that they were unable to reach criterion. On the other hand, 10% of subjects showed perfect visual learning in only one trial.

Table I shows the results of 15 studies with normal subjects which have compared all four modality conditions in terms of proportion-correct or error rates, and in which no substantial delay was interposed between presentation of the standard-and-comparison sets. When presentation was successive, the ordering of cross-modal comparisons was typically either VT > TV (Cashdan, 1968; Freides, 1975; Goodnow, 1971a; Jackson, 1973; Jones & Robinson, 1973; Koen, 1971; Lobb, 1965; Milner & Bryant, 1968) or VT = TV (Abravanel, 1971; Garvill & Molander, 1973; Goodnow, 1971a; Jones & Robinson, 1973). Where VT = TV, subjects are either adults or the older age groups in the sample. There is sufficient suggestion, therefore, that the ordering becomes VV > TT = VT = TV as subjects grow older. Interestingly, the ordering VV > VT > TV > TT was found with adults or adolescents when the stimuli were nonsense forms (Freides, 1975; Koen, 1971; Lobb, 1965) and the order was VV > TT = VT = TV when the subject explored three-dimensional objects (Abravanel, 1971; Garvill & Molander, 1973; Goodnow, 1971a), thus partly confirming the suggestion that three-dimensional objects may be more suited to tactile exploration than two-dimensional cutouts. Furthermore, with simultaneous presentation the ordering is in

Table I. Results of Cross-Modal Matching Experiments Without Memory Demands

Author(s)	Subject age group(s)	Stimuli	Presentation mode	Order of modality conditions
Abravanel (1971)	Adult	Nonsense objects	a. Sequential same-different	a. VV>TT=VT=TV
			b. Sequential 3 F.C. Simultaneous 2 F.C.[a]	b. VV>VT=TV>TV VV>TV>VT>TT
Bryant & Raz (1975)	3:5–4:8 years	Nonsense forms		
Cashdan (1968)[b]	Adult	Nonsense forms	Sequential 5 F.C.	(1) VV>VT>TT>TV (2) VV>TV>VT>TT
Freides (1975)	Adult	Nonsense forms	Sequential same-different	VV>VT>TT>TV
Garvill & Molander (1973)	Adult	Nonsense objects	Sequential same-different	VV>VT=TT>TV
Goodnow (1971a)	(i) Adult	Nonsense objects	Sequential same-different	(i) VV>TT=VT=TV
	(ii) 9- to 10-year-olds	Cyrillic characters	Sequential; subject chose correct match for 5 standards from 10 comparisons	(ii) VV>VT=TT>TV
Jackson (1973)	(i) 10-year-olds (ii) 8-year-olds (iii) 6-year-olds	Nonsense forms	Sequential 3 F.C.	(i) VV>VT>TV>TT (ii) VT>TV=VV>TT
Jones & Robinson (1973)	(i) 5-year-olds (ii) 12-year-olds	Nonsense forms	(a) Simultaneous same-different (b) Sequential same-different	(i)a. VV>VT>TV>TT (ii)a. VV>VT=TV>TT (i)b. VV>TT=VT=TV (ii)b. VV>VT=TT>TV

Koen (1971)	Adult	Nonsense forms	Sequential same-different	VV>VT>TV>TT
Lobb (1965)	14-year-olds	Nonsense forms	Sequential 3 F.C.	VV>VT>TV>TT
Millar (1972a)	(i) 7:7–9:4 years (ii) 5:4–6:8 years (iii) 3:0–4:6 years	Nonsense forms	Simultaneous 3 F.C.	(i) VV>TV=TT>VT (ii) VV>TV=VT=TT (iii) VV>TV=VT=TT
Milner & Bryant (1968)	(i) 7-year-olds (ii) 6-year-olds (iii) 5-year-olds	Geometrical forms	Sequential same-different	(i) VV>VT>TV=TT (ii) VV>VT>TV=TT (iii) VV>VT>TV>TT
Rose et al. (1972)	3-year-olds	Geometrical forms	(i) Simultaneous 2 F.C. (ii) Successive 2 F.C.	(i) VV=TT=VT=TV (ii) VV>TV=VT>TT
Rudel & Teuber (1964)	(i) 5-year-olds (ii) 4-year-olds	(a) "Simple" nonsense forms (b) "Difficult" nonsense forms	Sequential 5 F.C.	(i)a. VV>VT>TV>TT (ii)a. VV>TV=VT>TT (i)b. VV=VT>TV>TT
Rudel & Teuber (1971)	5:6–9:9 years	(a) "Simple" nonsense forms (b) "Difficult" nonsense forms	Sequential 5 F.C.	a. VT=VV>TT=TV b. VV>VT>TT=TV

[a] 2 F.C. is a two-forced-choice experiment, that is, the subject was required to choose the correct match for one standard form from two comparison forms. 3 F.C. is a three-forced-choice experiment in which the subject chooses the correct match from among three comparisons and so on.

[b] Cashdan (1968) performed two random replications of the same experiments with two different results.

general TV > VT (Bryant & Raz, 1975; Jones & Robinson, 1973, in the case of 5-year-olds; Millar, 1972a; Rose et al., 1972). In other words, the order of mean error rates for modality conditions is strongly related to presentation conditions and to a lesser extent to the kind of stimulus used for tactual exploration.

In principle, interposing a retention interval between presentation of the standard-and-comparison sets should produce an ordering of conditions similar to that of any other method of successive or sequential presentation. Some authors have suggested that differences between vision and touch are more pronounced when the task makes heavy memory demands (e.g., Goodnow, 1971a; Rose et al., 1972), since they have expected information derived from touch to be less stable. However, Garvill and Molander (1973) found no significant effects of 1-, 10-, or 30-sec retention intervals on any of the four cross- and within-modal visual and tactual conditions, and in a later study (Garvill & Molander, 1977) they showed that a visual interfering task during the retention interval had comparable effects on all modality conditions. In consequence they argue in favor of some common form of storage for visual and tactual information. Differences between modality conditions under memory demands might then be parsimoniously explained much as I have tried to explain the basic cross-modal matching paradigm on the basis of the interaction between the relative efficiency of visual and tactual pickup of information and presentation conditions.

Table II shows orderings from four experiments in which a retention interval varying from 5 to 30 sec was interposed between the standard and the comparison sets. Studies by Rose et al. (1972) and Milner and Bryant (1968) for two of three age groups, and Abravanel (1972) for the youngest age group show the relationship VT > TV expected on the basis of successive presentation. Eight-year-olds and adults in the Abravanel study show no significant differences between conditions except that visual matching is superior, confirming his previous results without a retention interval. The results from Millar's (1972a) extensive study are ambiguous. No age group or delay condition can be consistently ordered. Four of the nine cells in Millar's design show the predicted VT > TV relationship and three show TV > VT. Summarizing across age groups for successive conditions, we get the ordering VV > TT = VT = TV, whereas data from the simultaneous conditions summarized across age groups give VV > TV > TT = VT.

3.4. Cross-Modal Matching of Texture

It might perhaps be argued that form perception is not of the essence of touch (Taylor, Lederman, & Gibson, 1973), and hence cross-modal comparisons of form will inevitably show visual superiority. Changing

Table II. Results of Cross-Modal Matching Experiments with Memory Demands

Authors	Subjects	Stimuli	Delay	Order of modality conditions
Abravanel (1972)	(i) Adults	Nonsense objects	15 sec.	(i) VV>TT=VT=TV
	(ii) 8-year-olds		Unfilled delay	(ii) VV>TT=VT=TV
	(iii) 5-year-olds			(iii) VV>VT>TT>TV
Millar (1972)	(i) 7:7–9:4 years	Nonsense forms	a. 9 sec	(i)a. VV>TT=VT>TV
	(ii) 5:4–6:8 years		Unfilled delay	b. VV>TT>TV>VT
	(iii) 3:0–4:6 years		b. 9 sec	c. VV>TV–TT>VT
			Digit	(ii)a. VV>TV>VT=TT
			c. 9 sec	b. VV>VT>TT>TV
			Visual	c. VV>TV=VT>TT
				(iii)a. VV>TV=TT=VT
				b. VV>VT=TT>TV
				c. VT=VV>TT=TV
Milner & Bryant (1968)	(i) 7-year-olds	Geometrical forms	a. 5 sec	(i)a. VV>VT=TT=TV
	(ii) 6-year-olds		Unfilled delay	b. VV>VT=TV=TT
	(iii) 5-year-olds		b. 30 sec	(ii)a. VV>TT=VT=TV
			Unfilled delay	b. VV>TT=VT=TV
				(iii)a. VV>VT=TT>TV
				b. VV>VT=TT>TV
Rose et al. (1972)	3-year-olds	Geometrical forms	15 sec Unfilled delay	VV>VT>TV>TT

the task to texture perception could change the relative efficiency of VV and TT matching and hence change the pattern of cross-modal matches. However, the few studies which have compared visual and tactual judgments of surface texture show that visual judgments are typically more efficient, being either more accurate (Rose *et al.*, 1972), less variable (Björkman, 1967), or more rapid (Brown, 1960). Two studies have compared visual-tactual cross- and within-modal matching of texture (Björkman, 1968; Rose *et al.*, 1972). Rose *et al.* used the same 3-year-old subjects as in their form experiment; once again the study is difficult to evaluate since error rates were very low and probably modally zero in every cell of the design. Björkman (1967) reported variability of same-different judgments as an index of efficiency in discriminating sandpapers of different grit. Presentation was sequential. VV matching was considerably less variable than TT matching. Interestingly, VT judgments were rather more efficient than TV judgments, suggesting that cross-modal matching of texture can be explained, like cross-modal matching of form, on the basis of more efficient processing of visual information.

There is, in sum, strong evidence that cross-modal matching of form, and perhaps, surprisingly, of texture, between vision and touch may be determined by our efficiency in making visual judgments and our relative inability to make the same judgments through touch. There is little doubt that within-modal visual matching is more accurate than tactual matching, particularly in children (see Table I), and the cross-modal comparison, VT, tends to be more accurate than the converse TV task when standard and comparison items are not simultaneously present. We might reasonably conclude, therefore, that visual perception of the standard allows the more efficient pickup of information about the comparison sample in both the within- and the cross-modal conditions.

4. Visual and Nonvisual Judgments of Length

If a theory based upon visual efficiency and presentation-order effects has some success in accounting for cross-modal matching of form and texture, I shall argue that no general explanation of visual and nonvisual cross-modal matching of length should be attempted. Many different operations have been included under the rubric of tactual, or more usually, since cutaneous pickup is not always involved, of kinesthetic perception of length. For example, an object may be held between the fingers (e.g., Teghtsoonian & Teghtsoonian, 1965, 1970), may be passively moved through a given distance (e.g., Diewert & Stelmach, 1977), or the subject himself may actively move through the distance (e.g., Connolly & Jones, 1970; Jones & Connolly, 1970; Legge, 1965; Marcell & Allen, 1975; Millar, 1972a; Newell, Shapiro, & Carlton, 1979). I shall concentrate on visual-kinesthetic and visual-proprioceptive cross- and within-modal judgments of distance, which have made use of a reproduction paradigm (see Teghtsoonian & Teghtsoonian, 1970, for a brief review of various psychophysical comparisons of proprioceptive and visual judgments of length).

A developmental comparison of visual and kinesthetic combinations in judgments of length was made by the present author in collaboration with Kevin Connolly (Connolly & Jones, 1970). We presented standards of different lengths, visually by a mechanical system and kinesthetically by requiring the subject to draw a line between fixed stops. For visual reproduction the line was again produced mechanically until the subject judged that the length was equivalent to the visual or kinesthetic standard. For kinesthetic reproduction the subject drew a line which he again judged to be equivalent in length to the standard. There were thus four modality conditions, visual-visual (VV), kinesthetic-kinesthetic (KK), visual-kinesthetic (VK), and kinesthetic-visual (KV). Subjects were age 5 years to adult. All conditions showed improvement with age and there was no evidence for differential development of cross- and within-modal conditions. In fact at all age levels within-modal performance was more accurate than cross-modal. We also noted that KV performance was consistently more accurate than VK (so-called cross-modal asymmetry).

These findings were essentially replicated by Freides (1975) with adult subjects and to some extent by Millar (1972b) with 4-year-olds, though she observed the ordering VK > KV in 8-year-olds. Following Posner (1967) we suggested that kinesthetic memory is relatively unstable and we assumed further that any input is translated into the reproduction modality. Thus storage in the VV and KV conditions would be in a more stable visual form. On this basis we should have observed the ordering VV = KV > VK = KK. To explain the relation VV = KK > KV > VK, therefore, we had to hypothesize a noisy translation between modalities resulting in greater loss of information in the two cross-modal conditions. Though we did obtain some confirming evidence (Jones & Connolly, 1970), on the whole the model has stood up very badly to experimental tests (Jones, 1973; Marcell & Allen, 1975; Newell et al., 1979). Marcell and Allen interpolated a visual or a kinesthetic interfering task (judgments of curvature) between standard and reproduction. They hypothesized on the basis of our model that kinesthetic interference should lead to a greater decrement in accuracy of reproduction under KK and VK conditions and that visual interpolations should similarly interfere with VV and KV performance. None of these predictions was confirmed. Newell et al. informed the subject about the reproduction modality either before or immediately after presentation of the standard, or immediately prior to reproduction. This manipulation had no effect on the ordering of conditions, though on our model delaying instructions about the mode of reproduction should presumably have affected cross-modal translation. Newell et al. obtained evidence that the order KV > VK may only be obtained when the surround is visible to the subject during kinesthetic conditions.

I had earlier made a number of conceptual criticisms of our model (Jones, 1973), particularly on the ground that it included no description of the initiation and control of movement. In the KV condition the subject makes a "constrained" movement between stops whereas in the VK condition the movement is purely voluntary. Without going into detail, I have argued (Jones, 1972) that "constrained" movements differ from voluntary movements in that the latter but not the former are potentially ballistic and preprogrammed. The two so-called cross-modal conditions are simply different rather than asymmetric. VK matching involves the generation of efferent control signals in terms of the visual display (and not some translation between sensory codes). KV matching, however, involves retention of an artifactual movement and comparison with visual extent. Similarly the KK condition may be seen as a matching of two different patterns of motor output rather than of two sets of sensory input.

If the arm is moved passively through a given distance, information must be derived from proprioceptors in muscles, joints, and tendons. Intersensory comparisons with visual perception of length are therefore possible, and it has been shown that the two cross-modal conditions (visual-proprioceptive, VP, and proprioceptive-visual, PV) may not differ in accuracy (Diewert & Stelmach, 1977; Jones, 1973). Only Diewert and Stelmach have made comparison of VV, PP (proprioceptive-propriocep-tive), and the two cross-modal conditions. Overall the ordering of conditions was VV = PP > VP = PV, though differences between conditions tended to become more pronounced as the standard distance increased.

If it is typically found that within-modal visual and proprioceptive matching is more accurate than the two cross-modal conditions, it may be that the two systems function to some extent independently. However, experience of passively generated movements which must be precisely correlated with spatial information derived from vision is presumably a laboratory artifice, and it will be difficult to generalize effectively from such experiments. Moreover, since many different operations are cor-rectly described as "kinesthesis," no comprehensive explanation of visual-kinesthetic within- and cross-modal matching of length will be successful. In a length-matching experiment, the four conditions—VV, KK, VK, and KV—may each reflect quite different processes, and the VV condition clearly involves a sensory-equivalence judgment.

5. Visual-Auditory Matching

There have been fewer studies of auditory-visual matching than of visual-tactual matching, perhaps because auditory-visual correspond-ences are often more than a little contrived.[7] Recognition and discrimi-nation of objects may be more efficient visually, but by and large the visible and tangible aspects of an object (shape and texture) are one and the same. On the other hand, the audible aspects generally provide *new* information. Though we may know what something is from its sound, we do not directly perceive its shape through hearing. Consequently the first problem in comparing vision and hearing is of specifying perceptually relevant dimensions for both modalities, a problem which still resists truly satisfactory solution.

[7] A number of studies have investigated auditory-visual cross-modal matching in so-called slow readers (e.g., Birch & Belmont, 1964; Bryden, 1972; Jones, 1974). Since this literature raises special problems of sampling, I shall overlook it here. There is, in any case, no evidence from properly controlled studies (e.g., Bryden, 1972; Jones, 1974) that reading difficulty is related to a specific deficit in auditory-visual integration. Bryden's study is especially thorough.

It has often been suggested that vision is preeminently the spatial sense (e.g., von Senden, 1960; Warren, 1970), whereas hearing is preeminently temporal. (There is little doubt that subjects, whether children or adults, do in fact process auditory temporal sequences more efficiently than vsual temporal sequences; see, e.g., Cole, Chorover, & Ettlinger, 1961; Klapper & Birch, 1971.) Of course auditory patterns are not necessarily composed of elements in a temporal sequence. Harmony, after all is basic to European music. But no visual equivalent of chords exists, and studies of auditory-visual matching have invariably used some form of sequential presentation of sounds either in temporal or spatiotemporal patterns. Attempts have been made to construct quasi-melodic auditory analogues for visual patterns by treating visual height and length defined in Cartesian coordinates as equivalent to auditory frequency and temporal duration (e.g., Brown, Condon, & Hitchcock, 1966; Kinney, 1961; Williams & Aiken, 1977). Both adults (Brown *et al.,* 1966) and children (Williams & Aiken, 1977) can treat cross-modal presentation of such patterns as equivalent, though purely visual matching tends to be more efficient. There are at least three possible overlapping explanations for visual superiority. Visual processing may be preeminently spatial; therefore subjects would be more efficient when spatial patterns are presented visually, One might also argue, along the lines of our account of visual-tactual matching, that the auditory-visual task may confound modalities with presentation conditions. The visual pattern is presented holistically while the auditory pattern is by definition a temporal sequence. However, an alternative account may be rather more interesting. Visual processing may be superior because the concepts of length and height are given for normal persons in terms of visual exemplars, and the subject may not always consistently apply the relatively contrived correspondence rules—height = ordinal frequency and length = duration (cf. Goodnow, 1971b).[8]

Our discussion of visual-tactual matching centered in the end upon variations in ways in which the standard and comparison forms could be presented. The problem of presentation conditions occurs in even sharper relief here, since changes in the method of presentation may change the task from a spatial to a temporal one. Goodnow (1971b) has argued that development of auditory-visual cross-modal matching may be based upon acquisition of conventional correspondence rules for representing spatial intervals by temporal ones rather than upon changes in intersen-

[8] An experiment by Harvey (1973) with adult subjects does in fact suggest that visual position and auditory position on a frequency scale are not regarded as precisely equivalent concepts, or at least that visual position and auditory frequency may not be processed in the same way.

sory liaison. A test devised by Birch and Belmont (1964) will provide a useful focus for comparison of the two perspectives. The tester taps out a sound pattern varying the number of taps and/or the duration between taps over trials. The child is required to choose the correct match for the auditory pattern from an array of three horizontally spaced dot patterns. Birch and Belmont took failures with such problems to indicate failures of intersensory integration. They found that performance was no better than chance in kindergarten children and that the most marked developmental improvement occurred between kindergarten and the first grade. Thus Birch and Belmont argued that intersensory liaison, though not complete in preschoolers, was well on the way to maximum development in 6-year-olds.

Again one can question this conclusion, since no within-modal matching control conditions were included in the experiment (Bryant, 1968). Birch and Belmont themselves noted and attempted to discount the possibility that failures on the test could have been due to failures of auditory memory on the ground that recall of spoken digits was adequate in groups who were deficient on the test. While this may argue against general auditory memory deficit, it does not rule out specific memory problems given the particular test items. Although Goodnow (1971b) replicated Birch and Belmont's finding that performance on their test shows a sharp improvement between kindergarten and first grade, Rudel and Teuber (1974), who included all four within- and cross-modal matching conditions based upon Birch and Belmont's auditory and visual procedures, found no significant differences between conditions with subjects age 5 to 9 years. When Rudel and Teuber (1974) changed the basic task by presenting visual patterns as a sequence of elements (i.e., temporally), they simply replicated the common finding that auditory temporal matching is superior to other conditions (see also Cole et al., 1961; Klapper & Birch, 1971; Rubinstein & Gruenberg, 1971). Jones (1974) and Jones and Alexander (1974), using a spatiotemporal task (tones alternated between right and left earphones and subjects made same-different judgments of two four-element patterns), again found that all four conditions—VV, AA, VA, and AV—were performed with equal efficiency at a given age group and that all four showed comparable improvement with age (Jones & Alexander, 1974). There is nothing here to suggest that deficiencies on Birch and Belmont's test, or in auditory-visual matching in general, necessarily involve failure of intersensory integration, nor to suggest that intersensory liaison improves with age.

Perhaps of more interest is Goodnow's (1971b) argument that the principle requirement for adequate performance on Birch and Belmont's test is for the child to be aware of the conventional adult equation of spatial and temporal intervals. In one experiment she had kindergarten as well as first- and second-grade children write out a tapped auditory series, telling them only to "use a dot to show where the tap comes in the message" (p. 1192). Only 1 kindergarten child in 10 used a visual space to stand for an auditory interval, compared to nearly three-quarters of the sample of first- and second-graders. A further experiment, in which children were required to tap out an auditory pattern to match a simultaneously available visual standard, indicated complementary development. Older children (median age, 8:1) were more likely than younger children (median age, 7:5) to use a temporal interval to represent spatial distance, though both groups included children who represented spatial distance in the visual standard by varying the spatial distance between taps. Goodnow also noted that children who did not apply conventional adult "time for space" or "space for space" rules nevertheless tried to apply a particular principle consistently. For example, some children would use a motor pause between written dots to represent the auditory interval. In other words, development "improvement" in this as in other situations lies in part in the child's realization that only some of an indefinite range of internally consistent and reasonable rules are likely to be accepted by adults.[9]

> . . . kindergarten children do not perceive the spatial intervals in the visual series as equivalent to the time intervals in the auditory series. Older children are aware that the substitution is possible and, over time, aware that this is the only substitution required for a matching to be called "correct" . . . these children have learned that only certain properties of the stimulus need to be considered and that a particular kind of translation is the ault norm. (Goodnow, 1971b, p. 1198)

Only one study, by Alexander (1977), seems to provide evidence which would support the notion that developmental improvement in cross-modal matching is independent of changes in within-modal matching and hence that cross-modal matching could index developmental gains in intersensory liaison. Alexander argued that the rate of presentation of auditory and visual patterns could be an important variable in determining the relationship between cross- and within-modal conditions

---

[9] Rudnick, Martin, and Sterritt (1972) argued against the position, which they took to be implicit in Goodnow (1971b), that temporal-spatial integration would be more difficult than purely temporal matching. They found for a group of first-grade children that temporal-spatial matches were no more difficult than auditory or visual temporal-temporal matches. However, it is important not to confuse the ordering of conditions *within* age groups with the ordering expected *between* age groups to which Goodnow's (1971b) suggestions apply. In fact on the basis of her results one might argue that Rudnick's (Rudnick *et al.,* 1972) first-graders would have understood temporal-spatial correspondence rules, so that no differences between temporal-spatial and temporal-temporal tasks should have been expected.

over time, and there is evidence from adults that rate of presentation might effect ordering of conditions (Rubinstein & Gruenberg, 1971). Alexander followed our previous work (Jones & Alexander, 1974) in using four-element spatiotemporal patterns presented at either a "fast" or a "slow" rate. With "slow" presentation the results confirmed our previous finding (Jones & Alexander, 1974) that cross- and within-modal matching tend to develop in parallel. However, with "fast" presentation the two cross-modal conditions showed a substantially faster rate of development between first- and third-graders than the within-modal conditions. Since this result is unusual, it obviously merits attention.

One could take the result at its face value and argue that only one particular kind of cross-modal integration (auditory-visual spatiotemporal patterns) becomes more efficient over the course of time. Another possibility is more parsimonious. I have already discussed theories of auditory- (temporal) to-visual (spatial) matching in terms of appropriate correspondence rules (Goodnow, 1971b) rather than strictly modality relations. In Alexander's experiment the problem of which rule to apply does not seem to arise, since both visual and auditory patterns were spatiotemporal. Suppose, however, that the younger children in Alexander's sample were more likely to regard auditory patterns as equivalent to temporal patterns and visual patterns as equivalent to spatial patterns, whereas older children take both to be spatial patterns. The younger child is just beginning to apply the correspondence rule that duration can represent spatial distance and may in consequence attempt to match interval structure between auditory and visual patterns. Physically all intervals were constant; but psychophysically this was not necessarily the case. If younger children pay attention to interval structure and if the psychophysical scale values of auditory and visual intervals do differ, we should expect cross-modal matching by these children to be less accurate than within-modal matching. Older children may realize that they can ignore subjective interval structure, so that even if auditory intervals do not correspond perceptually to visual intervals the child knows that this is not a factor in the matching judgment. Thus cross- and within-modal efficiency should now be approximately equivalent. When the rate of presentation is slow, both younger and older children may have sufficient time to adequately encode and rehearse the spatiotemporal characteristics of pattern so that uncertainty about interval scaling is no longer an important factor. Admittedly this account is quite *ad hoc*. However, it does explain Alexander's results without having to assume a specific and perhaps unique course of development for visual-auditory spatiotemporal equivalence judgments.

One can argue, therefore, that auditory-visual cross-modal matching can be explained along lines analogous to our account of visual-tactual matching. When the task is temporal, AA matching is likely to be superior to other conditions. When the task is spatial, VV matching is likely to be superior particularly when standard and comparison patterns are presented simultaneously (e.g., Bryden, 1972; Rudnick, Martin, & Sterritt, 1972). Where temporal and spatial problems are confounded with presentation modality, development may be based fundamentally upon the acquisition of temporal-spatial correspondence rules (Goodnow, 1971b) rather than upon some hypothetically increasing intersensory efficiency (pace Birch & Belmont, 1964).

6. Conclusions

Rudel and Teuber (1971) thought that an analysis of stimulus-presentation conditions and their interaction with modalities would provide a clearer understanding of cross-modal matching, though they believed that no single factor could predict cross-modal effects. My analysis here has also drawn attention to presentation conditions, but it has suggested that the pattern of results from cross-modal matching experiments is explicable from processing within the modality which is the more efficient for a particular task. I have concentrated rather more on visual-tactual matching than upon other modality comparisons, since the stimulus dimensions of form and texture have direct relevance to both modalities. Visual processing is clearly the more accurate and immediate. In normal circumstances vision provides information on shape and texture (e.g., Abravanel, 1972a). Visual shape comparisons are often highly accurate in children as young as 3 or 4 years (e.g., Bryant & Raz, 1975; Millar, 1972a), whereas tactual comparisons may be at chance or little better (Goodnow, 1971a; Millar, 1972a). VT and TV comparisons allow subjects to use visual information to guide tactual exploration. In other words, tactual form perception is a motor skill in which visual information is used to control manual processes. The method of presenting standard and comparison forms is crucial to the ordering of cross- and within-modal conditions since it determines whether visual control of manual exploration is possible.

Visual-auditory comparisons again demonstrate the need for analysis of presentation conditions, though for the somewhat different reason that presentation conditions now determine whether the task is a spatial or a temporal comparison.[10] As with visual-tactual matching I have tried to

---

[10] Lashley (1951) noted that "in cerebral functions it is difficult to distinguish between spatial and temporal functions" (p. 128). In fact he regarded tactual shape perception as involving the translation of a temporal sequence into a spatial concept.

suggest that cross-modal effects are determined by within-modal efficiency, with subjects in general more accurate for auditory than for visual temporal judgments (Cole *et al.*, 1961; Klapper & Birch, 1971), and more accurate for visual spatial than for auditory spatial judgments (e.g., Williams & Aiken, 1977). Development of auditory-visual integration may involve the acquisition of conventional correspondence rules for temporal and spatial intervals (Goodnow, 1971b) rather than increased intersensory efficiency; that is, changes in the relationship between presentation conditions, not changes in the relationship between modalities.

All in all there is little to support the notion (Birch & Lefford, 1964) that human development is characterized by increasing cerebral intercommunication between initially independent modalities. This account seems to me, in fact, the final residue of the "law" of specific nerve energies, of the belief that perception is somehow to be explained by reference to peripheral receptors and their rigidly fixed cortical terminations. On this view intersensory relations are only intelligible on the basis of constant associations between correlated visual and tactual and visual and auditory information. In contrast we might find it more useful to take our ability to make cross-modal judgments to be a human given which develops according to particular experiences, including specifically within-modal experiences.

7. References

Abbott, C. The intelligence of batrachians. *Science*, 1882, *3*, 66–67.

Abravanel, E. Active detection of solid-shape information by touch and vision. *Perception and Psychophysics*, 1971, *10*, 358–360.

Abravanel, E. How children combine vision and touch when perceiving the shape of objects. *Perception and Psychophysics*, 1972, *12*, 171–175.(a)

Abravanel, E. Short-term memory for shape information processed intra- and inter-modally at three ages. *Perceptual and Motor Skills*, 1972, *35*, 419–425.(b)

Alexander, R. Pattern rate and interpattern interval in development of matching simple auditory-visual patterns. *Developmental Psychology*, 1977, *13*, 332–335.

Allen, T.W., Walker, K., Symonds, L., & Marcell, M. Intrasensory perception of temporal sequences during infancy. *Developmental Psychology*, 1977, *13*, 225–229.

Armstrong, D.M. *Bodily sensations*. Routledge & Kegan Paul: New York, 1962.

Aronson, E., & Rosenbloom, S. Space perception in early infancy: Perception within a common auditory-visual space. *Science*, 1971, *172*, 1161–1163.

Berkeley, G. *A new theory of visions*. Dent: London, 1925.

Birch, H.G., & Belmont, L. Auditory-visual integration in normal and retarded readers. *American Journal of Orthopsychiatry*, 1964, *34*, 852–861.

Birch, H.G., & Lefford, A. Intersensory development in children. *Monographs of the Society for Research in Child Development*, 1963, *28* (5), Whole No. 89.

Birch, H.G., & Lefford, A. Two strategies for studying perception in "brain-damaged" children. In H.G. Birch (Ed.), *Brain damage in children.* Williams & Wilkins: Baltimore, 1964.

Birch, H.G., & Lefford, A. Visual differentiation, intersensory integration and voluntary motor control. *Monographs of the Society for Research in Child Development*, 1967, *32* (2), Whole No. 110.

Björkman, M. Relations between intra-modal and cross-modal matching. *Scandinavian Journal of Psychology*, 1967, *8*, 67–76.

Blank, M. Cognitive functions of language in the pre-school year. *Developmental Psychology*, 1974, *10*, 229–245.

Börnstein, W. On the functional relations of the sense organs to one another and to the organism as a whole. *Journal of Genetic Psychology*, 1936, *15*, 117–131.

Brower, T.G.R. The visual world of infants. *Scientific American*, June 1966, 80–92.

Bower, T.G.R., Broughton, J.M., & Moore, M.K. The coordination of visual and tactual input in infants. *Perception and Psychophysics*, 1970, *8*, 51–53.

Bridger, W.H. Cognitive factors in perceptual dysfunction. In D.A. Hamburg, K.H. Pribram, & A.J. Stunkard (Eds.), *Perception and its disorders.* Williams & Wilkins: Baltimore, 1970.

Brown, I.D. Visual and tactual judgments of surface roughness. *Ergonomics*, 1960, *3*, 51–61.

Brown, D.R., & Owen, D.H. The metrics of visual form: Methodological dyspepsia. *Psychological Bulletin*, 1967, *68*, 243–259.

Brown, D.R., Condon, C.F., & Hitchcock, L., Jr. Stimulus equivalence of auditory and visual patterns in an intermodal discrimination task. *Perceptual and Motor Skills*, 1966, *22*, 823–832.

Bryant, P.E. Comments on the design of developmental studies of cross-modal matching and cross-modal transfer. *Cortex*, 1968, *4*, 127–137.

Bryant, P.E., & Raz, I. Visual and tactual perception of shape by young children. *Developmental Psychology*, 1975, *11*, 525–526.

Bryant, P.E., Jones, P., Claxton, V., & Perkins, G.M. Recognition of shapes across modalities by infants. *Nature*, 1972, *240*, 303–304.

Bryden, M.P. Auditory-visual and sequential spatial matching in relation to reading ability. *Child Development*, 1972, *43*, 824–832.

Buser, J., Borenstein, P., & Bruner, J. Etude des systemes "associatifs" visuels et auditifs chez le chat anesthesie au chloralose. *Electroencephalography and Clinical Neurophysiology*, 1959, *11*, 305–324.

Cashdan, S. Visual and haptic form discrimination under conditions of successive stimulation. *Journal of Experimental Psychology*, 1968, *76*, 215–218.

Cole, M., Chorover, S.L., & Ettlinger, G. Cross-modal transfer in man. *Nature*, 1961, *191*, 1225–1226.

Connolly, K., & Jones, B. A developmental study of afferent-reafferent integration. *British Journal of Psychology*, 1970, *61*, 259–266.

Cronin, V. Cross-modal and intramodal visual and tactual matching in young children. *Developmental Psychology*, 1973, *8*, 336–340.

De Leon, J.L., Raskin, L.M., & Gruen, G.E. Sensory-modality effects on shape perception in pre-school children. *Developmental Psychology*, 1970, *3*, 358–362.

Denner, B., & Cashdan, S. Sensory processing and the recognition of forms in nursery-school children. *British Journal of Psychology*, 1967, *58*, 101–104.

Diewert, G.L., & Stelmach, G.E. Intra-modal and inter-modal transfer of movement information. *Acta Psychologica*, 1977, *41*, 119–128.

Drager, U.C., & Hubel, D.H. Responses to visual stimulation and relationship between visual, auditory and somatosensory inputs in moise superior colliculus. *Journal of Neurophysiology*, 1975, *38*, 640–713.

Ettlinger, G. Analysis of cross-modal effects and their relationship to language. In F.L. Darley & C.H. Millikan (Eds.), *Brain mechanisms underlying speech and language*. New York: Grune & Stratton, 1967.

Fantz, R.L. Pattern perception in young infants. *Psychological Record*, 1958, *8*, 43–47.

Fishman, M.C., & Michael, C.R. Integration of auditory information in the cat's visual cortex. *Vision Research*, 1973, *13*, 1415–1419.

Freedman, S.J. (Ed.), *The neuropsychology of spatially oriented behavior*. Homewood, Illinois: Dorsey Press, 1968.

Freides, D. Information complexity and cross-modal functions. *British Journal of Psychology*, 1975, *66*, 283–287.

Garvill, J., & Molander, B. Verbal mediation in cross-modal transfer. *British Journal of Psychology*, 1971, *62*, 449–457.

Garvill, J., & Molander, B. Effects of standard modality, comparison modality and retention interval on matching of form. *Scandinavian Journal of Psychology*, 1973, *14*, 203–206.

Garvill, J., & Molander, B. Effects of interference on intra-modal and cross-modal matchings of form. *Umea Psychological Reports*, 1977, No. 124.

Goodnow, J.J. Effects of active handling, illustrated by uses for objects. *Child Development*, 1969, *40*, 201–212.

Goodnow, J.J. Eye and hand: Differential memory and its effect on matching. *Neuropsychologia*, 1971, *9*, 89–95.(a)

Goodnow, J.J. Matching auditory and visual series: Modality problem or translation problem? *Child Development*, 1971, *42*, 1187–1201.(b)

Gottfried, A.W., Rose, S.A., & Bridger, W.H. Cross-modal transfer in human infants. *Child Development*, 1977, *48*, 118–123.

Gottfried, A.W., Rose, S.A., & Bridger, W.H. Effects of visual, haptic and manipulatory experience on infant's visual recognition memory of objects. *Developmental Psychology*, 1978, *14*, 305–312.

Green, D.M., & Swets, J. *Signal detection theory and psychophysics*. New York: Wiley, 1966.

Harvey, N. Does intermodal equivalence exist between hetero-modal stimulus dimensions or between stimulus value on these dimensions. *Quarterly Journal of Experimental Psychology*, 1973, *25*, 476–491.

Hermelin, B., & O'Connor, N. Recognition of shapes by normal and subnormal children. *British Journal of Psychology*, 1961, *52*, 281–284.

Hershenson, M. Development of the perception of form. *Psychological Bulletin*, 1967, *67*, 326–336.

Jackson, J.P. Development of visual and tactual processing of sequentially presented shapes. *Developmental Psychology*, 1973, *8*, 46–50.

Jones, B. Outflow and inflow in movement duplication. *Perception and Psychophysics*, 1972, *9*, 118–120.

Jones, B. When are vision and kinaesthesia comparable? *British Journal of Psychology*, 1973, *64*, 587–591.

Jones, B. Cross-modal matching by retarded and normal readers. *Bulletin of the Psychonomic Society*, 1974, *3*, 163–165.

Jones, B., & Alexander, R. Developmental trends in auditory-visual cross-modal matching of spatio-temporal patterns. *Developmental Psychology*, 1974, *10*, 354–356.

Jones, B., & Connolly, K. Memory effects in cross-modal matching. *British Journal of Psychology*, 1970, *61*, 267–270.

Jones, B., & Robinson, T. Sensory integration in normal and retarded children. *Developmental Psychology*, 1973, *9*, 178–182.

Jung, R. Neuronal integration in the visual cortex and its significance for visual information. In W. Rosenblith (Ed.), *Sensory communication*. Cambridge: MIT Press, 1961.

Kinney, J.S. Discrimination in auditory and visual patterns. *Perceptual and Motor Skills*, 1961, *14*, 529–541.

Klapper, Z.S., & Birch, H.G. Developmental course of temporal patterning in vision and audition. *Perceptual Motor Skills*, 1971, *32*, 547–555.

Koen, F. Verbal mediators in cross-modal form discrimination. *Canadian Journal of Psychology*, 1971, *25*, 103–110.

Lashley, K.S. The problem of serial order in behavior. In L.A. Jeffress (Ed.), *Cerebral mechanisms in behavior: The Hixon symposium*. New York: Wiley, 1951.

Legge, D. Analysis of visual and proprioceptive components of motor skill by means of a drug. *British Journal of Psychology*, 1965, *65*, 243–254.

Lobb, H. Vision versus touch in form discrimination. *Canadian Journal of Psychology*, 1965, *19*, 175–187.

Lyons-Ruth, K. Bimodal perception in infancy: Response to auditory-visual incongruity. *Child Development*, 1977, *48*, 820–827.

Marcell, M., & Allen, T.W. *Memory effects and sensory integration: A test of Connolly and Jones' model of intersensory functioning*. Paper presented at the Biennial Meeting of the Society for Research in Child Development, 1975.

Marks, L.E. On colored-hearing synthesis: Cross-modal translations of sensory dimensions. *Psychological Bulletin*, 1975, *82*, 303–331.

Millar, S. Visual and haptic cue utilization by preschool children: The recognition of visual and haptic stimuli presented separately and together. *Journal of Experimental Child Psychology*, 1971, *12*, 88–94.

Millar, S. Effects of interpolated tasks on latency and accuracy of intramodal and cross-modal shape recognition by children. *Journal of Experimental Psychology*, 1972, *96*, 170–175.(a)

Millar, S. The development of visual and kinaesthetic judgments of distance. *British Journal of Psychology*, 1972, *63*, 271–282.(b)

Milner, A.D., & Bryant, P.E. Cross-modal matching by young children. *Journal of Comparative and Physiological Psychology*, 1968, *71*, 453–458.

Newell, K.M., Shapiro, D.C., & Carlton, M.J. Co-ordinating visual and kinaesthetic memory codes. *British Journal of Psychology*, 1979, *70*, 87–96.

Owen, D.H., & Brown, D.R. Visual and tactual form discrimination: Psychophysical comparison within and between modalities. *Perception and Psychophysics*, 1970, *7*, 302–306.

Pick, A.D., Pick, H.L., Jr., & Thomas, M.L. Cross-modal transfer and improvement of form discrimination. *Journal of Experimental Child Psychology*, 1966, *3*, 279–288.

Posner, M.I. Characteristics of visual and kinesthetic memory. *Journal of Experimental Psychology*, 1967, *75*, 103–107.

Rose, S.A., Blank, M.S., & Bridger, W.H. Intermodal and intramodal retention of visual and tactual information in young children. *Developmental Psychology*, 1972, *6*, 482–486.

Rubinstein, L., & Gruenberg, E.M. Intramodal and cross-modal sensory transfer of visual and auditory temporal patterns. *Perception and Psychophysics*, 1971, *9*, 385–390.

Rudel, R.G., & Teuber, H.L. Cross-modal transfer of shape discrimination by children. *Neuropsychologia*, 1964, *2*, 1–8.

Rudel, R.G., & Teuber, H.L. Pattern recognition within and across sensory modalities in normal and brain-injured children. *Neuropsychologia*, 1971, *9*, 389–399.

Rudnick, M., Martin, V., & Sterritt, G.M. On the relative difficulty of auditory and visual, temporal and spatial, integrative and non-integrative sequential pattern comparisons. *Psychonomic Science*, 1972, *27*, 207–210.

Sherrington, C.S. *Man on his nature*. New York: Macmillan, 1941.

Taylor, M.M., Lederman, S.J., & Gibson, R.H. Tactual perception of texture. In E. Corterette & M. Friedman (Eds.), *Handbook of perception*. Vol. 3. New York: Academic Press, 1973.

Teghtsoonian, M., & Teghtsoonian, R. Seen and felt length. *Psychonomic Science*, 1965, *3*, 465–469.

Teghtsoonian, R., & Teghtsoonian, M. Two varieties of perceived length. *Perception and Psychophysics*, 1970, *8*, 389–392.

von Hornbostel, E.M. The unity of the senses. *Psyche*, 1927, *4*, 83–89.

von Senden, M. *Space and sight*. London: Methuen, 1960.

Vurpillot, E. The development of scanning strategies and their relation to visual differentiation. *Journal of Experimental Child Psychology*, 1968, *6*, 632–650.

Warren, D.H. Intermodality interactions in spatial localization. *Cognitive Psychology*, 1970, *1*, 114–133.

Wickelgren, B.G. Superior colliculus: Some receptive field properties of bimodally responsive cells. *Science*, 1971, *173*, 69–72.

Wilson, W.A., Jr. Intersensory transfer in normal and brain-operated monkeys. *Neuropsychologia*, 1965, *3*, 363–370.

Williams, T.M., & Aiken, L.S. Development of pattern classification: Auditory visual equivalence in the use of prototypes. *Developmental Psychology*, 1977, *13*, 198–204.

Zung, B.J. Cross-modal matching among normal and retarded children. *Child Development*, 1971, *42*, 1614–1618.

PART II

Higher-Order Integration

Introduction

This section is concerned with higher-order integrations in intersensory development and sensory integration. All of the research reported in these chapters, with the exception of some in the Fraisse chapter, was carried out with adults. The chapter by Lackner shows that adaptation to altered sensory information, as in prism-adaptation experiments, is a very complex process, one that involves the whole body and especially that unknown territory for most of us, the proprioceptive system. Cohen considers in more detail the proprioceptive system, describes it, and illustrates its various receptors. He concludes with research in extreme environments, those of zero gravity and those of markedly increased or hypergravity. Fraisse describes the complexity of research with rhythm, and how rhythm affects the entire body. Cutting and Proffitt lead the reader on a quest for the underlying variables that differentiate the walking gait of male and female walkers. This research topic, an obviously pleasant one, has, like any good mystery story, a surprise ending.[1] Would you believe that gait perception has an underlying basis that is similar to the basis for the perception of aging in faces?

The chapters by Cohen and Lackner are best considered together. Both leave one with an appreciation of the complex interrelation of the human organism with its environment. We ordinarily think of ourselves as visual animals, or even as auditory animals as well, and we generally tend to ignore the complex interrelations of all of the senses, particularly the senses (and even separating them can be suspect) related to the

[1] The mind, as someone remarked, can be debauched by learning. One of the editors, a long-time student and admirer of the differences in gait of assorted walkers, found, after reading this chapter, that it was difficult to tell the sexes apart on the basis of differences in gait.

milieu interne as it interacts with the outside world. We call these the proprioceptive senses.

Lackner aptly discusses the concept from the classical work by L. J. Henderson, *The Fitness of the Environment* (1913). We think of ourselves as adapting to the environment, a Darwinian notion, which Henderson turned around to ask what qualities of the environment made it a "fit" environment for life. Lackner means that the organism must have strategies for adaptation to the existing environment during development or when it confronts unusual and unexpected changes in the environment. The focus is as much on the environment as on the organism.

Cohen considers the classical or Sherrington (1906) view of proprioception, and he contrasts it with more modern views such as the Gibsonian (1966) one. Sherrington's view was essentially a division between exteroceptors and proprioceptors; the exteroceptors are stimulated by the outside environment and the proprioceptors respond to stimulation from within the organism. This relegates proprioception to a secondary role since it mainly reacts to requirements posed by exteroception. This view, complex enough, and advanced for its time, has not proved adequate for modern research. The Sherrington view rests on the classical doctrine of specific nerve energies wherein each sense system is served by specific receptors that project to specific sensory centers in the brain. Intersensory interaction is the concept by which multisensory stimuli of the real world (e.g., rhythm) are integrated in the brain. These interrelations, as proposed, have proved inadequate. Sensory Tonic Field Theory (Werner & Wapner, 1949) is one attempt to account for complex organismic environmental interactions. The Gibsonian approach (Gibson, 1966, 1979) has proved more influential.

Gibson notes that perceptual systems cannot be gracefully categorized in terms of specific sensory systems, that under natural conditions many senses respond and interact to environmental stimulation, and the organism itself is initiating rather than reacting to events. This means that intersensory perception and integration are not specialized higher-order complex reactions, but are the rule for all perception. The task of the perceptual psychologist is no easier if one follows Gibson, but the focus is away from simple systems toward more complex natural life events.

Both the Cohen and Lackner chapters discuss various aspects of this complexity.

The chapter by Lackner shows the complexities of the process of the response of the body to unusual forms of stimulation. The posture of the body is dependent on many sources of sensory information and the physical patterns of stimulation are interpreted in interaction with auditory and visual stimulation. Thus, a stationary sound may be interpreted as being a moving sound when the subject's body is moving. An error in one's interpreted body posture means an error in sensory localization, or aberrant sensory stimulation may lead to an error in apparent posture. The postural system interacts in complex ways with unusual sensory stimulation in its attempt to adapt to the altered environment. All of this complexity shows that the old theories, such as those based on notions of reafference, are inadequate.

Cohen considers visual-proprioceptive interactions and provides a valuable illustrated review of the proprioceptors: the muscle proprioceptors, the joint and cutaneous proprioceptors and the labyrinthine proprioceptors. The muscle and joint proprioceptors in the neck cooperate with labyrinthine proprioceptors so that spatial behavior can be disrupted by a lesion in the neck. We cannot localize visual objects without concurrently processing proprioceptive information about our postural orientation, a point also made by Lackner. Thus, "the perception of spatial location and visual direction . . . depend critically on processes that involve intersensory interaction and intersensory integration" (Cohen, p. 189).

The complex interaction of visual perception and internal bodily processes is dramatically demonstrated in environments where gravity is altered: zero-gravity environments or hypergravity environments. In a zero-gravity environment visual objects appear below where they really are while in a hypergravity environment visual objects seem to be above their true position. The astronaut and the jet pilot represent individuals exposed to such unusual conditions. The pilot catapulted off an aircraft carrier is exposed to hypergravity and visually the instruments appear too high; if he pushes the nose down both the pilot and the aircraft will crash into the sea. The illusions do not diminish with experience, but experienced pilots learn to pay attention to their instruments and ignore the "evidence" of their senses. Here we have intersensory interaction with survival at stake.

Like Lackner, and, indeed, like many authors in Part III, Cohen does not find existing theories adequate. The Gibsonian theory is the most useful because it is an ecological one and it tries to consider the senses not in isolation but as interacting systems. Cohen's own research well supports that view.

The chapter by Fraisse deals with rhythm, and rhythm, so appropriate for music, poetry, and dance, is both multisensory and intersensory, calling on vision, audition, touch, and kinesthesis. The chapter shows a certain natural congruence between the auditory modality and motor movements—namely, that the auditory environment naturally induces motor movements. One can even think of a cruel experiment, in which subjects are forbidden to accompany a lively auditory rhythm with motor movements; the difficulty of such an experiment would be obvious, though its purpose, so much against "nature," escapes us. Clearly, to pose the questions is to show the importance of motion for auditory rhythms.

Infants, as Fraisse points out in mentioning the research of Condon and Sander (1974) apparently even synchronize their movements naturally with adult language, even to a language like Chinese which they have never heard before. This happens soon after birth, and infants begin to kick their feet to music before the age of 3 months and rock the entire body to it by the age of 6 months. The developmentally retarded are also retarded in rhythmically relating to music.

Rhythm also has its affective components. The military band is no accident of the martial arts since lively music can make tired soldiers forget their fatigue—music is a necessary component of good morale. At the other extreme, music can also lull to sleep; the lullaby is no accidental evolutionary offshoot.

While we may also accompany visual rhythm with movements, it is not as natural to do so; but, as Fraisse points out, experiments which use flashing lights are not as effective a visual stimulus as those which use the moving hand. The most effective visual stimulus may be the most meaningful one.

Fraisse points out that perceptual laws may be the same no matter in which modality they occur. This is a fascinating topic for more research. Many years ago Revesz (1950) wrote that the gestalt laws of perceptual organization do not apply to touch. In her chapter in this volume Millar (Part III) points out the difficulty of symmetry for tactual perception, though symmetry is easily perceived by vision. The research point is as follows: What perceptual laws are common to the modalities? What perceptual laws are different? Do intersensory relationships show different "laws" or principles than single modalities do? Research on such questions might give us a shorthand way of describing the different modalities and their relationships.

The chapter by Cutting and Proffitt describes their research on event perception where the event is that of a moving figure, more specifically of male and female figures. These figures are presented so abstractly, with points of light, following a technique pioneered by Johansson (1973), that the static display is never identified as a human being—a Christmas tree is a common response to the static display. Johansson found that only a fraction of a second (about one-fifth of a second or two to three frames, much less than one full step) is required to identify these moving lights as human beings, while Cutting and Proffitt found that a two-step cycle or four full steps was required to discriminate the two sexes. Somewhat surprisingly, no particular points on the human frame are necessary for the identification of the sexes. They describe a process by which they arrive at a description of the "center of moment" for the human figure, and the center of moment differs for males and females. The center of moment is not to be confused with the center of gravity since females have a lower center of gravity than males do, yet females have a higher center of moment.

Their analysis of the center of moment is also applied, somewhat surprisingly, beyond the perception of gait to other dynamic events, including the rolling of wheels, aging in faces, Gibsonian flow fields, and the migration of birds in the night sky. One cannot help but wonder what other fruitful applications they might find for their center-of-moment research.

The Cutting and Proffitt chapter should inspire more research on event perception, research well inspired by Gibson (1966, 1979) and Johansson (1975), yet often hard to get a handle on in terms of future research possibilities. Many of us are well acquainted with Koffka's analysis of wheel motion, but we now realize we accepted it without realizing its rich research possibilities. Similarly, Johansson's films (Maas, Johansson, Jansson, & Runeson, 1970, 1971) were an inspiration to many of us, while Cutting and his collaborators were both inspired and able to carry out creative research as well. One leaves Cutting and Proffits's chapter optimistic about the many possibilities of research on event perception.

For example, following Cutting and Proffitt, since individuals are recognized by their gait as well as by their sex, one wonders at what age infants might recognize their principal caretakers by gait. Recent research has shown that infants can recognize the mother at a few weeks of age by voice and odor. Perhaps the invariant of gait is recognized before the face is recognized. Also, when can children identify the invariant gait of males and females? What does the gait of children look like at various ages (is there a 4-year gait, an 8-year gait, etc., that is easily recognized as we suspect?), and at what age are males differentiated from females by their patterns of movement? These are natural questions, and these researchers, or others, may already have answered them. The Johansson technique as adapted by Cutting and Proffitt has wide applicability as a research tool.

References

Condon, W.S., & Sander, L.W. Synchrony demonstrated between movements of the neonate and adult speech. *Child Development*, 1974, *45*, 456–462.

Gibson, J.J. *The senses considered as perceptual systems*. Boston: Houghton Mifflin, 1966.

Gibson, J.J. *The ecological approach to visual perception.* Boston: Houghton Mifflin, 1979.

Henderson, L.J. *The fitness of the environment.* New York: Macmillan, 1913.

Johansson, G. Visual perception of biological motion and a model for its analysis. *Perception and Psychophysics,* 1973, *14,* 201–211.

Johansson, G. Visual motion perception. *Scientific American,* 1975, *232* (6), 76–88.

Maas, J.B., Johansson, G., Jansson, G., & Runeson, S. *Motion perception.* Part I (Film). Boston: Houghton Mifflin, 1970.

Maas, J.B., Johansson, G., Jansson, G., & Runeson, S. *Motion perception.* Part 2 (Film). Boston: Houghton Mifflin, 1971.

Revesz, G. *Psychology and art of the blind.* London: Longmans, Green, 1950.

Sherrington, C.S. *The integrative action of the nervous system.* New Haven: Yale University Press, 1947.

Werner, H., & Wapner, S. Sensory-tonic field theory of perception. *Journal of personality,* 1949, *18,* 88–107.

5

Some Aspects of Sensory-Motor Control and Adaptation in Man

JAMES R. LACKNER

1. Introduction

The control of human movement and spatial orientation is notably complex. The body is multiply articulate and as the trunk and limbs change their orientation with respect to the gravitational-force vector, the forces necessary to move a limb through a given angle also change. Moving the forearm back and forth through the same angular distances in a vertical and then in a horizontal plane represents a simple example of this. Even though the motor commands necessary to bring about the "same movement" in the two cases differ because of the load and orientation changes, one nevertheless, unless fatigued, experiences little or no difference in the effort required to bring about the movements. This means that the skeletomuscular system is "calibrated" such that body movements of a given extent are perceived as equivalent in terms of apparent force despite often radical differences in the actual forces involved. Such a calibration is possible only through a continual monitoring of the relative configuration and orientation of the body in relation to the substrate of support and the gravitoinertial-force vector. Actually, as Mach (1897) pointed out long ago, the eyes are really the only movable parts of the body that can be controlled by means of innervation sequences that bring about the same movements regardless of body

JAMES R. LACKNER • Department of Psychology, Brandeis University, Waltham, Massachusetts 02254. This chapter is dedicated to Hans Wallach.

orientation.[1] The relationship between eye movements and oculomotor commands is so direct that Bahill and Stark (1979) have been able to show that it is possible when given the dynamic characteristics of particular eye movements to reconstruct what the pattern of neural innervation to the extraocular muscles must have been.

The rest of the body, however, is not subject to such a privileged manner of control. External and internal conditions fluctuate continuously. Bernard (1865) and Cannon (1963) identified "constancies of internal milieu" such that body chemistries and temperatures vary only within certain limits, and homeostatic processes for maintaining these constancies. Homeostatic processes by which changes in the shape of the body are adjusted for over time also must exist. Since the body is often in motion in relation to a changing substrate, and sometimes carrying objects of considerable mass, dynamic adjustments in movement and postural control must continually be made in normal behavior. In the case of injury, compensation must also be possible. For example, loss of a limb not only affects possible modes of coordination but also displaces the center of mass of the body. Katz (1953) has described the rapid return of locomotion in animals that have been deprived of several or even all of their limbs—in the latter case they locomote by rolling their bodies or by pulling with their jaws. The great decrement in motor and postural control in humans after loss of vestibular function is well known; adaptation requires weeks or months for completion. The severe consequences of vestibular dysfunction are attributable not only to the disruption of vestibuloocular and vestibulospinal reflexes, but also to the loss of direct information about head orientation—and derivatively, therefore, to information about trunk orientation—in relation to the gravitoinertial-force vector. As can be appreciated from our mention of the changing demands of movement control under different postural conditions, such knowledge of head and trunk orientation is critical.

2. Adaptation to Sensory Rearrangement

It should be clear from the foregoing considerations that a state of dynamic adjustment to changing internal and external configurations characterizes locomotion and coordination whether terrestrial, aquatic, or aerial. Little surprise should arise, therefore, from the fact that

[1] This is a slight oversimplification. Reflex innervations of the eye muscles related to head orientation—for example, influences from tonic neck reflexes and the otolith organs—do affect eye position so that identical voluntary commands being issued with different head positions would not necessarily bring about identical eye movements.

adaptation can be achieved when specific aspects of sensorimotor coordination are intentionally distorted in a systematic way. To develop and to survive over time an organism must be so structured that accommodative changes are made when errors in sensory or motor coordination significantly disrupt performance. Given the fact of adaptation, it is of interest to determine (a) under what circumstances compensatory adjustments are made, (b) the range and nature of possible compensations, and when particular ones are used, and (c) the spatial and temporal properties that a sensory or motor rearrangement must have before adaptation is possible. It may be expected that different species will vary in the extent and in the fashion to which they can adapt to comparable rearrangement conditions; however, such differences will not concern us here.

3. Some Limitations on the Nature of Possible Compensatory Changes in Sensory–Motor Control

When sensory-motor coordination is disrupted—for example, by placing in front of the eyes prism spectacles that laterally deviate the visual array—a systematic and regular degradation of performance results. Presumably critical to the initiation of compensation is the "recognition" of the need for adjustment. That is, the system must determine at some level of representation that the canons under which it has been operating are inadequate. Prima facie, it would seem that as general a transformation as possible would be used in compensating for errors. This assumption implies that during exposure to a sensory or motor rearrangement, the nature of the exposure situation will affect markedly the form of adaptation achieved because it determines the extent to which information about the generality of the rearrangement is available. Given the constraints imposed by the exposure condition, it is likely that the "lowest level" adjustment possible will be made to restore accurate sensorimotor control. This point will become clearer as we proceed.

Because of the complexity of movement control, only certain forms of compensations for sensory rearrangement are functionally practical. Some examples will make this more apparent. For each position of an external object in relation to our body there is a potentially infinite set of movements that we could make to bring us in contact with the object. Consider the case of an object such as a pen lying on a table in front of which we are standing. It is possible to pick up the pen using a great variety of distinct movement patterns involving different combinations of hand, wrist, forearm, shoulder, trunk, leg, and head movement. If we wished, we could spin about our body axis twice or even 5,000 times before leaning over to get the pen. Although some of the potential movements associated with picking up the pen are unusual or bizarre, they are nevertheless functionally equivalent in the sense that their end result—picking up the pen—is the same. Although there is likely a shortest possible movement, both in time and distance, for picking up the pen, there is no longest movement in time or distance; although there are practical limitations such as fatigue, attention, life span, and so on.

The purpose of this example, even though intentionally exaggerated, is to show that movement and locomotion are flexible, infinitely variable processes. In fact, the same considerations that in linguistic theory led to the development of transformational generative grammars apply as well to sensorimotor control (cf. Lackner, 1970). In linguistic behavior there are a variety of transformational and generative rules that lead to an infinite variety of possible sentences and sentences of indeterminate length, but that are nevertheless linguistically well formed (Chomsky, 1957, 1965). These rules or mechanisms make possible self-embedding, concatenation of adjectives or adverbs, apposition of relative clauses and prepositional phrases, and so on. As I have tried to make clear with the example of reaching for a pen, analogous mechanisms exist in normal sensorimotor coordination. Just as language is governed by rules, so sensorimotor coordination is governed by rules, although the constraints involved are of a different nature. For example, we do not normally attempt to make limb movements in which the movement, if completed, would lead to extension or flexion beyond the anatomical range of motion of the joints. Similarly, we do not normally make head and trunk movements that lead to a loss of balance so that we fall over. In other words, the reflex and voluntary mechanisms involved in the generation of motor activity must automatically take into account the ongoing spatial configuration of the body, its "allowable states," and its relation to the direction of the gravitational-force vector. Otherwise, there would be times when "impossible" movements would be attempted or loss of balance would result because of failure to adjust for the change in center of gravity of the body.

It is likely that some form of simplicity metric could be developed to describe the way in which particular patterns of movements are generated when we reach for objects in different spatial positions. For example, when an object is in front of our body and close by we reach and pick it up with an arm movement; when it is farther away we bend the trunk forward from the waist as well; at still farther distances, we step forward and reach for the object. Presumably there is some lawfulness in the switch from one "mode" of reaching to another, where the distance of the object and its apparent mass are important in relation to the dimensions of the reacher's body. It is also necessary in the course of development, as the lengths and masses of the arm, trunk, and other body parts increase, that the switch from one mode to another—for example, reaching while bending from the waist rather than just reaching—occur at different distances of the object.

Similarly, when a visual target to be foveated is slightly to one side of the body midline, we simply turn our eyes; but as the eccentricity of the target is increased, both head and eyes will eventually be turned. Head movements come into play long before the eyes have reached the limit of their possible excursions. Presumably this is also a situation for which there are specifiable principles that determine the relative participations of eyes and head, as well as when torso movements and turning of the entire body will be used.

Such considerations are of concern because some potential compensations for sensory displacement or rearrangement might affect movement-component generation, thereby altering the selection patterning for the recruitment of body elements. An adaptive compensation that changes selection transitions could potentially interfere both with coordinated movements to the body itself and with the maintenance of stable balance. Accordingly, additional compensations would be necessary to correct for the unwanted consequences of the initial adjustment.

A clear example of this occurs when a subject views one of his arms through displacing prism spectacles and moves it back and forth. Initially the subject is inaccurate in reaching for external objects, but after adaptation is achieved he will be accurate in reaching with the "adapted" hand for external visual objects. However, if the subject reaches rapidly to touch part of his body, his nose for example, he will be inaccurate. In other words, he has compensated for the visual displacement of the external world at the expense of being inaccurate when reaching to parts of his own body. No one has yet studied how he then regains accuracy of reaching to his body. In the event the initial compensation is a reinterpretation of arm position, that is, a change in position-sense representation of arm posture, it seems likely the second change would have to be in the form of a transformational motor change. That is, a different infinite set of possible movements would be associated with touching other body parts with the adapted arm.

4. Conditions for Adaptation to Sensory Rearrangement

Adaptation to sensory rearrangement or displacement can only occur if the necessity for performance correction is "recognized" at some level of representation. A detailed analysis of adaptation to visual rearrangement will make this point explicit and highlight the complexity of the factors influencing adaptation.

Some of the earliest systematic experiments concerning the factors affecting adaptation to visual rearrangement were those of Held and his colleagues. An important feature of these studies was the introduction of a device that allowed measurement of a subject's accuracy in pointing, without sight of his hand, to the virtual images of targets (Held & Gottlieb, 1958). The same apparatus allowed the subject to see only his hand during exposure to visual displacement. A quantitative measure of adaptation was derived by comparing the accuracy of post- and preexposure pointing responses to visual targets. Because in this paradigm the subject sees only his hand during the exposure period, it is not possible for him to develop conscious compensatory strategies from seeing misreaching errors. Nevertheless, subjects who are only allowed sight of their voluntarily moved arm readily show adaptation (Held & Hein, 1958). This means that feedback information from misreaching errors to visual targets is not essential in order for adaptation to occur.

Extensive additional studies (Held, 1965; Held & Bossom, 1961; Held & Freedman, 1963; Held & Hein, 1958; Held & Schlank, 1959) using the same and related exposure paradigms suggested that only active movement of the subject's arm or body was effective in eliciting adaptation. Passive movements of the subject—even when of related frequency and amplitude to the active movements—failed to elicit adaptation. These reports suggested that there was something critically important about voluntary movement, and led to the notion that subjects, in adapting to visual displacement, must monitor their motor outflow and relate it to the changing sensory input that results. Steinbach and Held (1968) and Steinbach (1969) provided further support for this notion of efference monitoring through studies of eye–hand tracking. They found that subjects were able to track active hand movements much more accurately than passive hand movements. Tracking of the passively moved hand was found to be little better than tracking of an external target light moving in comparable fashion (Steinbach & Held, 1968).

In a related series of experiments, Held and Hein (1963) had earlier studied the influence of active and passive exposure conditions on the development of sensory-motor coordination. Here the experimental animals were kittens that were kept in darkness from birth except when in the exposure apparatus. This ingenous device was a "kitten carousel," in which the motion of an "active kitten" was communicated through a harness-and-linkage system to a gondola on the opposite side of the carousel, in which another kitten was restrained and passively transported. Whenever the active cat walked, it moved the passive cat in the gondola through a comparable distance. The active cat accordingly received correlated information about patterns of visual change related to its voluntary activity, whereas the passive cat did not. In later testing using the visual cliff (Gibson & Walk, 1960) and a visual-placing test,

Held and Hein found that kittens who had received active exposure behaved like normally reared cats, whereas the passively reared ones did not.

These converging lines of evidence suggest that relating sensory feedback from voluntary movements (reafferent feedback) and corollary-discharge (i.e., von Holst's "efference copy" [1954]) information is an important element in the development of sensorimotor coordination, normal coordination, and adaptation to sensory displacement. In an early model developed to explain the importance of efference monitoring, Held (1961) introduced the notions of "correlation storage" and "comparator" mechanisms.

> The Correlation Storage acts as a kind of memory which retains traces of previous combinations of concurrent efferent and re-afferent signals. The currently monitored efferent signal is presumed to select the trace combination combining the identical efferent part and to reactivate the re-afferent trace combined with it. The resulting revived re-afferent signal is sent to the Comparator for comparison with the current re-afferent signal. . . . Evidence for progressive adaptation to rearrangement implies that the selection from storage by the currently monitored efferent signal must be weighted by recency of trace combinations when alternatives are available. Thus, for example, if the conditions that make for typical combinations of signals are systematically changed, as they are by rearrangement, then new combinations will be stored.

These initial studies, and the theoretical formulation just cited (see also Held, 1968, for a related formulation), led to additional experiments concerned with identifying precisely how sensory and motor factors influence adaptation to sensory rearrangement in situations in which only sight of the hand is permitted. In one of the first of these studies, Kravitz and Wallach (1966) found that they could increase adaptation by enhancing the position sense of the arm seen during exposure. This observation pointed to the importance of a sensory discordance between the seen position of the arm and its proprioceptive representation. Several investigators (Howard, 1968; Lackner, 1974; Wallach, 1968) suggested that this discordance might be the factor responsible for adaptation. This makes sense logically because when the hand is viewed through prism spectacles, the discrepancy between its true and seen position is a constant (except for slight asymmetries in the optical displacement when the subject moves his eyes in relation to the prisms). Consequently, there is no need to recorrelate motor information associated with hand movements and the resulting visual feedback from these movements, because whenever the hand is voluntarily or passively moved, its visual image will be seen to move appropriately. The problem is actually one of detecting the constant discrepancy between the true and the seen position of the hand regardless of whether it is stationary or moving.

To evaluate the sensory-discordance hypothesis, Lackner (1974) used the apparatus illustrated in Figure 1. This apparatus permits the independent variation of the visual and the tactile-proprioceptive direction of targets. During the exposure condition, the subject sees visual targets, and without sight of his hand reaches and touches their apparent downward continuations out of the field of view. However, either the visual positions or the apparent tactile-proprioceptive loci of the targets can be displaced, either gradually or in a single step, thereby creating visual or proprioceptive rearrangements. In the case of a visual displacement, the top and bottom target pins are in register but the visual direction of the upper pins is displaced by having the subject look at them through prism spectacles; for a proprioceptive rearrangement, the bottom pins are displaced systematically in relation to the top pins, thereby providing false proprioceptive and motor information about the position of the upper targets.

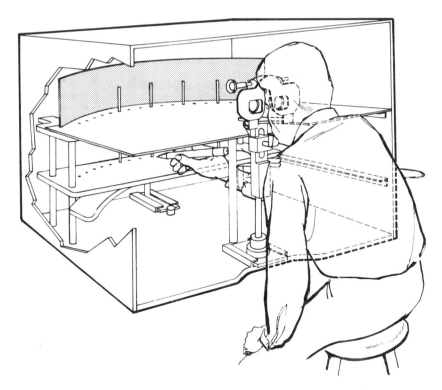

Fig. 1. Illustration of apparatus used to create visual-proprioceptive discordances. The apparatus is set for an exposure condition involving a visual displacement of the upper targets.

The results showed that both types of rearrangements were equally effective in eliciting adaptive changes in pointing behavior. Adaptation is not dependent on the conscious detection of a discordance between the seen and "felt" directions of the targets, because if the discordance is introduced very gradually, adaptation still occurs. (Howard [1968], Dewar [1971], and Lackner and Lobovits [1978] have shown, too, that when a visual displacement of the hand is introduced very gradually, adaptation also occurs. Moulden [1971] has used stroboscopic illumination of a subject's moving arm to show that the perception of visual movement during exposure is not necessary for adaptation to occur.) Welch (1978), using a related experimental paradigm, has also found that visual-proprioceptive discordances elicit adaptation, but to a lesser extent than when direct sight of the hand is permitted.

To evaluate directly whether efference monitoring plays a part in adaptation to visual displacement, Mather and Lackner (1975, 1977) made use of the tonic vibration reflex (TVR). A TVR can be elicited by vibrating the tendon of a skeletal muscle: the vibration activates the muscle spindle receptors within the muscle and thereby leads to a reflex contraction of the vibrated muscle (Hagbarth & Eklund, 1966). Accordingly, flexion of the forearm can be reflexly induced by vibrating the biceps, and extension by vibrating the triceps. Mather and Lackner compared the amount of adaptation elicited when subjects were allowed to watch their hand through prism spectacles as it was moved reflexly up and down by the action of TVRs, and when it was moved voluntarily through the same trajectory at the same frequency. Some of their many control conditions included viewing the stationary hand, viewing the stationary hand while the outer margins of the elbow were vibrated, and viewing the passively moved forearm. They found that the amount of adaptation elicited by reflex movements of the forearm was equal to that produced by active arm movements. In fact, significant adaptation occurred in all the experimental conditions except one in which the subject just fixated a target light in front of his body in an otherwise dark room. The results can be described by a simple rule: Adaptation diminishes as the richness of proprioceptive information about arm position is decreased.

Further support for this rule is provided in studies by Mather and Lackner (1980a,b) concerning the relationship between the accuracy of eye–hand tracking during visual rearrangement and adaptation. In these experiments, both active and passive control of limb movement were used and a wide range of movement frequency and predictability conditions was explored. Unlike earlier studies reporting a vastly superior visual tracking of active compared to passive limb movements, few differences were observed, and passive movements were sometimes tracked more accurately than active ones. What most affected the accuracy of visuomotor tracking was predictability of hand trajectory. Just as there were generally only trivial differences in the accuracy of eye–hand tracking for active and passive movements, so too there were few significant differences in the amount of adaptation elicited. No support was provided for the notion that efference monitoring is a critical factor in enhancing eye–hand tracking or in adapting to visual rearrangement.

In a final study related to the issue of what sensory and motor factors influence adaptation to visual rearrangement, Mather and Lackner (1980c) allowed subjects only sight of their hand and a target light. In separate experimental sessions they studied the relationship between tracking accuracy and adaptation when (a) the subject attempted to track his hand as it was moved passively; a target light was stationary at the midpoint of the arc, (b) the subject fixated the target light while his arm was moved passively, (c) the subject fixated his stationary arm while the target light was moved, (d) the subject's arm was stationary and he attempted to track the target light as it moved, and (e) the subject's arm was out of the field of view and he tracked the target light as it moved. Movement frequency was always 1 Hz and movement amplitude, 30°. During each condition, a continuous record of the subject's eye movements was made for comparison with the motion of the target. The results allowed a systematic assessment of the contribution to adaptation of limb proprioception, oculomotor pursuit, retinal-image displacement, and attention. The findings are presented in Table I. Adaptation to visual rearrangement only occurred when there was a discrepancy between the visual and the proprioceptively specified direction of the hand. Given the presence of such a discrepancy, adaptation was increased through enhancing position sense of the arm by passively moving it, maximizing

Table I. Adaptation to Visual Displacement in Degrees when Subjects Fixated or Tracked Their own Hand or a Target Light[a]

	Hand moving, light still, hand tracked	Hand moving, light still, light fixated	Hand still, light moving, hand fixated	Hand still, light moving, light tracked	Hand absent, light moving, light tracked
Mean adaptation	1.9°[d]	1.1°[c]	0.8°[b]	−0.3°	0.0°
Standard deviation	1.3°	1.2°	1.2°	0.7°	.9°

[a] Movement amplitude was 30°, movement frequency, 1 Hz. Hand movement was passively produced. ($N = 10$)
[b] Significant at $p < .05$.
[c] Significant at $p < .01$.
[d] Significant at $p < .001$.

accuracy of visual tracking by having the subject track his hand rather than the target light, and focusing attention on the hand rather than the target light.

The studies that have been described point to a common conclusion. A spatial or sensory discordance must be present before adaptation can be elicited.[2] The range of factors that influence adaptation is great and subsumes all elements, including "attention," that affect the accuracy of registering visual-spatial conflicts about limb position or external target positions. Efferent information about limb position is neither essential nor sufficient to elicit adaptation.[3]

Earlier studies that emphasized the importance of efference monitoring in adaptation likely did so because they failed to include control conditions that differed only in the presence and absence of efference monitoring. In this context, it is notable that Walk, Shepherd, and Miller (1978) have reexamined the role of active and passive movements in the development of visuomotor coordination. Their findings show that *attention* is a critical variable. Passively transported kittens who attend to the environment develop normal visuomotor coordination.

5. Factors Influencing the Form of Adaptation

The complexity of sensory-motor control places constraints on the forms that adaptive compensations can take and the kinds of models that can adequately describe motor performance. It has been popular in recent years to develop models of the adaptation process which involve correlations of present patterns of efferent and reafferent activity with stored traces of previous patterns. Similarly, motor control has been described in terms of finding appropriate entries in tables or matrices of muscle length–tension values; in this way, for example, particular configurations of the arm in pointing to an external target are thought to be brought about.

Such assumptions about adaptation and motor control represent a

---

[2] Finke (1979) has reported that some subjects show changes in movement control after "imagining" the presence of a sensory discordance. His study involved pointing movements to visual targets with sight of the hand. It remains to be determined whether an imagined discordance can elicit adaptation if only sight of the hand is allowed during the exposure period.

[3] Although corollary-discharge information appears not to play a role in adaptation to visual rearrangement, there is nevertheless strong evidence that it has an important function in other aspects of sensorimotor control. Lackner and Tuller (1979) have demonstrated that efference monitoring figures prominently in the control of speech production and in the perceptual representation of self-produced speech sounds.

profound underestimation of the complexity of human and animal movement. Most movement patterns, even seemingly "stereotyped" movements, are novel or unique in their structure. There is every reason to believe that even if it were possible to produce precisely the same pattern of voluntary efferent commands to a given skeletal muscle group, this would not necessarily produce a constant movement of the appendage in question unless the rest of the body were fixed in position. Bernstein (1967) made this point when he indicated the absence of an invariant relationship between patterns of efferent activity and the resulting movements of the body. This absence is attributable to both the changing orientations of the limbs in relation to gravity and the different mechanical advantages involved with varying configurations of the body. Thus an animal who controlled his behavior by means of "looking up" appropriate length–tension coordinates in stored lists or matrices would need an infinite set of lists.

Such considerations have direct implications for all memory-storage models of prism adaptation (cf. Held, 1961, 1968; Welch, 1978). It would rarely if ever be the case that identical motor commands would be issued before and during exposure to visual rearrangement. Therefore, the likelihood that an efferent trace that could be matched would be stored is extremely small; the fact that movement is so infinitely variable in its composition would require the storing of a virtually infinite number of efferent "memory traces." Perhaps equally restricting, however, is the problem that even if efferent traces were stored and matched with efferent commands issued during exposure to visual displacement, then one could predict adaptive shifts only for the efferent and reafferent trace combinations that were remapped during exposure. The practical implication of this is that to achieve full adaptation the animal would have to reduplicate much of its exposure history.

In this context, it should be noted that the recent revolution in linguistic theory initiated by Chomsky (Chomsky, 1959) revolved about similar issues. Learning theorists had argued that we understand speech on the basis of identifying sentences or constituents of sentences that had been learned earlier on the basis of various exposure and reinforcement contingencies. Chomsky's objection to this view is that language is infinitely varied; identical patterns are rarely encountered twice except in artifically contrived situations and certain automatisms. The same is true of human and animal movement. Consequently, theories of speech production and speech comprehension and theories of movement control and adaptation have to be generative in character, making possible the creation and recognition of an infinite but systematically restricted set of patterns, and in doing so making use of finite means. As we proceed it will become clear that adaptation to sensory rearrangement often takes the form of "postural remappings" (i.e., changes in the apparent position of parts of the body in relation to one another) rather than motor remappings. It is likely that this occurs because a postural remapping is a single transformation that eliminates the need for more complicated generative motor transformations. Motor remappings have so far been described only for eye-movement control, which, as we have seen, differs from the control of the limbs.

The occurrence of adaptation to sensory rearrangement and its form depend on the nature of exposure, including (a) how rapidly the rearrangement is introduced, (b) whether the subject is free to move, and (c) how long exposure lasts. Many other factors influence adaptation as well, but these three exemplify possible general principles.

5.1. Incremental Exposure to Sensory Rearrangement

Graybiel (1969) has demonstrated that subjects can readily adapt to highly stressful patterns of vestibular stimulation if the stressor level is increased gradually. For example, when subjects in a slow-rotation room make head movements nonparallel to the axis of rotation, they are exposed to Coriolis and cross-coupling accelerations that create bizarre patterns of vestibular stimulation and lead to illusory motion of the body and the visual world. If head movements are made at high velocities of rotation, for example, 10 RPM, then severe motion sickness will soon develop and the subjects will have to remain still. Thus, in a slow-rotation room, subjects are exposed to a highly stressful form of sensory rearrangement in which the relationship between active or passive movements of the head and trunk and the resulting pattern of vestibular and kinesthetic feedback is altered. With continued exposure some subjects gradually adapt so that head movements no longer elicit aberrant visual and apparent body motion. The nature of this adaptation will be considered in more detail later. The important point is that if the velocity of the slow-rotation room is gradually increased, and many head movements are made at each dwell velocity, nearly all subjects can be brought up to velocities that otherwise would be highly stressful. Graybiel and Wood (1969) found that incremental exposure or stepwise adaptation also enhances the rate at which adaptation is achieved and how long it lasts.

Lackner and Lobovits (1977, 1978) and Yachzel and Lackner (1977) have carried out a series of visual studies based on Graybiel's observations on vestibular adaptation. They found that incremental exposure to visual rearrangement also facilitates adaptation and retention of adaptation. A curious finding in both of these studies, not previously mentioned, is that subjects in the incremental-exposure condition (but not the single-step condition) reported as the exposure condition proceeded that their heads began to feel deviated on their torsos. Apparent head deviation resulted even though subjects were only permitted sight of their hand during the exposure condition, a situation that usually results in adaptive changes restricted to the hand seen during exposure (Harris, 1963). This observation suggests that the rate at which a visual displacement is introduced may affect the adaptive compensation that is made.

Yachzel and Lackner (1977) evaluated the effects of repeated incremental and single-step exposures on adaptation to visual rearrangement by giving subjects an exposure session every two days until five sessions had been completed. Their results showed carry-overs of adaptation from one session to the next with incremental exposure being superior in retention as well as acquisition of adaptation. Subjects who participated showed significant aftereffects 2 full weeks after their last exposure session. These aftereffects were manifest both when the subjects pointed (without sight of their hands) using arm movements similar to those used in the exposure condition, and when they pointed using very different patterns of elbow and shoulder motion. Despite these long-lasting aftereffects, none of the subjects noticed any disruption of visuomotor coordination in everyday situations in which they had sight of their hands.

Aftereffects from repeated incremental exposure to visual rearrangement thus appear to be situation-specific (pointing without sight of the hand), but not exposure-specific, as are some of the well-known visual aftereffects such as the McCollough effect (cf. Skowbo, Timney, Gentry, & Morant, 1975). In all relevant respects, adaptation to visual rearrangement achieved with incremental exposure resembles the adaptation to bizarre patterns of vestibular stimulation achieved with incremental exposure. These similarities suggest that enhancement of adaptation and retention of adaptation by incremental exposure may be characteristic of all forms of sensory rearrangement, hence reflecting a general property of adaptive sensory-motor reorganization.

5.2. Influence of Exposure Condition on Adaptation

The form adaptation takes is contingent—at least initially—on the character of the exposure condition. This is especially clear in exposure to visual displacement. In situations allowing the subject whole-body movement and locomotion, adaptation may initially involve a reinterpretation of head–trunk position (Harris, 1963; Hay & Pick, 1966; Lackner, 1973) although with longer exposure periods, lasting days rather than hours, the eye–head relationship may be reinterpreted (Hay & Pick, 1966). It is commonly observed, for example, that subjects walking about while wearing prism spectacles will begin to deviate their heads in the direction of the visual displacement. This deviated head posture compensates for the lateral displacement of the visual field. Without head deviation, a subject experiences the world as rubbery when he walks because objects directly in front of him and successively encountered appear to change position. This effect occurs because the prisms displace the images of objects to one side. As the subject walks toward an object, its displacement in degrees of visual angle remains the same but the lateral distance subtended diminishes; consequently the subject perceives the object moving in toward his midline as he walks toward it.

Such a deviated head position, if interpreted as the straight-ahead position of the head on the trunk, also restores accurate visuomotor coordination to external objects. For example, before a 10°-leftward visual displacement is compensated for by a change in registered head position, a subject will orient and reach incorrectly for external objects. After adaptation, the head will be perceived as straight ahead when it is physically deviated 10° to the left. This "postural remapping" is exactly compensatory for the visual displacement and reestablishes accurate coordination to external objects. The subject will both walk toward objects correctly and reach for them accurately with either hand.

It should be noted that a reregistration of apparent head position has implications for the reflex mechanisms related to head posture. It has been known since the work of Magnus (1924) that if an animal's head is maintained in a deviated position on its trunk, reflex modulations of posture and eye position result. For example, with the head deviated to the right there is a tendency for the eyes to be displaced to the left in relation to the head.

Teixeira and Lackner (1976) made use of the existence of tonic neck reflexes to determine whether changes in apparent head posture during adaptation to visual displacement are treated by the central nervous system as if they were true physical deviations of the head. In their experiment, they measured the average return position of the fast phase of optokinetic nystagmus for subjects first with the torso and head aligned and then with the trunk deviated in relation to the head. Deviation of the head to one side shifted the average return position of the optokinetic nystagmus to the opposite side in relation to the values obtained without head deviation. The subjects then wore and adapted to prism spectacles that laterally displaced their visual world 13° leftward. They were then retested with optokinetic stimulation while their head and trunk were physically aligned in the straight-ahead position. Each subject, however, felt as if his head were physically deviated to the right because of the postural remapping during adaptation. Only when the head was deviated 13° leftward in relation to the torso did it feel straight-ahead. The nystagmus records of these subjects showed a leftward deviation of the eyes just as if the head had in fact been physically deviated to the right (see Figure 2). This observation demonstrates that "errors" in the interpretation of true head position are treated with respect to the reflex modulation of posture as if they are physical shifts in head position. It shows, too, that the action of tonic neck reflexes is

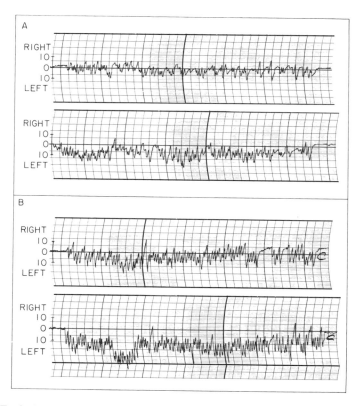

Fig. 2. Typical optokinetic-nystagmus patterns recorded for the two experimental conditions. Calibration legends indicate eye positions 10° leftward and 10° rightward with respect to the head median plane. (A) Representative 30-sec trials from one subject in physical head-deviation condition. Upper trace was recorded with the subject's head fixed straight ahead with respect to the trunk. Lower trace was recorded with the head deviated 45° to the right of the trunk median plane. (B) Representative 30-sec trials from one subject in apparent head-deviation condition. Upper trace and lower trace were both recorded with the subject's head oriented straight ahead in relation to his trunk. The upper trace was recorded prior to the subject's being exposed to a 13° leftward displacement of his visual world for 3 hrs. The lower trace was recorded after the subject had adapted to the visual rearrangement and the prisms had been removed; under this circumstance, the subject experiences his head to be deviated rightward although it is physically aligned with the median plane of his trunk.

dependent on registered head position in relation to the trunk rather than true head position, indicating plasticity and modifiability of the tonic neck "reflex."

Other reflexes that are normally compensatory for changes in true body position can also be elicited by changes in apparent body orientation. For example, when a blindfolded subject undergoes angular acceleration he shows a compensatory nystagmus with his eyes drifting slowly in the direction opposite acceleration and beating back to the direction of acceleration. Also, when the body axis is tilted, there are compensatory changes in eye position through ocular countertorsion. Lackner and Levine (1979) have described an entire class of *vibratory myesthetic illusions* in which illusory changes in whole-body orientation and visual localization are elicited by skeletal muscle vibration. By vibrating the appropriate postural muscles it is possible to elicit illusory motion of the stationary body in virtually any desired direction. Subjects experiencing such illusory motion often exhibit compensatory oculomotor and postural reflexes just as if the body were in motion or had been tilted. These findings indicate that compensatory oculomotor activity is not contingent on true motion of the body but on an internal representation of body motion, an internal representation that may not correspond to the true status of the body in relation to its surroundings. This "plasticity of possible representations" is one reason that adaptation to sensory rearrangement is possible.

5.3. Adaptational Specificity

The kinds of adaptive changes that can be adopted in response to sensory rearrangement are dependent on the nature of the rearrangement. For example, exposure to delayed auditory feedback of one's voice has a very disruptive effect when the delay is on the order of 200 msec (Fairbanks, 1955). There is an increase in speech duration and in frequency of articulatory errors. Katz and Lackner (1977) have provided strong evidence that subjects can adapt, at least partially, to auditory delays of 200 msec if exposure continues at least an hour. Such "adaptation" persists for periods at least as long as 30 days, so that when again exposed to delayed auditory feedback, subjects show markedly less disruption.

Adaptation to delayed auditory feedback cannot be achieved by sensory or postural remappings. Instead adaptation is achieved through the development of various "strategies," some of which subjects are not aware they are using. These strategies include speaking more rapidly or more slowly than normal, speaking in spurts to "outrun" the delayed auditory feedback, concentrating on the details of articulation, or imposing a rhythm. This latter example is considered not because adaptation to delayed auditory feedback is similar to adaptation to other forms of sensory rearrangement, but rather because it is different and shows that the introduction of virtually any kind of sensory rearrangement or delay is associated with the development of compensatory adaptations.

5.4. Intersensory Factors and Adaptation: Constancies of Auditory and Visual Direction

Normally, during head movement, stationary visual and auditory targets are perceived as remaining stationary because the ensuing change in auditory- and visual-receptor activity is ascribed to self-motion rather than to motion of or within the external world. That is, constancies of auditory and visual direction are maintained during body movements. Wallach has conducted an extensive series of studies in which he has altered the relationship between patterns of visual and auditory cues at the eyes and the ears and the motion of the head. In these studies, the position of an external visual or auditory target is linked to the motion of the subject's head, so that the target is displaced by a fractional amount of the head movement in the same (or opposite) direction.

In the first of these experiments, Wallach and Kravitz (1965) found that if an external visual target was displaced by more than a certain fraction of a subject's head movement, the subject would report that it moved when he moved his head. However, after many head movements, the subject would see the target's motion diminished. If, after this adaptation was achieved, the visual target was then left stationary during the head movements, the subject would see the target move but in the direction opposite that experienced before adaptation. Using auditory rather than visual targets, Wallach and Kravitz found similar adaptation and negative aftereffects. Moreover, adaptation resulted regardless of whether the subject's head was moved actively or passively during the exposure period.

In an elegant study, Wallach and Kravitz (1968) exposed subjects to altered relations between head movement and visual-target motion until adaptation was achieved, and then tested to see whether adaptation transferred when an auditory target was substituted for the visual one. No evidence of transfer appeared. However, when the reverse experiment was performed and subjects were exposed to abnormal auditory motion during head movements, then tested for transfer with visual targets, transfer of adaptation was found (Lackner, in press).

This pattern indicates that the form of adaptation differs for the visual and the auditory exposure conditions. In the case of exposure to the visual displacement, a change occurs in the relationship between head and eye motion and constancy of visual direction. For example, normally if there is a target in the midline of the body and the head is turned 15° to the right while foveal fixation is maintained, the 15° deviation of the eyes in the head coupled with the 15° registered deviation of the head on the torso indicates that the target has remained stationary in the median plane of the body. When the target is displaced in the direction of the head movement by a constant fraction, say one-third, the eyes will move only 10° leftward in the head when the head moved 15° rightward on the torso. Initially the subject will see the target move rightward, but after adaptation is complete there will be a change in the calibration of the eye–head–torso linkage. When this change is complete, a visual target will be perceived as stationary during head movement only if it is in physical motion, for example, during the 15°-rightward head movement the target would have to displace 5° rightward to be seen as stationary. Because the changed relationship between head movement and eye movement does not affect the interpretation of head position in relation to the trunk, transfer of adaptation to auditory targets does not occur.

By contrast, when the subject adapts to the auditory displacement the relationship between the auditory cues at his ears and the apparent position of his head on his torso is altered. This means that there is a change in the registration of the magnitude of head movement in relation to the trunk; consequently, transfer of adaptation to visual targets is to be expected. Such transfer occurs because the relationship between eye displacement in relation to head displacement is affected through the changed interpretation of head deviation in relation to the torso. Accordingly, adaptation is "automatically" present for visual-target displacement because it can be compensated for through changed interpretations either of eye–head or head–trunk relations. By contrast, the only postural remapping that can compensate for modification of the normal relationship between head movement and auditory change is an alteration in the readout of head position with respect to the trunk.

In another series of studies, Wallach and Bacon (1977) have modified the relationship between retinal-image displacement and eye motion. In these experiments, when the eye moves in relation to a stationary visual target the magnitude of the resulting image displacement on the retina is optically manipulated. Subjects exposed to this situation initially experience visual movement of the truly stationary target, but with longer exposure again experience perceptual stability. Apparent visual motion of opposite sign results when the optical transformation is eliminated. These observations show that the relationship between retinal-image motion and eye movement on the one hand and the perception of visual stability on the other can be systematically modified. Here the adaptation consists of a change in the magnitude of registered eye displacement for particular oculomotor innervation patterns. This finding may well represent the only clear-cut instance of a motor remapping. In this context, it should be recalled that the eyes are the only parts of the body that can be controlled by more or less invariant patterns of motor commands. It should, therefore, come as no surprise that it is with regard to oculomotor control that a genuine motor remapping seems to have been generated.

5.5. Adaptation to Coriolis and Cross-Coupled Angular Accelerations

As mentioned earlier, subjects exposed to Coriolis and cross-coupling accelerations experience aberrant postural and visual motion. For example, a subject facing the center of rotation of a clockwise-revolving slow-rotation room will, on tilting his head to his right shoulder, experience his head and trunk as being displaced rightward and backwards; simultaneously, the visual world will seem to undergo related motion. If the subject is in darkness when he makes the tilting head movement, his eyes will exhibit a compensatory nystagmus. After adaptation is complete, head movements will no longer elicit aberrant visual or postural motion, or nystagmus. However, when the slow-rotation room is stopped, aftereffects of opposite sign will occur when the subject tilts his head and he will again experience aberrant body motion and visual motion. If the subject's eyes are closed, a nystagmus of opposite sign will appear during tilting head movements (Graybiel, Guedry, Johnson, & Kennedy, 1961). These observations indicate that adaptation to an altered relationship between vestibular and proprioceptive information about body orientation is possible, and is brought about through modifications of the vestibuloocular reflex, a change of gain and reversal of sign, and remappings of proprioceptive patterns associated with particular postures.

6. Intersensory Interactions

Characteristic of the adaptation studies that have been described is a close relationship between sensory localization and postural representation. How intimate this relationship is can be appreciated from a consideration of several recent studies which show that: (1) errors in the interpretation of ongoing posture are associated with errors in sensory localization of similar time course and magnitude, and (2) unusual patterns of sensory stimulation can elicit errors in the interpretation of posture (which in turn affect sensory localization). Two experimental paradigms that illustrate these interactions will be considered: Z-axis recumbent rotation and vibration of postural muscles.

6.1. Z-Axis Recumbent Rotation: Importance of Touch and Pressure Cues

Constant-velocity rotation of recumbent subjects about the long axis, or Z-axis, of their body, is commonly used as a way of studying the dynamic response properties of the otolith organs. The Z- or mid-body axis is the long axis passing through the body's center of gravity. Investigators have argued that during such "barbecue spit rotation" the otoliths are the primary if not sole determinant of perceived orientation and oculomotor responses (cf. Guedry, 1974). The basis for this belief is that at constant-velocity rotation, the semicircular canals will not be differentially activated because they respond primarily or exclusively to angular acceleration. The otolith organs will be dynamically active, however, because they are sensitive to linear acceleration and are being continually reoriented in relation to the gravitational-force vector.

Nevertheless, Lackner and Graybiel (1978a,b) have recently found that at rotary velocities above 7–10 RPM, a blindfolded subject's apparent orientation and pattern of compensatory eye movements are actually determined by the patterns of touch and pressure stimulation of his body surface, not by otolith activity. The touch and pressure stimulation arises from the contact forces of support provided by the apparatus in opposing the action of the gravitational force-vector, which would otherwise accelerate the subject's body downward. During clockwise rotation the patterns of pressure change in a counterclockwise direction in relation to the subject's body, and he experiences a counterclockwise orbital motion with his head facing in a constant direction. The pressure cues on the surface of his body are interpreted as preserving his orbital motion by preventing him from flying out of the orbit. The relationship between the subject's experienced orientation and his actual orientation is illustrated in Figure 3.

A subject undergoing constant-velocity rotation about his horizontal Z-axis can often influence dramatically his apparent orientation by manipulating the pressure cues acting on his body surface. For instance, if he puts pressure on the soles of his feet, he may feel upright as he describes an orbital path. Pressure on the top of his head may make him feel upside-down while traversing his orbit. Accordingly, there is a "coalescence" of the touch and pressure cues in determining apparent orientation. By increasing the pressure on the front of his head, the

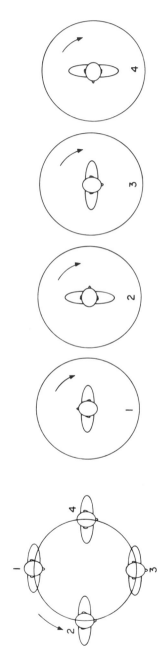

Fig. 3. The far left illustration depicts the orbital motion experienced by a horizontal, blindfolded subject who is being rotated at constant velocity about the Z-axis, or long axis, of his body. The numbered illustrations to the right show the relationship between the subject's true horizontal position and his experienced orbital position. For example, when the subject is actually faceup, Illustration 1, this corresponds to Position 1, in the representation of the orbit.

subject can increase the diameter of his apparent orbital motion, whereas decreasing the pressure decreases the orbital diameter. Such changes in apparent orbital diameter are associated with changes in the subject's apparent velocity, because one revolution of his orbit is completed each time he actually rotates through 360°. Consequently, when the orbit increases in diameter, the subject's apparent velocity increases pari passu. The magnitude and frequency of the nystagmus exhibited by the subject are also dependent on his apparent velocity; consequently, these parameters change when the subject's apparent velocity changes, even though his true rotary velocity is unchanged.

Further evidence for the importance of touch and pressure cues in orientation has been provided by experiments involving flight movements to generate periodic variations in gravitoinertial force. In these experiments, a KC-135 aircraft was flown through a series of parabolic maneuvers, thereby generating alternate periods of free fall, "O-g," and increased gravitoinertial force (approximately 2 g), lasting 30 sec each parabola. Lackner and Graybiel (1979) found that blindfolded subjects undergoing Z-axis recumbent rotation experienced a doubling of their apparent orbital diameter and orbital velocity in the 2-g phase of flight. By contrast, in the free-fall, or 0-g, phase of flight, when there was no pressure stimulation of their body surface, the subjects lost all sense of body movement and orientation. They were aware only of the relative configuration of their body and had no sense of orientation to the external environment. These findings indicate that one's perceived orientation in space is highly dependent on patterns of exteroceptive stimulation. Accordingly, in the absence of somatosensory, vestibular, visual or auditory information, no sense of orientation to the environment can be derived.

Under ground-based testing conditions, if a blindfolded subject is undergoing clockwise rotation, and there is a continuously emitting sound source lateral to his head and stationary in the experimental chamber, he will experience an interesting illusion. The subject will hear the sound source as moving in a counterclockwise orbit about his head as he goes through his own apparent orbital motion. The position and diameter of the sound-source orbit remain constant in relation to the subject's apparent head position even when he brings about a change in his apparent orientation by applying pressure to different parts of his body.

These observations indicate that the auditory cues from the stationary sound source—which are actually changing in a counterclockwise direction in relation to the subject because he is physically turning in a clockwise direction about his recumbent Z-axis—are being related to the subject's apparent ongoing orientation. Because his apparent motion is orbital while he is facing in a constant direction, the systematically changing auditory cues at his ears are being attributed to motion of the sound source. If a stationary visual target is substituted for the auditory one in an otherwise dark experimental chamber, the subject will perceive the visual target as moving in a counterclockwise orbit about his head. It is clear, therefore, that both the auditory and the visual patterns of stimulation are being related to the subject's apparent rather than true orientation. This means that the perceived directions of sensory stimuli in relation to the body are dependent on a computation involving conjoint analysis of apparent body orientation and physical patterns of auditory and visual stimulation.

6.2. Skeletal Muscle Vibration: Illusory Postural and Visual Motion

A further illustration of this same point is exemplified by the oculobrachial illusion (Lackner & Levine, 1978). If a subject's forearm is restrained in position and his biceps muscle is vibrated with a physiotherapy vibrator, he will experience illusory extension of his forearm; vibration of the triceps elicits illusory flexion (Goodwin, Mc-Closkey, & Matthews, 1972). Lackner and Levine (1978) found that if a small target light is attached to the hand of a subject experiencing illusory flexion or extension, the subject will see the stationary target light as moving down or up in keeping with the apparent motion of his arm. This was true even though eye-movement recordings showed that the subject's eyes were maintaining stable fixation of the target light and not moving. On the basis of this experiment and others, Lackner and Levine concluded that, even though physically stationary, the subject's eyes were being centrally interpreted as in motion, on the basis of an abnormal signal about arm position influencing the registration of eye position.

A further effect was noted in these experiments—namely, a bidirectional interaction between apparent posture and sensory localization. Just as an illusory change in arm position affected the visual direction of a target light attached to the hand, so did the presence of a target light attached to the hand affect the magnitude of the illusory motion of the arm. When the target light was present the magnitude of the arm illusion was diminished by approximately 25%.

If various postural muscles are vibrated instead of muscles of the arm (Lackner & Levine, 1979), then apparent motion of the stationary body can be elicited, as described earlier. If, in this situation, a stationary target light or auditory target is presented in the dark experimental chamber, the subject will see the visual target and hear the auditory target as moving in keeping with his own apparent motion.

Observations such as these emphasize the dependence of apparent posture on ongoing patterns of sensory stimulation, and the dependence of sensory localization on a correlation of ongoing apparent body orientation with visual and auditory cues at the eyes and ears. A model representing some aspects of these interactions is presented in Figure 4. It should be noted from this model that many patterns of sensory stimulation are ambiguous in terms of the body motions that can be associated with them. For example, if we are upright or seated and undergoing constant-velocity linear or angular motion, the vestibular organs and touch–pressure receptors are stimulated in the same way as when we are stationary because they respond to accelerative motion of the body and cannot distinguish stationarity from constant-velocity motion. Accordingly, it is natural that, if the input from another modality, for example vision, audition, or proprioception, is changing continuously, then this change can be attributed to constant-velocity motion of either the body or the environment, or some combination thereof. This is precisely what happens during exposure to constant-velocity visual stimulation: visually induced illusory self-motion soon results. The same effect can be achieved with constant-velocity auditory stimulation (Lackner, 1977), proprioceptive stimulation (muscle vibration) (Lackner & Levine, 1979), or somatosensory stimulation (as in the Z-axis rotation experiments just described).

However, in any situation involving induced apparent motion of the stationary body, if the subject is allowed to make head movements out of the axis of apparent motion, he will by so doing usually attenuate or abolish his illusory self-motion (Lackner, 1978; Lackner & Teixeira, 1977). The reason for this appears to be that such head movements, when made during actual motion of the body, are associated with Coriolis and cross-coupling accelerations; the absence of these accelerations serves as information to the nervous system that the body is actually stationary. This distinction appears to represent a general principle of spatial orientation: Absence of expected patterns of stimulation can be as important as ongoing patterns of stimulation in conveying information about ongoing body orientation.

Another illustration of this same theme is provided by observations of Lackner and Graybiel (in press) concerning optokinetic stimulation. If an optokinetic drum is accelerated from 0°/sec to constant velocity, visually induced self-rotation only results after the subject's compensatory nystagmus is no longer increasing in slow-phase velocity. This means that the absence of a change in vestibular stimulation coupled with an increasing eye velocity "informs" the subject that the visual world rather than he is moving; when eye velocity no longer changes, the situation is again ambiguous.

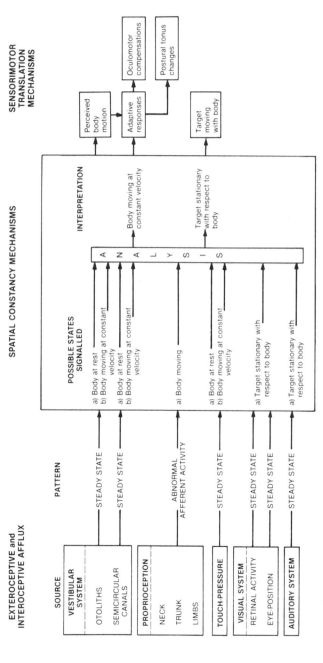

Fig. 4. This schema represents some of the sensory factors that affect the computation of apparent posture and shows how changes in apparent posture influence sensory localization and lead to compensatory motor adjustments. The pattern of inputs depicted would be associated with illusory motion of the body. A complete model would include (1) recurrent pathways allowing the interpretations derived by the spatial-constancy mechanisms to influence perceptual representations assigned to incoming patterns of sensory stimulation, (2) a specification of how postural adjustments can modify incoming sensory patterns, and (3) a representation of corollary-discharge signals that could indicate intended or ongoing voluntary movements. These important elements have been omitted to promote ease of visualization.

7. Conclusions

Two interrelated themes connect the experiments on adaptation to sensory rearrangement and on sensory interaction that have been described. The first theme is that of a complex interrelation between the representation of ongoing posture and sensory localization. Ongoing apparent posture is dependent on multiple sources of sensory information from both exteroceptive, proprioceptive, and interoceptive sources of stimulation. The interpretation of the visual or auditory direction of a target is jointly dependent on the physical patterns of stimulation created by these sources as well as the ongoing interpreted orientation of the body. Consequently, whenever there is an error in the interpretation of ongoing body posture (e.g., head–trunk relations), then errors in sensory localization result as well; similarly, unusual patterns of sensory stimulation can elicit errors in apparent posture so that there is a bidirectional interaction.

In many situations involving adaptation to sensory rearrangement, the following process seems to be occuring. The presence of the rearrangement leads to errors in sensory-motor coordination and orientation. When these errors exceed a certain magnitude, adaptive changes are made with compensation often taking the form of a postural remapping, for example, changes in the representation of the position of the head on the trunk or the eyes in the head. These postural remappings affect sensory localization, producing changes in localization that are compensatory for the rearrangement that initiated the process in the first place.

The second unifying theme is a variation on Henderson's concept of "the fitness of the environment" (1913). Henderson argued that just as an organism must have certain characteristics to be adaptable to changing environmental conditions, so must the environment have certain regularities and potentialities before life in it is possible. The same is true for adaptation to unusual sensory and force environments: the organism must have adaptive capacities to cope with changes in its own weight and dimensions during development and through life, and when carrying objects or tools or encountering different terrains. However, adaptation can only take place if the new sensory or force environment is "fit" in the sense of regularity, predictability, and persistence over some period of time. Given these constraints, it then appears that adaptation takes place when initiated by the presence of sensory or motor discordances in movement and orientation. The adaptive changes that take place appear to compensate for the precise disruption in performance encountered at the lowest level possible, and are, accordingly, highly dependent on the characteristics of the exposure condition and the modality being affected. One consequence of this apparent specificity is that compensation for one disturbed relation may lead to disrupted performance in other situations. As mentioned earlier, in exposure conditions involving sight of one hand alone, adaptation may take the form of a change in the interpretation of arm position in relation to the trunk. This change restores accurate reaching with that arm to external targets, but at the cost of errors in pointing to other parts of the body. It may be expected, therefore, that as the subject is also allowed to touch his body, the form of compensation will be altered or augmented to restore an adequate fit of the organism to itself as well as to the environment.

8. References

Bahill, A., & Stark, L. The trajectories of saccadic eye movements. *Scientific American*, 1979, *240*, 108–117.

Bernard, C. *Introduction a l'Etude de la Médecine Expérimentale*. Paris: J.B. Baillière et fils, 1865.

Bernstein, N. *The co-ordination and regulation of movements*. Oxford: Pergamon Press, 1967.

Cannon, W.B. *The wisdom of the body*. New York: Norton, 1963.

Chomsky, N. *Syntactic structures*. The Hague: Mouton, 1957.

Chomsky, N. Review of Verbal Behavior by B.F. Skinner (1957). *Language*, 1959, *35*, 26–58.

Chomsky, N. *Aspects of the theory of syntax*. Cambridge: MIT Press, 1965.

Dewar, R. Adaptation to displaced vision: Variations on the "prismatic shaping" technique. *Perception and Psychophysics*, 1971, *9*, 155–157.

Fairbanks, G. Selective vocal effects of delayed auditory feedback. *Journal of Speech and Hearing Disorders*, 1955, *20*, 333–345.

Finke, R. The functional equivalence of mental images and errors of movement. *Cognitive Psychology*, 1979, *11*, 235–264.

Gibson, E., & Walk, R. The "visual cliff." *Scientific American*, 1960, *202*, 64–71.

Goodwin, G., McCloskey D., & Matthews, P. The contribution of muscle afferents to kinesthesia shown by vibration induced illusions of movement and by the effects of paralysing joint afferents. *Brain*, 1972, *95*, 705–748.

Graybiel, A. Structural elements in the concept of motion sickness. *Aerospace Medicine*, 1969, *40*, 351–367.

Graybiel, A., & Wood, C. Rapid vestibular adaptation in a rotating environment by means of controlled head movements. *Aerospace Medicine*, 1969, *40*, 638–643.

Graybiel, A., Guedry, F., Johnson, W., & Kennedy, R. Adaptation to bizarre stimulation of the semicircular canals as indicated by the oculogyral illusion. *Aerospace Medicine*, 1961, *32*, 321–327.

Guedry, F. Psychophysics of vestibular sensation. In H. Kornhuber (Ed.), *Handbook of Sensory Physiology*. Volume VI/2: *Vestibular System*. Part 2: *Psychophysics, Applied Aspects and General Interpretations*. New York: Springer-Verlag, 1974, pp. 3–154.

Hagbarth, K.-E., & Eklund, G. Motor affects of vibratory stimuli in man. In R. Granit (Ed.), *Muscle Afferents and Motor Control*. Stockholm: Almqvist & Wiksell, 1966, pp. 177–186.

Harris, C. Adaptation to displaced vision: Visual, motor, or proprioceptive change. *Science*, 1963, *140*, 812–813.

Hay, J., & Pick, H. Visual and proprioceptive adaptation to optical displacement of the visual stimulus. *Journal of Experimental Psychology,* 1966, *71,* 150–158.

Held, R. Exposure-history as a factor in maintaining stability of perception and co-ordination. *Journal of Nervous and Mental Disease,* 1961, *132,* 26–32.

Held, R. Plasticity in sensory-motor systems. *Scientific American,* 1965, *213,* 84–94.

Held, R. Action contingent development of vision in neonatal animals. In D.P. Kimble (Ed.), *Experience and Capacity.* New York: New York Academy of Sciences, 1968.

Held, R., & Bossom, J. Neonatal deprivation and adult rearrangement: Complementary techniques for analyzing plastic sensory-motor coordinations. *Journal of Comparative and Physiological Psychology,* 1961, *54,* 33–37.

Held, R., & Freedman, S. Plasticity in human sensorimotor control. *Science,* 1963, *142,* 455–462.

Held, R., & Gottlieb, N. Technique for studying adaptation to disarranged hand-eye coordination. *Perceptual and Motor Skills,* 1958, *8,* 83–86.

Held, R., & Hein, A. Adaptation to disarranged hand-eye coordination contingent upon reafferent stimulation. *Perceptual and Motor Skills,* 1958, *8,* 87–90.

Held, R., & Hein, A. Movement-produced stimulation in the development of visually guided behavior. *Journal of Comparative and Physiological Psychology,* 1963, *56,* 872–876.

Held, R., & Schlank, M. Adaptation to disarranged eye-hand coordination in the distance dimension. *American Journal of Psychology,* 1959, *72,* 603–605.

Henderson, L.J. *The fitness of the environment.* New York: Macmillan, 1913.

Howard, T. Displacing the optic array. In S. Freedman (Ed.), *The neuropsychology of spatially oriented behavior.* Homewood, Illinois: Dorsey Press, 1968, pp. 19–36.

Katz, D. *Animals and men.* London: Penguin Books, 1953.

Katz, D., & Lackner, J. Adaptation to delayed auditory feedback. *Perception and Psychophysics,* 1977, *22,* 476–486.

Kravitz, T., & Wallach, H. Adaptation to displaced vision contingent upon vibrating stimulation. *Psychonomic Science,* 1966, *6,* 465–466.

Lackner, J. *Influence of posture on the spatial localization of sounds.* Ph.D. thesis, Massachusetts Institute of Technology, 1970.

Lackner, J. The role of posture in adaptation to visual rearrangement. *Neuropsychologia,* 1973, *11,* 33–44.

Lackner, J. Adaptation to displaced vision: Role of proprioception. *Perceptual and Motor Skills,* 1974, *38,* 1251–1256.

Lackner, J. Induction of illusory self-rotation and nystagmus in stationary subjects with a rotating sound field. *Aviation, Space, and Environmental Medicine,* 1977, *48,* 129–131.

Lackner, J. Some mechanisms underlying sensory and postural stability in man. In R. Held, H. Leibowitz, & H.L. Teuber (Eds.), *Handbook of sensory physiology.* Vol. 8: *Perception.* Berlin: Springer Verlag, 1978, pp. 805–845.

Lackner, J., Adaptation to constancy of auditory direction transfers to visual direction. *Aviation, Space and Environmental Medicine,* in press.

Lackner, J., & Graybiel, A. Postural illusions experienced during z-axis recumbent rotation and their dependence upon somatosensory stimulation of the body surface. *Aviation, Space, and Environmental Medicine,* 1978, *49,* 484–488. (a)

Lackner, J., & Graybiel, A. Some influences of touch and pressure cues on human spatial orientation. *Aviation, Space, and Environmental Medicine,* 1978, *49,* 798–804. (b)

Lackner, J., & Graybiel, A. Relationship between slow-phase velocity of optokinetic nystagmus and the visual induction of illusory self-rotation. *Aviation, Space and Environmental Medicine,* in press.

Lackner, J.R., & Graybiel, A. Parabolic flight: Loss of sense orientation. *Science,* 1979, *206,* 1105–1108.

Lackner, J., & Levine, M. Visual direction depends on the operation of spatial constancy mechanisms. *Neuroscience Letters,* 1978, *7,* 207–212.

Lackner, J., & Levine, M. Changes in apparent body orientation and sensory localization induced by vibration of postural muscles: Vibratory myesthetic illusions. *Aviation, Space, and Environmental Medicine,* 1979, *50,* 346–354.

Lackner, J., & Lobovits, D. Adaptation to displaced vision: Evidence for prolonged aftereffects. *Quarterly Journal of Experimental Psychology,* 1977, *29,* 65–69.

Lackner, J., & Lobovits, D. Incremental exposure facilitates adaptation to sensory rearrangement. *Aviation, Space, and Environmental Medicine,* 1978, *49,* 362–364.

Lackner, J.R., & Teixeira, R. Optokinetic motion sickness: Continuous head movements attenuate the visual induction of apparent self-rotation and symptoms of motion sickness. *Aviation, Space, and Environmental Medicine,* 1977, *48,* 248–253.

Lackner, J., & Tuller, B. Role of efference monitoring in the detection of self-produced speech errors. In E.C.T. Walker & W.E. Cooper (Eds.), *Sentence Processing.* Hillsdale, New Jersey: Erlbaum Associates, 1979, pp. 281–294.

Mach, E. Contributions to the analysis of the sensations. Chicago: Open Court Publishing, 1897.

Magnus, R. Korperstellung. Berlin: Springer-Verlag, 1924.

Mather, J., & Lackner, J. Adaptation to visual rearrangement elicited by tonic vibration reflexes. *Experimental Brain Research,* 1975, *24,* 103–105.

Mather, J., & Lackner, J. Sensory factors in adaptation to visual rearrangement. *Quarterly Journal of Experimental Psychology,* 1977, *29,* 237–244.

Mather, J., & Lackner, J. Visual tracking of active and passive movements of the hand. *Quarterly Journal of Experimental Psychology,* 1980, *32,* 307–316. (a)

Mather, J., & Lackner, J. Adaptation to visual rearrangement with active and passive limb movements: Effect of movement frequency and predictability. *Quarterly Journal of Experimental Psychology,* 1980, *32,* 317–324. (b)

Mather, J., & Lackner, J. Adaptation to visual displacement: Contribution of proprioceptive, visual, and attentional factors, 1980, in submission. (c)

Moulden, B. Adaptation to displaced vision: Reafference is a special case of the cue-discrepancy hypothesis. *Quarterly Journal of Experimental Psychology,* 1971, *23,* 113–117.

Skowbo, D., Timney, B., Gentry, T., & Morant, R. McCollough effects: Experimental findings and theoretical accounts. *Psychological Bulletin,* 1975, *82,* 497–510.

Steinbach, M. Eye tracking of self-moved targets: The role of efference. *Journal of Experimental Psychology,* 1969, *83,* 366–376.

Steinbach, M., & Held, R. Eye tracking of observer-generated target movements. *Science,* 1968, *161,* 187–188.

Teixeira, R., & Lackner, J. Influence of apparent head position on optokinetic nystagmus and eye posture. *Experimental Brain Research,* 1976, *24,* 435–440.

Teixeira, R., & Lackner, J.R. Optokinetic motion sickness: Attenuation of visually induced illusory self-rotation by passive head movements. *Aviation, Space, and Environmental Medicine,* 1979, *50,* 264–266.

von Holst, E. Relations between the central nervous system and the peripheral organs. *British Journal of Animal Behaviour,* 1954, *2,* 89–94.

Walk, R., Shepherd, J., & Miller, D. Attention as an alternative to self-induced motion for the perceptual behavior of kittens. *Society for Neuroscience Abstracts,* 1978, *4,* 128, A395.

Wallach, H. Informational discrepancy as a basis of perceptual adaptation. In S. Freedman (Ed.), *The Neuropsychology of spatially oriented behavior.* Homewood, Illinois: Dorsey Press, 1968, pp. 209–229.

Wallach, H. *On perception.* New York: Quadrangle/The New York Times Book Co., 1976.

Wallach, H., & Bacon, J. Two kinds of adaptation in the constancy of visual direction and their different effects on the perception of shape and visual direction. *Perception and Psychophysics,* 1977, *21,* 227–242.

Wallach, H., & Kravitz, J. The measurement of the constancy of visual direction and of its adaptation. *Psychonomic Science,* 1965, *2,* 217–218.

Wallach, H., & Kravitz, J. Adaptation in the constancy of visual direction tested by measuring the constancy of auditory direction. *Perception and Psychophysics,* 1968, *4,* 299–303.

Welch, R. *Perceptual modification: Adapting to altered sensory environments.* New York: Academic Press, 1978.

Yachzel, B., & Lackner, J. Adaptation to displaced vision: Evidence for transfer of adaptation and long-lasting aftereffects. *Perception and Psychophysics,* 1977, *22,* 147–151.

6

Visual-Proprioceptive Interactions

MALCOLM M. COHEN

1. Introduction

1.1. Scope of Chapter

This chapter is intended to present diverse points of view and provocative discussions of selected problems underlying visual-proprioceptive interactions. I do not intend to restrict my descriptions of visual-proprioceptive interactions to the field of experimental psychology alone, nor do I intend to propose a singular and unique explanation of these interactions. Rather, historical, anatomical, neurophysiological, and psychological constructs and data will all be considered. Thus, the chapter will be largely eclectic.

Although broad in scope, the chapter is not comprehensive, nor is it intended to be. I shall not present an exhaustive review of the psychological literature concerning visual-proprioceptive interactions. To those investigators whose extensive research efforts I do not cite, I offer my sincere apologies; my intent is not to slight any of them, nor to suggest that their research is not relevant to the issues discussed.

1.2. Contents of Chapter

Beginning with Sherrington's classical exteroceptive-proprioceptive dichotomy, I shall examine some of the ways in which vision and proprioception may interact, and shall describe in some detail those

MALCOLM M. COHEN • Naval Air Development Center, Warminster, Pennsylvania 18974.

sensory mechanisms that traditionally have been regarded as "proprioceptive." Following this examination, I shall review some of the neurophysiological and conceptual underpinnings of the interactions and briefly present Gibson's alternative approach to the classical views. Next, I shall discuss some of the physiological mechanisms that subserve visual-proprioceptive interactions, particularly as they influence perceived visual direction and orientation. Finally, I shall review some of my own work on visual-proprioceptive interactions, paying particular attention to how these interactions are affected by the unique conditions encountered in the aviation environment.

2.   Classical Views of Proprioception

2.1.   Proprioceptive and Exteroceptive Fields

Nearly three-quarters of a century ago, Sherrington (1906a,b) first proposed the term, "proprio-ceptive field," as a general rubric to categorize those sensory systems that respond to stimulation arising from within the organism. The receptors of the proprioceptive field were considered to be particularly adapted to respond to mechanical forces within the organism, and their excitation to be primarily the result of some action or change in the spatial position of the organism. In contrast, Sherrington proposed the term, "extero-ceptive field," to categorize those sensory systems that respond to stimulation arising from outside the organism. The receptors of the exteroceptive field were regarded as being "rich in number and variety," as well as being exquisitely adapted to respond to the diverse sources of stimulation provided by events in the outside world.

Sherrington's general model is one in which the proprioceptors detect changes in the position of the organism resulting from motor activity, and provide the central nervous system with the particular information it requires to modify and coordinate subsequent motor activity. Thus, according to Sherrington, the functioning of the nervous system is essentially circular, and, to a large extent, spatial orientation, posture, and locomotion are considered to be under the continuous influence of what is currently termed "proprioceptive feedback."

Despite his assertions regarding the circularity of the nervous system and its integrative functioning, Sherrington relegated proprioception to a secondary role in processing information from the outside world. Because Sherrington regarded the initiation of motor activity primarily as a reaction to exteroceptive stimulation, his model required explicit mechanisms by which proprioceptive stimulation could come to influence ongoing motor activity.

The mechanisms he suggested are similar to those involved in descriptions of chained conditioned responses (Guthrie, 1935), as may be seen in Sherrington's (1906b) assertions that:

> Reflexes arising from proprio-ceptive organs come therefore to be habitually attached and appended to certain reflexes excited by extero-ceptive organs. The reaction of the animal to stimulation of one of its extero-ceptors excites certain tissues, and the activity thus produced in these latter tissues excites in them their receptors, which are *proprio-ceptors*. (p. 133)

Thus, Sherrington was able, simultaneously, to dichotomize the sensory nervous system and to preserve its integrative functioning by providing for intersensory interactions between the receptors of the proprioceptive and exteroceptive fields.

As we shall see, Sherrington's understanding of how the nervous system functions, although rather advanced for its time, is quite rudimentary in the light of more recent anatomical observations, neurophysiological findings, behavioral studies, and theoretical concepts. Sherrington was aware of, and attempted to elucidate in detail, the long neural chains involving exteroceptive afference, motor efference, proprioceptive afference, and subsequently modified motor efference, but he was unaware of the more subtle, and probably equally important, mechanisms involving central efferent monitoring (Chang, 1955; Li, 1958) and gamma efference (Granit, 1955); nor was he aware of the behavioral and developmental effects of total spinal deafferentation (Taub & Berman, 1968). Nevertheless, Sherrington's signal contributions to neurophysiology provided the first modern major paradigm for the functioning of the nervous sytem, a paradigm that has altered the course of twentieth-century neurophysiological research.

2.2. Anatomical and Physiological Considerations

Following Sherrington's general framework, the receptors of the proprioceptive field may be conveniently classified under three general groupings: (1) the muscle proprioceptors, (2) the joint and cutaneous proprioceptors, and (3) the labyrinthine proprioceptors. Because the proprioceptors are generally acknowledged to play a crucial role in the perception of spatial orientation and visual direction, as well as in spatially directed motor activity, their structure and function will be examined in the following sections. Throughout this examination, current views will be emphasized rather than Sherrington's earlier, and more limited, conceptions.

2.2.1. Muscle Proprioceptors. Two fundamental types of muscle proprioceptors, neuromuscular spindles and Golgi tendon organs, are incorporated in the gross structure of most striated muscles. The neuromuscular spindles are distributed among the bundles of contractile (extrafusal) fibers, and are essentially stretch receptors that respond to changes in the length of the fibers. As noted by Matthews (1962, 1968), the sensory neurons of the muscle spindles have characteristic rates of firing for specific degrees of stretch (tonic responses), as well as for specific rates of stretch (phasic responses). Although structural details of the neuromuscular spindles vary, they generally consist of fluid-filled capsules containing small intrafusal fibers.

Afferent innervation of the spindles is achieved when they are stimulated mechanically by stretching their intrafusal fibers. In addition to afferent innervation, the intrafusal fibers of the neuromuscular spindles are directly supplied with efferent innervation by small gamma motor neurons. Neural impulses from the gamma motor neurons produce localized contractions of the intrafusal fibers at the ends of the neuromuscular spindles, thereby altering the sensitivity of the spindles to both concurrent and subsequent mechanical stimulation (Granit, 1955; Houk, 1974; Matthews, 1962). Thus, gamma efference is of critical importance in the functioning of the neuromuscular spindles because it provides the spindles with a mechanism that allows them to retain a high degree of sensitivity and precision irrespective of muscle length or load.

The Golgi tendon organs are enclosed in small capsules that blend into the connective tissues at muscle–tendon junctions. Contractions of their muscles distend the tendon-organ capsules and distort fine sprays of unmyelinated nerve fibers within the capsules, thereby initiating afferent neural impulses. Since they are located at muscle–tendon junctions rather than distributed among the bundles of contractile muscle

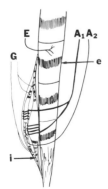

Fig. 1. Schematic representation of neuromuscular spindle. Efferent impulses from the motor nerve (E) cause extrafusal muscle fibers (e) to contract, thereby stretching the intrafusal fibers (i) within the neuromuscular spindle and initiating impulses along the afferent nerves (A_1 and A_2). Impulses from the gamma efferent nerves (G) produce localized contractions of the intrafusal fibers within the spindle, thereby altering the sensitivity of the spindle to subsequent stimulation.

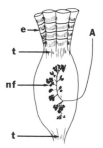

Fig. 2. Schematic representation of Golgi tendon organ. Contractions of the extrafusal muscle fibers (e) distort the nerve fibrils (nf) within the tendon organ, thereby initiating impulses along the afferent nerve (A). The muscle fibers and the tendon organ itself blend into the tendonous fibers (t).

fibers, the Golgi tendon organs are said to be arranged "in series" with the muscle fibers rather than "in parallel," as are the neuromuscular spindles. Due to their anatomical structure and location, and because their rates of firing increase with increased muscle loads for constant degrees of muscle contraction, the Golgi tendon organs appear to function as tension, rather than length, receptors (Henneman, 1974).

Despite the absence of gamma efference (Eldred, 1960), and despite their relative insensitivity to externally imposed stretch, the Golgi tendon organs are extremely sensitive when individual motor units of their respective muscles are electrically stimulated to contract (Henneman, 1974). The combined specificity and sensitivity of the Golgi tendon organs suggest that they are probably activated whenever their respective muscle fibers are contracting and working. Thus, the tendon organs appear to respond to localized tensions within their respective muscles rather than to the gross tensions of entire muscle groups.

Although it has been well established that the extraocular muscles of the human eye contain proprioceptive receptors similar to some of those described above (Bach-y-Rita, 1971; Wolter, 1955), and that these receptors can transmit afferent neural impulses to the brain (Cooper, Daniel, & Whitteridge, 1955), the inductive leap to the conclusion that these proprioceptors subserve the conscious awareness of eye position is probably unfounded. In fact, it is now generally accepted that these proprioceptors do not contribute to the conscious awareness of eye position (Henneman, 1974; Whitteridge, 1960). Nevertheless, it is highly probable that the muscle spindles provide the central nervous system with information used to adjust and to compensate for changes of eye position (Granit, 1971). The failure to distinguish between proprioception as a means of processing information regarding eye position and proprioception as the conscious awareness of that information has resulted in a considerable amount of confusion (Breinin, 1957). This issue will be discussed in greater detail when we examine "inflow" and "outflow" mechanisms for processing information about eye position.

2.2.2. Joint and Cutaneous Proprioceptors. The proprioceptive receptors of the joints, the skin, and the connective tissues vary widely in size, shape, and anatomical complexity. Further, many of them play a dual role, serving both as proprioceptors and exteroceptors. Despite their great anatomical variation and spatial distribution, they are all generally sensitive to pressure or changes in pressure resulting from mechanical distortions of their respective afferent nerve endings.

The joint proprioceptors include Pacinian corpuscles, Golgi–Mazzoni corpuscles, Ruffini spray receptors, and free nerve endings. With the exception of the free nerve endings, the joint proprioceptors consist of various amounts of fibrous tissue that surround either straight or branching afferent nerve endings. The Pacinian corpuscles, with their multiple layers of fibrous tissue, are rapidly adapting receptors found near joints, tendons, and in the deeper layers of the dermis (Geldard, 1972). Depending in part on their location, the Pacinian corpuscles respond to sudden movements of their adjacent joints, to vibration, and to pressure. The Golgi–Mazzoni corpuscles, structurally similar to the Pacinian corpuscles, but generally smaller and with fewer layers of fibrous tissue, are characterized by their widely branching nerve sprays, each supplied by its own afferent neuron. Generally found in close proximity to joint capsules, the Golgi–Mazzoni corpuscles respond to pressures resulting from displacements of their respective joints. The Ruffini spray receptors are found both in joint capsules and in the middle layers of the dermis; they adapt slowly, and are relatively insensitive to sudden movements. Although some investigators maintain that these receptors respond in proportion to the angle of joint displacement (O'Connell & Gardner, 1972), others (Clark, 1975; Grigg & Greenspan, 1977; Kelso, 1978) contend that they are generally activated only when the joints are displaced at or near the limits of their excursions. The free nerve endings are widely distributed around joints and throughout the dermis. In

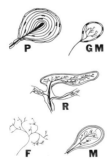

Fig. 3. Joint and cutaneous proprioceptors. Pacinian corpuscles (P), Golgi–Mazzoni corpuscles (GM), Ruffini spray receptors (R), free nerve endings (F), and Meissner corpuscles (M) are among the proprioceptive receptors found in the joints, skin, and connective tissue.

addition to being sensitive to pressure, they also appear to contribute to sensations of pain.

The cutaneous proprioceptors include Pacinian corpuscles, Ruffini spray receptors, and free nerve endings similar to those found near the joints and in connective tissues, as well as Meissner corpuscles. The Meissner corpuscles are encapsulated nerve endings located immediately below the epidermis; they are stimulated both by touch and pressure. Because of their spatial distributions over wide areas of cutaneous tissue, as well as because of the phasic nature of their responses (Eldred, 1960), the cutaneous proprioceptors appear to provide the central nervous system with temporally coded information associated with changes in distributions of pressure that result from changes in body posture and orientation.

An amusing demonstration of the importance of cutaneous proprioceptors in human spatial orientation has been attributed to an early pioneer in aviation medicine, Dr. Hubertus Strughold (1964). As the old adage states, ''Experienced pilots can fly by the seats of their pants.'' In a direct and straightforward attempt to test this assumed property of the nethermost parts, Strughold injected his own posterior with novocaine. When the anesthesia had taken effect, Strughold was carried aboard an aircraft, and served as an observer while the pilot performed a series of slow rolls, loops, and other aerobatic maneuvers. Although Dr. Strughold had acquired several hours of aerobatic flying experience in the course of his earlier studies, and although he had not previously experienced undue discomfort or severe disorientation, he reported that, in this study with his *derriere* anesthetized, he had lost all ability to orient himself.

Other experiments, perhaps less flamboyant and less humorous than Strughold's demonstration, have documented the importance of cutaneous proprioceptors in human spatial orientation (Brown, 1961; Nelson, 1968). In these studies, trained observers were totally immersed in water; with their eyes occluded, they were required to indicate the direction of the gravitational vertical. Under these conditions of total body immersion, the responses of the observers were exceedingly more variable than those obtained under terrestrial conditions. Since the pattern of stimulation to the cutaneous proprioceptors under water differs dramatically from that provided under terrestrial conditions, and since stimulation of the labyrinthine proprioceptors remains unchanged from that provided under terrestrial conditions, the dramatic increase in the variability of the responses can be attributed to the altered pattern of cutaneous stimulation.

2.2.3. Labyrinthine Proprioceptors. The labyrinthine proprioceptors, located in the nonauditory portions of each inner ear, are comprised of two types of highly specialized organs, the semicircular canals and the otolith organs. Collectively, these organs constitute an interactive receptor system, the vestibular system, that aids in the maintenance of equilibrium and posture, serves a crucial role in the perception of motion and spatial orientation, and elicits reflex responses in the extrinsic ocular muscles that help to stabilize the positions of the eyes relative to external space whenever the head is moved (Young, 1974).

Six semicircular canals are arranged in bilateral groupings of three curved tubes that are filled with endolymph, a fluid slightly more viscous than water. Although all three canals in each ear share endolymph in common with a single utricle, the endolymph in each canal constitutes a functionally complete and nearly independent fluidic circuit. The anatomical arrangement of the canals is such that the lateral, or "horizontal," canal slopes downward and backward in a plane forming an angle of approximately 30° with the horizontal plane of the head; the superior canal lies in a plane that is roughly orthogonal to that of the lateral canal, projecting forward and outward at an angle in the range of 35° to 45° from the medial plane of the head; the posterior canal, more or less orthogonal to both of the other canals, projects backward and outward at an angle of 45° to 55° from the medial plane of the head. The bilateral arrangements of the canals are such that the lateral canals in both ears are approximately parallel; the left superior and right posterior canals are roughly parallel, as are the left posterior and right superior canals.

In each of the canals, an enlarged region, the ampulla, houses a gelatinous wedge-shaped structure called the cupula. At its narrow distal end, each cupula tightly seals the ampulla of its semicircular canal, forming a flexible pendulous diaphram. At the base of the cupula, hair cells, the primary receptor elements of the vestibular system, are arranged in an arched epithelial layer termed the crista. Cilia from the hair cells of the crista project into the gelatinous cupula. The cilia are arranged in asymmetrical bundles that typically consist of one large and pliant filamentous hair, the kinocilium, and several smaller clublike hairs, stereocilia, that decrease in length with their distance from the kinocilium. This polarized arrangement of the cilia allows a directional sensi-

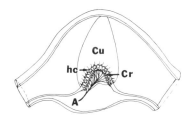

Fig. 4. Diagrammatic cross-section of ampulla of semicircular canal. Angular accelerations of the head cause the endolymph in the canal to displace the cupula (Cu), thereby bending the cilia of hair cells (hc) in the crista (Cr) at the base of the ampulla and altering neural activity of the afferent ampullary nerve (A).

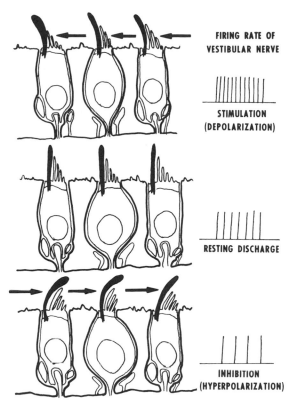

FIRING RATE OF
VESTIBULAR NERVE

STIMULATION
(DEPOLARIZATION)

RESTING DISCHARGE

INHIBITION
(HYPERPOLARIZATION)

Fig. 5. Schematic representation of hair-cell functioning. Stimulation of the hair cells is achieved by shearing forces that bend the stereocilia toward the kinocilium; inhibition results when shearing forces are directed in the opposite direction.

tivity in receptor response that depends on the orientation of the cells in the crista (Lowenstein & Wersall, 1959).

Forces that bend the stereocilia toward the kinocilium result in a depolarization of the hair cell and an increased firing rate of the vestibular nerve; forces that bend the stereocilia away from the kinocilium result in a hyperpolarization of the hair cell and a decreased firing rate of the vestibular nerve (Harris & Milne, 1966; Wersall, Gleisner, & Lundquist, 1967). In the cristae of the horizontal semicircular canals, all the hair cells are oriented with their kinocilia directed toward the utricle; in the cristae of the superior and posterior semicircular canals, all the hair cells are oriented with their kinocilia directed away from the utricle (Spoendlin, 1966).

According to classical theory, the adequate stimulus for the receptors of the semicircular canals is an angular acceleration of the head that has components acting in the plane of any canal. Because of its inertia, the endolymph in the canal initially lags behind the motion of the head, resulting in a temporary increase of fluidic pressure applied against the side of the cupula, thereby bending the cupula at its flexible distal end away from the direction in which the head is moved. Since the cilia of the hair cells in the crista project into the cupula, the bending of the cupula applies shearing forces to the cilia that, depending on their orientations, result in a depolarization or a hyperpolarization of the cells. These differences in polarization potentials of the hair cells result in differences in the rates of firing of the vestibular nerve (Lowenstein & Sand, 1940; Lowenstein & Wersall, 1959). When the angular acceleration of the head is terminated, elastic restoring forces within the cupula return it to its initial resting position, shearing forces cease to be applied to the hair cells, and the firing rate of the vestibular nerve eventually returns to its resting level (Dohlman, 1935; Steinhausen, 1931; Young, 1974).

Under appropriate conditions, stimulation of each semicircular canal results in binocular movements of the eyes that are exquisitely tuned to the motions of the head. For example, if an angular acceleration is applied that rotates the head to the right, both eyes move slowly to the left (slow-phase nystagmus), as though the eyes were attempting to maintain their direction in external space. The slow movements are immediately followed by rapid conjugate movements (quick-phase nystagmus) to the right, as though the eyes were attempting to acquire a new visual target upon which to fixate.

Depending on the specific semicircular canals stimulated, vestibular nystagmus can be elicited in a horizontal, vertical, or torsional direction. Thus, it appears that vestibular nystagmus represents an attempt to maintain a stationary image on the retina despite externally imposed motions of the head. Although the slow-phase vestibular nystagmus is by itself insufficient to compensate for externally imposed movements in the absence of visual targets, it is generally sufficient when coupled with optokinetic nystagmus in the presence of visual targets (Dodge, 1923; Wendt, 1936). With externally imposed movements, the vestibular component appears to serve as a trigger for the nystagmus, while the optokinetic component appears to provide enhanced precision regarding the magnitude of the nystagmus.

In summary, the semicircular canals may be viewed as highly specialized, fluid-coupled, angular accelerometers. Because of viscous damping of the endolymph in the canals, because of elastic restoring forces within the cupula, and because of the intricate morphology and neurological connections of the receptive elements, the semicircular canals are uniquely suited to cooperate in providing oculomotor responses that are well matched to the angular accelerations and velocities encountered in the natural terrestrial environment.

The other major receptive organs of the vestibular system, the otolith organs, may be viewed as linear accelerometers. Comprised of two pairs of eliptical sacs, the utricle and the saccule, the otolith organs contain hair cells that are virtually identical to those found in the semicircular canals; these hair cells are arranged in epithelial layers called maculae. The utricle, the larger of the otolith organs, lies in the upper portion of the nonauditory labyrinth and shares endolymph with the three semicircular canals through a series of openings in its walls. Lying slightly inferior, and connected to the utricle by a small endolymphatic duct, is the saccule (Hardy, 1934).

Although slightly curved like a cupped hand, the utricular macula slopes downward from its anterior wall at an angle of approximately 30° from the horizontal plane of the head (Corvera, Hallpike, & Schuster, 1958). The saccular macula, anatomically similar to that of the utricle, is located on its lateral wall; the nearly vertical macular surface lies in a plane that is directed forward and outward from the midline at an angle of about 10° (Larson, 1973; Spoendlin, 1966).

Both the utricular and saccular maculae are covered by a gelatinous mass that contains particles of calcium carbonate (otoconia). Since the gelatinous mass and its otoconia are more dense than the surrounding endolymph (Engstrom, 1968), changes in the direction of gravity as well as linear accelerations of the head shift the position of the mass relative to the macular surface. Because cilia from the hair cells of the utricular and the saccular maculae project into their respective gelatinous masses, shifts in the positions of these masses relative to their macular surfaces apply shearing forces to the cilia.

In both the utricular and saccular maculae, the cilia of the hair cells are arranged in asymmetrical bundles, as were the cilia of the hair cells in the cristae of the semicircular canals. Although the stereocilia and kinocilia are uniformly polarized over relatively large segments of the

Fig. 6. Morphological polarization patterns of right utricle. A boundary (b), originating at the upward-sloping anterior (a) section of the macular surface of the utricle (MSU), sweeping laterally (l) and curving back toward the medial (m) posterior (p) sections, separates the hair cells (hc) according to the orientations of their kinocilia (k). As shown in the insert, the kinocilia of hair cells on either side of the boundary stand in direct opposition to one another.

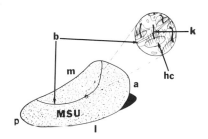

macular surfaces, the direction of polarization systematically changes. In the utricular maculae, the direction of polarization gradually spreads outward like a fan from the medial and anterior portion to a curved boundary, beyond which the polarization of the cilia is suddenly reversed; the kinocilia on either side of the boundary stand in direct opposition to one another (Spoendlin, 1965). Similarly, in the saccular maculae the pattern of polarization undergoes a sudden reversal at a curved boundary that runs from the anterior superior section to the posterior inferior section, but unlike the utricular maculae, the kinocilia of hair cells on either side of the boundary are directed away from one another, with the shorter stereocilia in direct opposition (Spoendlin, 1965).

Polarization patterns in the utricular and saccular maculae have effects that are similar to the polarization patterns of the hair cells in the cristae of the semicircular canals: Bending the stereocilia toward the kinocilium results in a depolarization of the hair cell and an increase in the firing rate of the vestibular nerve; bending the stereocilia away from the kinocilium results in a hyperpolarization of the hair cell and a decrease in the firing rate of the nerve.

Localized stimulation of either the utricular or saccular macula in specific regions elicits well-defined reflex displacements of the eyes that clearly depend on the particular region stimulated (Fluur & Mellstrom, 1970a,b). Further, natural stimulation of the otolith organs by linear acceleration results in directionally specific reflex eye movements. If the body is accelerated forward or upward, vertical eye movements in a downward direction are elicited; linear accelerations backward or downward elicit vertical eye movements upward; accelerations to the right result in eye movements to the left that are coupled with a clockwise rotation; accelerations to the left produce eye movements to the right that are coupled with a counterclockwise rotation (Fluur, 1970).

Subjects are typically unaware of the reflex eye movements elicited by linear accelerations, and the perceptual implications of these eye movements in determining the locations of visually perceived objects are profound. This issue will be discussed in greater detail when we examine some of the illusions encountered in the aviation environment.

Throughout the preceding descriptions of the labyrinthine proprioceptors, the semicircular canals have been characterized as pure angular accelerometers, and the otolith organs have been characterized as pure linear accelerometers. This classical separation of functions, although adequate as a first approximation, probably represents an oversimplication of the relevant facts (Benson, 1974; Lowenstein, 1974). Despite the exquisite sensitivity of the semicircular canals to angular accelerations, and despite the structural adaptation of the otolith organs to respond to linear accelerations, it is quite likely that both types of receptor organs are affected by both types of accelerations (Young, 1974). In view of these considerations, and with the further awareness that natural body movements in the real world generally involve both linear and angular accelerations presented simultaneously, it is perhaps more realistic to regard the semicircular canals and the otolith organs as interacting components of a highly complex receptor system that have both specialized and overlapping functions. The complete separation of functions and the total stimulus specificity implied by the classical model appear to be unwarranted.

Before concluding this section on the labyrinthine proprioceptors, an additional issue should be discussed. As shown by electron microscopy, the cristae of the semicircular canals and the maculae of the otolith organs contain two basic morphological types of hair cells (Wersall, 1956). Distributed most abundantly near the peak of the arched cristae and throughout the maculae, flask-shaped Type I hair cells are surrounded by an afferent nerve chalice formed from the dendritic endings of bipolar vestibular ganglion cells; synapses near the rounded bases of these cells apparently provide them with efferent innervation as well. The Type II hair cells are structurally more simple than those of Type I; they are roughly cylindrical in shape, and appear to receive both afferent and efferent innervation from individual nerve terminals near the base of each cell (Ades & Engstrom, 1965; Petroff, 1955; Wersall *et al.*, 1967). Ades & Engstrom have also identified some intermediate types of hair cells that share specific characteristics of the two basic types. To date, no clear-cut functional significance has been determined for the morphological differences described above.

It is extremely appealing to believe that efferent innervation to the hair cells plays a role similar to that of the gamma efference to the neuromuscular spindles. Although this role remains a definite possiblity, the full complexity and functional significance of efferent innervation to the hair cells are just now beginning to be understood (Precht, 1974; Precht, Llinas, & Clarke, 1971). For example, stimulation resulting from head movements changes the sensitivity of the labyrinthine receptors via

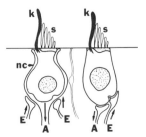

Fig. 7. Schematic representation of innervation of hair cells. At the left, a Type I hair cell is shown with its afferent (A) and efferent (E) innervation. Note the afferent nerve chalice (nc) surrounding the cell body and the efferent nerve endings at the base of the cell. At the right, a Type II hair cell is shown with its afferent and efferent nerve endings at the base. In both types of hair cells, forces that bend the stereocilia (s) and kinocilia (k) result in changes in firing rate of the afferent nerves.

their efferent connections, and while these changes in sensitivity might initially appear to be due to vestibular-proprioceptive feedback, the efferent impulses have been shown to precede the head movements themselves (Precht, 1974). Thus, it would appear that central efferent programs, rather than vestibular-proprioceptive feedback, subserve the changes in sensitivity.

2.3. Cooperative Functioning of Proprioceptive and Visual Receptors

As we have seen, the individual functioning of muscle, joint and skin, and labyrinthine proprioceptors allows the organism to determine the relative lengths and tensions of its muscles, the relative positions of its body joints, the differential pressures associated with various positions of its body relative to hard surfaces with which it is in contact, and the angular and linear accelerations undergone when its head is moved. The collaborative functioning of these receptors is such that it provides a substrate upon which exteroceptive stimulation impinges, and against which exteroceptive stimulation can be evaluated. The proprioceptive substrate itself is quite complex, involving both parallel and hierarchical integrations of the various inputs (Roberts, 1967, 1973, 1975; Sherrington, 1906a,b, 1918). For example, although labyrinthine proprioceptors provide information concerning the orientation of the head relative to gravitational-inertial space, muscle and joint proprioceptors in the neck are critical for specifying the orientation of the head relative to the trunk. Destruction of the labyrinthine proprioceptors causes serious disturbances in locomotion and spatially directed responding (Carpenter, Fabrega, & Glinsmann, 1959), but even when the labyrinthine proprioceptors remain completely intact, anomalies in the region of the neck such as muscle lesions, surgical deafferentation, or naturally occurring inflammatory processes seriously disrupt spatially directed behavior (L.A. Cohen, 1961; Cope & Ryan, 1959; Gray, 1956). Thus, to a very large extent, normal spatially directed behavior depends on the cooperative functioning of both the labyrinthine proprioceptors and the muscle and joint proprioceptors in the neck.

With our current understanding of visual sensory processes, it is little more than a platitude to assert that the visual perception of external objects requires adequate stimulation of the retinal receptors. Light emitted by or reflected from external objects traverses the space between the objects and the perceiver, passes through the lenses and humors of the eyes, strikes the photoreceptors of the retinae, and initiates a chain of neurochemical and neurological events that ultimately result in the detection and identification of the objects. The spatial locations assigned to these visually perceived objects, however, are not determined by retinal stimulation alone. Information concerning the loci of retinal activity, the positions of the eyes in their sockets, the position of the head with respect to the trunk, the position of the trunk relative to the lower torso, and the orientation of the entire body must be processed and integrated; only then can the spatial locations and the visual directions of external objects begin to be specified.

Clearly, the spatial localization of visually perceived objects requires the concurrent processing of proprioceptive information regarding the position and orientation of the perceiving organism. Further, this information must be combined and integrated with information arising from retinal stimulation. Thus, we may regard the perception of spatial location and visual direction as depending critically on processes that involve intersensory interaction and intersensory integration.

3.   Modern Views of Proprioception

3.1.   Historical Perspective

The sharp separation of sensory systems into exteroceptive and proprioceptive fields suggested by Sherrington (1906a) rests on an underlying assumption regarding the nature of the nervous system, the classical doctrine of specific nerve energies (Muller, 1838/1966). This doctrine asserts that each sensory system is subserved by a group of specialized receptors that excite their respective sensory nerves and project along particular afferent neural pathways to their unique centers in the brain (Bell, 1811/1966; Muller, 1838/1966). Except for their capacities to activate specific receptors and sensory nerves, the physical characteristics of the stimulus are considered to be of only secondary importance. Thus, according to this view, the separation of sensory qualities on the basis of specific nerves and their unique central projections appears to be quite reasonable.

From the perspective of the doctrine of specific nerve energies, proprioception may be regarded merely as the result of stimulation that affects "proprioceptive" centers in the brain, much as vision or audition may be regarded as the result of stimulation that affects "visual" or "auditory" centers. It follows that the senses in general may be regarded as discrete entities that derive their unique sensory qualities from the activation of specific neural centers in the brain. To bridge the gap between the discrete nature of the senses and a perceptual world comprised of multisensory real objects, the concept of intersensory interaction has been evolved. If we employ this concept, the senses can retain their discrete qualities, and the perceptual world can be regarded as resulting from the interactions and integrations of these qualities by additional processing in the central nervous system.

As noted previously, proprioceptive stimulation provides the substrate upon which exteroceptive stimulation impinges, and against which exteroceptive stimulation is evaluated. Further, the proprioceptive substrate itself is altered by exteroceptive stimulation. Conceptualizations such as the Sensory-Tonic Field Theory (Werner & Wapner, 1949, 1952) represent an early and pionneering attempt to account for these complex interrelationships. Perhaps because of its great generality, the Sensory-Tonic Field Theory has not been adopted by most psychologists interested in perception, but its acknowledgment of the cooperative, interdependent, and bidirectional nature of organismic state and environmental stimulation in determining perception represents an important advance in our understanding of intersensory interactions.

The classical views of sensory functioning generally regard the stimulus as an isolated and abstract construct; the "stimulus" is stripped of much of the information that could be provided by its unique physical characteristics. As a result, classical views of sensory functioning tend to remove the problem of "objectification" from sensory processing and assign this role to higher neural centers in the brain. In contrast, neurophysiological evidence provided by Hubel and Wiesel (1959, 1960, 1968) indicates that specific cells in the visual cortex respond only when particular patterns and shapes are projected to the retina; similarly, other cells respond only when particular orientations of linear stimulus objects are presented. Thus, considerable processing of stimulus characteristics must occur before the neural impulses arrive at the visual cortex, and, at least as far as vision is concerned, there is extensive intrasensory interaction that takes place at these earlier and more "sensory" stages.

Whether or not similar early processing takes place with respect to intersensory functioning is largely a matter of speculation. Although higher neural centers undoubtedly integrate information from exteroceptive and proprioceptive sensory channels, certain characteristics of the exteroceptors themselves can be directly altered by proprioceptive stimulation. For example, changes in the positions of the eyes have been shown to result from stimulation of the vestibular proprioceptors (Fluur, 1970; Fluur & Mellstrom, 1970a,b). These changes in eye position have definite visual consequences, since the perceived positions and orientations of seen objects are altered (Brandt & Fluur, 1967; Graybiel, 1952). Further, voluntary changes in eye and head position have been shown to alter the relationships between patterns of retinal stimulation and the apparent orientations of seen objects (Sherrington, 1918). Thus, intersensory interactions probably can occur at multiple neurological levels.

3.2. Contemporary Views

In reexamining the doctrine of specific nerve energies, Gibson (1966) has asserted that stimulation is by far more complex and rich in information than the classical views of a "stimulus" would permit. He has noted that stimulation from the environment under natural conditions does not impinge on single isolated receptor cells, but that entire populations of receptors and entire perceptual systems are affected, generally in highly complex patterns. Further, more than one sensory system is usually affected. We perceive multisensory objects, not stimuli.

For Gibson, the implied primacy of exteroception, the sharp separation of sensory systems into exteroceptive and proprioceptive fields, and indeed the entire characterization of proprioception according to the classical views derived from the doctrine of specific nerve energies are totally unacceptable. In noting that the classical exteroceptors of the eyes and the ears can register changes in the position of the organism as well as changes in the external world, Gibson has asserted that the detection of changes in body position or body movements need not depend on the activities of specialized proprioceptive organs or receptors. For example, Gibson noted that the eyes are highly sensitive to directional changes in the loci of retinal stimulation and to flow patterns on the retinae that accompany movements of the head. Conversely, externally imposed movements of the organism as well as self-initiated movements can be detected by proprioceptive receptors. As sentient organisms, we interact with our environment rather than being merely passive recipients of stimulation. Thus, the entire exteroception–proprioception dichotomy is called into question.

As a result of his analysis, Gibson has recast the problem of exteroceptive-proprioceptive interaction into more functional terms, and has asserted that:

> Proprioception considered as the obtaining of information about one's own action does not necessarily depend on proprioceptors, and exteroception considered as the obtaining of information about extrinsic events does not necessarily depend on exteroceptors. (p. 34)

The notion of independent and pure exteroceptive and proprioceptive fields is abandoned, and the major problem becomes one of exhaustively defining the entire array of stimulation, irrespective of the particular receptors involved. From a programmatic perspective, intersensory interaction is redefined in functional terms.

Whether we accept the classical exteroception–proprioception dichotomy proposed by Sherrington or Gibson's more functional description with its denial of the dichotomy and the increased importance of stimulus complexity in determining perception, the basic issues of inter-sensory interaction and intersensory integration nevertheless remain. Although the terms used to describe underlying relationships among sensory systems are altered, the precise nature, locus, and perceptual significance of the relationships must still be specified.

4. Mechanisms Subserving Visual Direction and Orientation

4.1. Background

It has long been recognized that the apparent directions and orien-tations of visually presented objects depend on both retinal and extra-retinal mechanisms; these mechanisms involve both patterns and loca-tions of retinal activity as well as the orientations of the eyes in their sockets. Early accounts of retinal and extraretinal components in visual space perception date at least as far back as Aristotle, who described the diplopia that results when binocular fusion is disrupted by depressing one eye with a finger while viewing an external object with both eyes (Ross, 1955). A single object appears to be located in two places simultaneously, giving the impression that two objects are present. This observation was correctly analyzed and interpreted by Smith (1738/1978), who suggested that the double image resulted from a displacement of the optic axis of the depressed eye, leading to noncorresponding stimulation of the two retinae. Both Bell and von Helmholtz repeated the above observation, and the role of eye position in influencing the apparent spatial locations of visually presented objects has been well acepted ever since their reports (Bell, 1803; von Helmholtz, 1866/1963).

Nevertheless, the precise mechanisms by which eye position influ-ences perceived visual direction have not been unequivocally determined to this day. Two explanations, based on *inflow* and *outflow,* respectively, have been vigorously debated for several years. The inflow theory maintains that afferent signals, probably from stretch receptors in the eye muscles, directly provide information concerning the positions of the eyes in their sockets; whereas the outflow theory asserts that information concerning the positions of the eyes in their sockets results from central-nervous-system monitoring of efferent impulses to the extrinsic eye muscles.

4.2. Inflow Mechanisms

The inflow theory has generally been attributed to Sherrington (1918), who speculated that muscle spindles in the extrinsic eye muscles provided information used in the perception of visual direction and orientation. Sherrington noted that three small spots, separated by a fixed distance and placed along a vertical axis in line with an observer's medial plane, remain in an apparently vertical orientation even when the spots are viewed from a different position and no longer lie in the observer's medial plane. Under these latter conditions, the image on the retina is no longer the same as when the spots were in the medial plane, but the spots are nevertheless still perceived as being vertical. Further, afterimages of targets fixated in different positions, each initially perceived as vertical, will intersect with currently perceived targets that are also regarded as being vertical. Different retinal images are assigned the same perceptual quality of being vertical. Thus, the orientations assigned to the retinal images must be altered with differing positions of the eyes and the head.

Sherrington, a physiologist by training, noted the perceptual effects described above, and stated that: "What we might suppose at first acceptance to be a purely visual perception is, in fact, the result of a fusion of retinal sensation with eye-muscle posture-sensation" (1918, p. 335). In citing the then recent findings of de Kleyn (1918), Sherrington suggested that changes in neck posture produce changes in the positions of the eyeballs, and that these positional changes play an important role in the determination of visual spatial perceptions.

It is perhaps unfortunate that the term "sensation" was employed by Sherrington to describe these intersensory effects, for the use of the term initiated a long series of experimental studies devoted to determining how accurately the changes in eye position could be "sensed." Thus, the problem was shifted from a determination of proprioceptive contributions to the spatial localization and orientation of visually presented objects to a determination of the conscious awareness and ability to control the positions of the eyes in their sockets, often in the absence of visual stimulation. Confusion has resulted from this shift in emphasis, because the processing of information regarding eye position as it affects "visual" perceptions is quite a different problem from that involving the conscious awareness of eye position itself. Proprioceptive information regarding eye position may very well influence the perceived locations and orientations of seen objects without being directly available to consciousness.

4.3. Outflow Mechanisms

The outflow theory has been ascribed to von Helmholtz (1866/1963), although Bell (1803) probably deserves most of the credit (cf. Wade, 1978). In his handbook of physiological optics, von Helmholtz (1866/1963) described a series of relatively straightforward observations that, when considered collectively, provide support for an outflow explanation of extraretinal contributions to perceived visual direction. The observations are summarized as follows:

1. Moving one eye by depressing it with a finger while viewing an object with both eyes causes a double image of the binocularly viewed object.

2. Depressing the eye when an object is viewed monocularly through that eye causes the object to appear to move.

3. Visual afterimages appear to remain stationary when the eye is similarly depressed.

4. Visual afterimages appear to move when the position of the eye is altered by natural contractions of the extrinsic eye muscles, as when the direction of the gaze is altered.

Based on the above observations, von Helmholtz concluded that:

> Thus, our judgment as to the direction of the visual axis is not formed either by the actual position of the eyeball or by the actual elongation or contraction of the ocular muscles that is the result of this position. (p. 245)

In addition, von Helmholtz strengthened his conclusion with an observation that patients with paralyzed eye muscles report that visually presented objects appear to move when the patients attempt to shift their direction of gaze, despite the fact that the eyes themselves do not move. Thus, he asserted that:

> These phenomena prove conclusively that our judgments as to the direction of the visual axis are simply the result of the effort of will involved in trying to alter the adjustment of the eyes. (p. 245)

Bruell and Albee (1955) employed the observations of von Helmholtz as a point of departure to develop a motor theory of visual egocentric localization. By assuming each retinal locus to have a space value or local sign associated with it for an initial orientation of the eyes in their sockets, Bruell and Albee suggested that the space value is systematically changed for each voluntary movement of the eyes so that a given angular shift in eye position results in a corresponding shift in the space value assigned to the retinal receptors. The net effect is one of position constancy whenever the direction of the gaze is voluntarily altered.

When the position of the eye is altered by externally applied forces or by nonvoluntary reflex responses such as the postrotary nystagmus that follows intense vestibular stimulation, the space values assigned to the retinal receptors remain unchanged, and visually perceived objects appear to move. The apparent movements of visually presented objects, resulting from the failure of externally applied forces or involuntary reflex responses to change the space values of retinal receptors, argue against an inflow interpretation. Thus, Bruell and Albee strongly imply that the space values assigned to the retinal receptors are determined by voluntary motor commands, or outflow.

4.4. Possible Hybrid Mechanisms

A general theoretical framework for a hybrid mechanism that would allow both inflow and outflow to play a role in the determination of perceived visual direction may be derived from the "reafference principle" developed by von Holst (1954) and elaborated upon by Teuber (1960). According to this view, efferent signals from higher neural centers provide corollary discharges, or efferent copies, to lower neural centers as well as initiating contractions of the extraocular muscles. Afferent signals from the eyes that result from the self-initiated movements of the eyes are fed back to the lower neural centers; these signals are termed "reafferent" because they are contingent upon immediately preceding efferent signals rather than upon extrinsic events. When the reafferent signals "match" the corollary discharges at the lower neural centers, the higher neural centers are signaled that the intended movement of the eyes has been completed, and efferent signals to the extraocular muscles are terminated. For voluntary self-initiated movements of the eyes, equivalence of the corollary discharge, or efferent copy, with the reafferent feedback allows the organism to distinguish between movements of the eyes and movements of external objects in the visual field. Thus, both central monitoring of efferent impulses and reafferent feedback resulting from the efferent impulses could play a synergistic role in the control and perceptual effects of eye movements.

Two distinct components of reafferent feedback are potentially available from movements of the eyes: (1) retinal components, consisting of both transformations and changes in the locus of stimulation as the image of a seen object moves across the retina, and (2) extraretinal components, consisting of changes in the firing rates from muscle spindles in extraocular muscles. Matin (1976) has suggested that the strongest support for an outflow interpretation of extraretinal components in visual space perception derives from the paralyzed-eye observation reported by von Helmholtz in 1866. Because the paralyzed eye does not move, it had been presumed that changes in activity of the muscle spindles could not be responsible for the apparent movements of objects in the visual field. However, as noted previously in this chapter, two distinct and different sources can modify the afferent signals from the muscle spindles: (1) changes in the lengths of the intrafusal fibers of the spindles when their parallel extrafusal muscle fibers stretch or contract, and (2) changes in gamma motor efference to the spindles that directly produce contractions of their intrafusal fibers.

Thus, Matin suggested that, although the extrafusal fibers of the eye muscles were paralyzed, the intrafusal fibers could have remained active. A possible consequence of this assumed condition is that a self-initiated voluntary attempt to move a paralyzed eye could, by means of gamma efference, contract the intrafusal fibers of muscle spindles in the agonist muscles. This consequence could modify the afferent signals from the muscle spindles in the agonist muscles relative to those from the muscle spindles in the antagonist muscles, thereby resulting in a directionally biased extraretinal signal that changes the relationship between perceived visual direction and retinal locus. Thus, a change in space values or retinal local signs could result from a mechanism such as that proposed.

Central efferent monitoring of voluntary motor commands need not be the exclusive mechanism underlying extraretinal contributions to perceived visual direction, but changes in afferent discharge from the muscle spindles due to altered gamma efference may play a crucial role. As with many other "either-or" formulations, the issue of inflow vs. outflow may have been stated in too simplistic a manner, and Matin's suggestion that both mechanisms might play contributory roles should be considered seriously.

From the perspective of Matin's suggestion, it may be conjectured that the "effort of will" invoked by von Helmholtz is directly reflected by gamma efference. According to this conjecture, when the paralyzed eye is "willed" to move, gamma efference changes the response of the muscle spindles, thereby resulting in a change of space values or retinal local signs; visually presented objects appear to move, although their images on the retina do not. When the "will" is not involved, as with involuntary or externally imposed eye movements, it is conjectured that gamma efference is either inappropriate or absent; under these conditions, movements of images on the retina are perceived as movements of objects in the external world. When the "will" is involved, as with voluntary eye movements under natural conditions, gamma efference to the muscle spindles is appropriate, and spatial position constancy is maintained. Although the relevant experimental studies examining these conjectures have not yet been conducted, their results could be important in helping to resolve critical problems in the understanding of perceived visual direction and position constancy.

5. Experimental Modification of Visual-Proprioceptive Relationships

5.1. Methodological Considerations

The relationships between visual and proprioceptive stimulation tend to be consistent in the terrestrial environment. Our senses provide us with coherent and integrated information from the external world, and our expectations of extrinsic events are usually confirmed. Spatial position constancy is the rule rather than the exception, and veridical perceptions of the external world are the typical result. We can readily distinguish the motions of our own body from motions of objects in the external world, and we seldom experience undue difficulty in coordination when we move about our environment; we function effectively as spatially responding organisms.

Anomalous conditions within the organism such as muscle paralysis, cervical diseases, nerve lesions, vestibular infections, etc., often can alter the relationships between visual and proprioceptive stimulation. Under these anomalous organismic conditions, spatial position constancy frequently breaks down, perceptual illusions commonly result, our expectations of extrinsic events are often incorrect, and we generally experience serious difficulties in coordination and locomotion. Although the relationships between visual and proprioceptive stimulation differ from those under normal conditions, and although the anomalous conditions give rise to altered perceptual effects, the basic mechanisms and principles underlying these effects remain essentially unchanged. It is largely through careful observation of the changes in perceptual functioning under anomalous conditions that we have achieved an understanding of the physiological mechanisms and principles that subserve perceptual functioning. Both normal and abnormal functioning are governed by the same rules; they differ only because of the special conditions under which the rules manifest themselves (Bernard, 1865).

Although anomalous conditions within the organism similar to those described previously can be produced experimentally by surgical interventions such as deafferentation, extirpation, and ablation, alternative nonsurgical and noninvasive methods are also available. These alternative methods, including sensory deprivation, sensory rearrangement, and systematic alteration of the physical environment, share the requirement that the organism function under atypical conditions (Held, 1961, 1968; Held & Bossom, 1961; Held & Hein, 1963; Ross, 1971). Thus, rather than examining the perceptual functioning of an anomalous organism in a normal environment, the alternative methods allow us to examine the perceptual functioning of a normal organism in an anomalous environment. Again, the same rules govern both normal and abnormal functioning, but the conditions under which the rules operate are changed. The perceptual effects of employing some of these techniques have been discussed in this volume (cf. Lackner's chapter) and elsewhere (Kornheiser, 1976; Pick & Hay, 1966; Rock, 1966; Ross, 1975; Welch, 1978).

Conceptually, the alternative methods rely on specific invariances between parameters of stimulation and parameters of perceptual functioning. The logic is straightforward: If a given parameter of stimulation is altered without altering a given parameter of perceptual functioning, then that stimulus parameter, over the range of its alteration, is irrelevant to the parameter of perceptual functioning under investigation; if alteration of a given stimulus parameter does alter a given parameter of perceptual functioning, then that stimulus parameter is relevant to the parameter of perceptual functioning under investigation. For example, either immersing a subject in water (Ross, 1971; Ross & Lennie, 1968) or requiring a subject to view external objects through prisms (Kohler, 1951/1964, 1962) generally changes the apparent visual locations of seen objects and results in a loss of visual position constancy when the subject moves his head. Both of these conditions, by altering the refractive medium through which light from the external object must pass before it arrives at the retina, change the direction from which the light strikes the retina, and thereby necessitate a change in the position of the eye to maintain foveal vision. Because the perceived location of an external object is altered under these conditions, we may conclude that the direction from which light is projected to the retina serves as a stimulus parameter for visual location. Further, head movements under both of these conditions produce differences in the thickness of the refractive medium through which the light must pass, thereby systematically changing the direction from which light strikes the retina during the head movements. Compensatory eye movements that formerly were associated with given head movements under natural conditions are no longer appropriate to maintain foveal vision, and apparent movements of objects in the visual field are the result. Because visual position constancy is lost during head movements under these conditions, we may conclude that systematic changes in the direction from which light is projected to the retina serve as a stimulus parameter for visual position constancy during head movements, and that alterations of these systematic changes are responsible for the loss of visual position constancy.

5.2. Visual and Proprioceptive Illusions in Altered Gravitational-Inertial Fields

One of the critical environmental parameters underlying visual-proprioceptive interactions is the gravitational-inertial field in which the organism is required to function. Changes of the gravitational-inertial field produced by acceleration result in altered stimulation to the muscle and cutaneous proprioceptors, as well as to the otolith organs of the vestibular system.

For example, consider a man in a zero-gravity environment such as that encountered in an orbiting spacecraft. His tonic muscular contractions are inappropriate, and there is a strong tendency for his arm to elevate spontaneously and involuntarily; the muscular activity that was formerly employed to overcome the terrestrial force of gravity is now superfluous. His Golgi tendon organs register reduced tensions in the muscles that formerly supported his weight in the terrestrial environment; because he is weightless, the tensions in his muscles now result primarily from muscular contractions that are opposed by counteracting forces. His cutaneous proprioceptors are no longer stimulated by the constant pressures that result from the weight of his body; because he is weightless, their stimulation now results most frequently from body movements that bring about contacts with external surfaces. Because the otoconia of his otolith organs are weightless, the otolith organs no longer indicate the orientation of his head relative to a reference gravitational-inertial field; in the zero-gravity environment, no reference field is present, and, except for efferent neural stimulation of the hair cells, the otolith organs are now stimulated by accelerations and decelerations of his head whenever it is moved.

Next, consider a man in a hypergravity environment such as that encountered in a human centrifuge, an aircraft recovering from a dive, or a spacecraft during launch into orbit. His arms are pulled sharply downward as his body musculature strains under the increased load; because the muscular activity formerly employed to overcome the terrestrial force of gravity is now inadequate, increased activity is required. His Golgi tendon organs register increased tensions in the muscles that support the weight of his body; because the weight of his body is now increased, additional tensions are produced in the antigravity muscles. His cutaneous proprioceptors are now stimulated by increased pressures resulting from the increased weight of his body; because his weight is increased, changes in pressures and deformations of the cutaneous proprioceptors that result from body movements are likewise increased. The increased weight of the otoconia in his otolith organs produces increased shearing forces against the hair cells; because the shearing forces are increased, a given change in the orientation of his head provides a greater change in stimulation to his otolith organs than under terrestrial conditions.

As a result of altered stimulation to the otolith organs, the natural resting position of the eyes is altered, and motor impulses to the extrinsic eye muscles required to maintain foveal vision are altered as well. In a zero-gravity environment, visually perceived objects appear to be below their true physical positions; in a hypergravity environment, visually perceived objects appear to be above their true physical positions (M.M. Cohen, 1973; Niven, Whiteside, & Graybiel, 1963; Roman, Warren, Niven, & Graybiel, 1963; Schone, 1964; Whiteside, 1961). Without a visual target upon which to fixate, the eyes tend to rotate upward in a zero-gravity environment, and downward in a hypergravity environment (Fluur, 1970; Gerathewohl, 1952).

It should be noted that individuals exposed to these unusual environmental conditions are typically unaware of any changes in the resting positions of their eyes that result from the altered stimulation to their otolith organs. It is quite likely that visual fixation reflexes that compensate for displacement from the natural resting positions of the eyes and maintain foveal vision are responsible for the changes in the apparent locations of visually perceived objects described above. For example, without the visual fixation reflexes, the eyes would be displaced downward in a hypergravity environment due to the increased stimulation of the otolith organs. Motor outputs previously associated with an upward direction of the gaze would result from the visual fixation reflexes employed to maintain foveal vision. Thus, if the otolith-oculomotor reflexes responsible for the downward rotation of the eyes in the hypergravity environment do not provide a change in the space values associated with the locus of retinal stimulation, but the upward visual fixation reflexes do yield a change in space values, there need be no net change in the actual positions of the eyes to produce displacements in the apparent locations of visually perceived objects.

5.2.1. The Elevator Illusion. Changes in the apparent locations of visually perceived objects that result from exposure to altered gravitational-inertial forces have been shown to depend on two distinct parameters of the forces: (1) their magnitude, and (2) their direction.[1]

As we have noted, stationary visible objects appear to rise when gravitational-inertial forces are increased in magnitude. The change of apparent elevation that results when these forces are altered in magnitude alone has been termed the *elevator illusion* (Whiteside, 1961); the elevator illusion is similar to the *oculogravic illusion* (Graybiel, 1952), which results when gravitational-inertial forces are altered in both magnitude and direction. Although similar mechanisms are undoubtedly involved in both illusions, differences in the degree to which they depend on labyrinthine proprioception have been demonstrated. For example, when

---

[1] The magnitude of force imparted by a gravitational-inertial field is expressed in units of G, where 1 G is the force per unit mass resulting from an acceleration of 1 g, the acceleration due to the earth's gravity (approximately 9.81 meters per second per second). The generally accepted convention regarding the direction of G forces is as follows: $+ G_x$ designates a force that displaces internal organs and fluids in the body from the chest toward the spine; $+ G_y$ designates a force that displaces internal organs and fluids from the right toward the left side of the body; $+ G_z$ designates a force that displaces internal organs and fluids from the head toward the feet. Thus, for example, a 1.50 G_z environment is one in which 1.5 times the terrestrial force of gravity acts along an observer's head-to-foot, or Z, body axis.

subjects with damaged labyrinthine proprioceptors experience gravitational-inertial forces that are altered in both magnitude and direction,
they report the oculogravic illusion in a modified form (Graybiel & Clark,
1965), but when they experience gravitational-inertial forces that are
altered in magnitude alone, they do not report the elevator illusion at all
(Niven et al., 1963). Thus, these findings suggest that, although labyrinthine activity is important for the oculogravic illusion, it is necessary for
the elevator illusion.

As noted previously, anatomical studies have shown that the macular
surface of the utricle slopes anteriorly upward by an angle of approximately 30° from the frontal-occipital axis of the head (Corvera et al.,
1958). If stimulation of the utricle is accomplished by shearing forces
along the macular surface (Schone, 1964), or if it is modified by a
combination of shearing forces and compression (Correia, Hixson, &
Niven, 1968), changes in the orientation of the head relative to gravitational-inertial forces should produce changes in stimulation of the utricle.
Also, if the apparent elevation of visually perceived objects depends on
stimulation of the utricle, the apparent elevation should be different for
different orientations of the head.

To minimize changes in the apparent elevation of visually perceived
objects when the orientation of the head is changed, signals from
proprioceptors in the neck independently adjust the positions of the eyes
in their sockets (L.A. Cohen, 1961; Cope & Ryan, 1959; de Kleyn, 1918).
For example, reflex changes in eye position remain after bilateral extir-

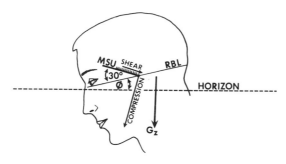

Fig. 8. Shear and compression of the utricular receptors. Changes in the orientation of the
head produce different amounts of shear and compression of the utricular receptors. The
macular surface of the utricle (MSU) slopes anteriorly upward by an angle of approximately
30° from Reid's baseline (RBL), an anterior-posterior plane passing from the lower orbit of
the eyes through the center of the ear canals. The angle, $\emptyset$, represents the inclination of
the head; when $\emptyset = 30°$, the macular surface of the utricle is approximately perpendicular
to G_z accelerative forces, and changes in the magnitudes of the forces primarily result in
changes of compression rather than shear.

pation of the labyrinthine receptors; when extirpation is followed by cervical lesions, the reflexes are eliminated (de Kleyn, 1918). Similarly, cervical diseases that leave the labyrinthine receptors unaffected often result in vertigo and disorientation (Cope & Ryan, 1959). Thus, in the normal terrestrial environment, it appears that signals from propriceptors in the neck are balanced with signals from the otolith organs to allow the apparent (and retinal) positions of visually perceived objects to remain relatively stable for different orientations of the head. When gravitational-inertial forces are altered, the delicate balance is disrupted, and visually perceived objects appear to move whenever the orientation of the head is altered (Guedry, 1968).

A study conducted on the Naval Air Development Center's human centrifuge examined how the apparent elevation of visually perceived targets is influenced by the magnitude of gravitational-inertial forces acting on an observer and by the orientation of the observer's head relative to his trunk (M.M. Cohen, 1973). Each of nine volunteer subjects attempted to keep a visual target at his apparent horizon in an otherwise totally darkened environment while he was exposed to altered gravitational-inertial forces. His head was positioned with the aid of a biteboard so that it was fixed at each of three orientations with respect to his trunk: a normal erect position, pitched 15° forward, and pitched 30° forward.

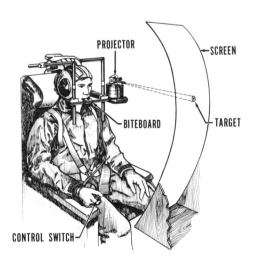

Fig. 9. Apparatus used to measure the apparent elevation of a visual target. The target, an annulus of light with an outer diameter of 25 mm, was continuously driven upward or downward on the screen by an electric motor. The subject attempted to keep the target at his apparent horizon by repeatedly activating his control switch to reverse the direction in which the target was driven. Thus, the subject attempted to bracket the position that he believed to be at his horizon.

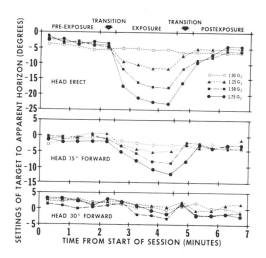

Fig. 10. Settings of the target to the apparent horizon during experimental sessions.

These three head orientations were combined with four different magnitudes of gravitational-inertial forces: 1.00, 1.25, 1.50, and 1.75 G_z, to provide a total of 12 experimental conditions. For each subject, the experimental conditions were presented in separate sessions, and in random order. Each session lasted for 7 min, and consisted of five parts: (1) a preexposure period of 2 min at 1.00 G_z, (2) a transition period of 30 sec in which the centrifuge arm was accelerated to produce the experimental level of gravitational-inertial force, (3) an exposure period of 2 min at steady-state gravitational-inertial conditions, (4) a transition period of 30 sec in which the centrifuge arm was decelerated until it came to rest, and (5) a postexposure period of 2 min at 1.00 G_z.

When the subject's head was erect, and when it was pitched 15° forward, the subject lowered the target by increasing amounts as the gravitational-inertial force was increased. Since the subject attempted to keep the target at his apparent horizon, it may be inferred that a stationary target would appear to rise under these conditions, and the greater the gravitational-inertial force, the higher the apparent elevation of the target. In contrast, when the subject's head was pitched 30° forward, he did not change the position of the target with changes in the gravitational-inertial force acting on his body. Since the macular surface of the utricle is approximately horizontal and perpendicular to G_z forces when the head is pitched 30° forward on the trunk, shearing forces to the utricle are virtually eliminated, and increases in the gravitational-inertial field essentially serve only to increase compression. Thus, the 30° forward pitch of the head should allow increases in the gravitational-inertial field without corresponding increases in shearing forces to the utricular receptors.

The rate at which the elevator illusion changed with increased G_z was reduced as the head was pitched forward on the trunk by increasing amounts. With the head erect, the elevator illusion changed at a mean rate of 20.4°/G_z as determined by a method of least squares linear fit to the data; with the head pitched 15° forward on the trunk, the elevator illusion changed at a mean rate of 9.1°/G_z; with the head pitched 30° forward on the trunk, the apparent elevation of the target did not undergo any significant changes with changes in G_z. Thus, for different orientations of the head, the same gravitational-inertial forces resulted in different apparent elevations of the visual target.

At the magnitudes of G_z examined in this study, the target appeared lower when the head was pitched forward on the trunk than when it was erect. Schone (1964) also reported that visual targets appeared lower when the head was pitched forward, but only when gravitational-inertial forces exceeded 1.00 G_z. According to Schone, the apparent position of visible objects remains constant in a 1.00 G_z (terrestrial) environment, irrespective of the orientation of the head. According to the present data, and those of DeLage (1886), the apparent position of visual targets differs for different orientations of the head, even in a 1.00 G_z environment. This finding suggests that the influences of neck proprioception and otolith-organ activity are not balanced absolutely, and that visual position constancy is only approximate, even in a 1.00 G_z environment.

5.2.2. Oculogravic and Posturogravic Illusions. When an aircraft is catapulted from the deck of a carrier, the pilot is exposed to a sudden and dramatic change in the accelerative forces acting on his body. He is pushed sharply back in his seat as the aircraft hurtles forward, accelerating rapidly to attain adequate airspeed. Although the acceleration is of but brief duration, lasting for only 2–4 sec, it is of sufficient intensity that the pilot may be seriously disoriented during its application and for

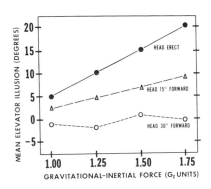

Fig. 11. Mean elevator illusion for three orientations of the head during exposure to altered gravitational-inertial forces. These data were derived by reversing the signs and computing mean values from each set of four measures obtained during the periods designated "EXPOSURE" in Figure 10.

some time thereafter. The G_x (chest-to-spine) forces that result from the forward acceleration of the aircraft are vectored with the force of the earth's gravitational field, and the combined gravitational-inertial force vector is increased in magnitude and rotated in direction as the catapult accelerations are applied. At the end of the catapult stroke, the accelerative forces are reduced, and the vector approaches its initial G_z (head-to-foot) orientation.[2]

Exposure to changed gravitational-inertial forces such as these can result in both visual and postural illusions. The visual, or oculogravic, illusion causes seen objects to appear to rise above their true physical positions (Graybiel, 1952), and the postural, or posturogravic, illusion causes the pilot to feel that his body is being tilted backward (Clark & Graybiel, 1949). Thus, the entire array of cockpit instruments may appear to rise, and the pilot may feel that his aircraft is climbing in an excessively high, nose-up attitude.

Some investigators have argued that the oculogravic and posturogravic illusions are not really illusions at all, but merely reflect the actual change in the direction of gravitational-inertial forces acting on the subject; the subject perceives that he is tilted because, relative to the gravitational-inertial field, he really *is* tilted (Howard & Templeton, 1966). In addition, Howard and Templeton have argued that there is functionally no difference between actually tilting a subject and rotating the direction of a gravitational-inertial acceleration vector relative to the subject, as in a human centrifuge or in an aircraft undergoing a catapult launching. In terms of steady-state conditions, Howard and Templeton's point is quite reasonable; although there may be differences in the magnitudes of the forces involved, the orientation of the subject relative to the forces is essentially the same. In terms of *transitions* between steady-state conditions, Howard and Templeton are simply wrong. For example, when a subject is tilted relative to a fixed-reference gravitational field, a rotation of his body is required; this rotation must involve angular accelerations in the plane perpendicular to the axis about which the subject's body is rotated. The double integral of the angular accelerations

---

[2] When gravitational-inertial forces act simultaneously in more than one orthogonal direction, the net vector magnitude and direction can be calculated by the Pythagorean Theorem. For example, consider a catapult acceleration of 4.00 g_x; this acceleration results in a force of 4.00 G_x on the pilot's body. If the pilot is initially seated upright, $G_z = 1.00$. The magnitude of the net acceleration vector is given $(1.00^2 + 4.00^2)^{\frac{1}{2}} = (17)^{\frac{1}{2}} = 4.12$ G. Since the 4.00 G_x transient is applied while the 1.00 G_z force of gravity is present, the angle through which the net vector is rotated is given by $\tan^{-1} 4.12$, which equals 76°. Thus, at the maximum acceleration of 4.00 g_x on the catapult, the pilot experiences forces that are 4.12 times those encountered when he was at rest and that are rotated by 76° from their initial orientation.

must equal the angular change in the orientation of the body relative to the reference field; further, the magnitude of the reference field does not change as the subject's body is rotated. In contrast, when a gravitational-inertial acceleration vector is rotated with respect to the subject, as in a human centrifuge or in an aircraft, angular accelerations of his body in a plane perpendicular to the axis about which the vector is rotated need not be present; further, the magnitude of the total gravitational-inertial acceleration vector changes as it is rotated under these conditions.

In terms of the combined functioning of the semicircular canals and the otolith organs, rotation of the subject's body relative to a reference field provides coherent stimulation, since both the semicircular canals and the otolith organs signal that the subject's body is rotating. Rotation of the gravitational-inertial acceleration vector relative to the subject provides contradictory patterns of stimulation, since the semicircular canals indicate that the body is not rotating about a given axis, but the otolith organs signal that the subject's orientation is changing relative to the vector.

Finally, when the gravitational-inertial acceleration vector is rotated with respect to the subject, there is generally a delay in the perception of the changed orientation (Clark & Graybiel, 1966), and when the vector is returned to its initial orientation, there is also a delay in the perception (M.M. Cohen, 1976; M.M. Cohen, Crosbie, & Blackburn, 1973). These delays are not obtained when the subject is actually rotated with respect to a reference field. Thus, at least as far as exposures to transient rotations of the gravitational-inertial acceleration vector are concerned, Howard and Templeton's arguments do not apply, and there really is an oculogravic illusion and a posturogravic illusion.

The illusions can be exceedingly dangerous when they result in pilot control errors. On the one hand, if the pilot is unaware of the illusions, he may attempt to reduce the apparently excessive nose-up attitude of his aircraft by easing forward on the stick, thereby placing the aircraft in a shallow, unperceived dive. On the other hand, if the pilot is aware of the illusions, he may believe that a truly excessive nose-up attitude of the aircraft is merely an illusion, thereby allowing his airspeed to decay below the stall speed of the aircraft. In either case, the results can be fatal. Unquantified intellectual awareness of the illusions does not suffice to strip them of their peril, and several aircraft accidents have occurred immediately following catapult launchings, particularly at night when there is no opportunity for external visual cues to override the disorienting illusions.

For the most part, experimental research had been concerned with the effects of small amplitude and long duration, rather than large amplitude and transient accelerations. Because quantitative information concerning the effects of suddenly applied, short-duration accelerations on illusions of spatial localization was extremely limited, and because night postlaunch water-collision accidents had become a problem in Navy flight operations (Anon., 1971), a series of experiments was conducted on the Naval Air Development Center's human centrifuge (M.M. Cohen, 1976, 1977; M.M. Cohen et al., 1973).

In the study by M.M. Cohen et al., 12 volunteer subjects, six Navy pilots who had recently experienced catapult launchings and six nonpilots without previous catapult experience, were seated in the gondola of the human centrifuge and were exposed to an impulse acceleration of approximately 3.2-sec duration that provided peak accelerative forces of 4.00 G_x. The subjects attempted to keep a visual target at their apparent horizon before, during, and after their exposure to the accelerative forces, in much the same manner as in the study of the elevator illusion described previously. Settings of the target to the apparent horizon were monitored throughout the experiment.

The oculogravic illusions generally reached their maximum values approximately 10–15 sec after the accelerative forces were terminated; the illusions usually persisted for more than 30 sec. Despite the fact that the gravitational-inertial acceleration vector was rotated by more than

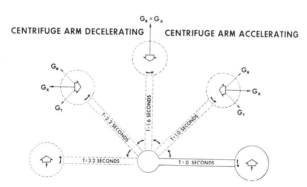

Fig. 12. Schematic representation of technique used to generate G_x forces on the human centrifuge. The subject is initially seated facing the direction of the open arrows. At T = 0 sec, the centrifuge arm begins to turn, leading to a rapid onset of tangential accelerative forces (G_T). As a velocity of the centrifuge arm increases, radial accelerative forces (G_R) are generated. The subject is rotated counterclockwise by the yaw gimbal of the centrifuge so that the vector resolution of G_T and G_R lies along his chest-to-spine (G_x) axis. At T = 1.6 sec, G_T approaches zero, and G_x is identified by G_R. At T = 3.2 sec, the centrifuge arm comes to rest. The subject is now facing in the same direction as he was at the beginning of the acceleration profile, having been rotated through approximately 180° by the centrifuge arm and 180° by the yaw gimbal.

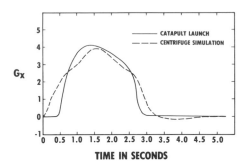

Fig. 13. Comparison of acceleration profiles encountered in actual aircraft catapult launchings and in centrifuge simulations.

75°, the peak magnitude of the oculogravic illusion seldom reached values of even 10°, and the mean peak illusion was only about 6°.

The illusions reported by the experienced pilots and the naive subjects were virtually identical, both in their magnitude and their duration. Thus, at least as far as perception is concerned, there is probably no significant effect of experience, and the major difference between highly experienced pilots and those with less experience probably would be found in the degree to which they monitor their flight instruments and the precision with which they control their aircraft.

In the second study (M.M. Cohen, 1976), changes in perceived body orientation were measured directly. Four experienced Navy pilots were required to control the pitch orientation of the centrifuge gondola in which they were seated, both before and after they were exposed to accelerations identical to those used in the previous experiment. The subjects were provided with a control switch that repeatedly changed the pitch orientation of the gondola at a rate of 5° per sec; their task was

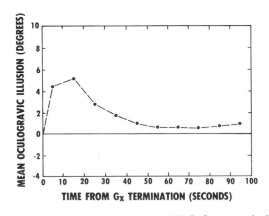

Fig. 14. Oculogravic illusions following exposure to 4.00 G_x forces on the human centrifuge.

to keep themselves in what they perceived to be an upright sitting position before and after the accelerative forces were applied. Because the control switch was active throughout each preexposure and postexposure session, the gondola was continuously driven in pitch to move either forward or backward, and the task was one of dynamic spatial orientation, without any opportunity for the subjects to remain stationary at any fixed position.

Like the oculogravic illusions obtained in the previous experiment, the posturogravic illusions generally attained their peak values about 10–15 sec after the accelerative forces were terminated; these illusions also persisted for several seconds after the accelerative forces had been removed. The subjects were firmly strapped in their seats throughout all segments of this study, and they actually pitched themselves forward and pressed against their restraint straps when they believed themselves to have been seated upright. Thus, the illusion appears to have been sufficiently compelling that even the increased pressures of their bodies against the restraint straps did not provide sufficient cues to eliminate it.

Clearly, the changes in magnitudes and directions of gravitational-inertial forces encountered in the aviation environment lead to powerful illusions that reflect the interactions of visual and proprioceptive receptor systems. When the proprioceptive receptors are stimulated by forces that are seldom encountered in the terrestrial environment, their influences on perceived spatial orientation and visual localization are felt nevertheless. The surprising aspect of this situation is not that pilots become disoriented in the aviation environment, but rather that they have come to function in it as well as they do.

Although the posturogravic illusion may alter the apparent orienta-

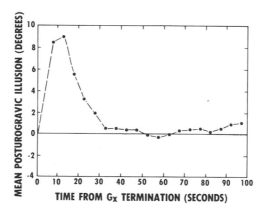

Fig. 15. Posturogravic illusions following exposure to 4.00 G_x forces on the human centrifuge.

tion of the pilot, and although the oculogravic illusion may alter the apparent visual location of the instrument panel, the readings of individual instruments on the panel should remain unchanged. The information presented by flight instruments requires visual-visual judgments—for example, the position of a needle relative to numerals on a dial. In contrast, the posturogravic illusion affects proprioceptive judgments, such as the orientation of the body relative to gravitational-inertial forces; and the oculogravic illusion affects visual-proprioceptive judgments, such as the apparent egocentric locations of visually presented objects. Thus, the flight instruments work because they essentially circumvent the visual-proprioceptive interactions. When the instruments operate correctly and when the pilot responds appropriately, the illusions need not be a matter of concern; it is primarily when the instruments do not operate, or when the pilot does not scan his instruments (M.M. Cohen, 1977), that the illusions can be deadly enemies.

As we have seen, acceleration conditions encountered in the aviation environment can produce unusual patterns of stimulation that result in extremely compelling visual and proprioceptive illusions. Not only can the acceleration conditions present hazards for aviators, and not only do they challenge the ingenuity of instrument designers and applied psychologists to overcome their disorienting effects, but they also provide a superb opportunity for researchers interested in visual-proprioceptive interactions to examine the effects of controlled atypical stimulation of the proprioceptive receptors on perceived spatial orientation and visual localization.

Although a thorough and comprehensive understanding of the mechanisms that subserve visual-proprioceptive interactions will most likely require more detailed neurophysiological investigations, the impetus and direction of these studies probably will arise from controlled behavioral investigations. Clearly, at least as far as visual-proprioceptive interactions are concerned, much exciting and intriguing research remains to be accomplished. The dramatic influence of acceleration conditions encountered in the aviation environment on visual-proprioceptive interactions represents an extremely powerful and largely untapped research tool that can be used to enhance our understanding of the interactive and integrative functions of the human nervous system.

ACKNOWLEDGMENTS

My sincere thanks to the editors of *Perception and Psychophysics* and to the editors of *Aviation, Space, and Environmental Medicine* for their kind permission to reproduce figures and extract segments of the text from articles that I had previously published in their journals. I thank Andrew H. Bellenkes for his efforts in creating the anatomical sketches presented in Figures 1–7.

6. References

Ades, H.W., & Engstrom, H. Form and innervation of the vestibular epithelia. In A. Graybiel (Ed.), *The role of the vestibular organs in the exploration of space.* Washington, D.C.: National Aeronautics and Space Administration, 1965.

Anonymous. Night post-launch accidents. *Approach,* 1971, *16,* 14–15.

Bach-y-Rita, P. Neurophysiology of eye movements. In P. Bach-y-Rita, C.C. Collins, & J.E. Hyde (Eds.), *The control of eye movements.* New York: Academic Press, 1971.

Bell, C. *The anatomy of the human body.* Vol. 3. London: Longman, Rees, Cadell & Davies, 1803.

Bell, C. Idea of a new anatomy of the brain: Submitted for the observation of his friends. In R.J. Herrnstein & E.G. Boring (Eds.), *A source book in the history of psychology.* Cambridge: Harvard University Press, 1966. (Originally published, 1811.)

Benson, A.J. Modification of the response to angular accelerations by linear accelerations. In H.H. Kornhuber (Ed.), *Handbook of sensory physiology.* Vol. VI/2. New York: Springer-Verlag, 1974.

Bernard, M.C. *Introduction a l'étude de la médecine expérimentale.* Paris: J.B. Baillière et fils, 1865.

Brandt, U., & Fluur, E. Postural perceptions and eye displacements produced by a resultant vector acting in the median sagittal plane of the head. *Acta oto-laryngologica,* 1967, *63,* 489–502.

Breinin, G.M. Electromyographic evidence for ocular muscle proprioception in man. *AMA Archives of Ophthalmology,* 1957, *57,* 176–180.

Brown, J.L. Orientation to the vertical during water immersion. *Aerospace Medicine,* 1961, *32,* 209–217.

Bruell, J.H., & Albee, G.W. Notes toward a motor theory of visual egocentric localization. *Psychological Review,* 1955, *62,* 391–399.

Carpenter, M.B., Fabrega, H., & Glinsmann, W. Physiological deficits occurring with lesions of labyrinth and fastigial nuclei. *Journal of Neurophysiology,* 1959, *22,* 222–234.

Chang, H.T. Activation of internuncial neurons through collaterals of pyramidal fibers at cortical level. *Journal of Neurophysiology,* 1955, *18,* 452–471.

Clark, B., & Graybiel, A. Linear acceleration and deceleration as factors influencing nonvisual orientation during flight. *Journal of Aviation Medicine,* 1949, *20,* 92–101.

Clark, B., & Graybiel, A. Factors contributing to the delay in the perception of the oculogravic illusion. *American Journal of Psychology,* 1966, *79,* 377–388.

Clark, F.J. Information signaled by sensory fibers in medial articular nerve. *Journal of Neurophysiology,* 1975, *38,* 1464–1472.

Cohen, L.A. Role of eye and neck proprioceptive mechanisms in body orientation and motor coordination. *Journal of Neurophysiology,* 1961, *24,* 1–11.

Cohen, M.M. Elevator illusion: Influences of otolith organ activity and neck proprioception. *Perception and Psychophysics,* 1973, *14,* 401–406.

Cohen, M.M. Disorienting effects of aircraft catapult launchings. II. Visual and postural contributions. *Aviation, Space, and Environmental Medicine,* 1976, *47,* 39–41.

Cohen, M.M. Disorienting effects of aircraft catapult launchings: III. Cockpit displays and piloting performance. *Aviation, Space, and Environmental Medicine,* 1977, *48,* 797–804.

Cohen, M.M., Crosbie, R.J., & Blackburn, L.H. Disorienting effects of aircraft catapult launchings. *Aerospace Medicine,* 1973, *44,* 37–39.

Cooper, S., Daniel, P.M., & Whitteridge, D. Muscle spindles and other sensory endings in the extrinsic eye muscles; the physiology and anatomy of these receptors and their connexions with the brain-stem. *Brain,* 1955, *78,* 564–583.

Cope, S., & Ryan, G.M.S. Cervical and otolith vertigo. *Journal of Laryngology,* 1959, *73,* 113–120.

Correia, M.J., Hixson, W.C., & Niven, J.I. On predictive equations for subjective judgments of vertical and horizon in a force field. *Acta oto-laryngologica,* 1968, Supp. 230.

Corvera, J., Hallpike, C.S., & Schuster, E.H.J. A new method for the anatomical reconstruction of the human macular planes. *Acta oto-laryngologica,* 1958, *49,* 4–16.

de Kleyn, A. Action réflexes du labyrinthe et du cou sur les muscles de l'oeil. *Archives Neerlandaises de Physiologie de l'homme et des animaux,* 1918, *2,* 644–649.

DeLage, Y. Études expérimentales sur les illusions statiques et dynamiques de direction pour servir à déterminer les fonctions des canaux demicirculaires de l'oreille interne. *Archives de Zoologie Expérimentale et Generale,* 1886, *4,* 535–624.

Dodge, R. Habituation to rotation. *Journal of Experimental Psychology,* 1923, *6,* 1–35.

Dohlman, G. Some practical and theoretical points in labyrinthology. *Proceedings of the Royal Society of Medicine,* 1935, *28,* 1371–1380.

Eldred, E. Posture and locomotion. In J. Field, H.W. Magoun, & V.E. Hall (Eds.), *Handbook of physiology.* Section 1: *Neurophysiology.* Vol. 2. Washington, D.C.: American Physiological Society, 1960.

Engstrom, H. The first order vestibular neurons. In A. Graybiel (Ed.), *Fourth Symposium on the Role of the Vestibular Organs in Space Exploration.* Washington, D.C.: National Aeronautics and Space Administration, 1968.

Fluur, E. The interaction between the utricle and the saccule. *Acta oto-laryngologica,* 1970, *69,* 17–24.

Fluur, E., & Mellstrom, A. Utricular stimulation and oculomotor reactions. *Laryngoscope,* 1970, *80,* 1701–1712. (a)

Fluur, E., & Mellstrom, A. Saccular stimulation and oculomotor reactions. *Laryngoscope,* 1970, *80,* 1713–1721. (b)

Geldard, F.A. *The human senses.* 2nd ed. New York: Wiley, 1972.

Gerathewohl. S.J. Physics and psychophysics of weightlessness: Visual perception. *Journal of Aviation Medicine,* 1952, *23,* 373–395.

Gibson, J.J. *The senses considered as perceptual systems.* Boston: Houghton Mifflin, 1966.

Granit, R. *Receptors and sensory perception.* New Haven: Yale University Press, 1955.

Granit, R. The probable role of muscle spindles and tendon organs in eye movement control. In P. Bach-y-Rita, C.C. Collins, & J.E. Hyde (Eds.), *The control of eye movements.* New York: Academic Press, 1971.

Gray, L.P. Extra labyrinthine vertigo due to cervical muscle lesions. *Journal of Laryngology,* 1956, *70,* 352–360.

Graybiel, A. Oculogravic illusion. *AMA Archives of Ophthalmology,* 1952, *48,* 605–615.

Graybiel, A., & Clark, B. Validity of the oculogravic illusion as a specific indicator of otolith function. *Aerospace Medicine,* 1965, *36,* 1173–1181.

Grigg, P., & Greenspan, B.J. Response of primate joint afferent neurons to mechanical stimulation of the knee joint. *Journal of Neurophysiology,* 1977, *40,* 1–8.

Guedry, F.E. Some vestibular problems related to orientation in space. *Acta oto-laryngologica,* 1968, *65,* 174–185.

Guthrie, E.R. *The psychology of learning.* New York: Harper, 1935.

Hardy, M. Observations on the innervation of the macula sacculi in man. *Anatomical Record,* 1934, *59,* 403–418.

Harris, G.G., & Milne, D.C. Input-output characteristics of the lateral-line sense organs of Xenopus laevis. *Journal of the Acoustical Society of America,* 1966, *40,* 32–42.

Held, R. Exposure history as a factor in maintaining stability of perception and co-ordination. *Journal of Nervous and Mental Disease,* 1961, *132,* 26–32.

Held, R. Dissociation of visual functions by deprivation and rearrangement. *Psychologische Forschung*, 1968, *31*, 338–348.

Held, R., & Bossom, J. Neonatal deprivation and adult rearrangement: Complementary techniques for analyzing plastic sensory-motor coordinations. *Journal of Comparative and Physiological Psychology*, 1961, *54*, 33–37.

Held, R., & Hein, A. Movement-produced stimulation in the development of visually guided behavior. *Journal of Comparative and Physiological Psychology*, 1963, *56*, 872–876.

Henneman, E. Peripheral mechanisms involved in the control of muscle. In V.B. Mountcastle (Ed.), *Medical Physiology*. Vol. 1. St Louis: C.V. Mosby, 1974.

Houk, J. Feedback control of muscle: A synthesis of the peripheral mechanisms. In V.B. Mountcastle (Ed.), *Medical Physiology*. Vol. 1. St Louis: C.V. Mosby, 1974.

Howard, I.P., & Templeton, W.B. *Human spatial orientation*. London: Wiley, 1966.

Hubel, D.H., & Wiesel, T.N. Receptive fields of single neurones in the cat's striate cortex. *Journal of Physiology*. 1959, *148*, 574–591.

Hubel, D.H., & Wiesel, T.N. Receptive fields of optic nerve fibers in the spider monkey. *Journal of Physiology*. 1960, *154*, 572–580.

Hubel, D.H., & Wiesel, T.N. Receptive fields and functional architecture of monkey striate cortex. *Journal of Physiology*. 1968, *195*, 215–243.

Kelso, J.A.S. Joint receptors do not provide a satisfactory basis for motor timing and positioning. *Psychological Review*. 1978, *85*, 474–481.

Kohler, I. [The formation and transformation of the perceptual world] (H. Fiss, trans.). *Psychological Issues*, 1964, *3*, 1–173. (Originally published, 1951.)

Kohler, I. Experiments with goggles. *Scientific American*, 1962, *206*, 62–86.

Kornheiser, A.S. Adaptation to laterally displaced vision: A review. *Psychological Bulletin*, 1976, *83*, 783–816.

Larson, C.A. *Otolith receptors: A mathematical description of their function*. Unpublished doctoral thesis, Drexel University, 1973.

Li, C.L. Activity of interneurons in the motor cortex. In H.H. Jasper, L.D. Proctor, R.S. Knighton, W.C. Norsbay, & R.T. Costello (Eds.), *Reticular formation of the brain*. Boston: Little, Brown, 1958.

Lowenstein, O. Comparative morphology and physiology. In H.H. Kornhuber (Ed.), *Handbook of sensory physiology*. Vol. VI/1. New York: Springer-Verlag, 1974.

Lowenstein, O., & Sand, A. The mechanism of the semicircular canal. A study of the responses of single-fibre preparations to angular acceleration and to rotation at constant speed. *Proceedings of the Royal Society; Series B Biological Sciences*, 1940, *129*, 256–275.

Lowenstein, O., & Wersall, J. A functional interpretation of the electron-microscope structure of the sensory hairs in the cristae of the elasmobranch Raja clavata in terms of directional sensitivity. *Nature*, 1959, *184*, 1807–1810.

Matin, L. A possible hybrid mechanism for modification of visual direction associated with eye movements—the paralyzed-eye experiment reconsidered. *Perception*, 1976, *5*, 233–239.

Matthews, P.B.C. The differentiation of two types of fusimotor fibre by their effects on the dynamic response of muscle spindle primary endings. *Quarterly Journal of Experimental Physiology*, 1962, *47*, 324–333.

Matthews, P.B.C. Central regulation of the activity of skeletal muscle. In I.A. Boyd (Ed.), *The Role of the Gamma System in Movement and Posture*. Rev. Edition. New York: Association for the Aid of Crippled Children, 1968.

Muller, J. [On the specific energies of nerves.] In R.J. Herrnstein & E.G. Boring (Eds.), *A source book in the history of psychology*. Cambridge: Harvard University Press, 1966. (Originally published, 1838.)

Nelson, J.G. Effect of water immersion and body position upon perception of the gravitational vertical. *Aerospace Medicine,* 1968, *39,* 806–811.

Niven, J.I., Whiteside, T.C.D., & Graybiel, A. *The elevator illusion: Apparent motion of a visual target during vertical acceleration.* Report No. 89. Pensacola, Florida: U.S. Naval School of Aviation Medicine, 1963.

O'Connell, A.L., & Gardner, E.B. *Understanding the scientific basis of human movement.* Baltimore: Williams & Wilkins, 1972.

Petroff, A.E. An experimental investigation of the origin of efferent fiber projections to the vestibular neuro-epithelium. *Anatomical Record,* 1955, *121,* 352–353.

Pick, H.L., Jr., & Hay, J.C. The distortion experiment as a tool for studying the development of perceptual-motor coordination. In N. Jenkin & R. H. Pollack (Eds.), *Perceptual development: Its relation to theories of intelligence and cognition.* Chicago: Institute for Juvenile Research, 1966.

Precht, W. Physiological aspects of the efferent vestibular system. In H.H. Kornhuber (Ed.), *Handbook of Sensory Physiology.* Vol. VI/1. New York: Springer-Verlag, 1974.

Precht, W., Llinas, R., & Clarke, M. Physiological responses of frog vestibular fibers to horizontal angular rotation. *Experimental Brain Research,* 1971, *13,* 378–407.

Roberts, T.D.M. *Neurophysiology of postural mechanisms.* New York: Plenum Press, 1967.

Roberts, T.D.M. Reflex balance. *Nature,* 1973, *244,* 156–158.

Roberts, T.D.M. Reflex contributions to the assessment of the vertical. *Acta Astronautica,* 1975, *2,* 59–67.

Rock, I. *The nature of perceptual adaptation.* New York: Basic Books, 1966.

Roman, J.A., Warren, B.H., Niven, J.I., & Graybiel, A. Some observations on the behavior of a visual target and a visual afterimage during parabolic flight maneuvers. *Aerospace Medicine,* 1963, *34,* 841–845.

Ross, D. De Insomniis. In *Aristotle—Parva Naturalia: A revised text with introduction and commentary by Sir David Ross.* Oxford: Clarenden Press, 1955.

Ross, H.E. Spatial perception underwater. In J.D. Woods & J.N. Lythgoe (Eds.), *Underwater science.* London: Oxford University Press, 1971.

Ross, H.E. *Behavior and perception in strange environments.* New York: Basic Books, 1975.

Ross, H.E., & Lennie, P. Visual stability during bodily movement under water. *Underwater Association Report,* 1968, *3,* 59–62.

Schone, H. On the role of gravity in human spatial orientation. *Aerospace Medicine,* 1964, *35,* 764–772.

Sherrington, C.S. On the proprio-ceptive system, especially in its reflex aspect. *Brain,* 1906, *29,* 467–482. (a)

Sherrington, C.S. *The integrative action of the nervous system.* New Haven: Yale University Press, 1906. (b)

Sherrington, C.S. Observations on the sensual role of the proprioceptive nerve-supply of the extrinsic ocular muscles. *Brain,* 1918, *41,* 332–343.

Smith, R. *A compleat system of opticks in four books.* As cited in Wade, 1978. (Originally published, 1738.)

Spoendlin, H.H. Ultrastructural studies of the labyrinth in squirrel monkeys. In A. Graybiel (Ed.), *The role of the vestibular organs in the exploration of space.* Washington, D.C.: National Aeronautics and Space Administration, 1965.

Spoendlin, H.H. Ultrastructure of the vestibular sense organ. In R.J. Wolfson (Ed.), *The vestibular system and its diseases.* Philadelphia: University of Pennsylvania Press, 1966.

Steinhausen, W. Uber den Nachweis der Bewegung der Cupula in der intakten Bogengangsampulle des Labyrinthes bei der naturlichen rotatorischen und calorischen Reizung. *Pflugers Archiv der gesamten Physiologie,* 1931, *228,* 322–328.

Strughold, H. (attributed to). Frozen rear-end causes disorientation. *Naval Aviation News,* July 1, 1964. Reprinted under title: Experiment shows pants-seat flying is OK method. *Johnsville Reflector,* 1964, *8,* (3).

Taub, E., & Berman, A.J. Movement and learning in the absence of sensory feedback. In S.J. Freedman (Ed.), *The neuropsychology of spatially oriented behavior.* Homewood, Ill.: Dorsey Press, 1968.

Teuber, H.L. Perception. In J. Field, H.W. Magoun, & V.E. Hall (Eds.), *Handbook of physiology.* Section 1: *Neurophysiology.* Vol. 3. Washington, D.C.: American Physiological Society, 1960.

von Helmholtz, H. [A treatise on physiological optics (Vol. 3)] (J.P.C. Southall, Ed. and trans.). New York: Dover Press, 1963. (Originally published, 1866.)

von Holst, E. Relations between the central nervous system and the peripheral organs. *British Journal of Animal Behaviour,* 1954, *2,* 89–94.

Wade, N.J. Sir Charles Bell on visual direction. *Perception,* 1978, *7,* 359–362.

Welch, R.B. *Perceptual modification: Adapting to altered sensory environments.* New York: Academic Press, 1978.

Wendt, G.R. The form of the vestibular eye-movement response in man. *Psychological Monographs,* 1936, *47,* 311–328.

Werner, H., & Wapner, S. Sensory-Tonic Field theory of perception. *Journal of Personality,* 1949, *18,* 88–107.

Werner, H., & Wapner, S. Toward a general theory of perception. *Psychological Review,* 1952, *59,* 324–338.

Wersall, J. Studies on the structures and innervation of the sensory epithelium of the cristae ampullares in the guinea pig. *Acta oto-laryngologica,* Suppl. 126, 1956.

Wersall, J., Gleisner, L., & Lundquist, P.G. Ultrastructure of the vestibular end organs. In A.V.S. de Reuck & J. Knight (Eds.), *Myotatic, kinesthetic and vestibular mechanisms.* Boston: Little, Brown, 1967.

Whiteside, T.C.D. Hand-eye coordination in weightlessness. *Aerospace Medicine,* 1961, *32,* 719–725.

Whitteridge, D. Central control of eye movements. In J. Field, H.W. Magoun, & V.E. Hall (Eds.), *Handbook of Physiology.* Section 1: *Neurophysiology.* Vol 2. Washington, D.C.: American Physiological Society, 1960.

Wolter, J.R. Morphology of the sensory nerve apparatus in striated muscle of the human eye. *AMA Archives of Ophthalmology,* 1955, *53,* 201–207.

Young, L.R. Role of the vestibular system in posture and movement. In V.B. Mountcastle (Ed.), *Medical Physiology.* Vol. 1. St. Louis: C.V. Mosby, 1974.

7

Multisensory Aspects of Rhythm

PAUL FRAISSE

1. Introduction

1.1. Rhythm in Antiquity

According to Plato in the *Laws,* "Rhythm is the order in movement."
This definition, concise as it may be, is still the best one available. With
it, Plato described what appeared in the numerous theatrical performances where the coryphaeus assured the coordination of the chorus'
songs and dances. Fragments of a dissertation by Aristoxène of Taranto
(born 360 B.C.), found at the end of the eighteenth century and annotated
by Westphal (1883) in Germany and by Laloy (1904) in France, provide
valuable information regarding this order of movement.

The order arose from the succession of *rhythmic times,* each of
which corresponded to a signal by the coryphaeus when he stamped his
foot. The *arsis* and the *thesis* were distinguished, the upbeat and the fall
corresponding to two times. These rhythmic times were regrouped into
more or less long bars which did not allow more than four signals. Today
we would assimilate them with the orchestra conductor's movements.

However, even though this aspect of the order corresponded to a
regularity, another aspect corresponded to the structural laws of durations. Recited poetry was constructed according to the metric principles
which opposed the long and short syllables, the long syllable being equal
to two or three short ones. Indeed, there are temporal differences

PAUL FRAISSE • Centre H. Piéron, Université René Descartes, 28 rue Serpente, 75006
Paris, France.

between the syllables in all spoken languages. However, in poetry, the distinction between short and long syllables becomes an ordering principle, especially when the poetry is *psalmodied,* or sung to the accompaniment of, for example, the cittern. Aristoxène, in order to describe rhythmic metric structures, invented a unit: the *basic time,* or the shortest duration which could contain only one syllable, note, or movement passage.

Thus, as soon as rhythm appeared in history, it had a multisensory character. There was a perception of the order of succession of recited poetry, dance, and music in an auditory, visual, and kinesthetic festival. Later on, the rhythmic arts became relatively independent, and consequently, it was possible to distinguish poetry from song, dance from music. However, there remained a number of connections between them, and they are reintegrated in our operas.

My purpose in this chapter is to analyze the role played by the different sensations in what we will call, using Ruckmick's (1927) phrase, the rhythmic experience.

1.2. Main Characteristics of Rhythms

Before investigating how rhythm is perceived by our different senses, it is necessary to specify its main characteristics (see Fraisse, 1956, 1974, 1978, for a fuller account).

1.2.1. Rhythm: Perception of an Order

It is necessary to differentiate between perceived rhythm and conceived rhythm. We speak of the rhythm of the seasons by referring to our multiple and recurrent experiences; we do not perceive it as we perceive the rhythm of a waltz.

Let us also, in order to avoid any possible ambiguity, distinguish rhythm from meter, and rhythmic from metric. The metrics, in poetry as well as in music, define the rules of the measure which guide the composer and the performer. These rules can guide us in the description of rhythmic stimuli. However, we are in the realm of psychology only when we proceed from what is perceived. What we perceive can have a close or remote affinity with what is described by the metrics.

Arrhythmia is opposed to rhythm, the perception of the order in a succession. The former corresponds to the perception of a succession of totally random events. The perception of the order enables one to anticipate what is to follow. Based on this anticipation, instrumentalists, dancers, singers, etc., can coordinate their movements.

1.2.2. Rhythm: Perception of Successive Groupings

We spontaneously group successive stimulations within the limits of our span of apprehension, also called short-term memory. The clause in a sentence, a telephone number, a short melodic tune, are groupings which belong to a psychological present before being relegated to the past, thereby being replaced by another grouping.

Rhythmic groupings are produced by the order of the stimulations. If we listen to a series of identical sounds which succeed each other at isochronous intervals, we do not perceive isolated sounds but groupings of two, three, or sometimes four sounds. One group succeeds another group. Although the intervals are isochronous, the interval between two groups has the characteristics of a pause. Also, the first stimulus of the group often appears to be more accentuated than the others. In this case, one speaks of *subjective rhythmization,* as the only thing that objectively determines the grouping is the subject's perceptual activity. Of course, if a periodic differentiation is introduced into this regular series of stimulations—either because a stimulus differs in intensity, pitch, or duration, or because one interval between the stimulations is longer than the others—this difference becomes the basis for the organization of the successive groupings. A lengthening of the duration of a stimulus or of an interval tends to determine the end of the group. A more intense stimulus tends to begin the group. A stimulus of different pitch is as often found at the beginning as at the end of a group.

1.2.3. The Internal Organization of Groups

Most often, the constituent elements of a grouping differ by one or several characteristics. Two fundamental distinctions dominate these organizations.

1.2.3.1. The Duration of the Elements. Rhythmic patterns are organized on the basis of the distinction between two, and only two, durations.

Greek and Latin poetry were based on the distinction between the breve and the long syllable. Music, in a given movement, uses in more than 80% of the cases only two durations of notes in a ratio of 1:2 or 1:3, for example,

$$\eighthnote \text{ and } \quarternote \quad \text{ or } \quad \eighthnote \text{ and } \dottedquarternote.$$

Only two durations, the dot and the dash, were used in order to create an alphabet based on durations. This limitation seems to be related to our incapacity to discriminate in an absolute way more than two durations in the range of perceived durations (from 10 to 200 csec).

1.2.3.2. The Accentuation. A grouping can be organized, as we mentioned, by one element being differentiated because it is more accentuated than the others. Accentuation is visible in subjective rhythmization; it can also be used in an objective way. There are accents in poetry as well as in music, and there are even hierarchies of accents. The periodic repetition of accents is a constitutive characteristic of the rhythmic experience.

Temporal organization is fundamental. Accentuation is always present, even though accentual structure may be less precise than temporal structure. Moreover, it is necessary not to separate duration and accent, since the long durations are often perceived as accentuated and the accentuated elements as longer.

The periodicity of the accents quite naturally induces movements — or incipient movements—which accompany the repetition of rhythmic patterns.

All of this does not lead, in the rhythmic arts, to uniform and monotonous repetitions. The variety of the organization of durations and accents gives rhythms their dynamic character. This is better described as a form of "variety in unity."

At this point we can adopt Ruckmick's (1927) statement:

> Rhythm may be defined as the perception of a temporal form or pattern in which individual members repeated periodically are consistently varied in any one or more of their qualitative and quantitative attributes.

2. Rhythms in the Different Sensory Modalities

2.1. Rhythm as Perception of the Succession

We are not able to perceive rhythms with all of our senses, as some of the senses are not adapted for the perception of successions. Thus, the inertia of the taste and smell receptors do not permit the perception of rapid successions.

By contrast, hearing, touch, and vision are adapted for this type of perception, although there exist notable differences between them. In order to perceive a succession, it is at least necessary to reach the threshold of temporal acuity; that is to say, a minimum of time is needed for the perception of the succession and temporal order of two stimulations from the same sensory field. Piéron (1952, pp. 296–297) indicated the following values: 2 msec between two identical sounds, 10 msec between two neighboring touches, 100 msec for vision in the best cases.

Hearing and touch are thus better adapted for the perception of rapid successions than is vision. The visual receptors, reacting photochemically, have an inertia regarding the establishment and the extinction of the sensation, thus diminishing the clearness of the short stimulations and thereby hindering the perception of rapid successions.

The reception of messages also occurs under different conditions depending on the sensory modality. Hearing intercepts sounds, whatever the position of the body may be; vision perceives only that which is in the retina's field; touch perceives only the mechanical or electrical stimulations which occur at the surface of the body. In the case of kinesthetic sensations, we no longer deal with the reception of stimulations which are external to the organism, but with the regulation of the organism's own movements. Either the subject can program his movements and control them, or else his movements are provoked by the environment. It is the same for rhythm: external stimulations not only create rhythmic perception but also induce movements which are generally isochronous. Rhythmic perception can result from purely kinesthetic perceptions, as in the case of an orchestra conductor's movements. Most often, however, kinesthetic perceptions are associated with tactile and auditory sensations, as in the play of percussion instruments, the dance, or a musical interpretation.

2.2. Rhythmic Groupings

The perception of groupings can result from auditory, visual, tactile, and kinesthetic sensations.

For audition, it is not necessary to demonstrate the evidence. One can, however, using this privileged example, study the intervals which allow or facilitate the grouping. As already mentioned, a lower limit exists which corresponds to the nondistinction of successive sounds. The upper limit, which is more interesting, is also more difficult to determine. A perceptual grouping of two or several sounds is possible only if the sounds are not independent events. All researchers agree that this limit is between 1.5 and 2 sec. We have proposed to retain an average duration of 1.80 sec. Beyond this limit, the grouping of two sounds within a rhythmic pattern is no longer possible. Similarly, a pause between two groups which is longer than this duration eliminates the linking of the rhythmic patterns. Between these two limits, an optimum duration of succession exists which has been estimated to be between 40 and 60 csec. These values do not seem to be characteristic of auditory perceptions. One also finds them in visual and tactilokinesthetic groupings. Whatever the nature of the stimulation, what counts is the capacity to perceive the organization of the succession.

In vision, the first problem studied was whether, using a succession of lights, the perceived subjective rhythms are analogous to those that are easily obtained using sounds. Meumann (1894) believed this to be true. The problem was investigated at the beginning of the century (see Ruckmick, 1913, 1917). Külpe (1895) thought that rhythm can only be perceived through the auditory modality, Titchener (1916) that it can only be perceived through kinesthetic modalities. Miner (1903) found that visual signals are organized into subjective rhythmic groups. Koffka (1909) found that subjective groupings of lights have the same character-istics as subjective groupings of sounds: that is, perception of regularity, perception of groupings of two, three, or four elements with a pause between two groupings, and accentuation of one of the elements. Werner (1919) confirmed these observations and, from a phenomenal point of view, insisted on the fact that the pause is integrated into rhythmic perception and that it does not simply constitute a ground. For this reason, he spoke of *Gestaltenverkettung*. However, all authors who have studied visual subjective rhythmization agree that it is established more slowly than auditory subjective rhythmization.

Tactile sensation has the same properties as auditory sensation, but it has been studied less because of its limited practical interest. The possibility of perceiving rhythmic patterns is also confirmed by the possibility of discriminating between two rhythmic patterns presented to the same sensory modality. C. E. Seashore (1938) used this principle in the construction of his test. Gault and Goodfellow (1938) applied it to three sensory modalities. Using the same patterns, the percentage of correct responses was 84.9% for hearing, 74.8% for vision, and 70.4% for touch. Training improved the results only by 2–4%.

In the motor field, experimentation is not necessary in order to demonstrate the possibility of rhythmic groupings. Walking, dancing, and rocking are all proof that rhythmic groupings exist. Moreover, these rhythms most often provoke tactilokinesthetic sensations. They exist by themselves, although most often, they are induced by auditory or visual rhythms. Thus, it is possible to perceive rhythm from auditory, optical, tactile, and kinesthetic stimulations.

2.3. The Spontaneous Tempo

The different sensory modalities can also be compared on the basis of tempo. It is possible to distinguish the *spontaneous tempo* (the speed of the succession of the most spontaneous and agreeable taps) from the *preferred tempo* (the speed of the succession of sounds or of lights which appears to be the most natural, that is, neither too fast nor too slow). Mishima (1956), testing the same subjects, found: (1) a spontaneous tempo corresponding to an interval of 46 csec, and (2) a preferred tempo of 54 csec for audition and of 68 csec for vision. These values are close and have a correlation of about .70. The tempos of the blind and of the deaf (excluding the defective sense) are of about the same magnitude, although they are slightly more rapid. Garner and Gottwald (1968), while investigating another problem, found that the optimal speed of succession in order to structure auditory and visual series was the same, that is, between 30 and 60 csec.

2.4. The Ontogenesis of Rhythms

It has always been known that children, even in infancy, perform rhythmic movements. These movements are evidently linked to motor development. However, they are present in neonates and probably prenatally, in the form of thumb or finger sucking.

Movements, most often the alternation of both feet (foot kicking) while the infant is lying on his back, appear toward 2.7 months (median value); body rocking appears at about 6.1 months. Also, head rotation or head banging can be observed in some, but not in all, infants (Kravitz & Boehm, 1971). This type of phenomenon is normal in infants and, moreover, appears at a later age in those suffering from cerebral palsy or from Down's syndrome (Kravitz & Boehm, 1971). These rhythmic movements seem to facilitate motor development and the construction of the body image. They also correspond to a release of tension, procuring satisfactions—which explains why, in certain cases, these behaviors persist. They are a prefiguration of the pleasant excitation created by all motor rhythms.

In order to demonstrate auditory (or visual) perception of rhythms in the neonate, it is necessary to find a way to show that they can discriminate between two patterns or between two successions of patterns. The most widely used technique is the habituation paradigm. A pattern is repeatedly presented to the infant. At first, an orientation reaction is elicited, which gradually tends to disappear; that is, there is habituation. If the pattern is then changed and if the orientation reaction reappears, one can conclude that the two patterns are discriminated. The orientation reaction can be passive (acceleration of the heartbeat or increase of the Galvanic Skin Response). It can also be an operant response in which the appearance of the stimulus is contingent upon visual fixation (Boyd, 1974; Demany, 1978; Demany, McKenzie, & Vurpillot, 1977).

It is well known that the neonate responds to auditory stimuli and particularly to the human voice. Listening to a recording of a heartbeat has a lulling effect on the infant. Certainly, the fetus was exposed to this stimulus during all of the gestation period. Demany, McKenzie, & Vurpillot (1977) demonstrated that infants between one-and-a-half and 3 months of age differentiate between a continuous sequence of identical 40-msec sound separated by 194-msec intervals, and another sequence of the same sounds having the same mean temporal density (194–97–194–291 msec). They also distinguish two patterns of three elements whose two intervals are inversed (97–291–582 msec and 291–97—582 msec). At 5 months, the infant can discriminate between two series of differing tones which are not in the same order or which, if in the same order, are not grouped in the same way: 2–4 transformed into 4–2 by displacing a 60 csec interval, the other intervals being 20 csec (Chang & Trehub, 1977). This result was confirmed using 7-month-olds, who very clearly distinguished sequences of three elements, one iambic, the other regular (Allen, Walker, Symonds, & Marcell, 1977).

Allen *et al.* also demonstrated that at the same age (7 months), infants discriminate between two patterns presented visually as well as they do when the same patterns are presented auditorily. Taken together, these results prove that temporal integration of stimulations into rhythmic patterns appears at a very early age, and seem to confirm the gestaltists' assertion that the structural laws are innate. In particular, the laws of proximity are pertinent in the perception of rhythmic patterns. Of course, perceptual discrimination improves with age, although it exists from birth.

3. Auditory and Visual Rhythms

Rhythmic organization is observed in the different sensory modalities. But does it always have the same characteristics? Most research has been carried out comparing auditory and visual rhythms; the results have depended on the methods employed.

3.1. The Differences

3.1.1. Discrimination Method. Unimodal comparisons of patterns, in which the subject has to decide whether two isolated patterns are the same or different, show that auditory patterns are easier to differentiate when the interstimulus intervals are short (Rubinstein & Gruenberg, 1971). This difference also exists for longer intervals, especially in young children. Klapper and Birch (1971), using patterns of 4 and 5 elements of 500-msec duration and intervals of 1 and 2 sec, found that the discriminability for both modalities was increasing with age (between 4 and 11 years), but that the task was easier with auditory than visual presentation, especially for the youngest. The difference disappears by 11 years. However, we believe that this result is less a matter of the differences between perceived patterns than of constructed temporal organizations.

3.1.2. Identification Method. The verbal description of the organization of a repetitive series of eight sounds, consisting of two different elements, is realized more quickly than that of two different lights. The difference is most distinct at an optimal tempo between two and three per sec (Garner & Gottwald, 1968). The role of tempo confirms our interpretation of Klapper and Birch's (1971) results. Handel and Buffardi (1969) also confirmed the role of tempo in an analagous experiment. The organization imposes itself on the listener at two to four elements per sec; at one element per sec the organization can be constructed and, thus, the difference between auditory and visual patterns disappears.

3.1.3. Learning Method. Nazzaro and Nazzaro (1970) compared the difficulty of learning Morse signals presented first auditorily and then visually (or vice versa). On the average, 10.5 presentations were necessary in order to learn a series of auditory signals, and 14.5 presentations were necessary in order to learn a series of visual signals. The second set of signals presented, whether auditory or visual, were always more easily learned, thereby demonstrating the generalization effect.

3.1.4. Motor-Reproduction Method. The subject hears or sees a pattern and is asked to reproduce it. An auditory pattern is always easier to reproduce than a visual one. Even with very simple patterns of two elements having different durations (from 0.5 to 2.5 sec), at the age of 5–6 years, the reproductions of auditory patterns are more accurate than are those of visual patterns. The difference diminishes with age, but does not completely disappear (Rosenbusch & Gardner, 1968). Moreover, Gault and Goodfellow (1938) found that with more complex patterns there is a substantial difference between different sensory modalities: 65.8% correct responses with an auditory presentation, 46.8% with a tactile presentation, and 31.2% with a visual presentation. However, what is most noteworthy is that after a 5-day training period, practically all of the differences disappear. We conclude that training, which hardly has any effect in a discrimination task, is effective when it permits the subject to use a mediator that acts as the verbal accompaniment of auditory, visual, or tactile sensations. This method equalizes the task's difficulty. We will propose the same explanation in our discussion of synchronization tasks.

However, the ease with which a subject perceives auditory patterns relative to visual patterns disappears if the visual task changes from the perception of a series of flashes to the perception of a series of *movements* (even if silent) of the hand (Thackray, 1969). This result is very interesting and supports the idea that the difficulty in perceiving static visual rhythms is due to the inertia of the sensory system. As soon as a visual rhythm has spatial dynamics, there is no longer a problem—as can be observed by watching dancers.

3.2. Resemblances

As soon as the difficulties linked to the character of the visual receptors are overcome, the principles of rhythmic organization seem to be of the same nature, whatever the kind of stimulation used. Since 1966, Garner and his colleagues have extracted the organizational principles of repeating series of from 6 to 10 stimuli. These series are made up of two different elements (for example, two different sounds) or of similar elements with variable intervals.

Preusser, Garner, and Gottwald (1970) have emphasized two primary principles:

> gap in which the pattern is organized so that the largest gap occurs at the end of the pattern; and run in which the pattern is organized so that it starts with the longest run . . . when the two principles are compatible in a particular pattern, a single organization is perceived or used; when the two principles are incompatible, more than one organization is used. (p. 167)

According to Preusser et al., the same principles apply to patterns having only one type of stimulus with different intervals, as well as to series of two elements, since in the latter case, one of the elements plays the role of figure and the other that of ground.

The existence of the organizational principles is supported by the observation that when sounds and lights are simultaneously used, rhythmic structuration is facilitated (Handel & Buffardi, 1969).

Another method of investigating whether the perceptual laws are the same for visual and auditory rhythms is to study the intersensory discrimination of rhythmic patterns. Allen et al. (1977) have demonstrated that a 7-month-old infant who is habituated to an auditory or visual rhythm has a new orientation reaction, manifested as an acceleration of the heartbeat and an increase of the skin potential when not only the sensory channel, but also the pattern, is changed. The infant reacts even more strongly if not only the pattern is changed, but there is also a shift from an auditory to a visual or from a visual to an auditory presentation. Rubinstein and Gruenberg (1971) found that cross-modal comparisons of patterns (auditory-visual or visual-auditory) are not more difficult than intramodal comparisons (auditory or visual), provided that the intervals have at least a 30-csec duration.

4. The Sensory-Motor Aspect of Rhythms

The close links between perceived rhythms and body rhythms were already pointed out in antiquity. For a long time, observers have noticed the tendency of infants (of about 1 year) to rock when listening to rhythmic music. Even in the neonate it is possible to film micromovements which correspond closely with the syllabic structure of an utterance (Condon & Sander, 1974). In the first experimental studies dealing with subjective rhythm, researchers were struck not only by the grouping phenomenon, but also by the spontaneous accentuation of the first element in a group. This accentuation corresponds, when the auditory perception is accompanied by taps, to differences in the intensity of the percussion (MacDougall, 1903). Also, artists as well as psychologists consider the motor aspect of rhythm to be essential.

Rhythms can be produced (I insist on the word "produced," as it can only be a matter of action) strictly on a motor basis in the absence of any auditory or visual context. Miyake attempted to do so in 1902, by having isochronous series of taps produced at a spontaneous tempo on a silent key. However, in this case, he found that the interval variability is a little larger than when the tap produces a sound.

I have studied (Fraisse, 1956, p. 43) the spontaneous structure of rhythmic patterns realized on a purely motor basis by using a silent-response key kept out of the subjects' sight. These rhythms have the same structures as patterns tapped in the same way but with an auditory control. In addition, I did not find that the individual variability was higher with only a motor control of movement than with an auditory-motor control.

I would now like to investigate the auditory-motor relations in rhythms. Afterward, we will investigate whether the visual-motor relations are of the same nature.

4.1. Auditory-Motor Relations

These are privileged relations. They appear above all in the spontaneous tendency to accompany auditory rhythms with patterns of rhythmic movements which occur *simultaneously,* that is, in synchronization with the auditory patterns, even though they sometimes differ from them. Thus, motor patterns are clearly induced by auditory patterns. For these privileged relations, we can go beyond the layman's common-sense observations and cite experimental proof.

4.1.1. The Immediate Character of the Synchronization. If subjects are asked to synchronize their taps with a series of sounds which repeat in an isochronous way, one notices that, if the subject hears the series before tapping, the synchronization is correct from the first tap on. This corresponds to observations of dancers following the music's rhythm as soon as they walk onto the dance floor. If the subject has to synchronize at the very beginning of the production of the series, the synchronization is acquired from the third sound on. If, instead of regular sounds, a succession of identical patterns is used, one also notices that synchronization exists from the audition of the third pattern on (Fraisse, 1966). Inversely, if subjects are asked not to synchronize their taps with the heard rhythmic series but to syncopate, that is, to tap at the same tempo as that of the stimulus series while interpolating their taps with the sounds, it is found that all subjects find the task difficult for intersound intervals of less than 1 sec. Nearly half of the subjects do not succeed: either the tendency to synchronize prevails, or else unorganized responses are given. For longer intervals, all subjects evidently can follow the instructions although, in any case, beyond 1.8 sec there is no longer rhythmic perception or real synchronization (Fraisse & Ehrlich, 1955).

4.1.2. *Correlations between Perception and Performance*. Everyone who uses C. E. Seashore's rhythm test, where the subject's task is to indicate whether two successive patterns are the same or different, has noticed that some subjects accompany the patterns of sounds with finger or hand movements in order to facilitate the task. R. H. Seashore (1927) established that there is a good correlation between the discrimination and execution of motor rhythms. Smith (1957) continued this work and found a correlation of .71 between the results of R. H. Seashore's discrimination-of-rhythmic-patterns task and the precision of the synchronization when these same patterns are repeated several times. The high correlation, greater than those found between various rhythmic tests (Hiriartborde & Fraisse, 1968) suggests that there is a motor component in the discrimination of auditory patterns. Thackray (1969) found a correlation of .655 between the results of a series of tests of auditory perception of rhythm and a test battery of rhythmic performance.

4.1.3. *Synchronization and Symbolic Transcription*. When subjects are asked either to synchronize with the successive repetition of a pattern or to graphically transcribe its organization in symbolic form, one notes that the synchronization is very fast and is globally apprehended, whereas the symbolic description is slower and develops by successive steps (Oléron, 1959). Preusser (1972) similarly found that it is possible to reproduce the organization of a series of (from 5 to 12) events by tapping long before it is possible to verbally describe this organization; the latency difference of the response is at least 1:2.

4.1.4. *Motor Accompaniment as a Phenomenon of Accentuation*. Motor induction, as attested to by the ease of synchronization, does not entirely explain the relations which exist between auditorily perceived rhythms and their motor accompaniment (perhaps we should say their motor "creation"). Let us return to the case of subjective rhythmization. The subject perceives the sounds as being grouped, and the first one as being more intense. These deformations of perfectly regular and identical stimuli are also found in the motor accompaniment of this subjective rhythmization.

However, in subjective rhythmization, as well as in synchronization with series of identical patterns, the temporal structures of the tapped rhythms are much more regular than are the intensive structures (Brown, 1911). An illustration of this law can be found in music. The notes' durations and the nature of their groupings into bars are exactly specified, although the accentuation is hardly suggested. The latter depends a great deal on the artist, who does not limit himself to the isochrony of the bars even though it is indispensable in allowing the synchronies of the polyphony. Accentuation also depends on the listener. Vos (1976) asked subjects to tap in synchrony with what appeared to them to be the beginning of perceived rhythmic groups. He used excerpts from a recording of Bach's *Well-Tempered Clavier* in a piano performance. The subjects sometimes followed the measure if it was not too long, but most often they structured the musical suite in regular patterns that were shorter than the measure; that is, they grouped the times without considering the bar of the measure. There is a dynamics originating in the subject himself, whether he be performer or listener.

4.2. Visuomotor Relations

We have seen that visual rhythms are more difficult to perceive than auditory ones. Their links with motor rhythms are also much less close. This phenomenon appears very easily when one compares the possibilities and the qualities of the synchronizations of, on the other hand, visual rhythms and on the other hand, auditory rhythms (Fraisse, 1948). In a synchronization task, using a visual or an auditory stimulus which repeats itself at intervals of 50 csec, I found that all of 10 subjects succeeded with the auditory stimuli, but only two out of the 10 with the visual stimuli. More precisely, only two out of 10 subjects were capable of tapping 20 taps while accompanying 20 stimuli. In synchronization with temporal patterns, all of the subjects succeeded with the auditory stimuli and only two-thirds of the subjects with the visual stimuli. Most important, perhaps, is the observation that with the auditory patterns the subject's response was almost immediate and global, whereas with the visual patterns the subjects needed approximately 1 min in order to identify the pattern. All subjects found the task with visual rhythms more difficult. They attributed this difficulty to the facts that, stimulations were hard to differentiate although they had a short duration (10 msec) and were separated by intervals of 250–800 msec, and that apprehending the structure of the form was difficult.

The subjects' comments revealed that they succeeded in this task by creating either a verbal mediate structure or a spatial mediate structure (slight displacements on the response key). Such creations seem to explain the progress through learning in the case of visual rhythms, a progress that was also found by Gault and Goodfellow (1938). They also explain that it is more difficult to synchronize with a cadence than with a rhythmic pattern, as shown in our research. Actually, it is easier to "construct" a pattern by, for example, counting, than to follow a cadence where only the motor induction is preeminent. This difference between motor synchronizations with auditory rhythms and with visual rhythms was demonstrated by the technique of delayed feedback which, of course, perturbs the verbal production. Karlovitch and Graham (1966, 1968), using this technique, found that subjects who accompanied a *visual* pattern with a delayed *auditory* feedback were very perturbed, while subjects who accompanied an *auditory* pattern were little perturbed by a delayed *visual* feedback. As Karlovitch and Graham would say, the auditory system controls the motor responses better than the visual system.

We have already underlined the fact that visual receptors are less adapted than auditory receptors for receiving successive stimuli. More generally, it is necessary to note that the optical apparatus is, on the whole, adapted to continuous luminous stimulations, and that successive stimulations are painful. Conversely, for the auditory apparatus, continuous stimulations are painful whereas the organ is adapted to perceive discontinuous stimulations or those that vary incessantly, as do the sounds of language.

Without being able to offer any proof, one can hypothesize that the perception of auditory patterns is directly organized at the level of the primary auditory area, while the organization of visual patterns requires the participation of the associative areas. It is necessary to add, although neurophysiology does not enlighten us here, that there seem to be more direct links between the auditory and the motor areas than between the visual and motor areas.

4.3. Sensory Cues in Synchronization

The immediacy of the synchronization between auditory and visual stimulations and motor responses is an important index in the analysis of rhythmic perceptions. This synchronization is perceived; that is, we perceive the simultaneity of the external stimulation and of the motor response. Nevertheless, this response has several sensory components. In effect, if it is a question of taps—as is most often the case—the taps supply kinesthetic cues (K), tactile cues (T), and auditory cues (S), or noises resulting from the tap. We have attempted to determine the respective role of these cues. In a first study, we recorded the EMG activity of the four limbs. The subjects were seated, their hands resting on a table. The stimuli were very rhythmic musical tunes such as a march or Ravel's *Boléro*. In most, but not all subjects a spontaneous motor induction was recorded which could extend to the four limbs. However, when the subject's posture was varied, for example, legs folded under the chair, arms hanging, one noticed that the motor activity was preferentially localized in the limbs which rested lightly on a surface, that is, when the position facilitated a slight tapping movement of the hands on the table or the feet on the ground. In these cases the cue appears to be tactile, as the movement did not produce any perceptible noise (Fraisse, Oléron, & Paillard, 1953). In another study, using complex apparatus, we were able to dissociate the different cues. Of course, as there was a motor response, the kinesthetic data were always present. If there is a movement in space (without a tactile cue) which (by cutting a beam of light) produces a sound that can coincide with the movement or be delayed by means of a timer, the subject does not privilege one cue at the expense of another but tries to compromise so that the two cues (K and T) are grouped as well as possible around the stimulus. On the contrary, if a conflict between the tactilokinesthetic cue given by the tap and the sound produced by this tap, which can also be delayed by an artifice, is created, one notes that the tactilokinesthetic cue is predominant in the synchronization (Fraisse, Oléron, & Paillard, 1958).

Results from these two studies indicate that the principal cue is tactile, although it is not possible to completely dissociate this cue from those supplied by the movement. Moreover, the synchronization's precision is relative. From the first studies of rhythm and subsequently (Dunlap, 1910; Miyake, 1902), it was found that the taps slightly anticipated the auditory stimuli, and anticipation which we have demonstrated in several ways (Fraisse & Voillaume, 1971), and which is of the magnitude of 30 msec. This duration is inferior to the threshold (60 msec) of the perception of the succession of two heterogenous stimuli (Hirsh & Fraisse, 1964), so that the time lag is not perceived.

We formulated the hypothesis that in reality this anticipation results from a physiological delay arising from the duration of the transmission of the peripheral tactilokinesthetic information to the brain. The main cue would be the cortical simultaneity of both auditory and tactilokinesthetic information. If this hypothesis is correct, the tap's anticipation in a foot–sound synchronization should be greater than that of a hand–sound synchronization. Indeed, we have found that the anticipation when the response was given by the foot is on the average 20 msec superior to that given by the hand. The induced motor response takes into account the physiological delays in the transmission of tactile information, in order to produce the final concurrence of the two cues (Fraisse, 1980).

The process of synchronization remains unclear. In general, our movements are responses to stimulations and follow them. Synchronization implies that we anticipate the moment when the stimulus appears in order to control the reaction in such a way that it coincides with the stimulus. Here, it is evident that we no longer speak of the slight time lag of the tap and the sound that we have just discussed.

The anticipation necessary for synchronization implies that the moment when the stimulus occurs can be predicted. Now, predictability, based on the order in the succession, is precisely the fundamental characteristic of rhythms. The coordination of musicians, singers, and dancers is only possible if some of them can anticipate what the others are doing on the basis of the perceived regularities. First, there is perception and also memory of the intervals. The synchronization is all the more exact and regular when the cadence's intervals are shorter (without being inferior to 200-300 msec as, in this case, sensorial or motor difficulties intervene). Synchronization depends on the precision of our memory of the intervals and on the corrections which are periodically made by the subject by relying on the information that the synchronizations supply him, these being more or less imperfect when the anticipation or the delay of the tap is too great. These corrections are made conspicuous by the fact that the autocorrelations between the successive intervals or responses synchronized with a simple cadence are slightly negative. This shows that intervals a little too short are followed by intervals a little too long (Fraisse, 1966; Fraisse & Voillaume, 1971).

Is the complexity of this mechanism responsible for the fact that this synchronization behavior is not found in animals?

4.4. The Role of the Nervous Centers

Relatively recent research dealing with the role of the different cortical centers, and particularly research dealing with the respective role of the two hemispheres, furnish precisions regarding the nature of sensory information in rhythm.

Two techniques are most often used: (a) the study of deficiency after localized brain injury, whatever the cause, and (b) the study of asymmetry in the reception of information by one ear or the other. Rosenzweig (1951) showed that if each ear had connections with the two auditory areas, for each area the connections with the counterlateral ear are more important than those with the ipsilateral ear.

The most important researches were carried out on normal subjects by comparing dichotic hearing with binaural hearing. Let us first note that we can perceive a rhythm and accompany it with hand clapping when the successive sounds are sent alternately to the right and to the left ears. According to Teatini (1968), 88% of the subjects succeed at the task, although in certain cases the sounds received by one ear are not accompanied by claps. Gregory, Harriman, and Roberts (1972) also used the alternate hearing of temporal sequences. The subjects had to manipulate a dial in order to locate the sound received by one ear exactly between the two sounds received by the other ear with a 1-sec interval. The task was accomplished with great precision (from +6 msec to −5 msec, the perfect bisection being 0 msec). The authors add that the result is slightly different if one ear receives weak stimuli close to the threshold, while simultaneously the other ear receives masking sounds. The integration of sounds arriving at each of the ears is the normal case.

The left hemisphere, according to the results of studies carried out on normal subjects (Efron, 1963b) and on subjects with left-hemispheric lesions (Efron, 1963a), appears to be specialized in the perception of temporal order. Carmon and Nachshon (1971) demonstrated that perception of temporal order is specific, as, in their experiment, the subjects had to identify, by the place where they occurred, from three to five successive stimuli, some of them colored lights (separated in space), others auditory (a different sound for each ear). By using as a criterion the speed of succession at which this order can be recognized, one sees that, for example, for four elements, an interval of about 240 msec between elements is necessary for normal subjects, 310 msec for those who have a right-hemispheric lesion, and 690 msec for those who have a left-hemispheric lesion. The subjects with right-hemispheric lesions differed little from normal subjects. However, the deficit is very pronounced for those with left-hemispheric lesions. The same authors found similar results by having the subjects identify the order of presentation of only three colored lights.

Since perception of temporal order depends mainly on the left hemisphere, it was assumed that the perception of rhythm would also depend on it, rhythm being a temporal organization. Robinson and Solomon's (1974) results verified this hypothesis. The subjects were presented dichotically a pair of patterns composed of four to seven identical sounds, some short (50 msec), others long (150 msec), separated by 50-msec intervals. The patterns were repeated three times. Four seconds after the presentation of the stimulus, the subjects heard binaurally four rhythmic sequences, two of them identical to the stimulus series, two of them different. The subjects had to indicate (forced choice) the two sequences which were the same as the stimuli. For 24 subjects, the percentage of correct responses was 62% with the right ear and only 55% with the left ear. However, the results were reversed for 6 subjects out of 24 who were all right-handed.

Natale (1977) investigated the problem of lateralization of subjects by computing an index of laterality from several manual tasks. He correlated this index with those of a dichotic task identical to that used by Robinson and Solomon (1974). The correlations between the indices of laterality and the results of the dichotic task are significant (r of .42–.64, depending on the laterality task).

This result seems to be well founded, at least for the ranges of durations used. Robinson and Solomon interpret their results by linking rhythmic perception and language perception, the latter implying the perception of an hierarchy of speech sounds (Martin, 1972). But the fact that the temporal order of stimulations when intervals are longer also depends on the left hemisphere shows that, if the perception of language depends on the perception of the temporal order, the perception of the temporal order does not necessarily depend on language.

Luria (1966), using more clinical as well as more advanced methods, contributed to the understanding of these problems. Subjects suffering from left (sometimes right) temporal lesions had trouble, after a delay, describing a simple or a complex rhythmic pattern when they were prevented from verbalizing during the audition. When the tempo was fast and when the same simple structure was repeated several times, the subjects suffering from these lesions were even less capable of succeeding at the task. This was so even though they were asked to distinguish groups of two sounds from groups of three sounds by a hand movement, thereby avoiding the use of language.

The reproduction of more-or-less rhythmic sequences is very difficult for persons suffering from right or left temporal syndromes. However, when the tempo is not too fast, the task is much easier

> especially if they are permitted to vocalize the rhythms out loud, counting off the corresponding taps in their proper sequence. When prohibited from vocalizing their reproduction of the rhythms is often much less satisfactory, and deprived of the aid of speech then patients will start to look for support based on the spatial organization of the process and will tap on different parts of the table. (Luria, p. 37)

Such behaviors are comparable to those of subjects who have difficulties accompanying visual rhythms.

Lastly, Luria states that subjects suffering from frontal lesions have a great deal of difficulty producing the requested rhythms and that they do not perceive the difference between what is requested and what they are doing.

> This indicates that the fundamental defect in the reproduction of rhythms by patients with a frontal syndrome is associated with a disturbance of the selective aspect of the motor act and the regulatory influence of the instructions originating it. (p.348)

The privileged role of the left hemisphere, as corroborated by Luria, should be opposed to the role of the right hemisphere, on which the perception of musical stimuli is more dependent. Milner (1962) demonstrated that C.E. Seashore's rhythm (and time) tests do not differentiate subjects with right from subjects with left temporal lobectomies. On the contrary, in the tests of tone and tonal memory, subjects with right temporal lobectomies made many more errors than those with left lesions. These results may, in fact, mean that in man the right hemisphere makes a greater contribution than the left in comparison of tonal patterns or judgments of tone quality. This result has been generalized by the work begun by Kimura (1964). She employed the dichotic listening of a series of numbers in one ear and a melody in the other. The best results were obtained when the numbers were presented to the right ear and the melody to the left; the results were not as good when the melody was presented to the right ear. These results seem to indicate that the right hemisphere is more concerned with the treatment of melody than the left. This result was confirmed by several authors, although it was invalidated by Bever and Chiarello (1974). Bever and Chiarello used melodic sequences of from 12 to 18 notes. A well-tempered 1½-octave scale was used. Each tone in a melodic sequence was exactly 300 msec long and was equal in intensity to the other tones. The subjects had a double task: first, to recognize whether two notes that they heard belonged to the initial musical sequence, and then, after a new audition of a melody identical to or different from the first, to indicate whether or not the sequence was heard earlier. The test was carried out using either the right or the left ear. There were two groups of subjects, one group musically naïve, the other group musically experienced. The naïve subjects did not succeed at the first task (discovering whether or not two notes belonged to the sequence) and succeeded at the task of recognizing the melody, although they were better at recognizing the melodies presented to the left ear than those presented to the right ear (54% vs. 36%). Inversely, the musically experienced subjects sometimes succeeded in identifying the two notes, and in the recognition of melodies there was right-ear superiority (57% for the right ear vs. 44% for the left ear). Bever and Chiarello interpreted their results by saying that the naïve subjects apprehended the melody as a whole whereas the experienced subjects were able to analyze the melody's composition. They concluded (referring to Jackson) that

> the left hemisphere is specialized for propositional analytic and serial processing of incoming information while the right hemisphere is more adapted for the perception of oppositional, holistic and synthetic relations.

The results, apparently contradictory depending on whether only rhythmic sequences or melodic sequences (with musically naïve subjects) are used, need to be clarified by further research. If confirmed, they will indicate a double system of musical perception, one being centered on the temporal rhythm, the other on melodic structures. The distinction corresponds, among other things, to the distinction between the melodic line and the accompaniment.

4.5. Rhythm and Affectivity

The privileged relations between auditory and motor patterns have consequences which go beyond the intersensorial framework. Whether the perceived rhythms are created by movements, as in the musical interpretation, or whether the perceived rhythms give rise to movements, as in the dance, the result is a harmony between the perception and the activity. This harmony, source of affective reactions, was pointed out by Wundt in numerous texts as well as by MacDougall (1902), Isaacs (1920), Ruckmick (1927), and others.

However, we would misunderstand the scope of rhythm if we limited ourselves to an isolated individual's reactions. The data supplied by rhythmic order and the motor induction which arises, permit a group of individuals to coordinate their actions. This is so in song, dance, music, and even in manual labor. The socialization of behavior multiplies the individuals' affective scope and is a source of excitations whose effects are attested to by numerous examples. At the end of a long march, tired soldiers stand erect again as soon as they are swept away by military music, and tired men after a day's work can dance all night. The applause after a performance is never as intense and prolonged as after a concert— it is as if an underlying tension needed to be exteriorized.

From a psychophysiological viewpoint, it can be noted that all sensations crossing the reticular formation influence the activity level. Rhythm's plurisensorality multiplies these effects and can partly explain the importance of rhythmic repercussions on activity and on affectivity.

5. Rhythmic Cues in Poetry and Music

Our preceding analyses attempted to point out the fundamental laws of rhythmic perception. The rhythmic arts—I will deal above all with poetry and music—have to respect these fundamental laws, although artistic creativity always attempts to go beyond the limits.

Poetry and music seem to belong only to the auditory domain, although poetry can be silently read. Poetic and musical rhythms that are perceived by the ear are issued (language and synthetic music excepted) by the word or by the musician's breath or motor play. Thus, poetic and musical rhythms depend on human activity.

The artist, whether he be creator or performer, establishes an order in the succession. However, this order should not be identified with a single isochronous repetition of structures. Metricians designate or look for the isochronism or, more generally, the repetition.

We have already underlined the difference between rhythm and measure. The perceived rhythm can be that of the measure, but it should not be confused with the latter even if the measure is often a condition for several performers playing together.

Rhythmic order implies periodicity, as does a bird's flight or the wind in the trees. However, this periodicity exists from the time that there is a type of structural redundancy on which the predictability and the anticipation of what is to follow is based. The plurality of possible periodicity cues enables the artist to use some of them. One may contest the importance of periodicity in the arts by pointing to the existence of free verse and the Gregorian chant. It is true that in free verse predictability is often foiled by the hiatus, the overrunning of a phrase into the next verse, and the absence of rhyme. But even though one does not find a metric in free verse, one can nevertheless detect the presence of rhythmic cells. In the Gregorian chant, there is also no metric. The notes or neumes do not have a differentiated duration, and everything is based on the variations in pitch and intensity of the successive patterns, which depend on the dynamics of the expiration's movement in a plain chant.

These are extreme forms of the rhythmic art. At the other extreme, we find the isochronous repetition of structures by the insistent recurrence of an intensive accent. The majority of artistic realizations are situated between these two extremes.

5.1. Music

In music, the durations of the elements are exactly specified, as any score will prove. Even though the possible number of these durations, from the quadruple quaver to the semibreve, is very great, in reality a musical movement is based on only two notes—for example, the quaver and the crotchet, or the quaver and the pointed crotchet, or two notes which are in a ratio of 2:3. They represent *80–95%* of the notes (Fraisse, 1956). The others have the evident aesthetic interest of breaking the monotony.

The notes are organized in measures which include a certain number of times. The measure gives a metric structure which allows either the accompaniment or a polyphony which is obtained through a coordination based on the synchronization of signals emanating from different sources. But let us again mention that if the measure is sometimes perceived— and thereby becomes rhythm—very often composers or performers, above all in the modern era, attempt to escape what seems to them to be a tyranny. Vos's (1976) previously cited research on Bach's preludes pointed out the variety of structures that are perceived from the same performance.

In contrast with the rigidity of the organization of the durations, musical scores give few indications regarding the intensity, and these are never specified. However, there are metric rules which require that the first (or the last) time of a measure be accented. But, justly, these rules are indicative and the art is to use them without being subjected to them. The accentive structure remains an essential foundation of musical rhythm. The accent, moreover, can be marked by slight temporal differences. In the playing of Chopin's sixth Nocturne, Henderson (1936), who recorded the duration and the intensity of the notes, noticed that very often (70–80% of the cases) in this piece, the accent was realized by a slight lengthening of the note (from 2% to 20%) and by a temporal delay, which amounts to marking the accent by the slight pause which introduces it.

The accent does not depend only on the intensity. Accentuation, in the widest sense of the term, can be indicated by the intensity, duration, pitch, and also by the accompaniment of the piano or of other instruments in an orchestra. The polyphony permits the play of rhythmic patterns by means of syncopations, enjambments, and countermeasures, which displace the accents or which replace them with a silence or with a holding note. Jazz is the most famous illustration of these variations.

The pitch of the sounds does not play an essential role in musical rhythm. The very large play of the pitch expands to the melody, which has its own organizational laws.

5.2. Poetry

Poetry is a repetitive language. Each verse is *versus*, that is, recurrence. In opposition to prose, *prorsus*, which advances linearly, the verse always comes back on itself (Cohen, 1966). The opposition is fundamental. Poetic rhythm consists of recurrences whose repetition is anticipated. "The decisive factor is not the strength but the repetition" (Jakobson, 1973, p.42). This statement does not prevent Jakobson (p. 491) from declaring, like Baudelaire before him, that this regularity is necessary in order to throw into relief "the disappointed anticipation," a discrepancy which is an essential part of the artistic effect.

Music can be similarly analyzed. However, the fundamental question presents itself: recurrence of what? We can attempt to answer this question by determining the variety of sensorial cues which permit the organization of the duration. By so doing, all possible structural analyses of poetry or of music will not be exhaustively studied. As Jakobson informed us, the periodic recurrences can be located at all levels of language; that is, at the level of the elementary structures (the phonemes), meters, assonances, or rhymes which enter into our field of study, as well as at the level of syntactic formulas or semantic themes which cannot be analyzed in terms of sensations. As in music, we can investigate the respective roles of the elements' duration, intensity, and pitch, and that of the silences.

5.3. The Human Voice

Poetry is the music of language. However, it has a single organ, the voice, which has specific constraints and a different material: phonemes, syllables, and morphemes.

The rhythmic cues are the same as those of music: duration, intensity, pitch. The first thing to point out is that the duration of the basic elements, the syllables (although one can begin the analysis at the phonemic level), is not as precise as that of musical notes. The duration of syllables is variable in all languages. It happens that the same syllable in a word can be short or long. In certain languages, such as Latin, the duration changes the meaning of the word: *mălŭm* means bad, *mālŭm* apple. In everyday language, the duration of the syllables and especially their organization can be random. But when the metrics intervenes in poetry, it imposes relatively strict temporal organizations. In Greek and Latin, the verse was determined by the number of feet and their composition, the feet having a group of different durations (in general, iambus u−, trochee −u, dactyl uv−, or anapest −vv). Each foot could be marked by a beat. Thus, the metric in part determined the duration of the syllables. French is a different example. In the Middle Ages, during the transformation of Latin into French, the distinction between breves and longs lost its perceptual value, resulting in the syllabical system. Poetry was constructed on the basis of the number and no longer the duration of the syllables. The system stressed the temporal cuts (or caesuras) and the recurrence of the rhyme, to the point that until the sixteenth Century, in French, rhyme and rhythm were confused. The syllabical system, moreover, was a theoretical construction. Today we know how to record the duration of sounds, and we are aware that French verse obeys a syllabic and accentual dynamics where the rhythmic patterns are constructed of atonic syllables whose average duration is 16 csec and of accented syllables whose average duration is 37 msec (Faure & Rossi, 1968).

We have just passed from the distinction between breve and long syllables to that between atonic and accented or tonic syllables. In reality, the duration, intensity, and pitch of the syllables in poetry are difficult to dissociate in all languages, as Lieberman (1960) showed.

One of the first studies (Wallin, 1901) to use English started with the fact that accentuation supplied by intensity or by pitch is a fundamental known quantity. Wallin measured the duration of the syllables and declared that the accented have, on the average, a 19-csec duration, the nonaccented an 11-csec duration. The ratio between them varies, according to the piece, between the extreme values of 1.5 and 2.5. In addition, Wallin pointed out that respiratory periods are the principle language divisions. He estimated their average duration to be 119 csec (with a mean deviation (MD) of 34%). The duration of the pause at the end of these periods is 44 csec (MD 29%). Lines of poetry have an average duration of 269 csec (MD 9%). The duration of the pause within lines of poetry is 34 csec (MD 25%) and that at the end of lines of poetry is 68 csec (MD 15%). The terminal pauses unify the lines of poetry and break the continuity of the organization of the accents. However, the regularity of the accents' recurrence remains the dominant rhythmic element, a theory that is again found, for example, in Martin (1972). Using more advanced techniques, Lieberman (1960) demonstrated that in a word

> the stressed syllable had a higher fundamental frequency than the unstressed syllable of the same utterance in 90% of the cases, a higher peak envelope amplitude in 87% and a longer duration in 66%. The stressed syllable compared with its unstressed counterpart in the other word of the stress pair had a higher peak envelope amplitude in 90% and a larger duration in 70% of the cases.

However, it is also necessary here to take into account what the psychoacousticians teach us regarding the effect of the duration on the intensity (Munson, 1947). The perceived intensity of a sound depends on its duration. For a 1,000-HZ sound of 70-dB intensity, the perceived intensity attains its maximum between 20 and 25 csec.

When one thinks that the vowels' duration can vary from 6 csec to 20 csec, one can imagine the simple repercussion of the duration on the intensity which can attain 10 phones. This law explains, at least partly, the connection between duration and accent.

Using Swedish poetry, Linde (1975) measured the relations between the stress of each syllable in several verses of various Swedish poems and its duration as measured by a spectogram. The subjects were asked to note, using free magnitude estimation, the stress of each syllable of the poems recorded on tape by the same actress. The correlations between the rated stress and the physical sensation varied, according to the poem, from .54 to .72. When subjects estimated the rated stress by silently reading the poems, their judgments were about the same (correlations of .70 to .88 for the 2-rated stress of the same poems).

Other analyses by the same author, using linguistic parameters such as the meter (division of the syllables into longs and breves) or prosodic stress (which is estimated from the duration, intensity, and intonation of the syllables), show that the rated stress is best predicted by a multiple correlation which takes into account physical duration and linguistic analyses.

Perceived accent or prominence (Jones, 1940) is not particularly linked to intensity but to a combination of the effects of intensity, duration, and intonation. The human voice is an instrument which poorly separates temporal, intensive, and tonal characteristics in the utterance of sequences of phonemes.

However, it is evident that a poet can more or less use one of the indexes, which thereby becomes prominent. This is striking even in spoken language, and we rightly speak of an Italian accent which is different from the English accent. However, the French accent, it seems, may remain undetected by the untrained ear. We quite rightly say that learning a language is learning its rhythm. Dooling (1974) demonstrated the importance of rhythm in the perception of short sentences perceived in noise. A set was induced by presenting a series of sentences that had the same syntax and rhythm. On a final test sentence either the rhythm alone or rhythm plus surface structure was changed. Changes in rhythm led to major disruptions in performance, whereas the effect of syntax alone was not significant.

Poetry reflects the characteristics of its language as well as the cultural models of its era. Classical Latin and Greek privileged both the duration of the syllables and the tonic accent. Toward the end of the Roman Empire, the tonic accent gave way to the intensive accent, and rhymes such as those already found in Plaute, Virgil, and Horace became more and more frequent. At the beginning of the Middle Ages, the syllabical principle appeared in church hymns and the distinction between breves and longs was lost. In languages such as French, where the syllabical principle is predominant, the pauses or caesuras inside as well as the rhyme at the end of the verses play a fundamental role.

Faure (1962) pointed out that the frequent confusion between stress linked with intensity and intonation linked with pitch comes from the fact that, although one empathizes with the speaker when he makes an effort to accentuate a syllable, the listener is actually more sensitive to differences in pitch. This reminds us that our ears' sensibility to pitch is much more refined than is our sensibility to intensities.

5.4. The Principal Psychological Characteristics

In addition to cue analysis, one can look for—by using adjectives, for example—general features which seem most characteristic of musical and poetic rhythm from the psychological viewpoint.

Two recent Swedish studies deal with this problem. They were performed by applying a variant of semantical-differential technique. Subjects judged the rhythmic qualities of musical or poetic passages, using pairs of adjectives previously chosen by specialists. All of these judgments were then factorially analyzed. After Varimax rotation, the principal factors appear to be as follows.

In music—although his work deals especially with dance—Gabrielsson (1973) distinguished four main factors: a factor linked to tempo named *vital-dull,* a second linked more to melodic and accentual structure named *uniformity-variation,* a third linked to *movement character* which may be characterized by opposites such as floating-stuttering or flexible-mechanical, and a fourth, *exciting-calm,* corresponding at the same time to tempo, a higher loudness level, and pronounced syncopations.

Linde (1975) found four main factors in poetry. The most important is *regularity-variation;* next come *melody* vs. lack of melody, *emphasis* vs. lack of emphasis, and *calmness* vs. agility. The names of these factors are self-explanatory. They do not exactly correspond to Gabrielsson's factors, but this can be quite easily explained. This type of analysis is always relative to the chosen stimulus and to the list of adjectives used. Furthermore, there is nothing surprising in the fact that the rhythmic characteristics of dance and poetry are not exactly the same.

However, since Gabrielsson's work, one can say that the rhythmic experience is linked: (a) to structural properties revealed in music by the factors uniformity-variation and in poetry by the factors regularity-variation and emphasis–lack of emphasis; (b) to movement characteristics in music which correspond to the factors calmness-agility in poetry.

The factors exciting-calm in music, linked to emotionality, and melody vs. lack of melody in poetry can be further specified. Musical rhythm surely has more emotional repercussions, and the melodic character itself is not taken into consideration when one judges musical rhythm as, in music, melody has its own specificity.

6.   Rhythms in Space

Rhythmic movement occurs in space each time that the human body produces, reproduces, or accompanies a temporal rhythm. But is there still rhythmic perception with points, lines, surfaces, and volumes which become organized in space? One is tempted to reply in the affirmative if rhythm is defined by order and proportion only, since order and proportion exist in spatial organizations as does reproduction of these orders. This can be verified in a building, a castle, or a cathedral.

In order to circumvent the problem, I will point out two differences in order to distinguish between rhythms in space and rhythms in time.

6.1.   The Structures

Order corresponds to the fact that temporal succession is always linear while in space there is a juxtaposition of lines, or more frequently, of surfaces and volumes.

Moreover, in the limiting case, space can be reduced to the linear. I wondered whether, in this case, the laws of structuration were the same. (Fraisse, 1956). I chose a three-interval structure. The first was short, the third was long and in a ratio of 2:5 with the first. The second interval varied from a duration almost equal to the short time to a duration 3.8 times that of the short time. This corresponded to a duration 1.53 times as great as that of the long time. These structures were presented in succession (audition) or simultaneously in space (vision).

In audition, the first short time was 18 csec, the third time 45 csec, and the second varied from 21 csec to 69 csec. The subject's task was, after having heard each structure once, to reproduce it as exactly as possible by means of a series of taps. In vision, the structures were the same. The first interval measured 9 mm, the third 22.5 mm, and the second varied between 10.5 and 34.5 mm. This linear structure was presented by tachistoscope during 30 csec, an adequate duration to assure a distinct global perception without permitting analytic evaluations.

The most interesting result was that the same systematic structured deformations were found in both situations, as can be seen in Table I. In order to facilitate the comparison of these ratios, the ratio of the second and third times was always calculated by dividing the longest of the two times by the shortest.

It seems that the deformations resulted principally from an underestimation of the ratios of the two times, except when the ratio of the model's time was greater than 1:6. In this case, the ratio was, on the contrary, overestimated. I interpreted these deformations according to a

Table 1. Ratio of Two Intervals for Spatial or Temporal Reproduction

Models	Reproduction	Ratio of the 2nd to the 3rd interval	Same ratio with spatial reproduction	Same ratio with temporal reproduction
9-10.5-22.5	10.2-11.6-25.7	2.14	2.22	2.57
9-13.5-22.5	10.8-13.9-25.7	1.67	1.85	2.02
9-16.5-22.5	11.2-18.6-23.6	1.36	1.27	1.26
9-19.5-22.5	11.5-21.4-22.9	1.15	1.07	1.04
9-22.5-22.5	12.4-24.9-24.0	1	1.03	1.01
9-25.5-22.5	11.5-25.6-24.0	1.13	1.04	1.02
9-28.5-22.5	11.7-25.3-21.9	1.27	1.15	1.14
9-31.5-22.5	11.6-26.9-24.5	1.4	1.11	1.20
9-34.5-22.5	11.7-29.4-24.0	1.53	1.22	1.21

double law of assimilation and contrast, tending to transform the complex and ambiguous structures into more simple structures corresponding to Gestalt analyses.[1]

The perceptual laws are thus the same no matter which sensory modality is used and in spite of the differences in the manner of reproduction: successive taps in audition, drawn dots in the vision of spatial forms.

However, we cannot conclude that rhythms in space are similar to rhythms in time. Our experiment proves only that there are common perceptual laws for the different sensory channels.

The structural laws are not the same for surfaces and for volumes. In particular, the ratio 1:68, the golden number, which one finds in forms and monuments and which has an almost magic quality (Fraisse, 1974), is precisely the ratio which in the temporal or linearly spatial forms that we have just spoken about is most deformed in one way or other.

6.2. Simultaneity and Succession

A second difference follows from the fact that spatial organization corresponds to elements which are perceived relatively simultaneously, while temporal organization is perceived successively. But would one say that the examination of a colonnade or a facade consists of successive

---

[1] This double law consequently brings the number of different durations in a structure to two. We have just seen above, in poetry as well as in music, that structures were principally constructed using only two durations. They also obey the double law of assimilation–contrast which adds to what I have already said (p. 219) regarding the difficulty of discriminating by absolute judgments more than two durations.

visual examinations? Certainly, but this succession is not an essential characteristic of spatial perception. A good understanding of, for example, an architectural structure implies a representational formation created from successive explorations not following a spatiotemporal order. At the limit, a single assessment perception of a small surface the size of a postcard can reveal order and spatial structure.

Thus, one cannot liken the perception of spatial order to that of temporal order. Temporal rhythms exhibit order, but they also exhibit a dynamic succession linked to explicit or implicit movements.

These differences prevent us from concluding in a syncretic way that rhythms exist in space as they do in time. There are laws of structure and proportion in both dimensions of our experience. Certain laws may be the same, but the rhythmic experience, linked to temporal perceptions, has a specificity which confers on it the close connections which exist in sensorimotor conjunctions, whether man produces the rhythms or whether he listens to them.

7. References

Allen, T.W., Walker, K., Symonds, L., & Marcell, M. Intrasensory and intersensory perception of temporal sequences during infancy. *Developmental Psychology,* 1977, *13,* 225–229.

Bever, T.G., & Chiarello, R.J. Cerebral dominance in musicians and nonmusicians. *Science,* 1974, *185,* 537–539.

Boyd, E.F. Visual fixation and voice discrimination in 2 month old infants. In F.D. Horowitz (Ed.), Visual attention, auditory stimulation and language discrimination in young infants. *Monographs of Society for Research in Child Development,* 1974, *39,* 63–77.

Brown, W. Temporal and accentual rhythm. *The Psychological Review,* 1911, *18,* 336–346.

Carmon, A., & Nachshon, I. Effect of unilateral brain damage on perception of temporal order. *Cortex,* 1971, *7,* 410–418.

Chang, H.W., & Trehub, S.E. Infant's perception of temporal groupings in auditory patterns. *Child Development,* 1977, *48,* 1666–1670.

Cohen, J. *Structure du langage poétique.* Paris: Flammarion, 1966.

Condon, W.S., & Sander, L.W. Neonate movement is synchronized with adult speech: Interactional participation and language acquisition. *Science,* 1974, *183,* 99–101.

Demany, L. *La perception de forme temporelle chez le nourrisson.* Paris: Thèse de 3ème cycle dactylographiée, 1978, 154 p.

Demany, L., McKenzie, B., & Vurpillot, E. Rhythm perception in early infancy. *Nature,* 1977, *266,* 718–719.

Dunlap, K. Reactions to rhythmic stimuli with attempt to synchronize. *Psychological Review,* 1910, *17,* 399–416.

Dooling, D.J. Rhythm and syntax in sentence perception. *Journal of Verbal Learning and Verbal Behavior,* 1974, *13,* 255–264.

Efron, R. The effect of handedness on the perception of temporal order. *Brain,* 1963, *86,* 261–284. (a)

Efron, R. Temporal perception, aphasia, and déjà vu. *Brain,* 1963, *86,* 403–424. (b)

Faure, G. *Recherches sur les caractères et le rôle des éléments musicaux dans la prononciation anglaise.* Paris: Didier, 1962.

Faure, G., & Rossi, M. *Le rythme de l'alexandrin: Analyse critique et contrôle expérimental d'après "le vers français" de Maurice Grammont.* Travaux de Linguistique et de Littérature, VI, 1, Paris: Klinsieck, 1968.

Fraisse, P. Rythmes auditifs et rythmes visuels. *L'Année Psychologique,* 1948, *49,* 21–42.

Fraisse, P. *Les structures rythmiques.* Louvain: Editions Universitaires, 1956.

Fraisse, P. L'anticipation de stimulus rythmiques: Vitesse d'établissement et précision de la synchronisation. *L'Année Psychologique,* 1966, *66,* 15–36.

Fraisse, P. *Psychologie du rythme.* Paris: Presses Universitaires de France, 1974.

Fraisse, P. Perception of time and rhythm. In F.C. Carterette & M.P. Friedman (Eds.), *Handbook of perception.* Vol. 8. New York: Academic Press, 1978.

Fraisse, P. Les synchronisations sensori-motrices dans les rythmes. In J. Requin (Ed.), *Fonctions anticipatrices du système nerveux et processus psychologiques.* Paris: Editions du C.N.R.S. 1980.

Fraisse, P., & Ehrlich, S. Note sur la possibilité de syncoper en fonction du tempo d'une cadence. *L'Année Psychologique,* 1955, *55,* 61–65.

Fraisse, P., & Voillaume, C. Les repères du sujet dans la synchronisation et dans la pseudo-synchronisation. *L'Année Psychologique,* 1971, *71,* 358–369.

Fraisse, P., Oléron, G., & Paillard, P. Les effets dynamogéniques de la musique. *L'Année Psychologique,* 1953, *53,* 1–34.

Fraisse, P., Oléron, G., & Paillard, J. Sur les repères sensoriels qui permettent de contrôler les mouvements d'accompagnement des stimuli périodiques. *L'Année Psychologique,* 1958, *58,* 321–338.

Gabrielsson, A.L.F. Similarity ratings and dimension analyses of auditory rhythm patterns. *Scandinavian Journal of Psychology,* 1973, *14,* 138–160.

Garner, W.R., & Gottwald, R.L. The perception and learning of temporal patterns. *Quarterly Journal of Experimental Psychology,* 1968, *20,* 97–109.

Gault, R.H., & Goodfellow, L.D. An empirical comparison of audition, vision and touch in the discrimination of temporal patterns and ability to reproduce them. *Journal of General Psychology,* 1938, *18,* 41–47.

Gregory, A.H., Harriman, J.C., & Roberts, L.D. Cerebral dominance for the perception of rhythm. *Psychonomic Science,* 1972, *28,* 75–76.

Handel, S., & Buffardi, L. Using several modalities to perceive one temporal pattern. *Quarterly Journal of Experimental Psychology,* 1969, *21,* 256–265.

Henderson, M.T. Rhythmic organization in artistic piano performance. *University of Iowa Studies in the Psychology of Music,* 1936, *4,* 281–306.

Hiriartborde, E., & Fraisse, P. *Les aptitudes rythmiques.* Monographies françaises de Psychologie. Paris: CNRS, 1968.

Hirsh, I.J., & Fraisse, P. Simultanéité et succession de stimuli hétérogènes. *L'Année Psychologique,* 1964, *64,* 1–19.

Isaacs, E. The nature of rhythm experience. *Psychological Review,* 1920, *27,* 270–299.

Jakobson, R. *Questions de poétique.* Paris: Editions du Seuil, 1973.

Jones, D. *An outline of English Phonetics.* New York: Dutton, 1940.

Karlovitch, R.S., & Graham, J.T. Effects of pure tone synchronous and delayed auditory feedback on keytapping performance to a programmed visual stimulus. *Journal of Speech and Hearing Research,* 1966, *9,* 596–603.

Karlovitch, R.S., & Graham, J.T. Auditorily paced keytapping performance during synchronous decreased and delayed visual feedback. *Perceptual and Motor Skills,* 1968, *26,* 731–743.

Kimura, D. Left-right differences in the perception of melodies. *Quarterly Journal of Experimental Psychology*, 1964, *16*, 355–358.

Klapper, Z.S., & Birch, H.G. Developmental course of temporal patterning in vision and audition. *Perceptual and Motor Skills*, 1971, *32*, 547–555.

Koffka, K. Experimentelle Untersuchungen zur Lehre von Rhythmus. *Zeitschrift Für Psychologie*, 1909, *52*, 1–109.

Kravitz, H., & Boehm, J.J. Rhythmic habit patterns in infancy: Their sequence, age of onset and frequency. *Child Development*, 1971, *42*, 399–413.

Külpe, O. *Outlines of psychology*. New York: Macmillan, 1895.

Laloy, L. *Aristoxène de Tarente et la musique de l'antiquité*. Paris: 1904.

Lieberman, P. Some acoustic correlates of word stress in American English. *Journal of the Acoustical Society of America*, 1960, *32*, 451–454.

Linde, L. *Perception of stress in auditively presented Swedish poetry*. Reports from the Department of Psychology of Stockholm, 1975, N 442.

Luria, A.R. *Higher cortical functions in man*. New York: Basic Books, 1966.

Mac Dougall, R. The relation of auditory rhythm to nervous discharge. *The Psychological Review*, 1902, *9*, 460–480.

MacDougall, R. The structure of rhythm forms. *Psychological Review, Monograph Supplements*, 1903, *4*, 309–416.

Martin, J.G. Rhythmic (hierarchical) versus serial structure in speech and other behavior. *Psychological Review*, 1972, *79*, 487–509.

Meumann, E. Untersuchugen zur Psychologie und Aesthetik des Rhythmus. *Philosphische Studien*, 1894, *10*, 249–332, 393–430.

Milner, R. Laterality effects in audition. In V. Mountcastle (Ed.), *Interhemispheric relations and cerebral dominance*. Baltimore: John Hopkins University Press, 1962, pp. 177–195.

Miner, J.B. Motor, visual and applied rhythms. *Psychological Review, Monograph Supplements*, 1903, *5*, 1–106.

Mishima, J. On the factors of the mental tempo. *Japanese Psychological Research*, 1956, *4*, 27–38.

Miyake, I. Researches on rhythmic activity. *Studies from the Yale Psychological Laboratory*, 1902, *10*, 1–48.

Munson, W.A. The growth of auditory sensation. *Journal of the Acoustical Society of America*, 1947, *19*, 584–591.

Natale, M. Perception of nonlinguistic auditory rhythms by the speech hemisphere. *Brain and Language*, 1977, *4*, 32–44.

Nazzaro, J.R., & Nazzaro, J.N. Auditory versus visual learning of temporal patterns. *Journal of Experimental Psychology*, 1970, *84*, 477–478.

Oléron, G. Etude de la "perception" des structures rythmiques. *Psychologie Française*, 1959, *4*, 176–189.

Piéron, H. *The sensations: Their functions, processes and mechanisms*. New Haven: Yale University Press, 1952, p. 469.

Preusser, D. The effect of structure and rate on the recognition and description of auditory temporal patterns. *Perception and Psychophysics*, 1972, *11*, 233–240.

Preusser, D., Garner, W.R., & Gottwald, R. L. Perceptual organization of two-element temporal patterns as a function of one-element patterns. *American Journal of Psychology*, 1970, *83*, 151–170.

Robinson, G.M., & Solomon, D.J. Rhythm is processed by the speech hemisphere. *Journal of Experimental Psychology*, 1974, *102*, 508–511.

Rosenbusch, M.H., & Gardner, B. Reproduction of visual and auditory rhythm patterns by children. *Perceptual and Motor Skills*, 1968, *26*, 1271–1276.

Rosenzweig, M.R. Representation of the two ears at the auditory cortex. *American Journal of Physiology*, 1951, *167*, 147–158.

Rubinstein, L., & Gruenberg, E.M. Intramodal and crossmodal sensory transfer of visual and auditory temporal patterns. *Perception and Psychophysics*, 1971, *9*, 385–390.

Ruckmick, C.A. A bibliography of rhythm. *American Journal of Psychology*, 1913, *24*, 508–519.

Ruckmick, C.A. Visual Rhythm. *Studies in Psychology: Titchener Commemorative Volume*. Worcester, Mass.: 1917, pp. 231–254.

Ruckmick, C.A. The rhythmical experience from the systematic point of view, *American Journal of Psychology*, 1927, *39*, 355–366.

Seashore, C.E. *The psychology of music*. New York: McGraw-Hill, 1938.

Seashore, R.H. Studies in motor rhythm. *Psychological Monography*, 1927, *36*, 142–189.

Smith, O.W. Relationship of rhythm discrimination to motor rhythm performance. *Journal of Applied Psychology*, 1957, *41*, 365–369.

Teatini, G. L'intégration bi-auriculaire des rythmes. *Les rythmes, Journal Français d'otho-rhino-laryngologie*, 1968, Supplément Automne 7, 115–126.

Thackray, R. *An investigation into rhythmic abilities*. London: Novello, 1969.

Titchener, E.B. *A textbook of psychology*. New York: Macmillan, 1916.

Vos, P.G. Identification of metre in music. Report 760N06, University of Nijmiegen, 1976.

Wallin, J.E.W. Researches on the rhythm of speech. *Studies from the Yale Psychological Laboratory*, 1901, *9*, 1–142.

Werner, H. Rhythmik, eine mehrwertige Gestaltenverkettung. *Zeitschrift für Psychologie*, 1919, *82*, 198–218.

Westphal, R. *Aristoxenus von Tarent Melik und Rhythmik des classischen Hellenenthums*. Leipzig, 1883.

8

Gait Perception as an Example of How We May Perceive Events

JAMES E. CUTTING and DENNIS R. PROFFITT

1. Time, Movement, and Their Place in Event Structure

In *An Essay Concerning Human Understanding,* John Locke (Locke, 1690/1959, II:8:9) listed five primary qualities of objects in the world around us: solidity, extension, figure, number, and motion. These attributes have served us well in the study of perception. Solidity, for example, has been studied in terms of transparency and depth in vision, texture in touch, and stereophony in audition—stereophonic literally means "solid sound." Extension, or size, has been very important, particularly in vision, where psychologists have studied effects of relative and absolute size, and proximal and distal size. Figure, interpreted as shape or form, has undoubtedly been the most important quality of objects for all perception, providing impetus for Gestalt and other psychologists. Number, especially when logically extended to include composition and the relation of parts to wholes, has also played an important role. Motion has also played some part; however, unlike the others, motion has most often been excised from the aggregate by the perceptual psychologist. It appears that we have spent most of our efforts in the study of *static* figures of a certain size, composition, and apparent solidity. It is clear that motion is a quality unlike the others; it

JAMES E. CUTTING • Department of Psychology, Uris Hall, Cornell University, Ithaca, New York 14853. DENNIS R. PROFFITT • Department of Psychology, University of Virginia, Charlottesville, Virginia 22901. Supported by NIH Grants MH33087 and MH35530.

invokes time. Our general purpose is to help integrate motion and time back into the study of perception.

Gibson (1950, 1966, 1979) and Johansson (1950, 1973, 1975) have argued that we should have spent more time with movement and less with static perception. Neisser (1976) and Turvey (1977) have lent the force of their recent apostasy from the usual tenets of information processing to reinforce the general views of Gibson and Johansson. It is amusing to note, however, that while these researchers have inveighed against the use of the tachistoscope to reveal psychological processes, the *inventor* of the modern tachistoscope, Raymond Dodge, presented this same view more than 60 years earlier:

> The tendency to reduce the physical exposure time to a minimum . . . is a methodological mistake, based upon a psycho-physical misconception. It introduces unusual conditions altogether foreign to the natural fixation pause, and leads, or may well lead, to a distorted analysis of the processes of apprehension; making the conclusion insofar as they are referred to normal perception, not merely valueless, but false. . . . (p. 32) Anything approximating a threshold exposure instead of simplifying the consequent psychological process, really complicates it and renders it more uncertain. (1907, p. 35)

Alas, fascination with the possibility of taking snapshots of mental life has left psychologists unmoved by Dodge's admonition. The reason for this may be twofold: First, psychologists have proceeded for the most part as if motion perception is achieved by simple compilation of static forms, much as a moving picture is assembled from separate frames; second, when somewhat more reflective, psychologists have simply stated that motion is too complex to be studied until we have a better grasp of the laws of form, composition, solidity, and size.

The first reason views dynamic forms as special cases of static forms. However, Gibson and Johansson suggest reversing this relation, and we agree. The value of considering static events as special cases of dynamic events is evidenced in the history of analytic geometry and calculus, mechanics, and physics. Johansson (1974, p. 142) has noted that, "The initial theoretical structure for physics was of a static type, and Zeno's paradoxes are well-known examples of the logical impossibility of dealing adequately with motion within this framework." He goes on to suggest that conventional approaches to perception are "rather similar to the pre-Galilean type of physics." Indeed, the conceptual breakthroughs of Galileo and Descartes were grounded in considerations of dynamic events, whereas the speculations of their predecessors related almost exclusively to statics (see Boyer, 1968; Mach, 1893). Thus, perhaps we should follow the lead of physics and consider dynamics to be primary with statics as a special case where time is held null.

The second reason for omitting motion from psychological study is equally damning. It asserts that psychologists are simply incapable at this time of a dynamic perceptual psychology. We think this is untrue. In our opinion, the basic elements necessary for a psychology of event perception are at hand.

Both reasons, however, converge on the same fact—the motion of relatively complex objects has remained largely unstudied. Our purpose in this chapter is to demonstrate that these two rationales are incorrect: (a) Movement is not the simple compilation of static forms, and (b) it is not so complex as to be unamenable to analytic study. In fact, we hope to show that there is a beautiful simplicity in dynamic forms that may contribute to their perception.

Our domain of study is that of *event* perception, so named by Johansson (1950). Before beginning our exposition, however, it behooves us to explain what we mean by an event. It seems best to follow Webster, where an event is defined as: "That which occupies a restricted portion of four-dimensional space-time." By extension, *perceptual* event would entail perception of movement or recognition of change in an object in one, two, or three spatial coordinates through the added dimension of time. What this definition accomplishes for us is that it states that events have a structure. Moreover, it implies that this structure separates an event from the rest of the world.

Wolfgang Köhler, among others, has parsed event structure. In speaking of objects and their movements, he stated

> In a physical system events are determined by two sorts of factors. In the first class belong the forces and other factors inherent in the processes of the system. These we will call the *dynamic* determinants of its fate. In the second class we have characteristics of the system which subject its processes to restricting conditions. Such determinants we will call *topographical* determinants of its fate. (1947, p. 107)

A *dynamic invariant* of an event can be thought of as some algorithm that describes change throughout the course of the event, and governs its temporal structure. A *topographic invariant* can be thought of as the abstract physical relations that remain constant throughout the event, governing its spatial structure. For a rolling ball, rolling can be said to be the dynamic invariant (subject to forces of gravity and impetus), and a spherical shape is the topographic invariant (subject to deformations by dynamics). Pittenger and Shaw (1975) have parsed events in a similar manner, postulating transformational and structural invariants. We prefer Köhler's terminology, because it is historically older and because the term *structural* as it includes dynamics, invites confusion of purely topographic concerns with all of event structure.

There are problems, however, with the type of parsing suggested by Köher and by Pittenger and Shaw. One problem is that this distinction systematically confuses two types of movements, those occurring within the object and those occurring with respect to the observer. Wallach (1965) calls these object-relative displacement and angular displacement. For our rolling ball, for example, the action of rolling has two components. One is object-relative. That is, the ball turns circles around itself. The other is observer-relative. That is, the ball moves through a visual angle of measurable degree as it passes in front of the observer. The differentiation of these two motions, rotation and translation, is important because, for event perception to occur, it appears that object-relative displacement is perceived *before* angular displacement, as suggested by Wallach (1965), and contrary to Johansson (1973). Proffitt, Cutting, and Stier (1979) and Proffitt and Cutting (1979) give a detailed account of why this is so. In the final two sections of this chapter we will discuss these two types of dynamic motions in more detail.

What is new to our approach to perceptual events is a factor that derives from topographic and from object-relative dynamic invariants: the center of moment. The center of moment is a functional point within the topography of the object, around which object-relative dynamics occur. For example, an axle is the center of moment for a wheel, and a fulcrum is the center of moment for a lever arm. Our plan in this chapter is to demonstrate that this point is perceptually useful and that, in fact, it appears to guide the viewer to perceive a dynamic whole. In this manner we capitalize on two of the term's meanings: that is, on *moment* as it refers to movement in the study of mechanics, and also as it refers to importance (as in the term *momentous*).

2. Gait Perception without Familiarity Cues

Using a technique that began with the work of Marey (1895/1933), Johansson (1973) mounted points of light on a person and observed that a perceiver had no difficulty determining the activity of that person, whether walking, running, bicycling, painting, doing push-ups, or dancing. We became fascinated with this kind of dynamic array. By placing lights on the joints and by darkening the surround, an experimenter can effectively remove all familiarity cues from the stimulus. In other words, the type of clothing, hairstyle, and facial expression of an individual are omitted, and only the relations among the moving points of light can be seen. Thus, one perceives the presence of a human being simply through the relational structure of the moving lights. This relational structure is, we believe, a deep structure, analogous to that of a sentence. In the final section of this chapter we will outline what we mean by this.

Our starting point in this research program was the commonly held belief that people can recognize friends by their walk. Unfortunately, this belief and the previously existing research on the topic (Wolff, 1943) are confounded by surface cues and probabilities of seeing someone at a given place and time. To counteract these contradictions, we employed six Wesleyan University undergraduates, three males and three females of approximately the same height and weight who lived together in university housing (Cutting & Kozlowski, 1977). We affixed glass-bead retroreflectant bicycle tape to their joints and videorecorded their gait as they passed in front of a television camera. A bright light was mounted near the camera and focused on the walking area. Contrast was turned to near maximum, brightness to near minimum, and the camera was placed slightly out of focus so as to make more circular the images of the reflectant patches. Figure 1 shows static representations of this technique, with brightness\turned up so that one can see where the tape is mounted on the walker. Two months after recording many examples of the gait of each walker, we randomized the dynamic-stimulus items on a test tape and presented the test to the subject. Their task was to identify each person in a 2.7-sec dynamic display of lights. Chance performance was near 17% and all viewers exceeded this value, with a mean of 38% correct identification across all trials. Without feedback, their performance improved over the course of the task from 28% on the first third of all trials to 59% on the last third. Thus, viewers can recognize themselves and others from a display that presents only the time-varying relational structure of gait, without the usual cues of hair style, clothing, and facial expression.

Although we continue to be fascinated with this result, we have not found it particularly amenable to further study. The problem lies in the fact that individual identity can be thought of as composed of many aspects: height, weight, age (all of which were controlled for in our study), gender, and various difficult-to-define personality variables. To further our study of gait perception, then, we chose to focus on one particular aspect of different walkers. We selected gender in part because Maas, Johansson, Jansson, and Runeson (1971) asked the following question on a study guide: "Do you think that subjects could detect male-female differences in the motion pattern of walkers, using the 'pinpoint of light' technique?" Aggravatingly, they did not answer the question, so it fell to us to do so experimentally (Kozlowski & Cutting, 1977).

We took the same videotape sequence used previously and presented it to 30 different undergraduates who had no knowledge of the identity of the six walkers. Where chance for determining gender would be 50%, performance was 63% correct, significantly better than chance. Moreover, when we replicated the results with 14 new walkers (seven males and seven females) and 57 new viewers, performance in judging males

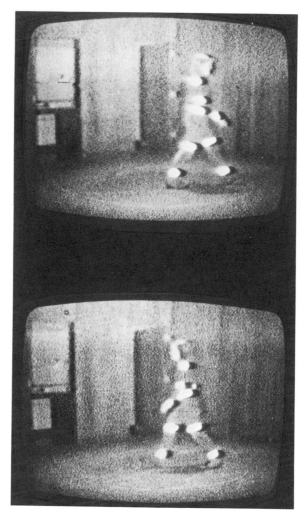

Fig. 1. A walker in two most-outstretched positions in the step cycle. Brightness of the image is turned up to reveal the approximate locations of the reflectant tape. Blurring and fuzziness result from the nature of the video medium.

and females was 67% correct (Barclay, Cutting, & Kozlowski, 1978). In general, across many experimental manipulations, observers, and stimuli, performance appears to hover between 60% and 70% on this task. Thus, while the effect is not large, it is systematic and generalizable.

Among these results were a number of interesting and surprising findings. First, static displays taken from the dynamic sequences were insufficient for revealing gender cues. In fact, most subjects had no idea that the constellations of lights represented human walkers—instead, they saw them as either clusters of stars or as Christmas trees viewed at night. Second, at least 2 sec of display time in the dynamic stimulus was necessary before viewers could give any accurate judgments of gender. This is an order of magnitude longer than the duration needed to see that the moving lights represent a human being (Johansson, 1976). From this fact we argued that two-step cycles, or four complete steps, appeared necessary for gender recognition. Third, no particular lights seemed sufficient for gender identification. It may be that even the ankles alone are sufficient (but see Kozlowski & Cutting, 1978), and certainly the ankles and right hip alone or the wrists, elbows, and right shoulder are sufficient.

These results suggested to us a number of things. First, the dynamic aspect of the display is crucial. Second, it took an extraordinarily long time for viewers to perform the task—at least with respect to the usual displays used in information-processing tasks. This generally excluded reaction time as a dependent measure and the use of brief displays as stimuli if we were to pursue our interest in this domain. Finally, and most importantly, the information available to the viewer appeared to be everywhere in the display, distributed from head to toe in the dynamic stimulus. This precluded the usual divide-and-conquer approach to cue finding in the stimulus array. Somehow the information that was relevant to gender identification was holistic in nature.

Initially, however, we ignored these implications and took a particularistic approach. Our first hypothesis was that arm swing might dictate to the viewer who is male and who is female. Indeed, we found that in our sample and in the normal population in general, women swung their arms more than men. Thus, we brought back our original set of walkers, and controlled arm swing. We found that viewers could recognize gender regardless of arm swing, though to a diminished extent. Thus, arm swing may be sufficient, but it is not necessary for gender recognition. Next, we thought that walking speed might suggest to the viewer who is male and who is female. Indeed, in our sample and in the general college population women take more steps per minute than men. We brought back our original walkers again, controlled walking speed, and found that viewers could still recognize gender, though again to a somewhat lesser degree. We also investigated step size—males generally take bigger steps than females—but this, too, was not a necessary cue. Thus, with such a particularistic approach we seemed to be thwarted at every turn. This, more than the logic of our previous results, forced us to drop back and reconsider the stimulus as a whole (Cutting, Proffitt, & Kozlowski, 1978).

2.1. A Search for a Biomechanical Invariant

We were convinced that there was something in the dynamic display that viewers were using to make their judgments. Thus, with no particular prejudice as to what we might find, we took a whole battery of physical measurements from our walkers—shoulder width, hip width, torso length, height, leg length, arm length, etc. Juggling these figures in virtually all possible ways, we rediscovered a fact that has been known since the beginning of art: Men have proportionately wider shoulders than women, and women have proportionately wider hips. This type of data can be found in Gray's Anatomy (1901/1977), Albrecht Dürer's sketches (Dürer, 1528/1972), and in contemporary sources such as Faust (1977, p. 67). The standard measure that reflects these differences is a ratio of shoulder width to hip width. Depending on where the measurements are taken, the ratio for men in our sample and for men in general is about 1.1, for women in our sample and women in general, about 1.0. This ratio for each of our walkers was highly correlated with a second measure, the percentage of all trials in which each was identified as male. That is, in general female walkers in our sample had shoulder–hip ratios near 1.0 or below and were identified as male on a mean of 35% of all trials. Male walkers, on the other hand, had ratios near 1.1 and were identified as male on a mean of 65% of all trials. This correlation across all walkers was remarkably strong, $r = .84$.

We thought that we might be well on our way toward describing a biomechanical invariant for gait perception, but then realized that there was a basic problem with our description: Viewers made judgments of walkers' gender from *sagittal* displays, where only one shoulder and one hip were visible at any one time. Thus, while our description accounted for most of the variance in our response measure, we were embarrassed by the fact that this description could not possibly be used, because it was not directly calculable from the visual display. We did feel, however, that we might be on the right track and that something related to the shoulders and hips may be invariant in sagittal, and perhaps other, displays.

Our second tack, then, was to determine what the shoulders and hips were doing in the step cycle. Studying the work of Carlsöö (1972), Murray (1967), and Saunders, Inman, and Eberhart (1953), we realized that the hips and the shoulders work in opposition to one another, as shown in Figure 2. *Torso* and *torsion,* after all, are derived from the same word. Thus, at the point within the step cycle where the right leg is forward and both feet are on the ground, the right hip is forward and the right shoulder is back. Both joints move counterclockwise along the path of an ellipse so that the next time both feet are on the ground, with

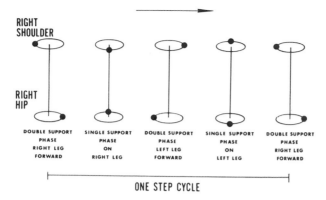

Fig. 2. A schematic representation of ellipsoidal movements of the right shoulder and right hip during one step cycle.

weight equally distributed, the right shoulder is forward and the right hip is back. Notice also that when the person is standing solely on the right foot, the length of the torso as measured from the hip to the shoulder on the right side is at its shortest extent, and that when standing only on the left, this length is at its greatest. This latter motion derives from a description by Murray, Kory, and Sepic (1970, p. 647). However, we concentrated on the former—the oscillation back and forth of the hips and shoulders. We argued that if male shoulders are broader than female shoulders, this difference ought to be visible as a greater shoulder swing for males than females. Moreover, if the shoulder difference is greater than the inverse difference in hip widths—and it is—then one could derive a measure of the various hip and shoulder swings from the visual display. This measure is shown in Figure 3.

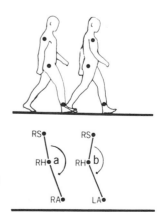

Fig. 3. Viewed from the side (as a sagittal projection), the torque in the torso can be measured by subtracting Angle B from Angle A. RS = right shoulder; RH = right hip; RA = right ankle; LA = left ankle.

Consider just three points of light: those for the right shoulder and the right hip, and that for the forward leg as it is planted on the ground. Connecting these points of light one can derive two angles, one when the right leg is forward and the angle is largest and one when the left leg is forward and the angle is smallest. The difference between these angles, we argued, would reflect the differences in the amount of shoulder swing, and hence might reflect gender. More particularly, male walkers should have larger angle differences than females. Indeed, careful measurement of all stimuli for all walkers yielded this difference. The correlation between this index and the percent of all trials in which each walker was identified as male was high, $r = .76$. This correlation is slightly lower than that for torso structure and identifiability, and it is as high as it is only because one walker was omitted from the sample. She was omitted because she did not swing her arms at all, had no difference between her two angular measurements, and was identified as male nearly 50% of the time. In other words, we argued, she was off the scale of angular differences—females had a mean of about 9° and males about 18°, and she was near 0°.

We were not happy with the need for her exclusion, but we were even more unhappy with our torsion index and its relation to a previous result. Remember, not all joints need to be represented in the dynamic display for accurate gender identification to occur. For example, the arms (shoulders, elbows, and wrists) are sufficient by themselves— leaving no hip and no ankles to be measured against. In addition, the legs (the hips, knees, and ankles) are also sufficient—leaving no shoulder to be measured against. Thus, while our torsion index may be appropriate for some standard displays in which all joints are represented by lights, it was clearly insufficient for others in which gender was determined almost as well as in the standard condition.

Although we believed that we were still on the right track, our description was surely not the most apt. We had come to believe that our biomechanical invariant should be one that was appropriate to all experimental conditions. Moreover, we began to be wary of the fact that, whereas our previous description might be appropriate to walkers, it was completely irrelevant to other types of moving displays. Thus, we wanted our invariant not only to capture the essence of the dynamics of gait, but to be applicable to other perceptual events.

2.2. An Invariant Found: A Center of Moment

Further study of existing research on the dynamics of gait revealed the systematic patterns involved. As one arm swings forward, the other swings back; as one leg swings forward the other swings back; crossed limbs work in phase synchrony; ipsilateral limbs work in opposition. Thus, dynamic symmetry is the key. It occurred to us, then, that if gait was symmetrical we should be able to find planes of symmetry. Certainly the midsagittal plane, the plane of biological symmetry, was important. However, we found two others: a horizontal plane of symmetry between the hips and the shoulders near the level of the navel, and a frontal plane dividing the front of the body from the back. These three planes intersect at a point, somewhere between the shoulders and the hips, so we began to focus on trying to find it.

Dividing the dynamic walker into planes is no easy feat, so it occurred to us that perhaps the environmental coordinates of the space around the walker may not be the most appropriate. We decided to consider the coordinates of the walker instead. This view assumes simply that the walker stays stationary and the environment moves around him or her. Functionally, it is identical to a description that assumes that the walker moves through the environment, but it turns out to have some notational simplicities about it, not captured by the other. Besides, Johansson (1973, 1976) had begun to use environmental coordinates in his vector-analytic approach to gait perception and, to us, it looked hopelessly cumbersome.

By using walker coordinates we assumed that there is a point within the walker around which everything moves. Indeed, this point will move through the environment, but this is an irrelevant concern at this time; we are simply interested in finding a "ground zero" for the movement of gait. It turns out that since the arms and legs are working in dynamic symmetry they can be temporarily omitted from consideration. That is, whatever movements happen to be going on in an arm are being counteracted by the other arm and the ipsilateral leg, but reinforced by the opposite leg. Forces and movements in the limbs nullify one another, leaving only the torso to be considered.

The torso has the general shape of an isosceles trapezoid, oscillating as a flat torsion spring. This general shape is shown in Figure 4 for a male walker and a female walker. When the torso oscillates, one can

Fig. 4. Schematic representation of the torsos of a male and female. In general, males have slightly wider shoulders and narrower hips than females. The intersection of stress lines across the diagonals of the torso is the center of moment. Note that this point is not the center of gravity.

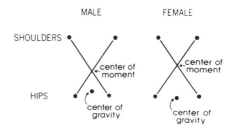

derive stress lines across the diagonals of the torso. These intersect at a point that we call the *center of moment,* a reference around which all movement in all parts of the body has regular geometric relations. Its relative location can be determined by knowing only the relative widths of the hips and shoulders. In general, males' center of moment is lower than females'. It is important to note, however, that for walkers the center of moment is *not* the center of gravity. The center of gravity concerns distributions of mass, whereas the center of moment concerns distributions of movement.

To make this point clear, consider a rolling wheel. The center of gravity for the wheel happens also to be its center of moment. That is, all motion occurs around the point around which all mass is distributed. However, consider these centers for a pendulum. Here, the center of gravity lies in the bob, oscillating back and forth, whereas the center of moment is the pivot. In similar fashion, the centers are separated in the human body. Certainly the center of gravity plays a crucial role in maintaining the balance in a human body, but we suggest that it is the center of moment that is perceptually the more important, because its location within the torso is strongly correlated with viewer performance, $r = .86$. Happily, this correlation includes the one difficult-to-identify female walker that was previously excluded.

However, a note of caution is in order. We acknowledge that there are an indefinite number of possible mathematical descriptions for our stimulus events, each of which would be similar to this one and account for the data just as well. Thus, there are at least two avenues of logic that we must pursue. First, we must garner some empirical evidence showing that our theory is plausible, and second, we must discover if our description applies to other types of perceptual events besides walking.

2.3. Gait Synthesis

We had found that fully three-fourths of all the variance in viewer judgments could be accounted for by a single variable. One should always be skeptical of such results, and we were. Thus, it behooved us to determine if this claim could be substantiated. The method that occurred to us was gait synthesis—an attempt to generate, on a computer display scope, constellations of dynamic light patterns that mimicked the movements of male and female walkers. Through this synthesis it would be possible to generate stimuli that differed *only* in their centers of moment. That is, the motions involved would differ only because of the difference in the place around which they were generated, constrained by the general forces of gravity and impetus.

Gait synthesis turned out to be relatively easy to accomplish (Cutting, 1978a,c), and it became possible to generate synthetic male and female walkers that were at least as identifiable as such on 80% of all trials. In addition, gait synthesis allowed us to replicate some of our previous results. For example, removing some of the lights from the display, such as the shoulder and the hip, decreased viewer performance to about 60%, yet it remained significantly above chance. Moreover, viewers judged that the synthetic versions of female walkers were more light-footed than the synthetic males. This result correlates nicely with naturalistic observations, and it makes good biomechanical sense. Females, with larger excursions of the hip, absorb more of the vertical bouncing motion of gait. This causes the carriage of the torso to be more even, and creates the appearance of gliding across the floor.

We were most pleased with our gait-synthesis venture by the fact that the synthesis routine is *exactly* that structure derived from our analysis of gait. This analysis-and-synthesis type of research program is analogous to that used so successfully in speech perception (Liberman, Ingemann, Lisker, Delattre, & Cooper, 1959). Its success can be taken as corroborating evidence that our description of the center of moment is theoretically plausible.

We are left, however, with the problem of generalizability. That is, would our center-of-moment analysis work for the perception of other types of events—for moving objects without shoulders and hips?

3. Perceiving Centers of Moment in Other Events

We do not have space to discuss fully our research on nongait movement, but we can indicate the perceptual utility of centers of moment in four domains, each quite different from walking.

3.1. Perceiving Centers of Moment in Wheel-Generated Motions

Consider first the Gestalt demonstration of the perception of rotary motion, or wheel-generated movement. From reading Koffka (1935) most of us remember that placing a light on the rim of a wheel, darkening the surround, and rolling that wheel across a flat surface yields the perception of a hopping light—but *not* the perception of a wheel rolling. Add some lights to the perimeter, or one to the center, and suddenly the dynamic event looks like a rolling wheel. Although the Gestalt psychologists were convincing in such demonstrations, we found little hard data on how good these rolling configurations of lights appeared to viewers. Thus, using a scaling technique, we investigated the apparent goodness for configurations of lights mounted on a rolling circular structure (Proffitt & Cutting, 1979; Proffitt *et al.*, 1979).

Two abstract centers are of importance here: one is the center of the wheel, and the other is the center of the configuration of lights, or centroid, which, in our view, is directly analogous to the center of moment in a walker. For a one-light configuration the centroid is simply the center of the single light; for a two-light system the centroid is the center of the triangle formed by the three lights, derived by the method of medians. This point is the point on which the triangle would balance if it were placed on top of a pencil tip. We discovered that it is the relation between these two points, the centroid and the center of the generating wheel, that dictates how wheellike the motion of lights will appear. That is, if the two centers are very far apart, the system of lights will appear to be a hobbling or bouncing structure. If, on the other hand, the two systems are very close together, the structure will look more like a rolling wheel. When the two centers are in exactly the same locale, viewers typically judge the stimuli to be perfect, or near-perfect, wheels. Thus, it is the center of moment (centroid) of a configuration of lights, and its relation to the center of the generating wheel, that perceivers appear to use in making their judgments of goodness concerning rotary motion.

3.2. Perceiving Centers of Moment in Aging Faces

A second nongait event in which we have found a center of moment useful is the perception of aging in human profiles. Pittenger and Shaw (1975) describe the process of facial aging as one of cardioidal transformation. That is, from the work of Thompson (1917) and Enlow (1975), they derived a mathematical description of the elastic shape changes undergone by the human skull. These changes are rather closely approximated by a heartlike (cardioidal) change in which the proportionately larger size of the cranium in the child is supplanted by a proportionately larger size of the lower face in the adult. Fortuitously, this transformation must occur about a point, and the most likely place for this point is somewhere inside the skull. Transforming the profile of an early teenager around a matrix of different points in sagittal space, and having viewers make judgments about the goodness of different transformed heads, we derived a point of best transformation (Cutting, 1978b). That is, this point would yield the transformed profiles judged as best examples of younger and older versions of a standard profile. Interestingly, this point corresponds almost exactly with a region found by Enlow from which aging changes are generated. This region is near the foramen magnum, the place where the skull meets the spinal column. Thus, for the perception of transposed heads—with apologies to Thomas Mann—there is a center of moment around which aging best occurs.

3.3. Perceiving Centers of Moment in Flowfields

A third nongait event of interest concerns the flowfield demonstrations of Gibson (1950, 1979). When flying over a terrain, or driving a car through it, one becomes aware that all textures in the visual world around the observer expand centrifugally from a point toward which one is hurtling. The perceptual utility of this point is that its location marks precisely the direction in which one is headed. (A complementary point can also be found directly behind the observer, indicating the direction from which he or she is coming.) Thus, the center of moment for a radiating flowfield can be useful to a perceiver, just as it is in the cases of a walker, a rolling wheel, and an aging face.

3.4. Perceiving Centers of Moment in the Night Sky

A fourth nongait event concerns celestial navigation by migratory songbirds. This entry in the domain of event perception pleases us because, for the first time in our discussion, it concerns points of light that are real objects (stars) rather than schematic representations of such objects. It appears that certain songbirds can use the clear night sky as an aid in migration. Prior to migratory flight, they typically sit in the branches of a tree for a period of hours, then suddenly take off— southward if it is fall and northward if it is spring. Ethologists had postulated that these birds might have some form of innate celestial map. Emlen (1975), however, thought this implausible and set out to discover what source of information in the night sky might aid migration. He suggested that birds watched the night sky rotate over a period of hours and through that rotation found the celestial north pole, Polaris (the North Star). To corroborate his point, he placed birds overnight in round cages within a planetarium, and found that over the course of hours they oriented with respect to the north pole. Moreover, when Emlen artificially rotated the night sky around Betelgeuse, the birds oriented anew as if it were the pole star. Our interest in this phenomenon is that the celestial north pole, whether there is a star there or not, is the center of moment for the rotating manifold of the night sky. Songbirds appear to extract it from the dynamic display, and use it to guide their migration.

Our delight in these disparate findings is that centers of moment appear to be useful in all types of events—those that are either slow or fast, rigid or nonrigid, reversible or irreversible, and biological or nonbiological. Moreover, underlying the richness of varied types of events there appears to be a common structure. This structure, we believe can be thought of as a deep structure, much like the deep structure of a sentence. In the next section we will outline what we mean by this.

4. Toward a Grammar for Perceptual Events

We are continually impressed in our research by the fact that the perceptual system seems to select one mathematical description for an event from among an indefinitely large set of possibilities. For example, two lights mounted opposite each other on the rim of an unseen rolling wheel are seen to revolve about the wheel's unseen center and also to move linearly across the visual field. This perception of *two* motion components for the two lights is one mathematical description of the event; however, the perception of each light moving independently on cycloidal paths is an alternative that is rarely seen. Depending upon the orders of extraction of information, the number of motion components sought, and the points taken as reference, this simple event could be specified in many different ways. In this section we offer a general description, a grammar if you will, for event perception. This "grammar" is an attempt to describe the information available in visual perception in terms of its analysis into the components that are perceived.

We call the information available to observers over time the visual scene.[1] Figure 5 is a deep-structure description of the parsing of the visual scene by the perceptual system. This diagram retains traditional descriptions of static perception by making them a special case of the more general perception of dynamic events. An emphasis is placed on the splitting of movements into two perceived components: internal dynamics within the figure and action of the figure as a whole. The remainder of this section is an elaboration of Figure 5, proceeding from the top of the diagram and working down.

The first division of the visual scene preserves the distinction between figure and ground while making figure a special type of event. Since the early work of Rubin (1915), perceptual psychologists have noted that objects, figures, and events are always embedded within contexts or grounds. Given that the term *figure* has static connotations, we prefer that the primary distinction be made between event and

---

[1] The visual scene presented to observers in our research to date is an admittedly restricted domain of moving dots of light presented on a two-dimensional TV screen; however, as there is ample evidence that depth can be perceived from similar experimental displays (see especially Green, 1961, and Braunstein, 1976), we take the limitations on the events studied to be less of a problem than might first be supposed.

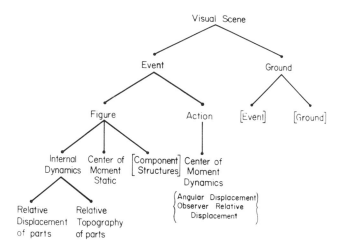

Fig. 5. A grammar for the perception of events, showing the manner in which we believe that the visual perception system parses events and extracts information.

ground. The information defining an event, let us say a walker, is extracted from the visual scene with residual information becoming ground. Within the ground further event–ground distinctions may be embedded. For example, a friend may be recognized walking on a crowded thoroughfare. The walking friend is an event embedded within the ground of the flowing pedestrian traffic. This ground would be rich in possibilities for extracting other events. If the event has no component of motion displacing it relative to the observer, then the event may be rewritten simply as figure. Thus, we define figure as an event without action.

By our account, an event is divided into two components, figure and action. A figure is a whole comprised of parts interrelated with static and dynamic invariants. For example, the dynamic configuration of lights that is recognized as a walker is a whole comprised of the lights which are its parts. The movement of the whole relative to the observer (that is, across the monitor screen) is its action.

Consider the pendulum drawn in Figure 6. As an event, a swinging pendulum consists of a bob, suspended below a pivot, that oscillates back and forth through an arc of angle θ. Considered as a whole this event has no observer-relative motion. That is, it may be adequately described as a figure with no action component. Remember, action is the dynamic whole that maintains a static relationship to a stationary observer. Thus, a pendulum is perceived to have motion, but its movements are not of the traveling sort.

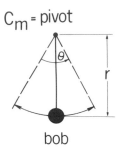

bob   Fig. 6. The movements and structure of a simple pendulum.

We find it convenient, as shown in Figure 5, to consider a figure as comprised of three components: internal dynamics, center of moment, and component structures. For some simple figures, such as a swinging pendulum, there are no component structures; thus, we bracket this constituent to show that it is optional, just as other events are optional in the whole of the visual scene. A walker, on the other hand, is perceived as a nesting of *many* component structures, a description of which entails the elaboration of the two required constituents.

As we see it, the internal dynamics for any figure is comprised of two constituents, relative displacement and relative topography of parts. These constituents are, respectively, dynamic and static relational invariants of figures. Generally speaking, the internal dynamics of a swinging pendulum consists of the motion of the bob about the pivot and the pivot-to-bob distance. More specifically, the relative displacement of parts is the acceleration-motion vector of the bob as it moves through arc θ of radius r about the pivot. The relative topography of parts is r, the length of the arm of the pendulum. If the pendulum were not swinging, the perception of this static figure would be wholly described by noting the positions of the pivot and the bob and the distance between them. Thus, for the special case of static perception, the available figural information in the visual scene is fully defined by the relative topography of the figure's parts.

The second constituent of figure is the center of moment as a static relational invariant. It is that point in space about which the internal dynamics of the figure are specified. The center of moment is the reference point, analogous to the point of origin in a coordinate system, for the description of the motions and locations of the parts of a figure. Its means of determination has been discussed in previous sections for each domain—walkers, wheels, aging faces, flowfields, or stars—that we have examined. As suggested earlier, the center of moment of a pendulum is its pivot.

For dynamic figures, we find that some shapes, like an aging face, change over time. Others, such as a pendulum, generally do not. Our description of figures allows us to state precisely the conditions for the perception of changing shape: If the internal dynamics of a figure has a period of identity, then it can be specified by a group of symmetry operations about the center of moment. A pendulum, for example, has a period of identity every 2θ of swing. A walker, likewise, has an identity period every two-step cycle. The circular rotations of lights on a wheel have a period of identity every 360° of rotation. So, too, do the circular paths of the stars moving about Polaris. In all of these instances the dynamics of the parts do not change the shape of the whole. However, in those cases where the internal dynamics of a figure do not have a period of identity, the figure will be perceived to change shape. An aging face is one instance of such an event.

Just as we do not perceive as separate the individual motions of parts of a rolling wheel, so, too, we do not perceive as separate the individual motions of parts of the body when viewing a human walker—a moving whole is seen in both cases. Figure 7 portrays the vector paths for the head, shoulder, elbow, wrist, hip, knee, and ankle of a computer-

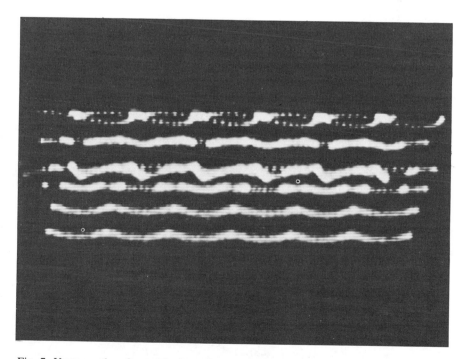

Fig. 7. Vector paths of a synthetic walker generated by the program of Cutting (1978c). The importance here is that we do *not* perceive the vector paths; instead, we perceive a walker. We do this, in part, by segregating relative movements of body parts from the action of the walker as a whole.

stimulated walker, generated from those used by Cutting (1978c). A similar set of traces may be found in Johansson (1973) for lights attached to a natural walker. We no more see this conglomerate of motion paths of a walker than we see the cycloidal paths of points on a rolling wheel. Event perception is clearly no such compilation of static frames. The grammar for event perception allows us to describe those motion components we do see in a walker by separating the available information into the required constituents and a nesting of component structures.

Figure 8 shows the analysis of the figural information for a walker presented as a dynamic display of lights attached to the joints. Because this figure is already rather cluttered, we have elected *not* to add the action component of the event, which would be the translatory motion of the whole figure relative to the observer. One may imagine the

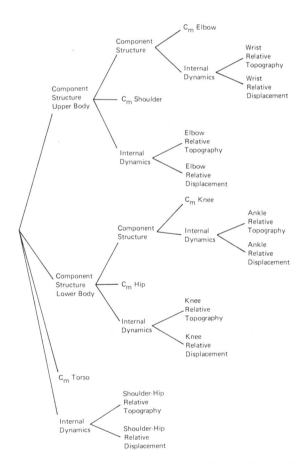

Fig. 8. A partial grammar for the perception of a walker. Only the elements under the heading *Figure* in Figure 5 are shown here.

description to be of a walker on a treadmill, sauntering along but getting nowhere. The motions of the lights attached to the walker are first analyzed into the constituents of the internal dynamics of the torso, the center of moment of the torso, and the component structures of the lower and upper body. The further analysis of these constituents yields a description of the relative motions and topography of the body parts as they are perceived.

The first extraction of information from the dynamic display describes the internal dynamics of the torso occurring about its center of moment. The torso is marked by two lights, one on the shoulder and the other on the hip. These two lights move, 180° out of phase, on elliptical paths of differing sizes. As discussed in Section 2.2, torso dynamics are described as the motions and locations of the hip and shoulder lights as they occur relative to the torso's center of moment. This center serves as a reference point for the figural description of the walker.

Once the perceiver extracts the movement from the hip and shoulders, these points now serve as static centers of moment for the analysis of the component structures of the lower and upper body. Considering first the lower body, one can see the hip as the center of moment for the knee, which moves in pendulum fashion about it. That motion shared by the hip and knee has been subtracted out; thus, the residual motion of the knee is described as an arc vector about the hip with a radius equal to the length of the upper leg. We suggest, as Figure 8 shows, that the internal dynamics of the knee is the relative displacement and location of the knee with respect to the hip. One perceives in the knee only its motion relative to the hip, rather than the more complex motion resulting from compounding this pendulum motion with the elliptical motion imparted to the knee by the hip. With the knee-to-hip relations described, only the component structure of ankle-to-knee remains. That is, the motion of the knee has been subtracted out, thus becoming a static center of moment for the description of the internal dynamics of the ankle. The ankle is related to the knee, roughly as a pendulum bob to its pivot. The internal dynamics of the ankle is described as an arc vector, the knee being its center, of radius equal to the length of the lower leg. The ankle is perceived to move in half-pendulum fashion rather than manifesting the motions imparted to it by the dynamics of the knee and hip. In a similar manner, the motions of the upper body component structures are described as a nesting of pendulum swings. Thus, all of the component structures of the lower and upper body are described as a nesting of pendulums, the knee and elbow being described both as bobs, relative to their hip and shoulder pivots, and as pivots, relative to their ankle and wrist bobs.

We suggest that in perceiving a human walker from a dynamic display of lights attached to joints, we extract information in logical steps that result in the parts of the body being perceived as a system of dynamic nested dependencies. The motions and locations of the hip and shoulder are extracted first as they are related to the body's deepest center of moment, that within the torso. Each step of information extraction that follows takes the previously described part as the center of moment for the determination of dynamic relations of other parts. The tree diagram presented in Figure 8 shows the steps followed in extracting information, and the terminal elements define the perceived components of motion and spatial location for each joint marked by a light.

Recall that we chose to describe a walker in Figure 8 as if he or she were on a treadmill. These motions are also preceived when viewing a walker traversing a terrain. In this latter case, however, one additional component of motion is perceived—the motion of the walker relative to the observer. As early Hollywood productions have shown, a person filmed walking on a treadmill and one filmed walking on solid ground will be indistinguishable if the background in the former situation is moved appropriately. The pendular movements of the arms and legs, together with the torsion of the hips and shoulders about their center of moment, are perceived as wholes in both cases. The motion of a walker relative to an observer is not imparted to each of the body's parts; rather, it is perceived as a distinct component describing the dynamics of the whole.

Remember, we define the movement of a figure relative to an observer as its action. A figure is defined by motions and locations of its parts relative to its center of moment; thus, for the purpose of figural description, the center of moment is a static point of reference. However, with respect to the motion of the figure as a whole, the deepest center of moment serves as that point embodying the dynamics of the whole. The action of a walker is the movement of the torso's center of moment and is described by a fairly uniform translational vector. (The slight up-and-down motion of the torso's center of moment was, since it is an action, ignored in the previous discussion of the treadmill walker, but see Cutting, 1978a, Experiment 5.) Some events have no action, and may thus be adequately described in figural notation. A clock's pendulum, for example, has no action except when the whole clock is moved. Other events, such as walkers, rolling wheels, or falling leaves, are perceived to move relative to the observer and these have both figural and action specifications.

5. Summary

We suggest that event perception proceeds through a logical series of steps for extracting stimulus information, each step resulting in the definition of distinct components. The first step isolates an event from the ground in which it is embedded. The second step divides the event into the components of figure and action. A figure is described by the internal dynamics of its parts about its center of moment taken as a static entity. Action is the dynamic property of the figure's center of moment. Our account is in accord with the Gestalt dictum that one does not perceive the motions of a uniform whole by perceiving individually the motions of its various parts; however, we go further in asserting that the motions of a whole are perceived as the movements of parts. *More particularly, the internal dynamics of a whole are perceived as the movement of parts about a center that is analytic to the whole, whereas the observer-relative displacement of the whole is perceived as the dynamics of that point.*

We believe that this general description holds for a whole variety of events, including the perception of humans walking, wheels rolling, faces aging, oneself flying, and the night sky revolving. We have only begun to explore the domain that we call event perception; we recognize that there are myriads of questions that our analysis raises; and we anticipate that our grammatical analysis may not be appropriate to all those things that psychologists may want to call events. Nevertheless, we are excited about the prospect of a structural description of events that follows the organizing principles of visual perception. The cornerstone of this approach is the recognition that dynamics is primary and that static arrays must be fit into a dynamic scheme.

6. References

Barclay, C.D., Cutting, J.E., & Kozlowski, L.T. Temporal and spatial factors in gait perception that influence gender recognition. *Perception and Psychophysics,* 1978, *23,* 145–152.

Boyer, C.B. *A history of mathematics.* New York: Wiley, 1968.

Braunstein, M.L. *Depth perception through motion.* New York: Academic Press, 1976.

Carlsöö, S. *How man moves.* London: Heinemann, 1972.

Cutting, J.E. Generation of synthetic male and female walkers through manipulation of a biomechanical invariant. *Perception,* 1978, *7,* 393–405. (a)

Cutting, J.E. Perceiving the geometry of age in a human face. *Perception and Psychophysics,* 1978, *24,* 566–568. (b)

Cutting, J.E. A program to generate synthetic walkers as dynamic point-light displays. *Behavior Research Methods and Instrumentation,* 1978, *10,* 91–94. (c)

Cutting, J.E., & Kozlowski, L.T. Recognizing friends by their walk: Gait perception without familiarity cues. *Bulletin of the Psychonomic Society,* 1977, *9,* 353–356.

Cutting, J.E., Proffitt, D.R., & Kozlowski, L.T. A biomechanical invariant for gait perception. *Journal of Experimental Psychology: Human Perception and Performance,* 1978, *4,* 357–372.

Dodge, R. An experimental study in visual fixation. *Psychological Review Monograph Supplements,* 1907, *8*(4), 1–95.

Dürer, A. *The human figure: The Dresden sketchbooks.* New York: Dover, 1972. (Originally published, 1528.)

Emlen, S. The stellar-orientation system of a migratory bird. *Scientific American,* 1975, *233*(2), 102–111.

Enlow, D. *Handbook of facial growth.* Philadelphia: Saunders, 1975.

Faust, M.S. Somatic development of adolescent girls. *Monographs of the Society for Research in Child Development,* 1977, *42,* Serial No. 169.

Gibson, J.J. *The perception of the visual world.* Boston: Houghton Mifflin, 1950.

Gibson, J.J. *The senses considered as perceptual systems.* Boston: Houghton Mifflin, 1966.

Gibson, J.J. *The ecological approach to visual perception.* Boston: Houghton Mifflin, 1979.

Gray, H. *Anatomy, descriptive and surgical.* 15th Ed., 1901. (Facsimile Ed., New York: Bounty, 1977.)

Green, B.F. Figure coherence in the kinetic depth effect. *Journal of Experimental Psychology,* 1961, *62,* 272–282.

Johansson, G. *Configurations in event perception.* Uppsala, Sweden: Almqvist & Wiksell, 1950.

Johansson, G. Visual perception of biological motion and a model for its analysis. *Perception and Psychophysics,* 1973, *14,* 202–211.

Johansson, G. Projective transformations as determine visual space perception. In R.B. MacLeod & H.L. Pick, Jr. (Eds.), *Perception: Essays in honor of James J. Gibson.* Ithaca: Cornell University Press, 1974.

Johansson, G. Visual motion perception. *Scientific American,* 1975, *232*(6), 76–89.

Johansson, G. Spatio-temporal differentiation and integration in visual motion perception. *Psychological Research,* 1976, *38,* 379–393.

Koffka, K. *Principles of Gestalt psychology.* New York: Harcourt, 1935.

Köhler, W. *Gestalt psychology.* New York: Liveright, 1947.

Kozlowski, L.T., & Cutting, J.E. Recognizing the sex of a walker from a dynamic point-light display. *Perception and Psychophysics,* 1977, *21,* 575–580.

Kozlowski, L.T., & Cutting, J.E. Recognizing the gender of walkers from a dynamic point-light display: Some second thoughts. *Perception and Psychophysics,* 1978, *23,* 459.

Liberman, A.M., Ingemann, F., Lisker, L., Delattre, P.C., & Cooper, F.S. Minimal rules for synthesizing speech. *Journal of the Acoustical Society of America,* 1959, *31,* 1490–1499.

Locke, J. *An essay concerning human understanding.* New York: Dover, 1959. (Originally published, 1690.)

Maas, J.B., Johansson, G., Jansson, G., & Runeson, S. *Motion perception I: 2-dimensional motion perception.* Boston: Houghton Mifflin, 1971 (film).

Mach, E. *The science of mechanics.* 1893. Reprinted, LaSalle, Ill.: Open Press, 1960.

Marey, E.J. *Movement.* New York: Arno Press & New York Times, 1972. (Originally published, 1895.)

Murray, M.P. Gait as a total pattern of movement. *American Journal of Physical Medicine,* 1967, *46,* 290–333.

Murray, M.P., Kory, R.C., & Sepic, S.B. Walking patterns of normal women. *Archives of Physical Medicine and Rehabilitation,* 1970, *51,* 637–650.

Neisser, U. *Cognition and reality.* San Francisco: W.H. Freeman, 1976.

Pittenger, J.B., & Shaw, R.E. Aging faces as viscal-elastic events: Implications for a theory of nonrigid shape perception. *Journal of Experimental Psychology: Human Perception and Performance,* 1975, *1,* 374–382.

Proffitt, D.R., & Cutting, J.E. Perceiving the centroid of configurations on a rolling wheel. *Perception and Psychophysics,* 1979, *25,* 389–398.

Proffitt, D.R., Cutting, J.E., & Stier, D.M. Perception of wheel-generated motions. *Journal of Experimental Psychology: Human Perception and Performance,* 1979, *5,* 289–302.

Rubin, E. *Synoplevede figure.* Copenhagen: Gyldendalske, 1915.

Saunders, J.B., Inman, V.T., & Eberhart, H.D. The major determinants in normal and pathological gait. *Journal of Bone and Joint Surgery,* 1953, *35-A,* 543–558.

Thompson, D.W. *On growth and form.* 1917. Reprinted, London: Cambridge University Press, 1969.

Turvey, M.T. Contrasting orientations to the theory of visual information processing. *Psychological Review,* 1977, *84,* 67–88.

Wallach, H. Visual perception of motion. In G. Keyes (Ed.,) *The nature and the art of motion.* New York: George Braziller, 1965.

Wolff, W. *The expression of personality.* New York: Harper, 1943.

PART III

Sensory Integration in Special Populations

Introduction

This section is on sensory integration as related to special populations. Millar deals with the blind; Hermelin and O'Connor with the blind, the deaf, the autistic, and the mentally subnormal; Cratty with special populations, frequently mentally deficient though often simply "disabled," for whom extra perceptual-motor experience has been prescribed; and Samuel discusses individual differences, presumably experientially based, on perceptual tasks where the reference populations may be athletes, ballet dancers, or artists. All of these populations have important theoretical relevance to the topic of intersensory integration.

How information is coded by the sense modalities is discussed by Millar and by Hermelin and O'Connor. One position, that of E. J. Gibson (1969) referred to earlier, is that similar information is coded similarly by each modality. We see a ball and thus identify it visually as a ball, but we could also identify it by touch. Shape is coded both by vision and by touch. Cross-modal identification is the recognition of an object in another sense modality previously identified in the first. Millar reviews the various theories concerned with identifications that cross from one modality to another. These theories range from unity (a single perceptual mechanism, amodal perception of features that are invariant between modalities, and "stored" descriptions that depend on memory) to separateness (the separate modalities must be integrated after cognitive experience or after motor organization). Other theories regard vision as the primary modality, so that recoding must be in visual terms, and others stress mediation by language or by memory stores tied to the modalities. With such a plethora of theories about that visual-haptic ball, one wonders how it can ever be identified at all.

In her research, Millar contrasts blind with normal children, while Hermelin and O'Connor's research is concerned with the perceptually handicapped (blind, deaf) as contrasted with the cognitively handicapped (autistic children, those with subnormal intelligence).

Neither chapter permits any simple conclusions about the coding of information with or between modalities. We hardly realize, until Miller describes it, how much vision is the spatial modality par excellence. "Space" refers not only to one's ability to navigate in the environment, though that is important, but also to spatial relations in form perception that are far from obvious in a comparison of visual-haptic form perception. While we know, if we think about it, that the difference between a square and a diamond depends on up-down and left-right relations to the environment, this spatial aspect of the difficulty of haptic perception is far from obvious. Spatial organization is more difficult by touch because reference cues are often lacking.

We think of touch as relying on the physical features of tactual objects; yet braille is encoded verbally, so that experienced braille readers my have little idea of the spatial relations between dots. In fact, braille readers have difficulty generalizing to slightly larger braille letters. Thus, tactual coding is not the same as shape coding.

Millar finds no evidence for learned translations between modalities or of specific "stores" for a modality. Coding seems to depend on the information most easily available for a given task. Visual experience may help, but this does not mean visual experience is necessary for spatial tasks. However, in some tasks, where cues referring to the body (self-referent cues) were difficult, even those with minimal visual experience did better than the congenitally blind because they could use external spatial cues when blindfolded.

Millar does not feel that the sense modalities are either separate or unitary. They are some of both, complementary to each other, and information can be used flexibly from different modalities. The organism adapts to the task, and the blind are handicapped (though not totally so) in situations where prior spatial experience helps the blindfolded sighted.

Hermelin and O'Connor, similarly, find no one theory of intersensory coding sufficient. They provide evidence that, on tasks where the information is encoded specifically within one modality, all children are about the same, whether perceptually or cognitively impaired or not. Vision is the prime modality for space and audition for temporal stimulation. Thus, it is easier to try to discriminate whether a light may be to our left or right, a spatial task, than to try to discriminate a long or a short light, a visual temporal task. But long and short sounds are easily discriminated (temporal), whereas sounds to the right or left (spatial) are much less easy for children. The handicapped children (the blind with the two auditory tasks, the deaf with the two visual tasks, and the autistic and the subnormals) were all similar, on this modality-specific task, to the normals. But when the children had to code by "representation" the normals were much better. An example is that of tracing simple line drawings by the blind or blindfolded sighted. The blind were as good as the blindfolded sighted at remembering a forward trace that was demonstrated to them, yet they were much worse when the lines had to be traced backward. Here the blindfolded sighted seemed able to use spatial codes derived from visual experience.

Depending on the task, then, one gets modality-specific coding where handicapped populations do not differ from normals, or in instances where representational codes help the normals and not the handicapped. Note that the "representational" codes are available to both modalities in the tasks they use, yet normals derive some benefit from being able to code in the more efficient, yet unused, modality.

Hermelin and O'Connor do find some evidence for "amodal" codes in that phonological features can be coded either visually or auditorily with an assist from vision. The deaf cannot lip-read as well as the sighted because of the difficulty of words in the back of the mouth (a "gaggle of geese" would be harder for the deaf to lip-read, compared to the sighted, than a "peck of peppers"). Somehow hearing can transfer the difficult material from the lips into an auditory code. Yet amodality is shown by the ease with which the deaf can match similar-sounding words even though they look as similar as different-sounding words look (e.g., rain-reign compared to train-than). Hermelin and O'Connor regard this as evidence that phonological material is coded amodally.

The chapter by Cratty focuses on a fascinating aspect of sensory integration, that of the influence of perceptual-motor training on perception and intelligence. Yet this area, despite its promise, is also a very frustrating one to assess.

The basic hypothesis is reasonable enough. It starts with the emphasis on activity by theorists like Piaget and Held for normal cognitive and perceptual development. The inductive leap to the hypothesis (assertion is perhaps a better word) that increased perceptual-motor activity can lead to an improvement in both perceptual and intellectual abilities does not seem large. Obvious targets for such training are the developmentally retarded and those with learning disabilities. Unfortunately, the "Scotch verdict"—not proven—must be given to programs that seek to enhance perceptual-motor activity for such purposes. Cratty finds an excess of enthusiasm, coupled with neglected or shoddy experimental control. The results secured to date have been unimpressive.

But we all feel that motor activities are important for normal development. Does this mean that increased perceptual-motor activity for certain groups with deficiencies can be helpful? One suspects that too many apples and oranges have been lumped together, and that it would be difficult for even the most clear-eyed research to unravel the complexities. Cratty asks for better experimental designs with control for such factors as the "Hawthorne effect"—the finding many years ago that merely paying attention to people can improve their performance— along with better ways of measuring "perception." He concludes that focusing on populations that were often neglected in the past may both help them and enrich our psychological understanding of the populations themselves, as well as of complex perceptual-motor processes.

The chapter by Samuel refers to individual differences related to the processing of visual and proprioceptive information. These individual differences could be the result of training, so that the chapter relates naturally to the Cratty chapter as well as to the chapters by Millar and by Hermelin and O'Connor. Dancers, for example, when wearing prisms, adapt less to the felt location of their body parts (Kahane & Auerbach, 1973) and are better able to set a tilted room to the gravitational vertical (Gruen, 1955). The dancers, with years and years of intense perceptual-motor experience, are exquisitely attuned to their own bodies. Graphic artists, on the other hand, as Samuel's own research shows, are very adept at finding embedded visual patterns—according to Witkin, this is "field independence." This capacity of female artists to analyze embedded figures throws doubt on the notion that females are more "field dependent" than males. While females may not be as good as males, on the average, in finding such hidden patterns, the expertise of the female artists points to experience as an important precursor of a factor like field dependence, meaning that whatever male–female differences are found are probably the result of differential male–female experience.

Even using extreme groups, such as swimmers who spend hours and hours a day on their type of perceptual-motor experience, Samuel finds rather slight differences. This may be somewhat cautionary to those who do research on extra perceptual-motor experience as recorded in the Cratty chapter.

Another cautionary note of complexity in the Samuel research comes from her reference to the two-visual-systems hypothesis of Trevarthen and others, in which focal visual information is seen to be primarily concerned with form perception and ambient visual information (in the visual periphery) to be more attuned to spatial perception. This hypothesis is particularly related to the chapter by Cratty, since gross perceptual-motor training would seem to be particularly related to the ambient visual system as well as to spatial perception, and not to detail vision, the focal system. Thus, one might not expect any general perceptual benefits from such training. Training in detail vision seems, as

Cratty points out, to help in the specific training task; but this is a far cry from helping in a more general perceptual-cognitive sense. One cannot, however, use the two-visual-system hypothesis to discredit perceptual-motor training, since visual-perceptual-cognitive interrelations are far more complex than might be implied by a rather simple analogue to this hypothesis. The point is, rather, that in such programs a more detailed analysis of the types of training being offered might be considered, as the types of training might be related to any possible perceptual-cognitive benefits.

The conclusion one makes from this series of studies is that we are slowly beginning to understand the interrelationships of the sense modalities. Global generalizations do not seem to hold. No one current theory seems capable of encompassing the diversity of findings. But one does feel, after reading these chapters, that we are ripe for another theoretical effort that, built on the past, will use the research reported here to help formulate more sophisticated theories.

References

Gibson, E.J. *Principles of perceptual learning and development.* New York: Appleton-Century-Crofts, 1969.

Gruen, A. The relation of dancing experience and personality to perception. *Psychological Monographs,* 1955, 69 *(14),* Whole No. 399.

Kahane, J., & Auerbach, C. Effect of prior body experience on adaptation to visual displacement. *Perception and Psychophysics,* 1973, *13,* 461–466.

9

Crossmodal and Intersensory Perception and the Blind

SUSANNA MILLAR

1. Introduction

Performance by the blind has been of interest in understanding cross-modal recognition since Molyneux asked his celebrated question whether a blind man, made to see, would recognize by sight alone an object that he had hitherto perceived only through touch. Von Senden (1960) suggested that there is little transfer. But for complete restoration of sight some preoperative residual vision is necessary (Rapin, 1979; Riesen, 1975). Gregory and Wallace's (1963) patient had light perception preoperatively. After the corneal graft that restored his sight, he recognized uppercase letters that he had previously learned only through touch. But, despite an interest in tools, he could not easily identify relatively unfamiliar tools until after he had explored them by touch. Gregory (1974, p. 106) suggests that although his patient "came to use vision his ideas of the world arose from touch."

Gregory's findings raise important questions about the blind which are also basic to understanding crossmodal functions: What is the role of vision in spatial performance? Do ideas gained through touch and movement really differ from those of the sighted? How do they differ? Could this difference be explained by the amount rather than the type of information provided by different modalities? In other words, how do the blind and sighted code information about shape, distance, location,

SUSANNA MILLAR • Department of Experimental Psychology, University of Oxford, Oxford, England. The research for this chapter was supported by a grant from the Social Science Research Council of Great Britain.

and direction when the information comes through touch and movement? These questions have been one of my major concerns and will be the central issues discussed in this chapter.

1.1. Implications of Crossmodal Models for Blind Performance

Crossmodal theories are often divided into those emphasizing the "unity" vs. "separateness" of sensory modalities. Neither extreme is likely to be adequate. The elaborate specialization of sensory systems that exists in most mammals would hardly be required if all the senses provided the same information; but specialization does not entail complete separation. An organism that could not integrate information from different sources would not survive long in normal conditions. There can be little doubt that phenomenological qualities like the color of an object, the sound of a voice, or the feel of materials are specific to different modalities in man, but that what is perceived is not necessarily exactly equivalent to the physical stimulation (Gregory, 1974). So much, presumably, is common ground. The difference in emphasis has turned mainly on the question whether all inputs to a given modality are primarily coded, organized, and stored in terms of this system, so that a special translation or integrating mechanism has to be postulated; or whether inputs are processed, organized, and stored in the same way, regardless of input modality. Prima facie, predictions for crossmodal performance, performance in blind vs. sighted conditions, and development in sensory handicap would be expected to differ on the two types of models.

Theories that explicitly or implicitly stress "unity" vary from assumptions of a single general perceptual mechanism, for instance for form, or the direct perception of relational features which are invarient over modalities (Gibson, 1969), to "top-down" models in which unity is ascribed to cognitive factors (e.g., Neisser, 1976), or assumptions that perception depends on "stored descriptions" to which modality is irrelevant (e.g., Anderson & Bower, 1973; Pylyshyn, 1973; Schank & Abelson, 1977). The level at which complete interchangeability of information is assumed tends to differ. It is not always quite clear, either, whether the difference in "level" refers to processing by the organism, or to the level of generality of the theoretical description.

One of the most influential theories in accounting for performance by children in terms of "unity" is that of Gibson (1969). This theory assumes direct perception of "amodal" features or invariant relations. The processing level assumed in this theory differs from the "amodal perception" of Michotte (1964). Michotte refers to perception of details for which there is no sensory stimulation but which is determined by the total stimulation. Gibson's theory assumes that various levels of "higher order'' relations are progressively detected. Reported difficulties by blind children in detecting identity, similarity, and symmetry from touch alone are accounted for by the additional assumption of intermodal facilitation (from vision to touch) of these higher-order relations. It is not quite clear how this would operate. Gibson's important distinctions between amodal properties, intermodal similarity, and cross-modal transfer actually refer to task differences: those demanding reference to abstract relations, or matching for equivalence, or transfer of a learned discrimination to another modality, respectively. These differences do not explain how a child who cannot detect symmetry in a tactual pattern is helped by visually detecting it in the same pattern, unless he already knows that the two patterns are identical. Such prior knowledge must be essential if visual detection is to prime attention to the same features by touch. If higher-order relations are detected progressively with experience, the blind, who have so much more experience of tactual and movement perception than the sighted, should actually be better at detecting higher-order features through touch than the sighted. Differences in the rate of pickup of higher-order information between the modalities are postulated. But the mode of pickup should be irrelevant.

The mode of perception is irrelevant also in cognitive theories. Neisser (1976) postulates that knowledge of the world is mediated rather than direct—a hierarchical process of construction and synthesis, rather than one of detection and differentiation. The end process is seen by Neisser in terms of schemes in Bartlett's (1932) sense, or as cognitive maps (Tolman, 1948). These representations are conceived not merely as equivalent, but as identical, whatever the source of the information. This theory should produce the prediction that ''mental images'' of spatial relations are the same in the blind as in the sighted. Cognitive maps tend to be eschewed in theoretical descriptions based on analogies with computer functioning. But although modality systems are equally irrelevant, predictions for blind conditions are more difficult. Knowledge is stored in terms of abstract (nonverbal) ''propositions,'' accessed by procedural rules (e.g., Schank & Abelson, 1977). There is no a priori reason why lack of knowledge of the world or of procedural rules should issue merely in more errors. It might also alter the route by which information is accessed or organized. The only thing that is unclear is how knowledge of the world or knowledge of rules is achieved in the first place. Indeed, this matter is not relevant to this level of theoretical description. Crossmodal questions thus hardly arise. Rules for crossmodal differences and equivalence rules could always be written in.

Models based on inferences from the ''separateness'' of the sensory systems usually focus explicitly on development and learning. Differences between different sensory systems are assumed to be qualitative so that some form of mediation has to be acquired to match information across the senses. Predictions about functioning in blind conditions are not the same for all such models, however. Piaget's well-known theory of spatial development (Piaget & Inhelder, 1948) depends on the assumption that the organism constructs integrated cognitive schemes from active interactions with the environment. In infancy different sense modalities are organized into separate "schemes." These are then integrated into sensorimotor or action schemata which are progressively internalized, and finally become abstract logical "operations" by processes of assimilation and accommodation. Piaget allows some form of "prefiguring." But perception and memory depend primarily on the intellectual level which has been achieved and not on any sense modality. Moreover, the postulated sequence of spatial development from "egocentrism" to topological coding and finally to Euclidean coordinate systems is assumed to be invariant. Lack of information due to insufficient interaction with the environment would thus retard the sequence, but could not change it. The blind might operate at a lower level in the sequence, like younger children. But, if anything, in this system constructions from touch and movement are more important than memory for visual pictures. Absence of active interaction rather than deprivation of sight would be important.

Dependence on motor output, or movement organization, rather than on cognitive schemata has been postulated as the integrating factor by a number of workers (Jones, 1974; Zaporozhets, 1965; Zinchenko, 1966). Such hypotheses are somewhat difficult to test, since testing depends on responses which necessarily involve motor output of some kind. Moreover, perception depends on changes in stimulation. Immobilization makes it impossible to perceive anything at all via either the eye or the finger. While this fact clearly makes motor information necessary to perception, it does not necessarily make motor information the basis for all perceptual organization or integration. On hypotheses of motor output or outflow organization, improvements in exploratory and response activity would explain differences in performance levels. But, in principle, conditions of blindness should not present any special difficulties, unless motor activity is severely curtailed.

Completely different predictions follow from theories that vision is the primary modality which organizes and integrates spatial information. This assumption has been put forward in various forms by many researchers, particularly those concerned specifically with blindness (Hatwell, 1978; McKinney, 1964; Révész, 1950; Schlaegel, 1953; von Senden, 1960; Warren, 1977; Worchel, 1951). The implications are clear. In the absence of sight, spatial organization is not only poor; it is also different. Révész (1950), for instance, suggests that the blind do not understand external spatial coordinates, but code spatial information with reference to their own body. Haptic space, according to Révész, has its own organization. The hypothesis that visual organization integrates information from all modalities (Warren, 1974) also suggests that the blind may have difficulties in matching inputs from the remaining modalities, and thus have specific crossmodal problems. The major question raised is whether or not vision is a necessary, sufficient, or merely facilitating condition; and if so, how it operates.

A number of theories have postulated mediation by language, names, or verbal descriptions (Ettlinger, 1967). Since crossmodal matching by apes, monkeys, and preverbal children has been demonstrated (Bryant, Jones, Claxton, & Perkins, 1972; Davenport & Rogers, 1970; Davenport, Rogers, & Russell, 1973; Weiskrantz & Cowey, 1975), this mediation cannot be regarded as a necessary factor. It could, of course, in principle, facilitate matching to learn the same name for two perceptually different inputs, or to learn equivalence rules (Goodnow, 1971a). In the case of arbitrary or conventional connections, such matching may even be necessary. But this would be the case within as well as between modalities. However, learning a name or rule would not be sufficient without being able to apply it correctly in a given situation. For instance, to apply appropriately the rule that after a 180° turn, the criterion location is reversed, it is necessary to perceive and remember that this turn has occurred and to organize the response accordingly. It is not sufficient merely to know the name for the turn, and the verbal rule. Verbal mediation has often been considered the only means by which the blind can perform spatial tasks.

Translation via a long-term memory store containing equivalent entries of a quasidictionary (not necessarily verbal) type has been proposed by Connolly and Jones (1970). But Connolly and Jones also assume that visual and kinesthetic information from the input is held in separate, modality-specific, short-term stores with different retention characteristics, as suggested by Posner (1967). Haptic information is held in a fast-decaying store with little access to attentional or processing capacity, while visual information can be maintained across delays provided processing capacity is not preempted by a concurrent or interpolated difficult mental task. Connolly and Jones make the additional assumption that translation via the long-term dictionary occurs prior to short-term storage, so that modality-specific information is held in the short-term store of the response modality. Crossmodal performance would thus be asymmetric, depending on the retention characteristics of the response modality. Since translation is required, crossmodal performance would also be necessarily worse than intramodal performance, although it would improve differentially with age and with learning more

dictionary equivalences. Given the poor retention characteristics proposed for haptic information, it must be inferred that the blind would
have considerable difficulties, since they necessarily have to rely on
touch and movement to a much larger extent than the sighted.

Even this brief review shows that crossmodal models range from
implying that the blind rely on a completely different spatial organization,
to assuming identical coding; from predicting severe intersensory handicap, to deficits easily remedied by alternative sources of knowledge.
This discrepancy is not because the evidence on which the models are
based is necessarily inadmissible or faulty, but because it is assumed in
each model that its description holds equally for relations between all
modalities, all aspects of information, all task conditions, and all levels
of processing by the organism, and that each model is at the same level
of generality of theoretical description as every other. It is the great
advantage of blatant contradictions between theories that such fallacies
become obvious. The need for detailed examination is clear (Freides,
1974). The survey which follows, mainly based on findings from my own
studies of crossmodal and blind performance, is an attempt to identify
some of the conditions responsible for the contradictions.

1.2. Some Methodological Considerations in Assessing Blind
Performance

The main strategy in the studies to be discussed has been to ask
questions about the form in which information from different modalities,
especially touch and movement, is coded, and about the role of vision.
For this, comparison between the blind and sighted is often inevitable.
The main pitfall in such comparisons is that the blind and sighted may
differ on other factors than lack of vision. This fact is often given as a
reason for not attempting such comparisons at all, and for concentrating
instead on comparing various levels of visual defect. This is a mistake.
Precisely the same considerations apply to the latter comparisons.
Another reason occasionally put forward is that the blind are so totally
different from the sighted that comparisons are useless. But this argument
already assumes precisely what we need to know. There are, in any case,
important practical reasons for comparing blind and sighted performance–for instance, for integration into schools and into the sighted
community. The principles of matching are the same for these as for any
other group comparisons: as many relevant factors as possible must be
controlled. There is no doubt, however, that great care is necessary. This
applies particularly to measures used for matching. A point which has

not always received sufficient attention is that IQ measures alone are often misleading. Blind and sighted tests are standardized on different norms. This practice could lead to an overestimation of ability in the blind. The opposite hazard is no less real in matching on the basis of sighted scales. Deliberately used, matching higher-IQ blind with lower-IQ sighted can be a reasonable strategy for testing differences on criterion tasks, since it loads the dice against irrelevant factors in worse performance by the blind.

The use of convergent methods, that is, studying the same question with a variety of different methods, is probably the best means of guarding against accepting differences when there are none. It ensures that findings are replicable, and draws attention to concealed differences in task factors when findings differ. In the studies discussed here the author also used a number of different criteria in combination to ensure reasonable interpretations. One of these is to exclude blind subjects with known brain damage, severe additional handicaps, and mental retardation (scores below low average on IQ tests), since there will be more of these individuals in any unselected blind populations than in otherwise comparable sighted groups. Another possible method is to match on several tasks on which average profiles of blind and sighted populations are known to differ in both positive and negative directions. Major instances are vocabulary (blind children worse), forward digit span (blind children better), backward digit span (blind children worse). When the criterion task is spatial, it is especially useful to match on at least one nonspatial task which involves the same general skill as the criterion spatial task. For instance, backward digit span involves mental reorganization of a verbal input sequence. It is thus a particularly useful check in cases where the criterion task requires mental spatial reorganization. Examining patterns of performance in relation to more than one relevant variable is important; and so is including a level of the criterion task on which the blind perform as the sighted. Differences in performance may be due simply to delay with age and experience in achieving a skill, or they may indicate differences in functioning. It is therefore useful to test a wide range of age and performance levels so that patterns in relation to different factors can be compared at the same level of efficiency.

Details about the age of blinding and the degree of residual sight are often scanty in experimental reports (Warren, 1977). But they are exceedingly important in interpreting results. Children ascertained as educationally blind vary considerably. In studies by the author, only subjects who were either blind from birth or less than 20 months of age were included. The criterion for selection was either total blindness, or some perception of light, but none of shapes, colors, or even handmovements. It will be seen that even this amount of visual experience can make a difference. Guarding against wrongly inferring equal performance is as essential in this work as guarding against inferring differences where there are none.

2. Shape Recognition

2.1. Three-Dimensional Shapes in Touch and Vision

Given that the same shapes are recognized by touch and vision, it is really very puzzling that shape recognition by touch should generally be so much worse than by vision. It is usually pointed out that visual perception is simultaneous while successive tracing is necessary in touch. The answer is relevant, but does not solve the puzzle. The difference remains even when the shape is pressed on the palm so that tactual stimulation is simultaneous (Krauthammer, 1968). Another answer is that visual discrimination is better. Tactual spatial details are certainly often more confusing than visual ones. Yet extremely fine texture discriminations are possible by touch. It thus seems unlikely that the difference is simply due to better visual than tactual "acuity," or that touch is the same as "blurred vision" (Apkarian-Stielau & Loomis, 1975). It certainly does not seem to be due to differences in general experience with a given modality. Surprisingly enough, the blind are not better than the sighted in recognizing unfamiliar shapes by touch, despite their obviously greater tactual experience. This seems to be true of adults (Foulke & Warm, 1967) as well of children (O'Connor & Hermelin, 1975; Pick & Pick, 1966). in matching-to-sample and shape-fitting tasks, respectively. Only with braille has any reliable superiority on the part of the blind been reported (e.g., Foulke & Warm, 1967).

Gibson (1969) suggests that visual shape perception is better because vision picks up higher-order relations more easily than touch. But this theory does not predict asymmetries in crossmodal-intramodel error patterns without additional assumptions. One possibility, for which there is supporting evidence (Millar, 1971) is visual "facilitation." Preschoolers matched three-dimensional nonsense shapes better by touch when both visual and tactual information were present at input. This finding demonstrated intermodal facilitation at an early age. But visual facilitation was effective only when the dual information was present simultaneously. Otherwise crossmodal recognition was only as good as intratactual matching. This is important. It suggests that assumptions additional to relative accuracy between modalities are required.

The visual-integration hypothesis also needs additional assumptions since visual facilitation is not always found. Worchel (1951) suggested that "visualizing" is not required if subjects match on some prominent shape feature. But subjects could match on features in shape rotation also. This possibility could explain discrepancies. Irrelevant corners from the bissected shapes used by Worchel (1951) could have been more distracting for the blind; whereas lack of differences between the blind and sighted (e.g., Marmor & Zaback, 1976) could result from matching distinctive features. Shape rotation is not always the most difficult match in blind conditions (Pick & Pick, 1966). For these reasons, rotation of shapes is not a convincing test of "visualizing." But the basis of coding even for recognition cannot be inferred solely from a lack of difference in efficiency.

A somewhat more sensitive assessment of the role of vision can be made by comparing studies specifically designed to assess coding in intramodal-crossmodal shape matching (Millar, 1972a), and in tactual matching of the same nonsense shapes by blind and blindfolded sighted children (Millar, 1974). Both studies used difficult (verbal) and easy modality-specific (visual and haptic, respectively) interpolations during delays in Peterson (Peterson & Peterson, 1959) distractor designs. The results are instructive. Distractors disturbed intravisual, but not intratactual matching. The latter deteriorated only with delay in both types of study. Such findings are often cited as evidence for modality-specific "stores" with greater processing capacity for visual than haptic stores (e.g., Connolly & Jones, 1970; Goodnow, 1971b). However, the finding on touch was confined to conditions in which subjects had few trials with large numbers of different stimuli. With extended practice of a small subset of the same stimuli, tactual recognition was disturbed by interpolated distractors; and these effects were the same for blind and blindfolded sighted children.

Two implications are obvious. First, tactual processing can change with task conditions. Thus the fact that distractors disturbed visual but not tactual matching of unfamiliar shapes cannot be ascribed to fixed characteristics of modality-specific "stores." Second, the blind could not have relied on visual memory for tactual matching, yet distractors had the same effects as on the sighted. This finding is evidence against the hypothesis that tactual shapes are necessarily coded visually by the sighted, even though visual information can facilitate tactual recognition (Millar, 1971). Whether visual information is used either in touch or crossmodally seems to depend on task conditions rather than on factors inherent in all forms of spatial organization.

The fact that subjects use information flexibly was shown further by the finding that distractors related to crossmodal matching in some cases as in vision (e.g., memory decrements), while in others they resembled touch (i.e., no effect). This was so whether or not vision was the input or the response modality, contrary to Connolly and Jones' (1970) assumption. Moreover, there was no specific association of crossmodal performance with either age, delay, or memory load (Millar, 1972a). On a translation model, crossmodal difficulties should relate specifically to these factors.

Comparisons of the blind and blindfolded sighted suggest that Molyneux's question should be reversed to ask how far subjects actually do code modality-specific information. For vision, evidence for coding physical features is quite good (Brooks, 1967; Millar, 1972b; Posner, Boies, Eichelman, & Taylor, 1969; Tversky, 1969). In the cross-modal study (Millar, 1972a), interpolated pictures disturbed intravisual matching by preschoolers more than did difficult verbal tasks. For older groups the latter were more effective; this was probably due to task difficulty rather than to naming. But the major question is over the intratactual matches, and the change from sensitivity to delay to disturbance by distractors. The original interpretation—that with repetition the children evolved some form of "naming," so that distractors disturbed verbal rehearsal—is no longer altogether convincing. Modality-specific (movement) distractors were easier than verbal distractors, but produced just as large an effect. The question of tactual coding and its relation to naming is thus one of the main questions in the next section.

The evidence discussed so far does not support the "visual integration" hypothesis, or theories assuming that learned translation is necessary, or that any single factor at input or output mediates crossmodal matching. Task-dependent strategies were clearly important. But for touch it was not clear whether these involved naming or modality-specific coding.

2.2. Touch and Naming

Raised dot patterns are of particular interest in attempts to understand the relation of different perceptual modes in performance by the blind. The most obvious reason is that some of the patterns have well-learned names for the blind but are "nonsense" to the sighted, and may thus provide clues about tactual coding and its relation to naming.

Different methods converging on the problem of tactual coding were used. The first was an adaptation of Conrad's (1971) method. Conrad showed that if subjects code verbally, successive items with similar-sounding names are remembered less easily than items with dissimilar names. It was argued that if subjects code physical tactual features, successive items that are tactually similar should also show decrements compared to tactually dissimilar lists. Blind children were tested on lists of braille letters that either had similar-sounding names, but were tactually different; or the letters had dissimilar names but similar tactual features; or letters were dissimilar both phonologically and tactually (Millar, 1975b). Tests with "probe" letters from the memory set showed both phonological and tactual coding. Moreover, the two forms of coding related differently to the comparison list. Disturbance by phonological similarity increased with the number of remembered items on dissimilar lists. Disturbance by tactual similarity decreased with the number of remembered items on the dissimilar list. Similar results were obtained with objects instead of letters (Millar, 1975c). Thus physical tactual as well as phonological features of the letters were coded. Moreover, since they related differently to at least one other variable (set-size of the dissimilar list), the two forms of coding seemed to be independent.

An interesting finding was that children's speed in naming letters on pretest related not only to how much they could remember of the dissimilar lists, but also to tactual vs. verbal similarity. Fast namers remembered more, and were disturbed more by phonological similarity. Slow namers remembered less and were disturbed more by tactual similarity. Discrimination difficulty was not a problem. But the speed with which names were accessible in memory seemed to be at least one factor in whether subjects coded verbally or tactually.

The second design (Millar; 1978a) used the well-known fact that grouping verbal items improves memory. Pauses presumably help subjects to rehearse verbally. Naming was here varied by using braille letters and nonsense patterns. If blind subjects code braille letters verbally, grouping should improve recall. If they code unfamiliar shapes by tactual features, grouping should actually worsen recall, either because memory for unfamiliar tactual features deteriorates fast, or because moving fingers across the spaces by which items were grouped produces more tactual inference. The findings showed precisely these effects. Memory for braille letters improved with grouping; memory for nonsense shapes was not only worse but actually deteriorated with grouping. The same children performed both tasks; so there was no question of individual differences in ability or rehearsal facility. Only subjects who had been slow at letter naming on pretest treated the letters similarly to nonsense shapes in the memory task. This finding suggests again that speed of access to codes in memory may determine whether or not the codes are used. In any case, the findings of this experiment confirmed the predictions from the previous studies by a different paradigm. Thus physical tactual features as well as names are evidently coded by blind subjects.

One problem in the previous studies demonstrating tactual coding was that tactual coding depended on unfamiliarity of the input. To surmount this problem, the paradigm used by Posner (Posner et al., 1969) to demonstrate the persistence of physical visual features of familiar letters was adapted for braille-letter recognition by blind readers. Posner and his colleagues showed that matching successive letters which have the same physical form (AA or aa) is faster than matching letters that have the same name, but differ in physical visual form (Aa, aA). Since the visual form affected recognition of successive letters, it must have been coded in memory. Braille does not have upper- and lowercase letters, but it is usually taught in only one format (overall size and dot size). The question was, therefore, whether physical formats that alter the "feel" of the letters (slightly larger overall size or dot size) without changing their shape and nameability would affect recognition (Millar, 1977a). The answer was clearly positive. Blind braille readers matched successive letters faster when letters were in the same physical tactual format than when they differed in format. The result was obtained when a slightly enlarged format was used together with the normal braille format, and when two (equally fast) altered formats (size and dot-size differences) were used to produce physically identical and different letter pairs. The effect could thus not be attributed to familiarity. The more familiar normal format was somewhat faster; but the difference in speed between physically identical and physically different letter pairs with the same name occurred regardless of the degree of familiarity of the formats. Discrimination difficulty was not in question. Accuracy was extremely high. Also in this, as in previous studies, judgments depended on successive stimuli. The features affecting recognition must therefore have been coded in memory.

Findings from three different paradigms thus showed that physical tactual features, as well as names, are coded in memory. Moreover, tactual features can be used to speed matching.

Naming and relying on tactual features in matching are probably best regarded as alternative means of coding, rather than as inevitable or fixed steps in a processing or learning hierarchy. This idea is suggested by the fact that blind subjects can rely on tactual features not only when naming is difficult or slow (Millar, 1975b, 1978a), but can also code these when letter names are well learned (Millar, 1977a).

2.3. Names, Shapes, and Physical Features in Tactual Recognition

The relation between verbal and physical tactual features in raised-dot-pattern recognition has obvious importance for understanding the "equivalence" of tactual stimuli across modalities. The role of naming has been sufficiently obvious for some time with visually presented material. It is of interest that, evidently, naming is also a merely optional coding strategy with tactual stimuli. But precisely what is coded when subjects use physical tactual features is not so clear. Prima facie there are two possibilities. One is that tactual features in memory consist of no more than the persistence of the physical stimulation after offset. The second is that physical tactual features are coded as shapes or in terms of spatial features in exactly the same way as in vision. It will be argued below that neither of these answers is adequate.

Persistence of the effects of stimulation for very brief periods after the physical stimulus has ceased is a relatively robust phenomenon in vision (Sperling, 1963, 1967). This persistence also seems to occur in touch, and has been reported as a sort of "afterglow" or "tingling" in the stimulated area of skin (Melzack & Eisenberg, 1968). The phenomenon has been identified with a sensory register in which stimulation continues in uncoded form until it is read off into a limited-capacity, short-term store (Hill & Bliss, 1968). The phenomenon itself is not in doubt. But whether the tactual coding found here could be identified with either "afterglow" or with an "unlimited capacity store" in which the information is held in uncoded form is extremely doubtful. Any afterglow or persistence of stimulation would necessarily be distorted, overwritten or displaced by any subsequent stimulation to the same area of skin. It would be impossible to remember more than one stimulus to the same site even for milliseconds if another stimulus succeeded it. In fact, the tactual effects found here were found in paradigms using successive inputs to the same fingertip. Subjects who showed tactual coding (e.g., disturbance by tactual rather than phonological similarity, etc.) could actually remember up to three or four items presented successively to the same finger (Millar, 1975b,c, 1978a). This simply would not be possible if the subjects relied on physical aftereffects in quite uncoded form. It is thus extremely unlikely that all findings on memory for physical tactual features could be explained as persistent uncoded "sensations." Some form of coding which permits memory (as opposed to persistence) of physical tactual features for more than one successive input must be assumed.

The second explanation is that tactual patterns are coded as shapes. If so, the left hand should be better since the right hemisphere is specialized for spatial coding. Milner and Taylor (1972) found this to be the case for familiarized nonsense shapes by commissurized patients. So did Kumar (1977), although he used visual examples prior to tests. But not all tactual-discrimination studies show left-hand superiority. Fertsch (1947) and Foulke (1964) reported right-hand preference by experienced adult braille readers with fast reading speeds, and slower reading by a minority who preferred reading with the left hand. Hermelin and O'Connor (1971) showed faster left-hand braille letter recognition. Their blind children and adults were presumably less skilled than Foulke's subjects, who had between 12 and 49 years of braille experience. Millar (1977b, 1978b) found little evidence for hand differences early in learning braille letters, or in matching unfamiliar patterns which differed in symmetry or dot numerosity. Fertsch (1947) made the important point, on the basis of her findings, that "the better hand" depends on the level of reading skill.

Change in laterality with experience is not confined to touch. Experienced musicians have a right-ear advantage for music while for nonmusicians the left ear is better (Bever & Chiarello, 1974). The findings from changes in hand (and presumably hemisphere) involvement in tactual matching are entirely consistent with the findings from changes in tactual retention characteristics with familiarity (Millar, 1974) and naming speed (Millar 1975b, 1977a, 1978a). This fact strongly suggests that the manner in which information is coded is not invariable or fixed by the material or by the mode in which it is presented. But the findings also suggest that coding does not fall into a neat "verbal" vs. "spatial" dichotomy. Such a dichotomy would leave totally unexplained the absence of a reliable left-hand superiority early in learning (Millar, 1977b, 1978b), as well as the puzzling differences between tactual and visual recognition of unfamiliar patterns after short delays. If unfamiliar patterns are always coded as shapes by both vision and touch, and the only difference is in accuracy, one would expect more errors in touch. But there would be no reason to expect differences in relation to, for instance, distractor tasks. These puzzles disappear if it is assumed that *nonverbal tactual coding is not necessarily organized spatially.*

The first doubt that braille letters are perceived as "shapes" early in learning came from the unexpected finding that recognition by young blind readers did not generalize to slightly enlarged braille letters (Millar, 1977a) without some instruction and training. This was certainly not due to discrimination difficulties or to inaccurate naming of the same letters in normal format. Another indicative finding was that less experienced readers needed as much time to match identical as "different" letter pairs. If, as is usually assumed (e.g., Nolan & Kederis, 1969), braille patterns are perceived globally as outline shapes, then identical pairs should be matched faster (Krueger, 1973), as is indeed the case in vision. In an experiment to further test this possibility (Millar, 1977b), sighted children were taught to discriminate braille letters by touch. Even when the children's discrimination accuracy was fairly high, they showed no reliable left-hand superiority and did not judge identical pairs faster than "different" pairs. Visually they showed the usual advantage for identical matches. The fact that the children did not code the tactual patterns spatially was strikingly confirmed by their drawing of four letters that they had learned to name. Subjects had no idea of the spatial relations between the dots in a letter, much less of the letter's total configuration.

Further evidence that small raised dot patterns are not automatically coded spatially has been found in experiments using different paradigms (Millar, 1978b). Even relatively experienced blind readers did not match braille letters in terms of differences in the spatial location of the dots. For beginning blind readers, letters consisting of larger dot numbers are more difficult than letters made up for fewer dots. Visually, all the letters are very simple shapes. Judged on shape, therefore, the number of dots making up the shape should not have affected matching. A further study showed that both blind and sighted children matched raised dot patterns more easily when these differed in dot numerosity than when they differed in spatial symmetry. Difficulty in judging symmetry tactually has also been reported by Walk (1965). By contrast, even quite young children appreciate differences in symmetry by vision (Gaines, 1969).

The evidence from findings on "same-different" judgments, difficulties in generalizing to enlarged shapes, and from experiments examining effects of differences in dot location, dot numerosity, and symmetry consistently suggests that tactual coding is not identical with shape coding, but can be based on nonspatial tactual (possibly texture) features. This is an important fact. It points to an explanation that can resolve the apparent discrepancy in the crossmodal data, changes in laterality, and memory differences between touch and vision. This explanation will be discussed below.

2.4. Tactual Coding and Information from Other Sources

The fact that patterns are not as easily coded spatially by touch as by vision is actually not surprising. Spatial coding requires stable references to relate features within patterns. To explore unfamiliar raised dot patterns subjects use small, often rather rapid, unsystematic movements with the fingertip. They thus lose any "anchors" within patterns. Movements are too small to relate reliably to body (trunk) references. References have to be sought actively unless there is a delineated frame (e.g., vibrators strapped to an area of skin). Similarly, the stationary finger in an apparatus such as the optacon provides stable references which can be used to organize "feels" (tingles, sharp-smooth) in terms of spatial codes (up-down, right-left). In the absence of such frames, or of prior knowledge about anchors, the change from nonspatial to spatial coding probably depends on systematic exploration and planned movements (Berlá & Butterfield, 1977; Davidson, 1972).

Convergent information from other sources also seems to be important in some apparently very simple discriminations. Monkeys can discriminate straight-edged from cylindrical objects by blind hand grasp. This ability is the result of a particular combination of inputs from skin and joints converging into different units in the parietal cortex (Sakata

& Iwamura, 1978). Such "form perception" presumably involves discrimination of sharp from smooth. For the sighted there is also probably convergence from visual straight-curved discrimination (Frantz, 1975). This discrimination may be either preprogrammed or established early through correlated visual and proprioceptive feedback (e.g., Held & Bauer, 1967). Blind babies certainly attend less to external cues (Fraiberg, 1977). But vision is not required for making the crossmodal connection. A young congenitally totally blind child, tested by the author, easily discriminated round beads, but did not associate these with circles or circular movements. However, she understood the association quickly when shown the similarity once by systematic movements.

The importance of convergent information, especially from planned movements for spatial coding in blind conditions, was already recognized by Weber (1795–1878) in his treatise on touch (Weber, 1978). "Moving our limbs intentionally and consciously, we can by the movements we must make with our hands about the resistant object, build up a picture of the size and shape of the object." This need not, of course, imply that tactual shape perception necessarily involves conscious deliberation. Processing can presumably become automatic (LaBerge, 1975), so that the shape or its meaning is recognized immediately. But the evidence does suggest that spatial coding of tactual inputs requires convergent information from other sources.

2.5. Shapes, Names, and Familiarity: An Explanation

The results with raised dot patterns and braille letters suggest first that the blind have no special difficulty in attaching names to tactual patterns or in using covert verbal strategies. Second, not only names but physical tactual features can be coded and used. Third, the physical tactual features that are coded are at least of two kinds —coding in terms of spatial and "shape" features, and coding based on physical and "texture" differences. The latter is more frequent in conditions of relative unfamiliarity. It was argued that for spatial coding, convergent information from planned movements or reference to other cues is required.

From these results it is possible to construct a clearer picture of shape coding by touch, and to account for questions raised by findings from tactual and crossmodal matching of three-dimensional shapes. The main puzzle was why visual perception of unfamiliar shapes is usually so much better, and is also more sensitive to processing demands than tactual shape perception. This difference could not be attributed to fixed modality-specific "stores," because tactual recognition can also become sensitive to processing demands.

The explanation offered here is simple: Coding in terms of spatial features (e.g., line-curve) and dimensions (up-down, right-left) organizes a relatively large amount of information economically in terms of a few parameters (e.g., by coordinate axes or global form). Spatial codes are "higher order" in that sense, and not because they necessarily come late in a processing hierarchy. The main difference between vision and touch is that spatial organization is less easily achieved by touch since appropriate reference cues are often lacking. Touch may thus have to rely on physical features (e.g., texture differences) which cannot be coded as economically (by as few parameters). Coding is thus of a "lower order." Highly organized information, whether automatically available (LaBerge, 1975) or derived, can be maintained across delays, but requires processing capacity. "Lower order" codes do not require limited capacity and information is readily lost because the input is relatively poorly organized, not because it is tactual. Change from insensitivity to sensitivity to processing demands occurs when subjects have enough information to organize "lower-order codes" spatially (e.g., by constructing internal links through planned movements or by reference to external cues).

Both "lower" and "higher order" codes can, in principle, be used to make judgments either within or between modalities. They are not "amodal" but depend on aspects judged to be relevant in a given task. The view here is that modality-specific coding does not prevent crossmodal perception, but, on the contrary, provides complementary information.

3. Spatial Judgments

3.1. Movement and Vision in Length Judgments

It is of some interest that crossmodal deficits are reported more often in studies using length (extent) than in those using shapes. Gibson (1969) suggests that length judgments are more difficult crossmodally because unidimensional stimuli provide fewer higher-order properties. The explanation here is that judgments depend on the amount of information available to organize the input economically. It is important to realize, therefore, that there are considerable differences between visual and blind conditions in the amount of available information. In normal vision there are a host of background cues to which the length of a line can be related, and in terms of which it can, consequently, be coded. A visual line can be scanned and rescanned, and beginning points and end points can be anchored to external cues. In darkness and in blindness information is given only by movement extent. Rescanning is not possible. In the very act of moving, the original anchor is lost. It is, therefore, much less possible to code the input economically by two spatial axes.

The difference in available information when comparing visual and kinesthetic lengths is rarely recognized or controlled in crossmodal studies (e.g., Connolly & Jones, 1970; Posner, 1967). But it is extremely important. Thus, Millar (1972c) showed that the presence, and use, of position cues changes the relation between intramodal and crossmodal errors. Further, if visual information is confined to a point of light moving in darkness, crossmodal judgments are less, or not at all inferior to intramodal judgments (Diewert & Stelmach, 1977; Millar, 1972c). Millar (1975a) found that stimulus complexity did not relate differentially to crossmodal judgments, and that crossmodal-intramodal differences can actually be less for younger than for older children in some conditions. These findings are strong evidence against the theory that crossmodal length judgments depend on learned translations. It was also found that error patterns change with apparently trivial changes in order of presentation. The results indicate that both intramodal and crossmodal efficiency depends on the information available in tasks and experimental conditions and the extent to which subjects use it.

It is even more important to consider what information is available in different conditions in order to understand the effects of blindness, and to evaluate the evidence for modality-specific coding of discrete blind movements. Studies which extended Posner's important (1967) paradigm systematically varied position and length cues in blind conditions (e.g., Laabs, 1973) with sighted adults. The criterion movement either ended at the same location as the input movement, so that the end location was always invariant, or the criterion movement had to be reproduced from different locations, so that starting and end locations were never reliable cues. The crucial question is whether the input can be maintained without loss across delay, and is sensitive to processing demands from other tasks. This question is tested by the Peterson (Peterson & Peterson, 1959) paradigm. The rationale is that memory depends on processing capacity if it deteriorates only when delays are filled with difficult mental tasks, but holds up if delays are unfilled. Marteniuk (1976) argued that discrete blind movements with fixed end points require processing capacity. Length judgments without fixed positions do not, since they deteriorate even when delays are unfilled. He suggested that processing capability is required because movements with fixed positions are coded in terms of visuospatial references.

An alternative explanation is that movements require processing capacity when subjects organize them. The presence of location cues as such is not crucial; nor is "higher order" coding necessarily visuospatial. The author ran a series of experiments to test this explanation. It was argued that even when location cues are reliable, subjects may not realize this—for instance, if the movements are new. Coding should thus change with familiarity. Visuospatial coding was tested by comparing congenitally totally blind with blindfolded sighted children. Only discrete lengths with fixed starting and end locations were used. Two types of distractors were compared with unfilled delays: a difficult mental task to assess processing demands, and an easy irrelevant movement to test for movement coding. The first experiment showed that memory for new movements (different on every trial), and memory for a movement practiced prior to and during tests, was not sensitive to the difficult mental task. Memory deteriorated with unfilled delay, despite the fixed end locations of the movements. The irrelevant movement did have a deleterious effect, especially for the repeated input. A second study used a new movement that was repeated in all trials, as well as a movement that had also been practiced extensively prior to tests. The latter showed only effects from the irrelevant movement. Since there was no feedback, some form of "automatic" response may have been evolved. The main point was that only memory for the newly repeated movements was worse after delays filled with difficult mental tasks as well as interpolated movements. A third experiment showed that sensitivity to difficult distractors was due to the amount of repetition, and did not vary simply as a function of the specific lengths used. Two naïve subject groups judged the two criterion lengths from new, but repeated, movements and from movements that were only presented once during trials. There was a clear association between repetition and distractor effects. Memory for the two repeated criterion lengths was sensitive to distractors. Memory for the completely new lengths deteriorated only with delay. Subjects thus evolve some form of coding which demands processing capacity with repetition. A further experiment showed that this coding did not depend on visuospatial experience. Congenitally totally blind children who could not have had such experience showed exactly the same effects in the same conditions as blindfolded sighted children.

The findings make it clear that the matter of whether or not memory for movements demands processing capacity does not depend on the presence of location cues as such, or on visuospatial experience. The findings incidentally also disconfirm the hypothesis that only preselected (subject defined) movements are sensitive to distractors, while constrained movements are not (Jones, 1974). All input movements in the above studies were "constrained" (movements to a stop). Yet performance was disturbed by difficult mental tasks. Processing demands in memory depend on how subjects code movements, not on the input as such.

The important question was precisely how subjects did code movements that were repeated, but not extensively practiced. Visual strategies, as has been shown, were clearly not necessary. Verbal coding could also be ruled out. The subjects in this series of experiments were 8-year-old children, and children of nursery age. The preschoolers were, if anything, more affected by distractors than 8-year-olds. Yet preschoolers are known to use verbal strategies less (Conrad, 1971). If the distractor effects had depended on verbal strategies, therefore, the relation between age and such effects should have been in the opposite direction. Similarly, worse memory after irrelevant movements could not be attributed to persistence of uncoded peripheral stimulation, since it was more obvious with familiar imputs, and paralleled disruption by difficult mental tasks. Yet movements were clearly an important factor. The most reasonable explanation, therefore, was that subjects coded the criterion movements by self-reference. This strategy would improve with increased familiarity; it is equally available to the blind and sighted and at least as much for younger as for older subjects; and it is at the same time an economical spatial code and thus likely to require processing capacity. Moreover, disruption by irrelevant movements would be expected, if subjects code the end location of the hand movement relative to the body midaxis. The hypothesis thus explains all the results of this series of experiments.

This explanation assumes that self-referent coding is merely one among optional strategies available to subjects. Children use whatever is easiest in a given task. Coding hand location relative to the body midaxis is easier than using past experience about external frames. Hence, even the sighted used this strategy in blind conditions. If this explanation is correct, then the sighted should have recourse to past visual experience when self-reference is made unreliable. The blind should find tasks with unreliable self-referent cues differentially more difficult. The author tested this prediction in a further study. Blind and blindfolded sighted subjects judged discrete repeated movements after unfilled delays, and after delays filled with difficult mental tasks. Self-reference was made obvious and reliable by aligning the end position of the hand movement to the body midaxis of the subject. So that self-reference would be unreliable, the movements had to be judged by their length alone. The movements started (and ended) at different locations, none of which could be aligned to the body midaxis. The results supported the hypothesis. Both blind and blindfolded sighted children were most accurate with reliable self-referent cues, and these judgments were sensitive to processing demands during delays. Self-reference was thus a "higher order" code in the sense used here. When self-referent cues were made unreliable, the blind and sighted differed. The blind were worse and showed no sensitivity to processing demands in these conditions. Presumably, they had to rely on some form of "lower order" (movement) coding. By contrast, the sighted were more accurate in unfilled delays than under distractors, suggesting that they organized the movement input spatially on the basis of their past visual experience when self-referent cues were made obviously unreliable. In any case, coding clearly differed with past visual experience, and this difference depended on whether or not self-reference was reliable. It can be concluded, therefore, that subjects can use a number of different methods of coding kinesthetic lengths.

In summary, the studies discussed in this section provide evidence that notions of learned translations between the modalities and assumptions of modality-specific "stores" are not required for judgments of length either. Crossmodal matching depends on what information is available from vision and movement and how subjects code it. This is also the case within the kinesthetic modality. Memory for blind movements is sensitive to processing demands if subjects can organize the input spatially. Neither location cues nor visual experience determine this uniquely. Rather, coding seems to depend on what information, present or past, is most easily available and reliable in a given task. This is not merely a question of the *amount* of information. Coding also seems to differ in *form*. Three main forms of coding were found here: (1) spatial self-reference (when locations can be coded reliably relative to the body midaxis), which is relatively easy with repeated inputs but demands processing capacity; (2) movement coding (by blind and sighted with unfamiliar lengths, and by the blind when self-reference was disrupted), which seemed to be independent of limited capacity; and (3) spatial coding derived from visual experience which required processing capacity (for the sighted, only when self-reference was disrupted). Further evidence for these forms of coding will be considered in the context of tasks of location and direction.

3.2. Spatial Location and Direction

Differences between the blind and sighted have been reported most reliably for tasks that require mental spatial reorganization of external locations and directions (Hatwell, 1978; Millar, 1975d, 1976; O'Connor & Hermelin, 1975; Warren, 1977). In such tasks self-referent coding is almost always inappropriate, and coding in terms of movements is less adequate than reference to external directions.

Mental spatial-rotation problems are the most usual tests for self-referent coding. Piaget's "three mountains," or perspective, task is probably the best-known example (Piaget & Inhelder, 1948). Subjects are required to predict how a given spatial layout would look to a person situated at a location different from the subject's own viewpoint. In Piaget's view, young children are said to be "egocentric" (select a view similar to their own), and to become progressively less so, finally achieving an objective external-coordinate system. Recent studies have shown that even infants can solve rotation problems, provided external cues are present and salient (Bremner, 1978) and the material and layout are familiar (Acredolo, Pick, & Olsen, 1975; Fishbein, Lewis, & Keiffer, 1972), or the task involves a simple, obvious rule (Flavell, Manson, & Latham 1978). It is also quite easy to fool intelligent adults into making an "egocentric" error by making the task sufficiently difficult. A neat invariant progression from egocentrism to a Euclidean coordinate system cannot, therefore, adequately describe spatial development. Self-referent coding cannot, in any case, be regarded as some form of inferior anticipation of logical spatial coordination. It is important for most animals to know where their limbs are in relation to their head and trunk. Self-referent systems are extremely important at all ages. It is only when used inappropriately that they become maladaptive. Conditions of blindness elicit inappropriate strategies.

Spatial-rotation problems are complex, and impose a considerable "mental work" load. But it can be shown that spatial "ego-centrism" on the part of the blind is neither simply attributable to this factor, nor to developmental "lag." Millar (1979) used a very simple object "shift" task that did not involve mental rotation or any mental work load. Subjects merely had to shift objects between identical locations on identical easy or more difficult background shapes. The movements were either in the vertical (median plane) or horizontal (across the body midline) directions. In vertical shifts, the hand position in locating objects remained proportionately invariant relative to the body midline of the subject. In horizontal shifts, the relation of the object–hand position changed relative to the midline. Self-referent or movement coding thus led to errors. Blindfolded sighted children made no errors on these tasks beyond the age of 8 or 9. Four- and five-year-olds were not affected by the direction of the movements either, but made more errors with the difficult background shape. This showed that they used external cues from the background shapes to code object positions. Blind subjects who had some minimal visual experience also coded by external cues, although they made errors on the difficult shape at much later ages than the sighted, thus showing some "developmental lag." But the congenitally totally blind were affected by the direction of the movement shift, regardless of background shape. They made far more errors in horizontal shifts. This meant that they used self-reference and movement rather than external cues, although the latter were present and had been felt by them. This was clearly not because of "developmental lag." The totally blind actually did better than young sighted subjects in conditions where self-referent and movement coding were appropriate. Two conclusions may be drawn from this. First, even minimal visual experience seems to draw attention to external cues. Second, the difference between the sighted and the totally congenitally blind is not mainly a question of "accuracy." There are demonstrable differences in the *type* of information being used.

The results discussed in the previous section suggested that self-referent and movement coding differ. The distinction is important, especially as it is usually blurred by the general notion of spatial "egocentrism." It must be pointed out, therefore, that movement coding is "egocentric" only in the redundant sense that the information is from and about the subject's own body. Self-referent coding, on the other hand, refers to the subject's use of a body part (usually the trunk midline) as the point of origin or reference axis to which an external location is referred. Self-referent coding thus provides more organization than coding by movements. Self-reference was shown to be a "higher order" code (see previous section). Evidence that subjects can and do use movement information, and that this differs from self-reference, is given below.

The author tested for differences between movement and self-referent information in recent experiments with blind and blindfolded sighted children. A metal square with easily felt vertical and horizontal coordinates was used. Different toy figures marked the near and far ends of the vertical (raised) line. The right and left end of the horizontal ridge were test positions. Subjects moved a ring from one of the vertical ends to the test location by guided movements. To test for self-reference, the display was rotated by 180° prior to retrieving the ring. Responses to the opposite (original) half-field indicated self-referent (relative to the subject's midline) coding. For the congenitally totally blind the proportion of such responses was well above chance level up to the age of about 14. For the sighted, the proportion was below chance level even for 6-year-olds. Movement coding was assessed by a condition in which the test location remained invariant relative to the subject's midline, but the movement accessing it was changed from the near to the far (or vice versa) ends. Self-reference thus remained invariant while the accessing movement differed. Errors in this condition differed significantly both from errors under rotations, and from errors in conditions in which the response movement was the same as in presentation. Thus, there was clear evidence that movement information was coded.

It can be shown also that visually derived strategies differ in form, and not merely in accuracy, from strategies that depend on movement information. Two different paradigms were used (Millar, 1975d, 1976). Self-reference was made unreliable in both. One study (Millar, 1976) used mental rotation of a vertical (median plane) ridge on a rectangular table. Subjects walked around it in a clockwise direction to test positions (45° through to 315° in random order). They then reproduced the line as "seen" from the new position. It was argued that visual experience facilitates "mental map" or survey-type strategies. If this is so, errors by blindfolded sighted children should not differ between test positions. On the other hand, if subjects rely on memory for the movement sequence, they should make more errors on positions far from the starting point, and on locations that produce oblique directions. Obliques have to be specified by two coordinated directions, while for orthogonals one movement reference would be enough. Errors by the blind showed precisely these differences, whereas errors by blindfolded sighted children were consistent with predictions from a mental "survey map" strategy with quasi "equal access" to references from different locations. This does not mean that blindfolded, sighted children were accurate. Visually derived strategies are not necessarily the best method for solving such problems. Nevertheless, strategies derived from visual experience have advantages over movement coding for specific directions.

Similar results were found with a different paradigm (Millar, 1975d). Subjects traversed a five-sided mazelike figure with a stylus. Self-reference was made unreliable by presenting the layout unpredictably in different positions. Subjects had to reproduce the path to near or far locations on the maze either from the start, or backward from the end of the figure. With the mental "survey map" strategy, backward recall of the locations should not be worse than forward recall. On the other hand, coding in terms of the movement sequence should produce larger errors in backward recall, particularly for the longest path. The results were consistent with both predictions. Interestingly enough, the massive interactions between sighted status and the form of recall did not relate to age. Children improved within the coding strategies they were using. By contrast, using additional nonspatial information (cuing prior to input, or to response) was found to relate to age and not to blindness.

In summary, studies with spatial location and direction provided further evidence that blind movements can be coded in at least three different forms. Strategies based on self-reference, on memory for kinesthetic sequences, and on visuospatial organization were distinguished. In some sense, "modality-specific" information was involved in all of them. This was perhaps most obvious when only movements differed and both external location and self-reference remained invariant.

It showed also in the "survey map" strategies found in the error patterns of quite young, sighted children. It must be stressed that these strategies were far from accurate, and, therefore, certainly nothing like "photographic copies" (Neisser & Kerr, 1973) of the actual layout. But the findings were consistent with using references to relations between external directions which are more obvious in vision than through the other senses. The notion that the three forms of coding are in some neat developmental progression, and that the blind are merely a stage behind, can be discarded. Children improved with age in using any kind of information. But vision not only provides more information, it evidently also draws subjects' attention to external cues as means of reference. This does not mean that vision is either necessary or sufficient for spatial reorganization: in the studies here, some, if few, congenitally totally blind children solved such problems; some, if relatively few, sighted children did not. The difference between visual and blind experience was nevertheless an important factor in the type of information children used. Blind conditions foster strategies that neglect reference to external directions, and are thus often inappropriate, or inefficient.

3.3. Sound, Vision, and Movement in Large-Scale Space

There is no doubt that, in principle, spatial problems can be solved by inference from sequential information. Some blind people are excellent chess players. Intelligent blind adolescents can infer shortcuts in a familiarized layout (Leonard & Newman, 1967). In fact, however, blind children do have considerable difficulties with many spatial tasks (see above). These difficulties also occur in large-scale space. The question, thus, is not whether the blind have the ability to code spatially, but under what conditions they come to do so, and whether their spatial inferences can be guided by "cognitive maps."

Sound as the only remaining distal source is extremely important for the blind in large-scale space. The development of auditory and movement coordination is thus of considerable practical as well as theoretical interest. In fact, reaching to sound seems to be less well programmed than reaching to visual targets. There seems to be no auditory parallel to the visual control of posture and movement (e.g., Lee & Aronson, 1974) early in life. It is precisely these visually controlled postures and movements that are delayed in the congenitally totally blind (Fraiberg, 1977). Difficulties on the part of the blind in spatially integrating sounds and movements have been reported (Warren & Pick, 1970). To explain these difficulties, it is not necessary to assume that vision is essential to the integration of movement and sound. It is important to realize that, in vision, the view of objects changes continuously and reliably as the child moves. In blind conditions, feedback from external sources is neither reliable nor invariant, nor necessarily correlated with movements. To some extent this difference in feedback conditions can be minimized by echolocation. Some, although by no means all, blind children develop methods of obtaining echolocation—for instance, by stamping while walking, hand clapping, and the like.

It has been suggested that fitting babies with an echolocation device from early infancy can substitute for visual spatial information (Bower, 1977). Certainly, covariation of movements with sounds provides predictable external consequences which the blind can use to guide their movements. Even quite young totally blind children can learn to walk straight to a sound source. In a recent experiment, the author found that blind children use fixed sound cues to locate objects in space much more than the blindfolded sighted. A similar result was found by Juurmaa and Suonio (1975) for adults. Nevertheless, the sighted were better at the task. Reliable sources of sound and correlated feedback are obviously important. It is not so clear that they are sufficient to substitute for visual information. Vision provides concurrent information about the relation of planes, lines, and surfaces to each other. The findings discussed in the previous section suggest that it is precisely this information which enables the sighted to organize locations—however inaccurately—in terms of external spatial layouts. Even when sounds are rigged to differ between different planes and surfaces, their spatial relation to each other has to be inferred from successive inputs. This is true also with active exploration through movement. That spatial inferences can be made from such information is not in doubt. The question is what kind of conditions facilitate this. Some of these conditions are considered below.

Findings on sighted children (Acredolo, 1977; Acredolo et al., 1975; Kosslyn, Pick, & Fariello, 1974) suggest that the presence of landmarks, as well as familiarity are important. In studies discussed in previous sections, the presence of location cues and input familiarity were shown to elicit spatial coding with small-scale displays. To test whether the blind code large-scale space by external cues in these conditions, the author used a simple square area with distinctive toys at each of the four corners. Subjects were familiarized with the area by repeated guided walks around it in a clockwise direction, always starting from the same location. They were tested only when they could recite the sequence of the four toys correctly. Tests were on moving from one toy to another in either old (clockwise), new (anticlockwise), or inferred (one toy skipped) diagonal directions. Subjects also had to draw the space and indicate the toys on it. Below the age of 7, blind children could not cope with the tests at all, and seemed to have no idea that an enclosed space had to be represented, in contrast to blindfolded sighted controls. Above the age of 10, the blind were quite good even at inferrred directions, and usually caught on to the fact that the space had to be represented by a closed figure, although even these children made more use of a fixed sound cue than the sighted. Thus, with familiar landmarks in a known sequence, maplike representations are possible even for the blind. It has also been shown that the blind can represent the human figure by conventional, simple two-dimensional shapes (Millar, 1975e).

The fact that the blind can use maplike two-dimentional representations is important. It suggests another means by which the blind may be helped to understand and organize external spatial relations in large-scale space. The studies discussed above underline the conclusion that vision is not necessary for solving spatial problems, or even for spatial representations. The contributions of vision must not be underestimated, however. In the study with a known object sequence in a familiarized space, blind children with even only light perception, or any earlier visual experience, were much better than the congenitally totally blind. In total blindness, reference to external relations and maplike spatial organization has to be achieved by a much more circuitous route. Invariant correlations between sounds and movements, known sequences of landmarks, and symbolic representations of spatial relations seem to be at least some of the factors which facilitate this achievement.

4. Conclusion

My aim has been to understand how blind children perceive space, and to resolve some of the contradictions in crossmodal theories and predictions about the blind. For these purposes it was necessary to consider in some detail how children use information from touch and movement. I shall now consider some conclusions.

A reasonably clear picture emerges. Vision is neither necessary nor sufficient for spatial tasks. But it draws attention to external cues, and to directional connections between them which makes spatial coding easy. Tactual shapes were coded by name and by physical tactual features. These physical features were not organized spatially, unless the shapes were familiar. Reliable concomitant information from other sources was even more important for judging extent, location, and direction. Spatial coding means organizing information in terms of directions or configurations. Such organization requires stable references. In the absence of stable references, movements were coded by kinesthetic cues that were not spatially organized. Differences in information affect knowledge and coding strategies. This fact, it has been argued, explains most of the contradictions in crossmodal and blind behavior.

It should be stressed that children used several, demonstrably different coding strategies, but that these were not arbitary or unpredictable. The coding strategies related consistently to three main conditions: the type of references currently available, how reliable they were, and the ease and speed with which other codes could be accessed in memory. Verbal strategies related to naming speed; when physical tactual features could be used more easily, subjects coded these to speed matching. The type of spatial coding depended on whether current hand-to-body relations were invariant, or were made obviously inconsistent. The sighted must have had more knowledge of external relations than the blind. But they resorted significantly to configurational strategies derived from memory only when current easier cues were made obviously inappropriate. If external cues were present, the sighted used these more. When there were no immediately obvious anchors, subjects coded differences in feel and movement that were not organized spatially. These detailed findings from tasks set within a single modality confirm and extend the crossmodal data. Touch and vision differ in how easy it is to organize shapes as configurations. Consistent additional cues from another modality can help; unreliable, discrepant cues can hinder. Young children may use rather crude features and modes of coding. This can make it as easy to match across as within a modality. Modality-specific information was certainly coded. But it is no paradox that there was evidence against a "dictionary" of specially learned translations. The sense modalities cannot be regarded as either separate, or unitary. They are normally *complementary and convergent*. Children use information flexibly from several sources.

It is tacitly assumed in most theories that the sense modalities are either crucial, or else irrelevant for spatial tasks. The opposite is more nearly correct. No single sensory system is crucial; yet difference in modes of information affect knowledge and the way it is used. This is shown when a sense modality does not function. The fact that congenitally totally blind children have serious difficulties mainly when tasks demand reference to external cues and directions is perfectly intelligible. In blind conditions, connections between external sources are less obvious, and are not reliably correlated with movement. The blind will thus have less knowledge of external relations, and little reason to consider that they would help. But their responses are not chaotic. Révész (1950) was quite right. Congenitally totally blind children do rely to a very large extent on self-reference and movement sequences. These strategies were found even in quite simple tasks that did not involve mental rotation. But the blind are not retarded in a supposed sequence (e.g., Piaget) in which self-reference is necessarily prior. Their strategies are perfectly reasonable in the circumstances. Self-reference can also be easier because it uses current information. But even the youngest sighted used external cues when these were present. The strategies related to prior vision. Quite minimal visual experience made some difference. There is no doubt that the blind are capable of making inferences about external relations, even if the relevant knowledge has to be provided through more circuitous routes. Moreover, the inaccurate maplike strategies used by the sighted are not the best possible method. But as a heuristic they were more appropriate than the strategies which the blind derived from touch and movement. It can be concluded that vision is not necessary for spatial tasks, but that lack of vision affects knowledge of external relations, and promotes strategies that derive from particular modes of information.

The implication for intersensory and intermodal performance by the blind is that, in principle, these need not be impaired in the remaining modalities. In practice, there can be difficulties. These difficulties arise not because vision is necessary for crossmodal performance. The difficulties are in particular spatial tasks, when the remaining modalities do not naturally provide the information which makes it easy to code by external configurations. In large-scale space, sounds are essential as landmarks which make mobility possible in familiar environments. But such landmarks are not enough. Small-scale layouts which can be scanned and rescanned so that external relations are understood are probably more important for the blind than has often been recognized hitherto. Representing spatial relations by drawing may also encourage organization of larger-scale space by spatial form. *Planned movements are important.* It is no accident that the survey of findings in preceding sections ended, as it began, by considering shape.

The thesis here is that to understand spatial performance in blind conditions, three factors must be distinguished: (1) the amount of available information; (2) the form and flexibility of coding; and (3) how economically codes organize information. These factors are indirectly related, but they contribute differently to performance. Coding which uses few parameters to organize a lot of information makes demands on memory regardless of modality. But the form of coding is not "amodal." Like verbal coding, spatial coding by self-reference and by external references is "higher order" in the sense that it needs few parameters and is disturbed by irrelevant difficult tasks. But these codes differ in the type of information used, and in form. They also differ in their appropriateness to different tasks. Forms or modes of coding are selectively sensitive to different forms of modality-specific interference, and show response patterns characteristic of the mode of prior experience, irrespective of the level or economy of organization. Thus, "lower order" coding is less demanding, but loses information—not because it necessarily comes earlier in a processing sequence, or because the information is uncoded, or because modality effects occur only at this level, but because the information is not organized economically. Similarly, the fact that the sense modalities access different aspects and forms of information is not a handicap. The diversity increases knowledge as well as the number of possible alternative strategies. Modality-specific information is not merely coded in memory. It can be used flexibly and optionally to index or symbolize information. A name, an arrow, or a "feel" can mean the same, without necessarily being equally useful or appropriate to all tasks. This notion is intelligible if the theoretical distinction between "separateness" and "unity" is discarded. The sensory systems are complementary and converge. The correct analogy is not with a single type of organization, nor with the Tower of Babel, but with complex cross-reference systems and flexible means of indexing.

The implication of the thesis is that in crossmodal tasks, normally convergent information is temporarily disrupted. Performance depends on what current information there is, and on how easily this information elicits strategies that either complete or circumvent missing or discrepant information. In principle, the procedures are the same as in within-modal tasks under the same conditions. Similarly, the congenitally totally blind lack important aspects of information, and forms of organizing it that are easily derived from vision. These aspects mainly concern reliable information about the connections between external cues and the means to organize them in map-like configurations. In principle, most of this information and equal degrees of organization can be achieved by other routes. Whatever the preferred modes of indexing, eventually they can become equally efficient.

In conclusion, the evidence suggests that vision, touch, and movement contribute and emphasize different aspects of information about the world, and that these aspects affect both the manner and means of coding. But there is no special problem about combining information from different modalities. The explanation offered is that the sense modalities are normally complementary, and they converge at several levels of organization. Subjects use information, including modality-specific aspects, flexibly at all levels. When vision is lacking, much of the information needed for spatial organization is reduced. But it can be gained through other sources and can become organized efficiently, whatever mode of indexing is used. The point is that the manner in which information is gained, and how it is handled, explains the findings on children's crossmodal behavior, and the spatial difficulties of the blind.

5. References

Acredolo, L.P. Developmental changes in the ability to co-ordinate perspectives in large-scale space. *Developmental Psychology*, 1977, *13*, 1–8.

Acredolo, L.P., Pick, H.L., Jr., & Olsen, M.G. Environmental differentiation and familiarity as determinants of children's memory for spatial location. *Developmental Psychology*, 1975, *11*, 495–501.

Anderson, T.F., & Bower, G.H. *Human associative memory.* New York: Wiley, 1973.

Apkarian-Stielau, P., & Loomis, T.H. A comparison of tactile and blurred visual form perception. *Perception and Psychophysics*, 1975, *18*, 362–368.

Bartlett, F.C. *Remembering.* London: Cambridge University Press, 1932.

Berlá, E.P., & Butterfield, L.H., Jr. Tactual distinctive feature analysis: Training blind students in shape recognition and in locating shapes on a map. *The Journal of Special Education*, 1977, *11*, 336–346.

Bever, T.G., & Chiarello, R.C. Cerebral dominance in musicians and non-musicians. *Science*, 1974, *185*, 537.

Bower, T. *The perceptual world of the child.* London: Fonata/Open Books, 1977.

Bremner, J.G. Spatial errors made by infants: Inadequate spatial cues or evidence of egocentrism. *British Journal of Psychology*, 1978, *69*, 77–84.

Bryant, P.E., Jones, P., Claxton, V., & Perkins, G.M. Recognition of shapes across modalities by infants. *Nature*, 1972, *240*, 303–304.

Brooks, L.R. The suppression of visualization during reading. *Journal of Experimental Psychology*, 1967, *19*, 289–299.

Connolly, K., & Jones, B. A developmental study of afferent-reafferent integration. *British Journal of Psychology*, 1970, *61*, 259–266.

Conrad, R. Acoustic confusions in immediate memory. *British Journal of Psychology*, 1964, *55*, 75–84.

Conrad, R. The chronology of the development of covert speech in children. *Developmental Psychology*, 1971, *5*, 398–405.

Davenport, R.K., & Rogers, C.M. Intermodal equivalence of stimulation in apes. *Science*, 1970, *168*, 279–280.

Davenport, R.K., Rogers, C.M., & Russell, I.S. Cross-modal perception in apes. *Neuropsychologica*, 1973, *11*, 21–28.

Davidson, P.W. The role of exploratory activity in haptic perception: Some issues, data and hypotheses. *Research Bulletin, American Foundation for the Blind*, 1972, *24*, 21–28.

Diewert, G.L., & Stelmach, G.E. Intramodal and intermodal transfer of movement information. *Acta Psychologica*, 1977, *41*, 118–128.

Dillon, R.F., & Reid, L.S. Short-term memory as a function of information processing during the retention interval. *Journal of Experimental Psychology*, 1969, *81*, 261–269.

Ettlinger, G. Analysis of cross-modal effects and their relationship to language. In F.L. Darley & C.H. Millikan (Eds.), *Brain mechanisms underlying speech and language*, New York: Grune & Stratton, 1967.

Fantz, R.L., Fagan, T.F., & Miranda, S.B. Early visual selectivity: In L. Cohen & P. Salapatek (Eds.), *Infant perception from sensation of cognition*. Vol. 1. New York: Academic Press, 1975.

Fertsch, P. Hand dominance in reading Braille. *American Journal of Psychology*, 1947, *60*, 335–349.

Fishbein, H.D., Lewis, S., & Keiffer, K. Children's understanding of spatial relations: Coordination of perspectives. *Developmental Psychology*, 1972, *7*, 21–33.

Flavell, T., O'Manson, R.C., & Latham, C. Solving spatial perspective-taking problems by rule versus computation. *Developmental Psychology,* 1978, *14,* 462–473.

Foulke, E. Transfer of a complex perceptual skill. *Perceptual and Motor Skills,* 1964, *18,* 733–740.

Foulke, E., & Warm, T.S. Effects of complexity and redundancy on the tactual recognition of metric figures. *Perceptual and Motor Skills,* 1967, *25,* 177–187.

Fraiberg, S. Insights from the blind: Comparative studies of blind and sighted infants. New York: Basic Books, 1977.

Freides, D. Human information processing and sensory modality. *Psychological Bulletin,* 1974, *81,* 284–310.

Gaines, R. The discriminability of form among young children. *Journal of Experimental Child Psychology,* 1969, *8,* 418–431.

Gibson, E.J. *Principles of perceptual learning and development,* New York: Appleton, Century, Crofts, 1969.

Goodnow, J.J. Matching auditory and visual series: Modality problem or translation problem? *Child Development,* 1971, *42,* 1187–1201. (a)

Goodnow, J.J. Eye and hand: Differential memory and its effect on matching. *Neuropsychologica,* 1971, *9,* 89–95. (b)

Gregory, R.L. *Concepts and mechanisms of perception.* London: Duckworth, 1974.

Gregory, R.L., & Wallace, J.G. Recovery from early blindness: A case study. *Experimental Psychology Society Monograph No. 2,* 1963.

Hatwell, Y. Form perception and related issues in blind humans. In R. Held, H.W. Leibowitz, & W.L. Teuber (Eds.), *Handbook of sensory physiology. Vol. 8. Perception,* Berlin: Springer Verlag, 1978.

Held, R. & Bauer, J.A. Visually guided reaching in infant monkeys after restricted rearing. *Science,* 1967, *155,* 718–720.

Hermelin, B. & O'Connor, N. Functional asymmetry in the reading of Braille. *Neuropsychologica,* 9, 431–435.

Hill, J.W., & Bliss, J.C. Modelling a tactile sensory register. *Perception and Psychophysics,* 1968, *9,* 91–101.

Jones, B. Role of central monitoring of efference in short-term memory for movements. *Journal of Experimental Psychology,* 1974, *102,* 37–43.

Juurmaa, J., & Suonio, K. The role of audition and motion in the spatial orientation of the blind and the sighted. *Scandinavian Journal of Psychology,* 1975, *16,* 209–216.

Kosslyn, S.M., Pick, H.L., Jr., & Fariello, G.R. Cognitive maps in child and man. *Child Development,* 1974, *45,* 707–716.

Krauthammer, G. Form perception across sensory modalities. *Neuropsychologica,* 1968, *6,* 105–113.

Krueger, L.E. Effects of irrelevant surrounding material on speed of same-different judgments of two adjacent stimuli. *Journal of Experimental Psychology,* 1973, *98,* 252–259.

Kumar, S. Short-term memory for a nonverbal tactual task after cerebral commissurotomy. *Cortex,* 1977, *13,* 55–61.

Laabs, G.J. Retention characteristics of different reproduction cues in motor short-term memory. *Journal of Experimental Psychology, 100,* 168–177.

LaBerge, D. Acquisition of automatic processing in perceptual and associative learning. In P.M.A. Rabbitt & S. Dornic (Eds.), *Attention and performance.* New York: Academic Press, 1975.

Lee, D.N., & Aronson, E. Visual proprioceptive control of standing in human infants. *Perception and Psychophysics,* 1974, *15,* 529–532.

Leonard, J.A. & Newman, R.C. Spatial orientation in the blind. *Nature,* 1967, *215,* 1413–1414.

Marmor, G.S., & Zabeck, L.A. Mental rotation by the blind: Does mental rotation depend on visual imagery. *Journal of Experimental Psychology: Human Perception and Performance*, 1976, *2*, 515–521.

Marteniuk, R.G. Cognitive information processes in motor short-term memory and movement production. In G.E. Stelmach (Ed.), *Motor control: Issues and trends*. New York: Academic Press, 1976.

McKinney, J.R. Handschema in children. *Psychonomic Science*, 1964, *1*, 99–100.

Melzack, R., & Eisenberg, H. Skin sensory afterglows. *Science*, 1968, *159*, 445–447.

Michotte, A., Thinès, G., & Crabbe, G. *Les complements amodaux des structures perceptives*. Louvain, Belgium: *Publications, University of Louvain, 1964*.

Millar, S. Visual and haptic cue utilization by preschool children: The recognition of visual and haptic stimuli presented separately and together. *Journal of Experimental Child Psychology*, 1971, *12*, 88–94.

Millar, S. Effects of interpolated tasks on latency and accuracy of intramodal and crossmodal shape recognition by children. *Journal of Experimental Psychology*, 1972, *96*, 170–175. (a)

Millar S. Effects of instructions to visualize stimuli during delay on visual recognition by preschool children. *Child Development*, 1972, *43*, 1073–1075. (b)

Millar, S. Tactile short-term memory by blind and sighted children. *British Journal of Psychology*, 1974, *65*, 253–263.

Millar, S. Effects of tactual and phonological similarity on the recall of Braille letters by blind children. *British Journal of Psychology*, 1975, *66*, 193–201. (b)

Millar, S. Spatial memory by blind and sighted children. *British Journal of Psychology*, 1975, *66*, 449–459. (c)

Millar, S. Visual experience or translation rules? Drawing the human figure by blind and sighted children. *Perception*, 1975, *4*, 363–371. (d)

Millar, S. Spatial representation by blind and sighted children. *Journal of Experimental Child Psychology*, 1976, *12*, 460–479.

Millar, S. Tactual and name matching by blind children. *British Journal of Psychology*, 1977, *68*, 377–383. (a)

Millar, S. Early stages of tactual matching. *Perception*, 1977, *6*, 333–343. (b)

Millar, S. Short-term serial tactual recall: Effects of grouping on tactually probed recall of Braille letters and nonsense shapes by blind children. *British Journal of Psychology*, 1978, *69*, 17–24. (a)

Millar, S. Aspects of memory for information from touch and movement. In G. Gordon (Ed.), *Active touch*. New York: Pergamon Press, 1978. (b)

Millar, S. The utilization of external and movement cues in simple spatial tasks by blind and sighted children. *Perception*, 1979, *8*, 11–20.

Milner, B. In V.B. Mountcastel (Ed.), *Interhemispheric relations and cerebral dominance*, Baltimore: Johns Hopkins University Press, 1962.

Milner, B., & Taylor, L. Right hemisphere superiority in tactile pattern recognition after cerebral commissurotomy. *Neuropsychologica*, 1972, *10*, 1–15.

Neisser, U. *Cognition and reality: Principles and implications of cognitive psychology*. San Francisco: W.H. Freeman, 1976.

Neisser, U., & Kerr, N. Spatial and mnemonic properties of visual images. *Cognitive Psychology*, 1973, *5*, 138–150.

Nolan, C.Y., & Kederis, C.J. Perceptual factors in Braille word recognition. New York: American Foundation for the Blind, 1969.

O'Connor, N., & Hermelin, B. Modality-specific spatial co-ordinates. *Perception and Psychophysics*, 1975, *17*, 213–216.

Peterson, L.R., & Peterson, M.J. Short-term retention of individual verbal items. *Journal of Experimental Psychology*, 1959, *58*, 193–198.

Piaget, J., & Inhelder, B. *La representation de l'espace chez l'enfant*. Paris: Presses Universitaires de France, 1948.

Pick, A.D., & Pick, H.L., Jr. A developmental study of tactual discrimination in blind and sighted children and adults. *Psychonomic Science*, 1966, *6*, 367–368.

Posner, M.I. Characteristics of visual and kinaesthetic memory codes. *Journal of Experimental Psychology*, 1967, *75*, 103–107.

Posner, M.I., Boies, S.J., Eichelman, W.H., & Taylor, R.L. Retention of visual and name codes of single letters. *Journal of Experimental Psychology Monograph*, 1969, *79* (1, Part 2).

Pylyshyn, Z.W. What the mind's eye tells the mind's brain. *Psychological Bulletin*, 1973, *80*, 1–24.

Rapin, I. Effects of early blindness and deafness on cognition. In R. Katzman (Ed.), *Congenital and acquired cognitive disorders*. New York: Raven Press, 1979.

Révész, G. *Psychology and art of the blind*. London: Longmans, Green, 1950.

Riesen, A.H. *The developmental neuropsychology of sensory deprivation*. New York: Academic Press, 1975.

Sakata, H., & Iwamura, Y. Cortical processing of tactile information in the first somatosensory and parietal association areas in the monkey. In G. Gordon (Ed.), *Active touch*. New York: Pergamon Press, 1978.

Schank, R.C., & Abelson, R.P. *Scripts, plans, goals and understanding: An inquiry into human knowledge structures*. Englewood Cliffs, N.J.: Lawrence Erlbaum, 1977.

Schlaegel, F.F. The dominant method of imagery in blind as compared to sighted adolescents. *Journal of Genetic Psychology*, 1953, *83*, 265–277.

Sperling, G. A model for visual memory tasks. *Human Factors*, 1963, *5*, 19–30.

Sperling, G. Successive approximation to a model for short-term memory. *Acta Psychologica*, 1967, *27*, 285–292.

Tolman, E.C. Cognitive maps in rats and man. *Psychological Review*, 1948, *55*, 189–208.

Tversky, B., Pictorial encoding in a short-term memory task. *Perception and Psychophysics*, 1969, *6*, 225–233.

von Senden, M. *Space and sight: The perception of space and shape in the congenitally blind before and after operation*. London: Methuen, 1960.

Walk, R.D. Tactual and visual learning of forms differing in degree of symmetry. *Psychonomic Science*, 1965, *2*, 93–94.

Warren, D.H. Early vs. late vision: The role of early vision in spatial reference systems. *New Outlook for the Blind*, 1974, *68*, 157–162.

Warren, D.H. *Blindness and early childhood development*. New York: American Foundation for the Blind, 1977.

Warren, D.H., & Pick, H.L., Jr. Intermodality relations in localization in blind and sighted people. *Perception and Psychophysics*, 1970, *8*, 430–432.

Weber, E.H. [*The sense of touch.*] (D.J. Murray, trans.). London: Academic Press, 1978.

Weiskrantz, L., & Cowey, A. Crossmodal matching in the rhesus monkey using a single pair of stimuli. *Neuropsychologica*, 1975, *13*, 257–261.

Worchel, P. Space perception and orientation in the blind. *Psychological Monographs*, 1951, *65*, Whole No. 332.

Zaporozhets, A.V. The development of perception in the preschool child. In P.H. Mussen (Ed.), *European Research in Child Development. Monographs of the Society for Research in Child Development*, 1965, *30*, 82–101.

Zinchenko, V.P. *Perception as action in perception and action*. Proceedings of the 18th International Congress of Psychology, Moscow, 1966.

10

Coding Strategies of Normal and Handicapped Children

N. O'CONNOR and B. HERMELIN

1. Introduction

This chapter reports the results of experiments carried out with children who suffer from either specific perceptual or general cognitive handicaps. The studies represent an attempt to compare the effects of such specific sensory handicaps with general cognitive deficit, but they were also intended as a breaking away from the traditional role of psychology in relation to psychiatry, a role in which psychologists have tended to accept uncritically the classificatory framework of clinically defined groups or, alternatively, to reject such diagnostically defined groupings out of hand. A further source for these studies lay in the problems which characterize the psychological investigation of subnormality, which had for long been dominated by the important concept of intelligence. Although the experimental investigation of general cognitive handicap has proceeded in the last two decades by specific investigations concerned with learning processes, this particular departure from the traditional approach via the intelligence test could nonetheless be criticized. Explicitly or implicitly, most experimental workers in the field of subnormality have assumed the existence of a linear information-handling process, beginning with the focusing of attention and followed by perception and short-term retention of input. The categorization of this

N. O'CONNOR and B. HERMELIN • Medical Research Council (MRC), Developmental Psychology Unit, Drayton House, Gordon Street, London, WC1H 0AN England.

retained input in long-term memory, the selection of a verbal equivalent, and the subsequent verbal or motor output associated with the stimulus have been the other stages which have been presumed. Such a "chain reaction" was considered to be linearly organized, and in consequence, failure of one of the constituent processes could be held to affect all other subsequent stages. The weakness of the logic of such a model is that inefficiency at any one point in the processing chain does not in fact necessarily preclude the existence of similar deficiencies at another link. Consequently the failure of the total process cannot necessarily be assumed to arise from one source only. Nonetheless, the experimental approach following such a strategy has led a number of psychologists, such as Luria (1961), Ellis (1963), and Zeaman and House (1963), to conclude that a specified link of the assumed chain of linear information processing in the mentally handicapped is impaired. We ourselves have contributed to the same viewpoint (O'Connor & Hermelin, 1963). In making any new contribution to the study of developmental retardation, therefore, one faces a methodological problem. If the approach to the study of general cognitive deficit via the estimation of intelligence is unrevealing and perhaps circular, and if the experimental approach of investigating specific mental operations, based on a linear information-processing model, is logically hard to defend, what alternative remains? The strategy adopted in the experiments reported below is based on the assumption that an exploration of impairments due to specific causes could perhaps help us to understand the nature of defects due to general, central, and cognitive maldevelopment. If we were to compare children with specific, congenital sensory impairments with those with general cognitive defects, and were to find that some performance or behavior was similar in both groups in spite of a very different intelligence level, then it could be presumed that the behavior in question could originate independently of intelligence level. If, however, in any particular process or mental operation children with sensory-specific defects differed in their performance from those with general cognitive handicap, the cause of the difference might reasonably be attributed to a general intelligence factor. Thus, such a strategy has been adopted in the experiments described below. We had initially considered comparing localized brain damage with general cognitive handicap, but eventually concluded that to use children with specific brain lesions as subjects was contraindicated for a number of reasons. One of these reasons was that specific lesions in children may be compensated for by a transfer of function to the contralateral hemisphere, and as McFie (1976) has shown, such compensation following brain injury often occurs up to the age of 10. Another reason why children with localized lesions may not in our context be the best subjects is that the effect of lesions in early childhood can produce a more generalized form of defect than would be common in a nervous system in which specialization of function and its localization have already occurred. Therefore, the alternative was to select children who had suffered no known central damage, but showed instead a clearly defined peripheral impairment, such as is found, for example, in the congenitally blind or deaf. These groups, therefore, are referred to in subsequent pages as specifically handicapped, while in subnormal or autistic children we assume central cognitive deficit.

Our key concern was to observe whether or not the input of stimuli in one modality was encoded in terms of the modality of this input, or was instead processed in terms of images and representations based on a modality system which, for the task concerned, would be considered more appropriate. Such an alternative representational code might not be available to subjects with a restricted repertoire of perceptually based reference systems, or might not be readily accessible to those with cognitive deficits. Thus in subsequent work an attempt was made to examine the evidence for modality-specific memory coding, and to determine the conditions leading to the encoding of material presented in one modality in terms of another. Consideration was also given to dual and ''amodal'' coding processes, such as have been proposed by Paivio (1971) and by Gibson (1969).

2. Modality-Specific Memory Systems and Sensory Integration

The differentiation by a number of authors, such as Sperling (1960), Posner and Mitchell (1967), Conrad (1964), and Crowder and Morton (1969), of different sensory memories suggests that the sensory qualities of stimuli in terms of their specific modalities is preserved for at least brief periods. Evidence, such as that from Nilsson (1974), indicated that subjects often remembered the modality of presentation of a stimulus, even when faced with stimuli presented in different modalities in mixed order. Thus it seems well established that in some circumstances the modality-specific qualities of the stimulus material may be retained. A good deal of this evidence concerns either vision or audition, but Posner (1967), Abramsky, Carmon, and Benton, (1971), and Coquery and Amblard (1973), among others, have also demonstrated differences between visual and kinesthetic memory coding. The existence of such a differentiation gives rise to the question of whether particular modality-specific memory stores are more specialized than others for the appreciation of certain qualities or dimensions of percepts. There is, for example, an extensive literature, to be referred to in subsequent pages, which seems to indicate a tendency for vision to be specialized for the appreciation of space, and for audition to be predisposed to the organization of stimuli in successive temporal order. Paivio and Csapo (1971) appear to support such a view, although Lashley (1951) thought earlier that the mechanism that determined order was independent of specific neural traces. The question of whether ordering in motor memory follows a pattern similar to, or different from, the ordering in visual or auditory memory has been considered by such workers as Pepper and Herman (1970), who note that the accuracy with which a movement sequence could be recalled would decrease over time. The monitoring of motor programs was discussed by von Holst (1954) and Keele (1968) using a reeference model, and it seems clear that motor memory also has some qualitatively different features from those memory systems of other modalities.

Briggs (1974) opposed a simple modality-encoding hypothesis, and obtained evidence against any distinction between verbal and visual codes. This finding supports Aristotle, who had proposed the existence of a *sensis communis* which would link the information from the various sensory systems. Others, such as Berkeley 1709/1948 and Gibson (1969), have taken the view that sensory integration is only gradually acquired through experience. While Berkeley suggested that the sense of touch developed prior to that of vision, and in turn "taught" vision to reinvert the inverted visual image on the retina, Gibson (1966) holds that children become increasingly able to abstract "amodal" stimulus features which can thus be recognized in any sensory modality. One possible means for such amodal abstraction could be language, but, as cross-modal transfer has been demonstrated in apes and preverbal children, this is an unlikely hypothesis. It is possible, however, that those who presuppose sensory integration to be present at birth and those who stress the role of experience may both be correct. Bower (1974) has demonstrated that infants begin life with integration of the senses already developed through what he calls "supramodal object perception." However, at about the fifth month, vision and grasp become differentiated. The capacity to predict on the basis of one sensory experience that information to other senses is potentially available has to redevelop subsequently through associative learning. Bryant, Jones, Claxton, and Perkins (1972) have shown that this reintegration had at least partially occurred in 10-month-old infants, who were able to associate an object which they had previously felt when they saw it subsequently.

One aspect of sensory integration can be demonstrated by the phenomenon of "sensory capture," in which conflicting input to different sense modalities is often not perceived as such. Instead, the observer seems to resolve such conflict by making one sense impression conform with another dominant one. Thus when a subject views an object through distorting lenses and touches it at the same time, the tactual perception also becomes distorted in accordance with the visually presented information. Likewise, a sound may appear to originate from an apparent source which is visually present, when in fact it is emitted from somewhere else. Such "capture" of one sensory input by another is of interest because it suggests that there may be a degree of perceptual equivalence between various sensory information, so that the same stimulus qualities tend to be perceived in various modalities.

3. Temporal and Spatial Coordinates

The manner in which humans organize or appreciate time has been seen from two different points of view. The first, based on Aristotle's observation, concerns the appreciation of change in the external environment, and the recognition that such change can give rise to notions of succession, and of succession associated with duration. The second idea, which has contributed to our understanding of time, was proposed by Augustine, and concerns the awareness of the flow of events in the mind, whereby what is present in the mind at the moment disappears and is replaced by a subsequent state of consciousness. William James termed this state "the current present." The other thinker who has influenced our views of time is Kant, who, while realizing that the understanding of time—that is, time as a concept—was not innate, nonetheless believed that space and time were both a priori intuitions, by which he meant that they were the framework of our experience without which the experience could not occur.

James (1890/1950) took up the Augustinian notion of succession in thought, and proposed that we can "intuit" about 12 sec of time. He also proposed that overlapping and successively weakening events in short-term memory gave rise to our notion of time, thus indicating that time was not an a priori form of experience, as Kant had thought, but an awareness of the passage of events and, therefore, dependent on experience. Piaget (1927), one of the few psychologists who respected Kant's views, nonetheless thought that notions of time in children depended on the appreciation of causality, space, and velocity, and he proposed that the child's idea of time was initially linked to his idea of the space an object traversed and was, therefore, derived. He found that though speed was appreciated at age 6, the relationship between the amount of space traversed and the time taken to cover the space or distance was only fully appreciated by 9 or 10 years. Piaget regarded the appreciation of time as dependent on the conservation of motion and velocity, and on the capacity to seriate events. As these capacities are related to mental age, time as a determining notion in experience can, according to this view, occur only at a relatively late stage of mental development. Other workers who have tried to determine when notions of time occur in children's language have, not surprisingly, observed an increasing set of references to time with increasing age, and Cromer (1968, 1971) observed that children "decentered" time, that is, saw it as independent, at about the age of 4-1/2. Most investigators agree with Cromer in that, while drawing attention to the increasing use of time references in children's language, they would not necessarily claim that the appreciation of time is language-dependent.

While it would seem that the weight of evidence suggests that time concepts, and even the simple awareness of time passing, increase with age—and may also, develop later than the appreciation of space— children's awareness of the temporal order of a series of items or events has not been extensively studied. Most of such studies with adults, as those of Conrad (1965) and of Crowder and Morton (1969), have tended to emphasize the significance of audition in the development of notions of temporal order in memory. Other authors have drawn attention to the association between deprivation of auditory input and the disturbances of judgments of temporal duration. Examples include Goodfellow (1934), Hirsch, Bilger, and Deatherage (1956), and Savin (1967). Sensory deprivation, especially of audition, appears to decrease the awareness of duration, whereas increasing the number of stimuli would appear to increase it.

The perception of the passage of time at a macroscopic level may conceivably differ from the discrimination of very short time intervals, as Exner originally observed in 1875 (cited in James, 1950/1890). His claim was that only short intervals were better discriminated by ear than by eye. By ear, intervals of 2 msec could be determined, whereas by eye the minimum interval discriminated was 44 msec. Efron (1963) and Hirsch (1959, 1967), following Exner, assumed that in auditory perception sequential and temporal patterns probably play the same role as do form or shape in visual perception of space. Hirsch (1967), using a flicker-fusion technique, noted that vision was capable of resolving intervals of 20 msec whereas audition could resolve intervals of only 1 or 2 msec. These results confirm the auditory-visual differences observed by Exner.

James noted that the "current present" was unusually shortened in aphasics, thus indicating the importance of the auditory channel in the appreciation of durations. More recently, Tallal and Piercy (1973a,b) repeated the work of Efron and Hirsch with dysphasic (mildly aphasic) children. As in previous research, they found that the capacity of the dysphasic children in the auditory discrimination of intervals of short duration was defective, although their discrimination of visual durations was unaffected. Doehring (1960) measured the memory for the position of a point of light with deaf, normal, and dysphasic children. Duration of exposure and delay of response were both varied, and aphasics were shown to be worse than either of the other two groups. This finding conflicts with that of Tallal and Piercy, because it shows impaired visual as well as poor auditory performance. It is, however, fair to observe that the intervals used in this experiment were rather longer than those used by Tallal and Piercy.

Such resolution tasks differ from those involving the ordering of events which differ one from the other. In the former case events are similar, whereas the ordering of different items may conceivably be less related to the specific characteristics of the modality involved.

If we turn to studies of the ordering of different events, we must refer to the work of Conrad (1959), Baddeley (1966), and Morton (1970), who each stressed the influence of modality of input on the serial recall of differing items. Various theories for the causes of order errors as distinct from item errors were advanced by these authors, including misperceptions (proposed by Conrad), errors of reencoding from one processing stage to another, as claimed by Aaronson (1967), or errors of retrieval, as noted by Wickelgren (1969). The ordering of such verbal items must be distinguished from studies carried out with non-verbal sounds by R.M. Warren (1968), who showed that order errors in the recall of such items increased if the duration of the items was cut below 200 msec. Such an interval is much greater than that below which ordering of auditory verbal events results in increasing errors.

The retention of order may also be affected by an overloading of immediate memory, and by item interference in the short-term memory store. In addition, the correct recall of the order of a series of items may be associated with the perception of a predictable pattern in the presented material; and the awareness of duration, as well as that of succession, may depend on the amount and organization of the stimuli. Thus the psychological appreciation of time might be said to be based on coding processes, and in this sense we might be thought to construct our own time.

Turning to the appreciation of space, James 1890/1950, in order to illustrate the varying quality of information from different sensory sources, compared a sighted with a blind baby's spatial experience. The sighted baby's eyes would take in a whole scene at once, and single objects would then have to be discriminated from among many others. This discrimination, according to James, would have to occur through a process of analysis. In contrast, the blind baby, who has to explore objects piece by piece and successively, would have to perform a process of mental synthesis to arrive at a simultaneous representation of space.

Nevertheless, James thought that all senses were directly responsive to qualities, such as, for instance, volume, and he held that spatial qualities were inherent in perceptions. Wundt (1894), on the other hand, believed that such qualities as extent and distance were not given in sensations, but were inferences derived from experience. Both James's and Wundt's theories contrast, of course, with Kant's assertion that neither space nor time are either given in experience or inferred from it, but are a priori patterns in terms of which we experience the environment.

Whatever one thinks about the nature of space perception, our movement in space and manipulation of objects in space are restricted by the development and structure of the appropriate sensory systems and by the nature of the physical world. Perception of movement in space has to be distinguished from the perception of space when stationary, and the body's orientation in space is signaled by different receptors than those needed to perceive the spatial orientation of objects. The visual system appears to be the most effective means of acquiring spatial information, though Held and Hein (1963) and Held and Bauer (1966) have established that the absence of opportunity to correlate visual with proprioceptive and kinesthetic data may impair the control of visually guided movements. Nevertheless, it appears that space becomes primarily represented in visual terms. Renshaw and Wherry (1931), McKinney (1964), and Smothergill, Hughes, Timmons, and Hutko (1975) all concluded that children visualized when solving spatial problems, and Shepard and Metzler (1971) and Shinar and Owen (1973) found that adult subjects mentally manipulated visual images to solve object-orientation problems.

D.H. Warren (1973) has suggested three possibly critical periods for the development of visual-motor integration. The first of these occurs during the early months of life, when grasping and reaching come under visual control. The second sensitive period centers around the stage of crawling and walking, which become visually guided and directed. The final crucial period takes place during language development, which allows for the emergence of a conceptualized spatial framework. Certainly age of onset of blindness and impairment in spatial tasks seem to be correlated (Axelrod, 1959; Worchel, 1951), though in the first few months of life blind and sighted babies both track their hand movements with their eyes and show eye movements toward a sound source (Fraiberg, 1968; Freedman, 1964). This finding seems to confirm Bower's (1974) conclusion that such early behavior is not attributable to a differentiation between different sensory inputs, which at first are unified and undifferentiated. The disintegration of this apparently uniform visual-auditory-motor space takes place at the same time for sighted and blind babies. Reintegration of visual with other spatial stimuli occurs, of course, only in the sighted, though even for them it is not necessarily always a visual perception per se which proves crucial. Thus D.H. Warren (1970) reported that a hidden invisible sound source was more accurately located with open than with closed eyes, and he concluded that a visual mapping of an auditory stimulus provided an optimal strategy for locating sounds in space. Although having the eyes open seems to maximize such visual mapping, those who are sighted, even with eyes closed, still show greater accuracy in sound location than do the blind (Gomulicki, 1961). It is suggestive that at least in the cat, if not as yet in humans, Fishman and Michael (1973) have established that the same receptor cells in the visual cortex were responsive to both visual and auditory stimuli, thus providing a physiological basis for intersensory integration.

Von Senden (1932) thought that it was impossible to develop spatial imagery without sight, and in this he agreed with the eighteenth-century philosopher Platner, who thought that those born blind substituted a framework of time for that of space. Von Senden observed that patients with restored sight had an immediate visual appreciation of space, and that their reaching for objects, though at first involving over- or under-shooting, was qualitatively quite different from their groping when still blind. Gregory (1966), who observed a subject whose sight was restored by corneal grafting, reported that many objects, including letters, which had been tactually familiar were visually recognized at first sight. On the other hand the visual perception of things which could not have been tactually experienced, such as the height of a bus, or the distance between the ground and an upstairs window, was distorted. Qualitatively different rather than impaired coding of spatial relationships for visual and kinesthetic inputs has been reported by Pick, Klein, and Pick (1966). Blind, sighted, and sighted blindfolded children investigated shapes through touch or vision, and were asked which were "upside down." As the forms were nonsense shapes, there was no objectively incorrect orientation. For both the blind and the blindfolded subjects, judgments on the basis of touch were different from those made through vision. This finding suggests that different sensory systems may extract and code different spatial features from the same stimulus objects.

Thus, when we assess the evidence which has been obtained so far about the perceptual coordinates of temporal and spatial awareness and judgments, it seems fair to conclude that an association between time and hearing and between space and seeing is suggested. Regarding movement the issue seems more complex. On the one hand movements are a succession of events, and therefore occur according to a temporal-sequential pattern. On the other hand, movements occur in space and have therefore a strong spatial component. Generally, however, it can be concluded that different sensory systems tend to extract predominantly temporal or spatial features which become preserved in the resulting code.

4. Modality-Specific Processing

This section describes a number of our experiments in which the characteristics of the input modality tended to determine the manner in which the material was coded (O'Connor & Hermelin, 1978). The results from these experiments also tend to show that there is an association between the auditory modality and the temporal framework of perception and memory, and between the visual modality and spatial coding. The degree to which either sensory or cognitive handicap may prevent such encoding is also explored. The subjects of the reported experiments will, therefore, be congenitally deaf, blind, subnormal, and autistic children, together with normal controls.

The first experiment concerned the judgment of duration. Twenty subnormal children with a mental age of 7 years, and 10 deaf, 10 blind, and 20 normal children aged 7 years were taught to discriminate between two intervals, one lasting 2 and the other 6 sec. Tactile stimuli of these durations were administered to the subjects through a rotary probe in the palm of one hand, in pairs which were either the same (e.g., two stimuli of 2-sec duration, separated by half a second, or two stimuli of 6-sec duration, separated by half a second) or different (e.g., a stimulus of 2 sec followed by another of 6 sec, or a stimulus of 6 sec followed by another of 2). The subjects were required to learn the discrimination, and to indicate to the experimenter whether the two stimuli were the same or different. After this discrimination had been learned to a stringent criterion, similar pairs of stimuli but in different modalities were presented in random order. These were either two lights, or two sounds, given, respectively, to deaf or to blind subjects and their subnormal and normal controls. The discrimination between durations experienced through touch stimuli was not transferred to either light or sound. This was the case even though in many instances a verbal formulation of the principle of solution of the initial training task had been obtained in questioning after training trials.

Despite such an adequate description of the principle of solution, generalization to similar situations in other sense modalities did not occur in the above-mentioned experiment, and one must conclude, therefore, that duration is not a salient dimension at this age. This lack of salience was further illustrated by another experiment with subjects of approximately the same age. In this experiment, discrimination of duration was also required, for example, two successive signals of either 2- or 6-sec duration were presented, and the subjects were to judge their duration as same or different. The signal pairs were either two lights, two sounds, or a light paired with a sound. In addition, the two lights in a pair would be of the same or different colors, and the tones of the same or different pitches. The subjects were specifically required to judge the relative durations regardless of color, pitch, or modality. In this experiment, however, subjects were instructed that duration was the crucial dimension to be judged. As in the previous experiment, stimuli were matched for intensity on a scale developed by Stevens and Galanter (1957). The results showed that more "same" judgements were made when the two stimuli were in every respect identical than when they differed in modality, color, or pitch. In other words, the children tended to judge differences in terms of modality, color, or pitch rather than in terms of duration. This occurred despite the stress in the instructions on the relevance of durational judgments. One might conclude from these results that young children's judgments of duration are not readily transferred from the modality in which they were first appreciated, and that they may be easily disrupted by irrelevant stimulus dimensions.

Other experiments indicated that difference-processing strategies resulted from the stimulus exploration by either touch or sight. The first study was concerned with the appreciation of letters by congenitally blind, braille-reading children when the letters were "read" through either the right or the left hand. The results clearly demonstrated the superiority of the left hand, and the subsequent work of Rudel, Denckla, and Hirsch (1977) confirmed this finding with sighted but blindfolded children. Braille letters, unlike those from other alphabets, are differentiable on the basis of the spatial relationship of dots to each other. It appears that in braille reading the spatial component is first analyzed by the right cortical hemisphere before verbal coding occurs. The fact that the tactile exploration of braille also resulted in a left hand–right cortical hemisphere superiority in sighted children suggests that different features of the display may have to be extracted through tactile exploration rather than through visual reading, in which case a left cortical dominance is usually found. Such a conclusion is also suggested by the next experiment. In this we asked how several related spatial positions would be organized when vision was or was not available. Fifty subjects took part, 10 autistic and 10 blind, in addition to 10 sighted blindfolded and 10 nonblindfolded normal children. There were in addition 10 blindfolded adults aged about 20. The normal children had average IQs, and the IQs of the congenitally blind children averaged 118, while the average IQ of the autistic children was 85. The chronological age of the normal and blind children, and the mental age of the autistic children, was 8 years.

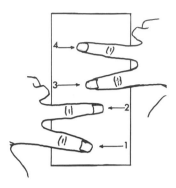

Fig. 1. Finger placement for hand reversal experiment.

The subjects were presented with a board on which the first two fingers of their left and right hands were arranged in succession, running away from the body in the midline (illustrated in Figure 1). Each finger was given a name, and the subject learned to call out this name when the appropriate finger was touched. After the association between a finger touched and its name had been learned, the subject's hand positions were changed, so that those fingers initially in Positions 1 and 2 in Figure 1 were now in Positions 3 and 4, while the changes were reversed for the fingers of the other hand. Trials went on without an interval, and without new instructions, so that the child now had the option of associating a name with the same finger as previously, but now in a new spatial position, or maintaining an association between name and position, regardless of which finger occupied the position.

The results fell into clear patterns, according to whether the task was performed by the subject with or without vision. Those children who could see their hands and the board retained a fixed pattern of responses to spatial positions, although the fingers were in new arrangements. Those children who performed the task by touch without vision gave responses to particular fingers rather than to fixed spatial positions. Thus, the visual presentation of the task favored a stable framework of Euclidean space, whereas tactile stimulation resulted in a relatively "egocentric" frame of reference. It is perhaps particularly surprising that adults with a lifetime of visual experience to draw on also reverted to this "egocentric" pattern of response when carrying out the task blindfolded.

In this experiment it seemed that the sighted blindfolded children did not make use of image codes derived from other sensory sources — that is, vision—but coded in terms of the modality in which the stimuli were presented.

The comparative effect of presenting sequences in the visual or the auditory modality was investigated in another study. Deaf and normal children were given visual displays, and blind and normal controls auditory displays. Three digits were presented, either from a box with three windows placed in a row, or auditorily from three loudspeakers arranged around the subject, to his left, to his right, and in front of him. The temporal-sequential order of the presentation of the digits was always incongruent with the left-to-right order, so that the first items never occurred on the left, the second never in the middle, and the third never on the right. Subjects were asked to either watch or listen to the three digits, and then to write down or call out the middle one. There were thus two possible response strategies for the child. He could either select the second digit which was presented, in which case he would opt for the temporal-sequential middle. Alternatively he might regard the spatial middle as relevant, and in this case he would respond to the stimulus placed between those to the right and left of it, though this would have been either the first or the last presented item. The question asked was whether visual and auditory presentation might lead to, respectively, spatially and temporally determined response strategies.

The visual material was presented to 10 deaf and 20 hearing children, matched for digit span and chronological age, and the auditory material was given to 10 blind and 20 sighted children, similarly matched. Ten of the hearing controls wore earmuffs, and 10 of the sighted controls were blindfolded. The mean chronological age of all the children was 13-1/2, and the average digit span of each group was more than five digits. Results showed that when the material was presented visually, all children, irrespective of the presence or absence of handicap, tended to select the spatially middle one of the three digits. When the material was presented auditorily from three loudspeakers, the results showed a strong tendency to opt for the temporal middle digit. Although it should be pointed out that the strategies which were adopted were elective, and alternative response patterns occurred when they were explicitly asked for, the spontaneous tendency was to associate auditory with temporally, and visual with spatially determined organization.

Results from another study reinforced this finding. This study was concerned with the presentation of a series of successive stimuli, either lights or sounds. These lights and sounds could either be presented from one centrally placed source, in which case they varied from one another in duration, being either long or short; or they could be presented from two sources, one to the left and one to the right of the subject. In this condition signals were all of the same length, but varied spatially. The procedure was to present to either the deaf or blind or normal or subnormal children two series of nine stimuli and ask the subject to judge whether the two series were the same or different. Deaf, normal, and subnormal children were significantly more often correct when the visual series were presented from two sources, that is, spatially distributed, than when the signals varied in duration; and in the case of the sound series, blind, normal, and subnormal children gave significantly more correct responses when the stimuli were presented from one source, and the items in a sequence differed from each other along a temporal dimension.

All results presented so far suggest coding differences of formally identical stimuli when presented in different modalities. They also show that when a code which is abstracted is modality-specific, all children, provided that the appropriate modality system is intact, respond similarly. Similar results were also obtained from the next series of experiments. The first of these was concerned with the memory for and the reproduction of the end position of an arm movement. Held (1961) proposed that certain limb movements were normally accompanied by a mental "copy" of previous visual records of the same kind of movement, and that the actual visual information from a current movement was compared with this visual scheme. If this were to be the case with limb position, the blind might be expected to be at a disadvantage at a task requiring such position estimates. To test this hypothesis, we carried out an experiment with sighted blindfolded normal and autistic children as well as congenitally blind children. The blind and sighted normal children in this experiment had a mean chronological age of 10 years, and the mental age of the autistic children was 10 years, 4 months, while their chronological age had a mean of 13-1/2.

The apparatus used in this experiment consisted of a 50-cm-long rod, vertically mounted, on which a pointer could be moved. A stopper could be set at any required height. The first task was the simple reproduction of a practiced standard movement, which varied in length from 10 to 30 cm in 5-cm steps. During practice the extent of the movement was marked by the stopper, but during test trials the stopper was moved and the subject was required to stop at the previous end point. The second task required the termination of a movement at the same end point as in the training trials, although a new starting point was selected by the experimenter. In this instance, therefore, the movement would be shorter or longer, but the end point would remain the same.

No significant differences between the groups were found in these two tasks. The end position of a previously experienced arm movement could be better estimated from an invariant than from a variant starting position, but the mean error even in the second condition was only 2-1/2 cm. As there are receptor cells in the joints and muscle spindles which signal the position of a limb in space, for both blind and sighted children proprioceptive information seemed to have been adequate for accurate estimation of end location.

The perception of the relationship between objects in space is signaled by different receptors from those indicating limb position. In experiments concerned with the mental manipulation of forms in space, two separate approaches have been used. One consists of the juxtaposition of separated forms, where the subject is required to indicate the total configuration resulting from bringing together the two shapes. The second approach makes use of object rotation and of the comparison of mentally rotated forms with an existing model. Worchel (1951) has exploited the former technique, and Ghent (1960), Shepard and Metzler (1971), Cronin (1972), and Shinar and Owen (1973) have used the latter. In a study with both blind and sighted children, we explored the capacity of these groups to judge whether or not two shapes fixed apart on a board would, when brought together, either unrotated or rotated, form a complete square. The subject was required to explore both shapes manually. The shapes were based on material used by Thurstone (1946) in his primary-mental-abilities test.

The results showed that blind and blindfolded children performed at the same level when deciding whether or not two shapes when fitted together would form a square. There thus appeared to be no advantage for the sighted in their previous visual experience when carrying out this task without vision, whether or not the shapes were rotated in relation to one another. The results seemed to indicate that the rotation was largely ignored by the children, and that judgments were made instead in terms of form characteristics. As shape differences, unlike orientations, can be well appreciated through manual exploration, such differences were used as distinguishing features. Thus, as in the other experiments described in this section, the findings suggested kinesthetically derived coding for blind and blindfolded children alike.

It would seem from the experiments presented in this section that in certain circumstances there is a strong tendency for problems to be solved in terms of the features extracted from the modality in which the stimuli were presented. This tendency was found irrespective of whether mental representations derived from other modality systems were available to the subject for adopting an alternative form of coding.

5. Representational Coding

We now come to a series of experiments, described in detail in our recent monograph (O'Connor & Hermelin, 1978), which showed differences between normal and impaired children, even when the stimulus was directed to an intact sensory-modality system. The findings indicated that in the following studies normal children used another code instead of, or in addition to, the one derived from the modality in which the stimuli were presented. Such recoding had first been demonstrated by Conrad (1964), who found that substitution errors in recalling visually presented words or letters were based on an auditory and not on a visual similarity with the initially shown items. He thus concluded that though presented visually, verbal material was stored in the form of an acoustic code.

We have already mentioned that different sensory codes tend to be organized along qualitatively different dimensions. Thus visual material seems to be retained in a spatially ordered form, and auditory material in a temporally ordered form. The question which was thus asked in the following study was whether visually presented verbal items would be organized according to the visual modality, or in terms of a verbal sequence. Normal, congenitally deaf, autistic, and subnormal children were tested. The normals had a chronological age of 8 years, matching the mental age of the other children. The subjects were shown a visual display of consecutively exposed numbers. However, the first-to-last order in which the items appeared did not correspond to the left-to-right order in which such items would normally be read. The display procedure is illustrated in Figure 2. However, in contrast with the task mentioned in the previous section, instead of selecting a single item the children had to remember all three digits.

Following the display the subject was shown a card on which two series of numbers were printed. In half the instances one series on the card reflected the spatial-display order (for example, 147) and the other series consisted of an order not previously shown (for example, 714). For the other instances, the randomly ordered items were shown together with the temporally ordered sequence (for example, 471). The child's task was to indicate the series of numbers he had just seen. The results showed that the great majority of normal children were able to recognize the temporally ordered sequences, but that they distinguished the left-to-right from the random order only at chance level. This pattern of results was reversed for the deaf, who recognized the spatial but not the first-to-last, temporal order of the displayed digits. The autistic children behaved very much like the deaf, but only those subnormal children with verbal IQs below 60 did so, whereas those with IQs above 60 followed the normal response pattern.

We concluded that these results demonstrated that the normal subjects, and also the subnormals with higher verbal IQs, had recoded

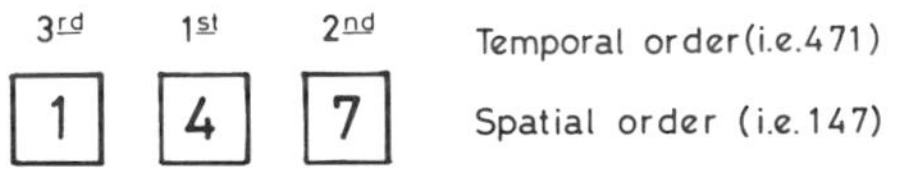

Fig. 2. Digit display for spatial and temporal order encoding.

the visually presented items into an auditory-verbal form. They consequently recollected the items as a temporal sequence. The deaf, the autistic, and the remaining subnormals had apparently processed the material in the form in which it had been presented, that is, as a visual display. As visually derived codes tend to be spatially organized, these subjects recognized the items as ordered from left to right rather than as from first to last. In these instances the material was not recoded into auditory verbal form.

It is of interest to note that these results differ from the one reported in the situation in the previous section, in which the "middle" digit had to be indicated from a similar display. In this single-item-selection task, the stimulus modality had determined the coding strategy. In the present instance, in which memory was more involved, the typically found recoding of visually presented verbal material into auditory verbal form occurred with the normal children. The two experiments are an illustration of the fact that task requirements as well as the nature of the stimulus display may determine which particular coding strategy is to be adopted.

The next experiment also showed that the verbal characteristics of the stimuli may lead to a temporal-sequential organization in memory. We showed normal children either three Roman or three Arabic letters, again presented successively in a temporally-spatially incongruent order. Thus the first-exposed item never appeared at the left, the second never in the middle, and the third never to the right. The recognition procedure was similar to that in the previous experiment. It was explained to the children that the letters would sometimes be familiar ones, but would sometimes be letters which they had never seen before. The Arabic letters could not be "read" and were therefore presumably perceived as nonverbal shapes. We predicted that the verbalizable Roman letters would be stored in auditory-sequential form, and would therefore be ordered from first to last, whereas the Arabic letters would be processed as a visual display, which would be spatially organized. The results confirmed this prediction. Roman letters were recognized predominantly as a temporally ordered sequence, and Arabic letters more frequently in a spatially ordered form. Thus these experiments showed that normal, but not language-impaired children tended to derive an auditorially based processing code from visually presented verbal material, whereas nonverbal items tended to be visually coded. However, language-impaired children treated all visually presented material, whether verbal or not, as a visually organized display.

In another experiment, we also presented hearing and deaf children with visually displayed series of letters. The letters appeared successively, either from left to right or right to left, and recall was required either in the same or in the reverse order. The results from this experiment were that for the deaf, but not for the hearing, backward recall was better than forward recall.

Where these letters had to be recalled backward, it was the last presented items which were recalled first, and a detailed analysis showed that the deaf were particularly good in remembering these last-presented, first-recalled items. The short delay between presentation and recall may have enabled them to make use of the fast-fading, short-term visual trace, and to utilize a partial visual image. However, unlike such a visual image, which can be inspected from any direction, a verbal-acoustic memory code, such as was presumably used by the hearing children, may be more unidirectional—for example, it is easy to spell one's name forward but quite difficult to spell it backward. Consequently, reversal of a temporally based sequence would constitute an additional mental operation, which may have canceled out the advantage of a short storage time for the last-presented letters. Thus, in this instance, the fact that for the deaf the series was not recoded into auditory form, but remained visual, led to an improved performance.

The next series of experiments deals with the question of whether blind, and in some instances sighted autistic children deal differently with kinesthetically presented information than the sighted. Congenitally blind children can have no visual image of what something looks like when they touch it, and may thus have a differently based code. A series of movements, unlike vision, but like hearing, is a temporal-sequential event. If, as we suggested, reversal is easier when it is based on a visually derived rather than on a successive auditory code, differential ease of reversal may also be evident in a successive series of movements. We presented blind and blindfolded sighted children, 12 years old, with 40 simple line drawings, consisting of either two, three, four, or five straight lines. Examples of these drawings are shown in Figure 3.

The child held a pencil, and his hand was then guided along a particular track. The task was to retrace what was drawn in either the

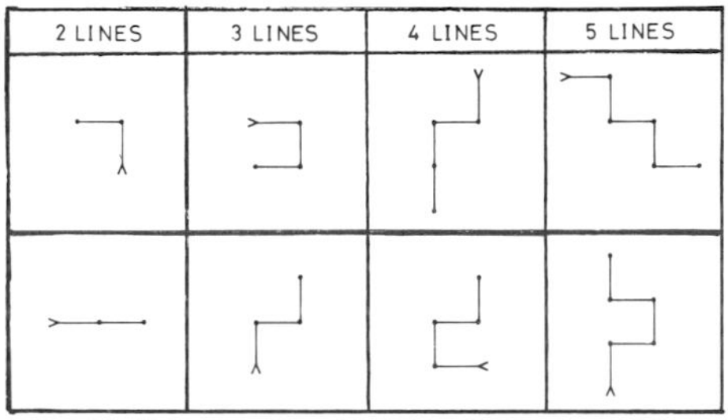

Fig. 3. Simple line drawings for motor recall experiment.

same, or the reverse direction to the previously guided movement. The results showed no differences between blind and blindfolded groups in forward tracing. However, with backward tracing the blindfolded were better than the blind, and this difference became increasingly marked with the longer tracks. Apparently a kinesthetically established trace provided sufficient information for the blind to retain and reproduce a sequence of movements. But when such movements had to be reversed, and particularly with longer sequences, the blind children became increasingly handicapped. Sighted children may have made use of information from visual representations, which, though the visual system was not stimulated directly, were nevertheless available to them through a visual-image code. The blind, who had no access to such a code, were dependent on modality-specific kinesthetic processing, which may have been coded into a motor program. This was an efficient enough strategy for a forward but not for a backward reproduction of the initial movement sequence.

A similar explanation may also account for some of the results of an experiment which has already been mentioned. In this experiment, blind and blindfolded normal or autistic children had to reproduce the previously experienced end position of an arm movement. All subjects, using presumably a kinesthetically based memory code, had succeeded in this task. In the present instance, however, it was not the end position but the extent of the movement which had to be reproduced. Following three training trials, in which the child had moved a pointer along a vertical rod until it encountered a stopper, the starting position of the pointer was changed and the stopper removed. The child was required to make a movement covering the same distance as in the preceding training trials, which, as it now began from a different point, would also terminate at a different position. Every effort was made to make the task requirements clear to the children, and the autistic children in particular needed considerable practice without being blindfolded prior to the experiment. In these distance estimates there were no invariant spatial points, and hence no invariant kinesthetic information was available. Consequently the sighted blindfolded normal children were significantly better able to match the extent of their previous movements than were the blindfolded autistic or the blind children. Though there are kinesthetic receptors for the position of a limb in space, no receptor cells which could signal distance information exist. Thus in the absence of kinesthetically reliable information, cues about distance could only have been derived from a code using an alternative representation, such as, for instance, visual images. No such code was available to the blind, and the autistic children, although they did not lack visual reference data, seem to have failed to make the necessary cognitive inferences from it. Thus these results illustrate again that a restriction of potentially available representational codes may occur as a consequence of perceptual as well as of cognitive impairments. Cognitive deficit may lead to a tendency to process information only in those terms in which it is directly presented, and to fail to access appropriate image codes.

Another study also illustrated the fact that sighted blindfolded children used codes derived from a visual-spatial framework. Plastic (fiberglass and resin) casts of right and left hands were given to blind and blindfolded 10- to 12-year-old children. The experimenter sat opposite the child and presented a right or left hand in one of various spatial positions and rotations. An illustration of the stimuli is given in Figure 4. The child was allowed to feel around the stimulus hand, and had to decide whether it was a right or left hand. An analysis of the results showed that the blind children made many more errors than the blindfolded sighted group. Thus, as in the experiment reported by Shepard and Metzler (1971), the sighted subjects seem to have accomplished the task through the mental manipulation of a visual image. As was pointed out in relation to the results from previous experiments, the facility to

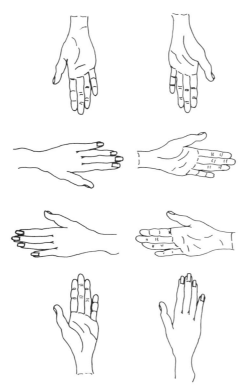

Fig. 4. Model hand used in kinesthetic judgment of right and left hands.

use such additional reference schemata in appropriate situations is severely restricted in children with congenital sensory impairments, and also, though for different reasons, in some instances of cognitive deficit. Gibson (1969) suggested that there is information in stimuli which is not tied to specific modalities, but is invariant over them and therefore amodal. If this notion applied to the experimental situations which we have presented here, we should not have found coding differences between children with and without specific sensory impairments. As we did obtain such differences, we have to conclude that the particular processing code which was used, whether it was derived from representations or from the presented stimulus characteristics, contributed to determining the qualities which were abstracted from a stimulus display.

6. Phonological Coding

That different features can be abstracted from different modality and image systems does not exclude the possibility that there are certain other qualities and characteristics of input which may be shared by different modalities. One example of such sharing can be found in the development of phonological speech codes, which have similar characteristics regardless of whether the input is auditory, or in the case of congenitally deaf children, visual—that is, derived—for example, from lipreading. A series of experiments concerned with lipreading has been carried out in collaboration with our colleague Barbara Dodd (O'Connor & Hermelin, 1978). In one of these studies, 10-week-old infants were presented with a mirror reflection of the experimenter's face as she spoke nursery rhymes. The speech sounds changes at 1-min intervals between being congruent with the lip movements, or being delayed by 400 msec, so that lip movements and speech sounds did not correspond. The infants' attention to the mirror was measured, and alternative subjects began with either the in-synchrony or the out-of-synchrony condition. It was found that significantly more sustained attention was paid in conditions where sounds and lip movements were in synchrony than when they were out of synchrony. As children of this age did not understand what was said, one must conclude that an integration of speech sounds and their corresponding lip movements is either present from birth, or acquired soon after.

That older hearing children could combine visual lip-read information and stored auditory information was shown in another experiment with 12 deaf and 12 hearing 12-year-old children. They were asked to lip-read nonsense words which were either produced at the front of the mouth (e.g., "milt"), and were therefore easy to lip-read, or came from the back of the mouth (e.g., "klug"), and were therefore more difficult to lip-read. There was no difference between the hearing and the profoundly deaf in perceiving the easy-to-lip-read words, but hearing children were better at recognizing those words which were hard to lip-read. As there is no a priori reason to assume that hearing children have better lipreading ability than those who are deaf, one may suppose that the hearing were able to supplement the visually perceived information with stored corresponding auditory features. The deaf could not do this, and, as in some previously mentioned studies, a reduced number of available perceptual reference systems thus affected the information processing even of those stimuli which were directed to an intact perceptual system.

If normal children use visual cues from lipreading to supplement information about phonological features derived from hearing, one might assume that the phonological systems of the deaf may also be based on lipreading. That phonological features of speech are appreciated by the congenitally deaf was shown in one of our experiments which compared the ability of deaf and hearing children to memorize paired associates of pictures when the names of both members of a pair either rhymed (e.g., chair-bear) or did not rhyme (e.g., girl-bus). The children were shown a display of 30 picture pairs, the names of half of the pairs rhyming and of the other half not rhyming. One member of each picture pair was then removed, and the position in the display of the remaining pictures was changed. The subject was then given cards containing one picture of each pair, and asked to place each next to its associate. Of the 57 children tested, 34 were able to extract the rhyme of the picture names as the relevant feature, and thus to perform the matching of the rhymed pairs significantly better than those which were randomly associated.

How did these congenitally and profoundly deaf children recognize rhymes? There were at least four possible explanations. The recognition could have been achieved through a visual similarity of the written forms of similar-sounding words, or by using articulatory cues which would be similar for similar-sounding words. Alternatively, the subjects may have remembered what they had been taught about certain words, or they might have gained phonological information by using a code which classified words according to how they looked when they were said.

In order to test these alternatives, 13 profoundly and prelingually deaf 13-year-old boys took part in the following experiment. In one condition 18 pairs of written homophones (e.g., reign-rain) and 18 pairs of randomly associated words (e.g., train-than) were used as stimuli. Each homophone pair was matched with a randomly associated pair for the number of shared letters in the same sequential positions. Subjects were shown a simultaneously presented display of these 36 word pairs and were asked to remember which two words belonged together. They were then shown a second display containing one member of each word pair, and were given cards with the remaining words. They were asked to place each card with the word it went with before. Significantly fewer errors were made with homophone pairs than with randomly associated pairs, and as no more letters were shared between one type of word pair than with the other, the superior performance with the homophones could not have been due to their more similar written forms.

Whether the code which was used by the deaf was derived from articulatory information was tested by asking them to read aloud a list of randomly ordered words containing the 18 homophones. However, the similar-sounding words were never in adjacent positions in the list. Responses were recorded and analyzed, and it was found that members of a pair of homophones were often pronounced very differently, thus demonstrating that the previous recognition of their sound similarity was unlikely to have been made on the basis of stored articulatory information.

Whether the recognition of homophones depended simply on previous lexical learning was investigated by presenting pairs of nonsense words, which were thus unfamiliar to the subjects, and which they were asked to identify as either rhyming or not rhyming. The mean correct score was 12 out of a possible 16 correct responses, which was significantly better than chance performance. Thus it is unlikely that the identification of rhymes depends solely on previous learning.

Finally, for testing whether the subjects used a code based on lipreading, they were shown a list containing one of the members of the previously shown 18 homophones. The experimenter then read out these words in random order, and the child had to identify the word he had lipread in his list. Nine of the words were easy to lip-read, for example, were easily visible when said, and 9 were produced at the back of the mouth and were consequently hard to lip-read. The analysis showed that significantly fewer errors were made in the identification of the easy-to-lip-read than of the hard-to-lip-read words. When these results were related to those in the first condition, where these words had to be matched with their homophones, it was shown that the words which had been easy to lip-read were the same as those which had been successfully matched with their homophones in the first condition. Thus the hypothesis that the deaf gain phonological information primarily from a code based on how words look when they are said seems to be supported by these findings.

Lastly, it was demonstrated that the phonological code used by hearing and deaf children showed many common features. Smith (1973) and Dodd (1974) have provided evidence that young hearing children's incorrect pronunciations are strictly rule governed. The rules according to which adult speech is changed include that of consonant harmony, a process by which a sound becomes similar to, or is influenced by, another sound in the same word. Cluster reduction refers to words in which specific members of a consonant cluster are deleted, and systematic simplification includes instances where, for example, unstressed syllables in a word are deleted. In the relevant experiment, 10 11-year-old prelingually and profoundly deaf children were asked to name 45 pictures, and their responses were tape-recorded. When the transcripts were analyzed, they showed that hearing was not essential for the acquisition of an extensive phonic repertoire, which was governed by rules which closely followed those found to operate in the speech development of young hearing children. Thus, independently of the particular perceptual system through which phonological information was perceived, the resulting phonological code was very similar. The coding of phonological features seems to be one instance of the existence of "amodal" features which can be extracted from auditorily as well as from visually perceived speech input.

7. Interpretation

How should we sum up and interpret the experimental results reported in this chapter? We began by asking whether the spatial and temporal frameworks within which perception occurs were in some way inherently associated with, or derived from, the structure of specific sensory-modality systems such as sight and hearing. We also suggested that though information was often processed in terms of the sense which had been stimulated, there were also situations where it proved more effective to use a processing system which was derived from a sense other than that of the stimulus modality. We hypothesized that if this were a valid model of information handling, those children who were restricted in the range of possible sensory experience either from birth or soon after, or those who lacked the cognitive capacity to draw inferences from perceptual representation, might use different coding strategies than children not so impaired.

Our results suggested that when a processing code which was adequate for the task's requirements could be abstracted from the modality system which had been stimulated, such modality-specific coding occurred. In other words, in these instances the sensory modality determined the coding characteristics when, and only when, the features which had to be abstracted in order to solve a particular problem were an inherent part of a particular modality system. Thus, because of the association between hearing and temporal sequences, tones tended to be temporally organized in memory. Similarly, because of the spatial nature of the visual system, light flashes were best recognized in terms of the spatial organization of the stimuli.

On a simple level, if the tasks required those judgments for which the necessary information was directly and effectively signaled by appropriate receptor cells, such as with limb position, such signals formed the basis of the memory code which was utilized. Whenever they used such stimulus-derived coding strategies, impaired and nonimpaired children, whether the former were perceptually or cognitively handicapped, responded similarly, provided the stimulation was directed toward an intact perceptual channel.

The problem becomes more complex when a code is derived not from direct stimulation, but from memory representations based on a different modality system. The first question which should be answered here is what determines such a representationally based, rather than a perceptually based, coding strategy. We think that the answer lies in the human brain's disposition to extract certain specific features from different modality systems. If, however, the task does not require the abstraction of those features which are associated with the modality of stimulation, then inferences will be made which are derived from remembered representations in terms of another perceptual system than that which is stimulated. In many situations such representational systems provide additional rather than alternative information. An example is the lipreading ability of hearing children. It has been demonstrated that while lipreading provides data for the place of articulation—for instance, allows such discriminations as between L and K—the manner of articulation—for instance, differences such as those between M and B—is best obtained through hearing. Consequently, deaf and hearing children can recognize easy-to-lip-read words—that is, those which have distinct place information—equally well. However, hearing children were better than deaf children in perceiving hard-to-lip-read words—that is, those with prominent manner characteristics—because they were able to supplement insufficient visual cues with stored auditory information.

In other instances, the observed strategy seems to imply substitution of the stimulus-modality code instead of one obtained from mental representations based on other modality systems. Thus, normal-hearing children organized visually presented verbal stimuli as if they were heard—that is, in a temporally ordered rather than in a spatially organized sequence. Similarly, they apparently used a visually derived framework to solve certain kinesthetically presented data. This occurred, for instance, when mental rotation of an object was required in order to ascertain its spatial orientation. Such an operation seems best carried out through visual rather than through kinesthetic imagery. Another relevant example was provided in the results from the backward tracing of line drawings. A visual image lends itself more easily to inspection from any direction, than kinesthetic memory of a series of sequential movements. Therefore blind children, to whom a strategy based on visual representations instead of on kinesthetic stimulation is not available, were found to be at a disadvantage in these tasks. This finding illustrates our conclusion that perceptually impaired children may have to rely on other codes than those not so impaired, even if the stimuli are directed toward intact modality systems. Similar effects, though for different reasons, could be observed in children with mental handicaps. Such subjects tended to remain "stimulus bound" and treated information only in those terms in which it was presented. Thus, although alternative representational systems were available to those children, they failed to access them even when such an image-based strategy would have been appropriate.

Lastly, the fact that coding strategies often seen either modality based or derived from perceptual images does not exclude the possibility that similar or identical features could not also be extracted from different perceptual inputs. Such codes, with shared features abstracted from different senses, could justifiably be termed "amodal," and were observed in such processes as similar phonemic development by the deaf and hearing and the discrimination of similar shape characteristics by the blind and sighted children. Whether a stimulus-modality code or one based on mental images is used, or whether coding is based on the abstraction of "amodal" stimulus features, depends on the nature of the stimulation, the task's requirements, and the capacities and predispositions of the subject.

8.   References

Aaronson, D. Temporal factors in perception and short term memory. *Psychological Bulletin*, 1967, *73*, 130–144.

Abramsky, O., Carmon, A., & Benton, A. Masking of and by tactile pressure stimuli. *Perception and Psychophysics*, 1971, *10*, 353–355.

Axelrod, S. *Effects of early blindness*. New York: American Foundation for the Blind, 1959.

Baddeley, A.D. Reduced body temperature and time estimation. *American Journal of Psychology*, 1966, *79*, 475–479.

Berkeley, G. (1709) An essay towards a new theory of vision. In A.A. Luce & T.E. Jessup (Eds.), *The works of George Berkeley Bishop of Cloyne*. New York: Nelson, 1948. (Essay originally published, 1709.)

Bower, T.G.R. *Development in infancy*. San Francisco: W.H. Freeman, 1974.

Briggs, R. Auditory and visual confusions: Evidence against a simple modality encoding hypothesis. *Memory and Cognition*, 1974, *2*, 607–612.

Bryant, P.E., Jones, P., Claxton, V., & Perkins, G.M. Recognition of shapes across modalities by infants. *Nature,* 1972, *240,* 303–304.

Conrad, R. Errors of immediate memory. *British Journal of Psychology,* 1959, *50,* 349–359.

Conrad, R. Acoustic confusion in immediate memory. *British Journal of Psychology,* 1964, *557,* 75–84.

Conrad, R. Order error in immediate recall of sequences. *Journal of Verbal Learning and Verbal Behaviour,* 1965, *4,* 161–169.

Coquery, J., & Amblard, B. Backward and forward masking in the perception of cutaneous stimuli. *Perception and Psychophysics,* 1973, *13,* 161–163.

Cromer, R.F. *The development of temporal reference during the acquisition of language.* Unpublished doctoral thesis, Harvard University, 1968.

Cromer, R.F. The development of the ability to decenter in time. *British Journal of Psychology,* 1971, *62* (3), 353–365.

Cronin, V. Orientation and position effects on mirror-image reversal discrimination of triangles by young children. *Perceptual and Motor Skills,* 1972, *34,* 707–711.

Crowder, R.G., & Morton J. Precategorical acoustic storage. *Perception and Psychophysics,* 1969, *5,* 365–373.

Dodd, B. *The acquisition of phonological skills in normal, severely subnormal and deaf children.* Unpublished doctoral dissertation, University of London, 1974.

Doehring, D.G. Visual spatial memory in aphasic children. *Journal of Speech and Hearing Research,* 1960, *3,* 138–149.

Efron, R. Temporal perception and aphasia and déjà vu. *Brain,* 1963, *86,* 403–424.

Ellis, N.R. The stimulus trace and behavioral inadequacy. In N.R. Ellis (Ed.), *Handbook of mental deficiency.* New York: McGraw-Hill, 1963.

Fishman, M.C., & Michael, C.R. Integration of auditory information in the cat's cortex. *Vision Research,* 1973, *13,* 1415–1419.

Fraiberg, S. Parallel and divergent patterns in blind and sighted infants. *Psychological Study of the Child,* 1968, *23,* 264–300.

Freedman, D.A. Smiling in blind infants and the issue of innate versus acquired. *Journal of Child Psychology and Psychiatry and Allied Disciplines,* 1964, *5,* 171–184.

Ghent, L. Recognition by children of realistic figures presented in various orientations. *Canadian Journal of Psychology,* 1960, *14,* 249–256.

Gibson, E.J. *The senses considered as perceptual systems.* Boston: Houghton Mifflin, 1966.

Gibson, E.J. *Principles of perceptual learning and development.* New York: Appleton, Century, Crofts, 1969.

Gomulicki, B.R. *The development of perception and learning in blind children.* London: The Psychological Laboratory of Cambridge University, 1961.

Goodfellow, L.D. (1934) An empirical comparison of audition vision and touch in the discrimination of short intervals of time. *American Journal of Psychology,* 46, 243–258.

Gregory, R.L. *Eye and brain: The psychology of seeing.* London: Weidenfeld & Nicolson, 1966.

Held, R. Exposure history as a factor in maintaining stability of perception and coordination. *Journal of Nervous and Mental Diseases,* 1961, *132,* 26, 32.

Held, R., & Bauer, J.A. Visually guided reaching in infant monkeys after restricted rearing. *Science,* 1966, *155,* 718–720.

Held, R., & Hein, A. Movement-produced stimulation in the development of visually guided behaviour. *Journal of Comparative and Physiological Psychology,* 1963, *56,* 872–876.

Hirsch, I.J. Auditory perception of temporal order. *Journal of the Acoustic Society of America,* 1954, *31,* 759–767.

Hirsch, I.J. Information processing in input channels for speech and language: The acquisition of serial order of stimuli. F.L. Darley (Ed.), in *Brain mechanisms underlying speech and language.* New York: Grune & Stratton, 1967, pp. 21–38.

Hirsch, I.J., Bilger, R.C., & Deatherage, B.H. The effects of auditory and visual background on apparent duration. *American Journal of Psychology,* 1956, *69,* 561–574.

James, W. *The principles of psychology.* Vol. 2. *The perception of space.* New York: Dover, 1950. (Originally published, 1890).

Keele, S.W. Movement control in skilled motor performance. *Psychological Bulletin,* 1968, *70,* 387–403.

Lashley, K.S. The problem of serial order in behavior. In L.A. Jeffress (Ed.), *Cerebral mechanisms in behavior.* New York: Wiley, 1951.

Luria, A.R. In J. Tizard (Ed.), *The role of speech in the regulation of normal and abnormal behaviour.* London: Pergamon Press, 1961.

McFie, E. *Assessment of organic intellectual impairment.* New York: Academic Press, 1976.

McKinney, J.P. Hand schema in children. *Psychonomic Science,* 1964, *1,* 99–100.

Morton, J. A functional model for memory. In D.A. Norman (Ed.) *Models of human memory.* New York: Academic Press, pp. 203–248.

Nilsson, L.O. Further evidence for organization by modality in immediate free recall. *Journal of Experimental Psychology,* 1974, *103,* (5), 948–957.

O'Connor, N., & Hermelin, B. (1963). *Speech and thought in severe subnormality.* London: Pergamon Press, 1963.

O'Connor, N., & Hermelin, B. *Seeing and hearing and space and time.* New York: Academic Press, 1978.

Paivio, A. *Imagery and verbal processes.* New York: Holt, Rinehart, & Winston, 1971.

Paivio, A., & Csapo, K. Short term sequential memory for pictures and words. *Psychonomic Science,* 1971, *24,* 50–51.

Pepper, R.L., & Herman, L.M. Decay and interference in the short term retention of a discrete motor act. *Journal of Experimental Psychology,* 1970, *83,* 1–18.

Piaget, J. [*The child's conception of time.*] (A.J. Pomerans, Ed. and trans.). London: Routledge & Kegan Paul, 1969. (Originally published, 1927.)

Piaget, J. *The origins of intelligence in children.* New York: International Universities Press, 1952.

Pick, H.L., Klein, R.E., & Pick, A.D. Visual and tactual identification of form orientation. *Journal of Experimental Child Psychology,* 1966, *4,* 391–397.

Posner, M.I. Characteristics of visual and kinesthetic memory codes. *Journal of Experimental Psychology,* 1967, *75,* 103–107.

Posner, M.I. and Mitchell, R.F. Chronometric analysis of classification. *Psychological Review,* 1967, *74,* 392–401.

Renshaw, S., & Wherry, R.J. Studies on cutaneous localization: III. The age of onset of ocular dominance. *Journal of Genetic Psychology,* 1931, *39,* 493–496.

Rudel, R.G., Denckla, M.B., & Hirsch, S. The development of left hand superiority for discriminating braille configurations. *Neurology,* 1977, *27* (2), 160–164.

Savin, H.B. On the successive perception of simultaneous stimuli. *Perception and Psychophysics,* 1967, *95,* 285–289.

Shepard, R.N., & Metzler, J. Mental rotation of three dimensional objects. *Science,* 1971, *171,* 701–703.

Shinar, D., & Owen, D.H. Effects of form rotation on the speed of classification: The development of shape constancy. *Perception and Psychophysics,* 1973, *14,* 149–154.

Smith, N. *The acquisition of phonology: A case study.* London: Cambridge University Press, 1973.

Smothergill, D.W. Hughes, F.P., Timmons, S.A., & Hutko, P. Spatial visualizing in children. *Developmental Psychology*, 1975, *11*, 4–13.

Sperling, G. The information available in brief visual presentations. *Psychological Monographs*, 1960, *74*, (11).

Stevens, S.S., & Galanter, E.H. Ratio scales and category scales for a dozen perceptual continua. *Journal of Experimental Psychology*, 1957, *54*, 377–411.

Tallal, P., & Piercy, M. Defects of non-verbal auditory perception in children with developmental aphasia. *Nature*, 1973, *241*, 468–469. (a)

Tallal, P., & Piercy, M. Developmental aphasia: Impaired rate of non-verbal processing as a function of sensory modality. *Neuropsychologia*, 1973, *11*, 389–398. (b)

Thurstone, L.L. *Primary mental abilities*. Chicago: Science Research Association, 1946.

von Holst, E. Relations between the central nervous system and the peripheral organs. *British Journal of Animal Behaviour*, 1954, *2*, 89–94.

von Senden, M. Raum und Gestalt Auffassung bei operierten Blindgeborenen vor und nach der Operation. Leipzig: Barth, 1932.

Warren, D.H. *Early versus late blindness: The role of early vision in spatial reference systems*. Paper presented at Society for Research into Child Development, Philadelphia, March, 1973,

Warren, R.M. Relation of verbal transformation to other perceptual phenomena. In Conference Publication No. 42 IEE/NPL, Conference on Pattern Recognition (Supplement, 8 pp.). Teddington, England: Institution of Electrical Engineers, 1968.

Wickelgren, W.A. (1969). Context sensitive coding, associative memory and serial order in (speech) behavior. *Psychological Review*, 1969, *76*, 1–15.

Worchel, P. Space perception and orientation in the blind. *Psychological Monographs*, 1951, *65* Whole No. 332.

Wundt, W. *Lectures on human and animal psychology*. London: Sonnenschein, 1894.

Zeaman, D., & House, B.J. The role of attention in retardate discrimination learning. In N.R. Ellis (Ed.), *Handbook of mental deficiency*. New York: McGraw-Hill, 1963.

11

Sensory-Motor and Perceptual-Motor Theories and Practices: An Overview and Evaluation

BRYANT J. CRATTY

1. Introduction

The use of movement to aid the human condition has a past lost in antiquity. The ancient Hindus and Chinese practiced various physical exercises to remedy a variety of illnesses and pathologies. Thousands of years before the coming of Christ, the Greeks and Romans, as well as physicians in the Arab nations, also included physical exercise in their medical kits (Licht, 1965).

As the Renaissance spread across Europe, common man began to perceive that he might have some control over his own destiny, rather than being solely at the mercy of the church and state. These feelings, along with the awakening of scientific endeavor, prompted efforts in several countries to change the unchangeable; to try to modify the seemingly fixed behaviors of the deaf, blind, emotionally disturbed, and retarded. These efforts, beginning in the middle and late eighteenth century, were at times marked by the inclusion of motor and sensory-motor activities in their total programs. Activities of this kind were used throughout the nineteenth century, and into the present century, as exemplified by the writings of Maria Montessori. This perceptive physician found such tasks useful when attempting to enrich the educational

BRYANT J. CRATTY • Department of Kinesiology, University of California, Los Angeles, California 90024.

progress of slum children in Rome around the turn of the century (Montessori, 1914).

In the 1880s the first experimental psychologists, including Wundt in Leipzig, Galton in England, and McKeen Cattell in the United States, employed sensory-motor and motor tasks in their experimental programs. They also attempted to evaluate human intelligence using these kinds of basic measures, including tasks which purportedly tested kinesthesis. Alfred Binet, during these same years, employed drawing tasks in his first attempts to assess "mental levels" in populations of French school-boys (Cratty, 1973).

During, and especially following, the second World War, two primary thrusts may be discerned in the literature dealing with physical abilities: (a) Wartime needs prompted Edwin Fleishman and others to study, in detail, the nature of human motor abilities, using factor-analytic techniques (Fleishman, 1964); and (b) in the early and late 1950s as well as in the 1960s, programs consisting primarily of movement tasks had been advocated by several persuasive writers as having a salutary effect upon academic potential and school achievement in children and youth, as well as aiding atypical children to function better in a variety of ways (Barsch, 1967; Delacato, 1964; Getman, 1952; Kephart, 1960).

The terms sensory-motor, perceptual-motor, as well as others linking input with output, began to appear in both these types of writings. Fleishman and others studying motor functioning in rather direct and straightforward ways coined the terms to indicate that seldom does a motor task function independently of sensory and/or perceptual components. He and others suggested that in the "real" three-dimensional world one must organize visual space both when monitoring one's own movements, as well as when attempting to deal with objects, and moving objects which may impinge upon one's "personal space." Extensive research programs, exemplified by that of K.U. Smith (1970) at the University of Wisconsin, further explored the nature of sensory-motor integration in a wide variety of tasks, including those requiring both larger and smaller muscle groups.

On the other hand, various remedial "educationalists" for whom movement was a paramount part of their programs used the terms sensory-motor and perceptual-motor in ways different from those employed by the experimental psychologists discussed above. These latter writers, including Getman (1952), Kephart (1960), and Barsch (1967) as well as others, suggested that the compound character of these terms denoted that not only were perceptual qualities and motor abilities linked functionally, but that *causal* relationships could be demonstrated between the exercise of these two facets of the human personality. These writers were emphatic in stating that one might change perceptual abilities and academic functioning by encouraging children and adolescents to engage in prescribed movement tasks.

During the 1960s, the "movement movement" truly "caught on." As the programs and writings appeared, several "schools of thought" began to emerge:

(a) Getman (1952), Kephart (1960), and others suggested that engaging in movement tasks would improve perceptual and academic operations and abilities: that physical awkwardness inevitably accompanied academic deficiencies, and thus by aiding a child to move better, improved schoolwork would result.

(b) Delacato (1964), and later Ayres (1972a), held similar goals for movement experiences, but aligned their approaches with their interpretations of developmental neurology. They published models which postulated that various rudimentary movement and sensory-motor tasks would first directly impinge in positive ways upon the higher centers of the brain, and that once this had occurred a variety of qualities mediated by these "improved" centers would also be changed for the better. They advocated, therefore, an approach which went against "symptom specific" education for children with learning disabilities and other kinds of sensory, motor, and academic handicaps. They proposed to change in direct ways the central nervous system, and this change in turn would rectify a number of differentiated abilities without necessitating the taking of direct actions with each deficiency possessed by a child or youth, as had traditionally been done.

(c) A third school of thought also began to emerge, whose membership took more of a cognitive approach to the use of movement in education. Pointing to the lack of substantiating evidence undergirding the previous two positions outlined, this latter group of writers suggested that movement might aid thought to the extent to which intellectual and perceptual qualities were ingrained directly in movement programs to which children and youth were exposed (Cratty, 1973; Mosston, 1972). This third, "cognitive-motor" approach will not be dealt with directly in this chapter.

The theoretical positions outlined above have spawned innumerable controversies, research articles, books, and, most important, thousands of school programs imposed upon hundreds of thousands of normal and atypical children, adolescents, and adults. Countless professionals have staked their reputations upon the veracity of the claims which undergird these models. The "movement movement" is a reality; it will not go away. Thus, in this chapter, an attempt will be made to try to sort out fact from fallacy, folklore from pragmatic realism, and in helpful ways to prompt those interested in perceptual development and associated qualities to examine closely the worth, and perhaps at times the worthlessness, of the models, operations, and programs which have been proposed.

In the next section a brief look will be taken at the theoretical issues linked to child development which underlie various assumptions about change by way of sensory-motor and perceptual-motor programs. In the succeeding portions of the chapter, literature examining possible changes in movement qualities as well as visual, visual-perceptual, and academic functioning will be reviewed. The final portion of the chapter contains a summary of important points, together with suggestions for further research, which appears needed.

2. Theoretical Issues and Child Development

The development of the human infant has been a fascinating object of attention for philosophers and scientists during the past centuries. Informal observations of childhood behavior, and of infant squirmings, have, within recent years, been accompanied by increasingly sophisticated methods of objectifying the sight, touch, thought, and audition of infants, as well as the ways in which the senses are combined with each other and are controlled by "higher" mental processes (Bower, Broughton, & Moore, 1971; Lipsitt & Kay, 1964; Siqueland, 1970).

Perhaps the most influential writer on this subject was Jean Piaget. When his works were translated into English in the 1950s, they not only inspired renewed interest in the sensory-motor bases of cognition, but also encouraged important research on the nature of the evolution of human intelligence, and on the development of thought in the maturing infant and child.

Piaget suggested the importance of a sensory-motor period within the early development of the human, and his thoughts on these matters have provided a rational basis for those advocating some of the perceptual-motor theories within the literature. In general outline, Piaget's model suggests that motor and sensory-motor behaviors provide the foundation for later cognitive development, and that direct action upon the environment by the maturing infant is an imperative and critical beginning for the elaboration of more complicated perceptual and intellectual behaviors.

Alternatives to the sensory-motor-based Piagetian model have also been postulated within the literature. For example, the present author (Cratty, 1979) formulated what he termed a "latticework" model for the development of human behaviors. This paradigm suggests that the beginnings of verbal, motor, sensory, as well as cognitive behaviors may be seen near birth, and that as the child matures various of these behaviors may function at times independently, and at other times in combination, in order to expedite the completion of developmental tasks.

Individual differences in the neurological makeups of developing children, as well as of mature humans, cause various training effects, attributed to any of the methods currently in vogue, to be highly unpredictable.

Supporting this second assumption is the evidence which has been obtained by Cohen (1969) using dogs of a similar species. Finding that similar peripheral movements produced different neurological activity (measured via implanted electrodes), Cohen concluded that his data pointed to the reasons why only *some* programs of movement therapy succeed *some* of the time, with *some* of the patients and clients exposed to them.

In conclusion, therefore, current and recent data obtained using infants as subjects place into serious question some of the basic assumptions held by perceptual-motor theorists. Movement may be an important component of the human personality, but may not be the basis for so-called higher cognitive functions. And finally, human development may be more complicated than most of the current theories imply (Bower, 1974; Cratty, 1979; Hammill & Weiderholt, 1972; Larson & Hammill, 1964; Whitsell, 1970).

3. Sensory- and Perceptual-Motor Programs and Changes in Movement Capacities

Before proceeding to evaluate whether or not sensory-motor or perceptual-motor programs of remediation alter "higher functions," it is important to consider first whether or not important intermediate objectives are met by such ministrations. It is not even entirely clear, for example, whether exposing a child or youth to the various programs containing movement tasks will change their movement capacities. Further, the infant may, according to Cratty (1979), engage in both thought and in perceptual behaviors independent of actions which may be taken; thus, adequate motor functioning is not an imperative precursor of adequate perceptual and/or cognitive behaviors.

In the often-cited visual-enrichment study of White and Held (1958), it was found that infants subjected to an enriched visual environment tended to evidence "hand regard" about 3 weeks later than did those who were not similarly "enriched." Thus, in this case visual stimulation, while perhaps promoting intellectual and perceptual processes, seemed to delay the infant's attempts to sight his own hand, and thus to use it in a useful way (Cratty, 1979; Bower, 1974).

Further evidence that motor activity is not a critical basis for perceptual activity comes from considering the finding of Held in his work on the influence of self-initiated movement upon the organization of movement in visual space. Held first suggested that his findings indicated that action was an imperative for the organization of visual space (Held & Freedman, 1962). However, Held, as well as others upon the collection of further data, decided that conceptual processes contribute as much or more to the organization of visual space as do direct actions taken by the individual (Fishkin, 1969; Kilpatrick, 1946; Wilkinson & Adrian, 1971).

Perhaps the data which instigate the most questions concerning the validity of a straightforward Piagetian model for the nature of sensory-motor functioning in the developing child are those produced in the late 1960s and early 1970s by Bower and his colleagues (Bower & Paterson, 1972; Bower et al., 1971; Bower, Broughton, & Moore, 1972). His studies, reviewed in his 1974 book *Development in Infancy,* seem to leave little doubt not only that the human infant engages in rather sophisticated cognitive and perceptual (visual and auditory) behaviors earlier in life than Piaget and others imagined, but that further, these behaviors may not only precede, but at times may be relatively independent of voluntary and coordinated movement of the larger and smaller skeletal muscle groups (Bower, 1974; Bruner, 1968; Lipsitt, 1964; Siqueland, 1970).

Moreover, Bower's data and interpretations present persuasive arguments against the traditional manner in which it was assumed that visual-manual behaviors evolve in the infant. White (White & Held, 1958), for example, has presented a sequence of acts which purportedly suggest that the child must evidence accurate voluntary movement of the upper limbs, before proceeding to act upon and perceptually deal with visual space. His sequences, presented below, are questioned by Bower (1974).

According to White and Held (1958):

   (a) Discovery of the child's hand by the child . . . leads to
   (b) looking at the hand, when accompanied by an object in the space field . . . leads to
   (c) crude "swiping" at the object . . . which then
   (d) becomes more precise and refined . . . which leads to . . .
   (e) the formation of increasingly sophisticated concepts about objects, objects in visual space, object permanence and associated conceptual behaviors and ideas.

Bower, on the other hand, presents evidence that suggests that an entirely different series of events may take place in the newborn. He has found that if infants are placed in an upright position near birth, so that their arms are free to move, they begin to swipe at objects with a 40% "hit rate" without evidencing hand-regard first; at the same time infants in this position evidence agitation when apparent objects (produced via illusions) are not contacted. In other studies Bower has found that, during months prior to the development of the ability to move their hands accurately, infants evidence surprise when hidden objects are not present when their covering is removed (Bower & Paterson, 1974).

Thus, upon reviewing this data, a critical assumption of the perceptual-motor theorists is placed in serious jeopardy—that movement is an imperative predecessor of both perceptual as well as cognitive behavior. Thus, Bower might suggest that infant development appears as follows, in contrast to the steps reflecting Piagetian (and perceptual-motor theorists') thought outlined previously by White and Held (1958).

(a) At birth there are inherent combinations of auditory-motor, cognitive-perceptual, and visual-motor behaviors, which manifest themselves if the infant is placed in positions and under circumstances which encourage their expression.

(b) Near birth the infant's cognitive qualities permit the assumption of the permanence of objects, independent of the ability of the infant to directly see the objects.

(c) At times, excesses in the opportunities to exercise a given group of qualities (i.e., visual-perceptual enrichment) may tend to delay the onset of other qualities (manual activity).

(d) At birth, vision dominates motor functions, as the mere sight of a real (or an illusionary) object instigates swiping behaviors.

In addition to the assumption that motor competencies are a necessary base from which other conceptual and perceptual behaviors emerge, there are other important hypotheses upon which the more "neurologically oriented" members of the sensory-motor family of theoreticians rest their arguments. Ayres (1972a) and the Doman–Delacato group (Delacato, 1964) believe that it is possible to elicit real and important changes in the higher centers by exposing the child to various kinds of relatively simple and basic activities involving primitive movement patterns seen in the young child and in lower forms of life. Ayres includes movement patterns, as well as tactual stimulation, and tasks intended to stimulate the vestibular centers in her program. However, most of the evidence these investigators cite for their claims is indirect. Studies of lower animals are frequently found in their writings; other evidence they present deals with purported modifications of behaviors which their programs have apparently elicited, rather than any direct measures of neurological adjustment, which are also purported outcomes of their treatments.

Some of the evidence which surrounds these theories will be reviewed later in the chapter. It should be pointed out here, however, that (a) there still exists a relatively large gap between what is known about neurological development in infants, and behavioral changes via peripheral stimulation and/or movement activities; and (b) there are individual differences relative to whether or not some movement-training programs change motor functions. The modification of movement capacities is a question of transfer. And while it is well known, and reasonably well documented, that practicing a specific motor task enhances performance in that task, it is not as clear what the range of transfer is from a *single* task to a *group of tasks*. It is not well known whether or not practicing a limited number of motor tasks really aids a wide variety of motor performances, as is claimed by a number of perceptual-motor theorists.

At the same time, the perceptual-motor theorists do not seem overly concerned with the question whether movement aids movement, but instead intellectually "jump over" that obvious intermediate point, and claim that visual, perceptual, and cognitive changes occur as the result of exposure to movement tasks!

At times the instigators of perceptual-motor programs seem to be stacking the cards in their favor. They both (a) design programs which are replications of the tests *they* have initiated to evaluate the worth of their own programs, and/or (b) present evidence based upon test batteries containing tasks which probably require primarily motor abilities (drawing), which are arbitrarily labeled indices of "perceptual functioning." Thus, they assume that the range of transfer from their training tasks is small, and fail to identify the real factors underlying the tests which purport to evaluate their programs' efficiency.

Further clouding the issue is the question of the manner in which the factor structure of motor abilities is found to change in various populations. For example, evidence from factor-analytic studies of motor abilities (also of cognitive and perceptual abilities) indicates that as one samples children of older ages and those with increasingly higher levels of mental functioning, a "differentiation effect" is seen. That is, performance on the various tasks by older children is more specific, less likely to show high intercorrelations, and more fragmented when subjected to factor analyses (Cratty, 1979; Rarick & Dobbins, 1975).

This trend in the data makes it highly possible that greater intertask-transfer effects will occur when a group of younger and/or less able individuals are exposed to a motor-training program, than will occur when an older or more able group are subjected to the same groups of motor tasks. If one obtains a "low level" group of individuals from the local state mental hospital, and subjects them to nearly *any* program in which they experience human contact and general stimulation, they will improve on measures of "development," containing simple evidences of improved attention and the like.

In more than one study, however, it has been found that exposure to perceptual-motor training programs does elicit changes in motor functioning, particularly in the tasks inherent in the program (Brekke, Burke, Landry, & Schaney, 1976; Cratty *et al.*, 1970; Hebbelinck, 1978; Werner, 1974). For the most part, however, these findings were ancillary to the main purpose of these investigators, which was to ascertain whether or not movement programs change academic functioning.

While difficult, it is possible to change significantly the movement capacities of awkward children (Cratty *et al.*, 1970). However, to elicit change, these programs should contain (a) a wide diversity of tasks within several categories identified via factor-analytic techniques, and (b) useful and relatively specific "splinter" skills helpful to older children when attempting to play with their peers. Motor skill is more specific in nature than is generally believed. Practice of gross-motor activities is not likely to transfer to printing and writing skills; while manipulative skills, the printing of letters, and the copying of geometric figures are often independent qualities in children as young as 5 years (Cratty, 1979).

It is remarkable that so few studies exist which have explored the degree to which training in movement tasks produces changes in motor capacities. The early work in this area sometimes involved co-twin control studies, (e.g., McGraw, 1966). The tasks taught to the "trained twin" involved climbing skills, ball throwing, swimming, and the like. When the untrained twin often quickly "caught up" with the sibling who was tutored, perhaps some were prompted to ignore this field of potentially fruitful investigation.

However, it could be argued that movement capacities are important facets of the child's overall behavior, and helpful contributors to school success. Precision of movement as well as good "motor planning" are needed if the child is to freely express his thoughts, and to play well with his peers in a school environment. Particularly important during the first year in school, is the ability to print (Keogh & Smith, 1967). It is hoped that the future will see more definitive work on these types of problems and training effects. Among the questions to be answered are: (a) Just how task-specific is the program content in relation to the tests constituted to evaluate change? (b) How broad a program of movement tasks is required to elicit change in useful school tasks? (c) How might programs of movement enrichment differ when working with younger vs. older populations, with more severely "involved" populations vs.

those with less serious motor and/or intellectual problems? (d) What program components or combinations of components contribute to changes in what? (e) What are the differential effects of exposure to a motor-development program vs. "special attention" given during the same time in which these programs are instituted?

4. Perceptual-Motor Programs and Visual and Visual-Perceptual Changes

Several of the sensory-motor programs, including those put forth by Delacato (1964) as well as by Getman (1952), have placed priority on the instigation of changes in the visual system, with accompanying modifications in visual perception. Additionally these writers, as well as others (Kephart, 1960), assume that modifications in visual-perceptual functioning inevitably lead to improvement in school tasks—notably reading.

Thus the main hypotheses under which such programs operate reflect the beliefs that:

(a) Movement tasks modify a variety of visual and visual-perceptual functions.

(b) Positive changes in visual-perceptual functioning contribute to reading success.

(c) Vision and movement are inseparable, and thus the exercise of one ability inevitably modifies, in a positive way, the other.

The evaluation of several of the presently popular programs is made difficult by the variety of ways in which such terms as vision, perception, visual training, and the like are employed (Cratty, 1979). For example, Getman uses the word "vision" in a rather global way, and at various times in his writings it may be taken to mean cognitive functioning, perceptual ability, as well as attributes reflected in ocular capabilities. However, Getman seems to feel that vision is a rather all-inclusive concept, as he states that

> visualization is an ability to ignore time and space . . . visual patterns are substitutes for action, speech, and time . . . visual perceptual organization is the ultimate process in the development of the child. (Getman, 1952)

Despite the rather romanticized view Getman and others may have of the nature of human vision, and of how it interacts with reading, there *is* available data which suggest that (a) reading problems may occur for reasons other than visual and visual-perceptual functioning (Gibson & Levine, 1975); (b) visual functions during reading are highly differentiated and complex (Taylor, 1965; Tinker, 1958); and (c) relatively few visual functions have been shown to be modifiable through visual training, much less by visual-motor training of various kinds (Cratty, 1979; Hammill & Weiderholt, 1972; Weiderholt & Hammill, 1971).

During reading, the eye makes a variety of rapid movements, including rapid jumps (or saccades) across the page occurring from three to eight times a second. Additionally, tiny accommodation-like movements occur, termed *fibrillations*. At the same time gross tracking movements of the eye occur as the eyes find their way from the end of one line of print to the beginning of the next. Finally, the eyes must fuse, at "near point," about 10 to 16 inches away, as the child inspects the printed page (Taylor, 1965; Tinker, 1958).

To further cloud the issue, there are numerous reputable authorities in the field of reading who insist that reading is largely an intellectual act, in which various "nonsense shapes" (words) must be translated into verbal and cognitive meanings. Many of these same scholars include the rate of information processing of the central nervous system as a critical quality which governs the speed with which a child can "decode" the printed page (Gibson & Levine, 1975).

Like the tasks in the programs of Kephart (1960) and Frostig (1964), the tasks contained in the publication by Getman (1952) are purported to produce a wide range of transfer. The programs contain motor as well as visual-perceptual training activities. For example, Getman includes quickly presented visual stimuli which must be remembered in order to improve visual memory.

When evaluating any of the programs discussed in this chapter, one should consult research studies which may reflect *behavioral changes*, despite any uneasiness over the theoretical rationales involved. The quality of the research studies should be carefully considered, as they vary greatly in the types of populations used, in the controls imposed, and in the sophistication of the statistical treatment of the data as well as of the research design used (Hammill & Weiderholt, 1972). In terms of these criteria, programs purporting to improve visual and visual-perceptual functioning through movement experiences seem to come up short. Getman's program has not been subjected to real scientific scrutiny, except in three articles—one of which contains two subjects, and the second of which did not appear in a monitored journal, but was authored by Getman and accompanies materials ordered from him. The third suffers from inadequate statistical treatment of the data, and vague descriptions of the dependent variables involved (Cratty, 1979).

Kephart's program as well as that of Frostig have been subjected to constant scrutiny by several scholars over the years. Critiques of the studies purporting to support the programs are severe, and do not result in high praise for the quality of the experimental work carried out (Cratty, 1979; Goodman & Hammill, 1973; Mann, 1970; Seefeldt, 1974). Changes which have occurred as a result of these programs have usually been confined to the actual content of the programs themselves, and are often modifications in hand–eye coordinations found in drawing tasks (Brekke *et al.,* 1976; Hebbelinck, 1978; Werner, 1974). In perhaps the most stringent test of the Kephart program, Hebbelinck, using over 500 children in Belgium over an 8-year period, found that application of the Kephart program changed some motor functions, but no academic abilities (Hebbelinck, 1978).

When attempting to ascertain what, if any, perceptual changes may occur as the result of the various perceptual-motor programs, it is most important to arrive at an operational definition of just what "perception" means, and how it may be measured. Recent research for the most part suggests that visual perceptual attributes are highly specific (Cratty, Apitzch, & Bergel, 1973; O.W. Smith & P.C. Smith, 1966) and include depth perception, static acuity, dynamic acuity, distance perception, depth perception, the ability to fractionalize space (to decide what is halfway between the observer and an object), as well as various measures of perceptual anticipation.

Thus, vague claims that movement programs somehow will aid "perception" are rather imprecise. Rather, one should specify just what perceptual attributes may vary as a function of the training procedures imposed. And perhaps most important, programs should indicate just *why* a given attribute or group of attributes should be changed with reference to specific academic skills and operations.

Also, as has been mentioned, many of the most-used tests of "visual perception" are in reality figure-copying tests. The Frostig Developmental Test of Visual Perception (Frostig, 1964), The Bender Visual-Motor Gestalt Test (Koppitz, 1965), as well as other tests of visual-motor integration are examples of these.

In the case of the above evaluative instruments, poor performance may be due to (a) faulty perceptions of what is to be copied; (b) difficulty in integrating what is perceived and what is to be drawn, and the drawing act itself; (c) physical awkwardness and/or a defect in motor planning when trying to execute the figure; (d) some combination of the above qualities (Friedrich, Fuller, & Hawkins, 1969).

Thus, the evaluation of whether or not a program of motor activities truly changes some perceptual capacity should be based upon "motor free" tests of visual perception. The instrument developed by Colarusso and Hammill (1972) is an example of these. These scholars, rejecting the premise that movement and perception are inseparable attributes, and finding fault with the then-available tests of visual perception, sought to formulate a measure which would be independent of the child's ability to draw. Their initial research, as well as follow-up studies by Newcomer and Hammill (1973), have resulted in data which reflect some of the ways in which children differ in their ability to process input, and "manage" output, in the form of drawing.

These "motor-free" tests of visual perception seem more reflective of academic achievement, IQ, and other intellectual operations, than do the "motor contaminated" tests of visual perception which have been traditionally employed. Not only are such "pure" tests of visual perception helpful in the evaluation of the perceptual abilities of motorically handicapped children, but they also produce scores which are independent of various copying tests which have been alluded to (Colarusso & Hammill, 1972; Johnson, Brekke, & Harlow, 1977).

Thus the purveyors of the theories that suggest that (a) movement aids perception, and that (b) improving perception somehow helps school success, seem in error on several counts. The fallacies under which they may be operating include the notions that copying tests of "visual perception" truly evaluate the degree to which a child organizes perceptual input, and that tests of visual perception tell us something about reading success (Gibson & Levine, 1975; Larson & Hammill, 1974).

Kephart (1960), Getman (1952), Frostig (1964), Barsch (1967), as well as others who may be classified as perceptual-motor theorists have thus had probably rather mixed effects upon the education of both typical and atypical children. During the 1950s and 1960s when these programs first became known, little was being done to remedy either learning difficulties or the problems of the physically awkward child. The fact that the tests' relatively simple techniques attracted a large number of both lay and professional workers probably helped to illuminate the fact that physical awkwardness was found in at least some children with learning difficulties, and the fact that at times motor ineptitude was a learning difficulty in and of itself, as the child could not communicate his thoughts with accuracy and efficiency.

At times the positive effects elicited in the programs were achieved in indirect ways. For example, when a child could engage in motor tasks for 2 days a week, instead of a stressful reading lesson, the practice of reading was spaced in time, and thus the rest periods may have produced positive changes in reading scores, due to the dissipation of inhibition toward the task of reading. Moreover, some motor tasks contained in these programs may have aided to prolong children's attention spans. For example, the balance beam, if used daily with distractable children, may help them to focus their attention on *something* (their feet walking the beam) for longer than they have paid attention to anything before!

In summary, those individuals still "caught up" with the "magic" of perceptual-motor training (and claims made by the instigators concerning the broad "transfer width" of these programs) should proceed with some caution. It should be realized that (a) movement and visual perception are developmentally and functionally often separable qualities; (b) many measures of visual perception are not highly predictive of school success and reading, but are actually tasks requiring hand–eye coordination rather than perceptual qualities; (c) special care should be taken when exposing awkward children to such programs in order to ensure that changes in their motor competencies will even transpire; (d) all awkward children are not learning-disabled; and (e) remediating motor ineptitude will not likely create any positive and direct changes in school achievement.

5. Sensory Integration and Neurological Organization

Perhaps the most dramatic approaches to the use of sensory-motor stimulation in the remediation of atypical children have been programs espoused by the Doman–Delacato group in Philadelphia (1958), and more recently the programs and techniques advanced by Jean Ayres (1972a). These two models have several common components, including the supposition that by exposing the child or adult to basic and rather rudimentary motor activities, and to tactual stimulation as well as balance tasks, direct influences will be exerted upon brain functions. Further, the models postulate that improvement of these functions will in turn positively change a wide variety of perceptual, motor, and cognitive tasks. These theorists thus espouse a more generalized approach to the academic and motor therapy of atypical children, in contrast to the traditional "symptom specific" approach which is often found in special schools.

Both models are types of recapitulation theories, which contend that by focusing upon basic processes, some of which are found in subhuman groups, positive changes in brain function of the human infant, child, and adult will take place. Thus they both suggest that phylogeny parallels ontogeny—that the development of the child parallels the evolution of the species; and that by the recapitulation of basic evolutionary functions, the development of the typical and atypical human infant will be neurologically enhanced. Both models further suggest that this neurological improvement will be reflected in real and measurable changes in useful academic behaviors.

The Doman–Delacato approach antedates that of Ayres. The first writings from the group in Philadelphia, composed of the Doman brothers, Delacato, and their colleagues, were in the form of small self-published monographs, appearing in the middle and late 1950s. A theory was espoused which can be historically traced to philosophical speculations occurring as early as the eighteenth century. The basic premise is that the development of the child resembles the manner in which the species emerged—from an evolutionary standpoint; and that if one exposes both normal and atypical children to motor activities which are purported to be mediated by primitive, intermediate, and higher centers of the brain (including crawling, creeping, and the like), not only will these "layers" be enhanced, but innumerable other qualities controlled by these layers (pons, midbrain, medulla, cortex, and neurocortex) will be similarly improved. Thus, like the perceptual-motor theorists, these theorists claim a remarkable range of transfer arising from the practice of a relatively limited number of movement activities. The majority of these activities resemble the stages which precede the assumption of an upright stance and walking behavior in the normal infant (Cratty, 1973; Delacato, 1964).

The Doman–Delacato method enjoyed great popularity in the 1960s, partly instigated by articles in the popular press. It was simple to follow, and promised results for individuals ranging from the severely brain damaged to graduate students. But by the end of the 1960s some doubters had begun to air their views, both in writings (Glass, 1967; Robbins & Glass, 1968; Whitsell, 1970) and in personal appearances. Funds offered by the Federal government to the Philadelphia group to test their methods were, surprisingly, refused.

The methodology seemed to be in a constant state of flux, making difficult the verification of the claims by other researchers. In 1969 a policy statement from leading national organizations concerned with the health and education of the handicapped urged caution. Further research continued in the 1970s, however, and again produced controversy (Neman, Ross, McCann, Menolascino, & Heal, 1974; Zigler & Seitz, 1975). Some still contend that exposure to the program's content produces positive changes in intelligence, movement capacities, as well as perceptual abilities; while others are equally adamant in refusing to accept the "evidence" that is placed before them.

Evaluating this program and others of a similar nature proved, and still proves, difficult. Volunteers for viable control groups are not easily come by. The methodology seems made of rubber, and its contemporary state is usually known to but a few intimates close to the program authors themselves. Evaluating the subtle movement capacities and reflex qualities of brain-injured children was and still is both an art and a science, whose outcomes may be more dependent upon the skill and integrity of the neurologist than upon the actual capacities of the children scrutinized.

The findings of the majority of the few well-controlled studies (Cratty, 1979; Whitsell, 1970) seem less than positive. Although recent positive change was recorded in a study by Neman et al. (1974), the study was soundly critized for faulty methodology and sampling techniques by Zigler and Seitz (1975).

The organized "movement" of the Delacato group has largely dissolved. Their approach is practiced now with a few parents in relatively isolated situations. The franchised "therapy centers" of the 1960s no longer exist. The program has been questioned severely on grounds which are both theoretical and practical (Cratty, 1979). From a theoretical standpoint, the methodology assumes that the nervous system is laid down in neat layers, a supposition which, while frequently found in the writings of neurologists in the nineteenth century, is not widely accepted today. The vertical integrators of brain function were ignored, as were data which have illuminated both the nature of hemispheric dominance and the manner in which the two hemispheres interact when the individual is faced with a complex task.

The practical outcomes of the method, as well as the nature of experimental findings focusing upon behavior changes, have also caused many observers serious concerns. Some children have had their motor functions reduced when exposed to some of the more rigorous methods contained within various applications of the program. Family life was, and is, often disrupted when large numbers of people enter the home to aid in the patterning of a hapless sibling on the dining-room table. It has been observed that when this type of social stimulation is withdrawn, if the method does not seem to be working, the child who has been "treated" may withdraw into what at times resembles a catatonic state.

In summary, reviews of the experimental findings by Robbins and Glass (1963), Whitsell (1970), and others suggested that the methodology is not viable. The instigators of the program failed to conduct well-controlled replicable studies, even when offered public funds to do so.

Although the methodology has fallen into disrepute, several interesting social-psychological lessons do emerge. These lessons reflect both positive and negative outcomes. First, increased attention began to be focused upon the more severely brain injured, as a result of the attention drawn by the Doman–Delacato movement. Subsequent methodologies reflect a more comprehensive approach to sensory-motor remediation and stimulation than was practiced by the Philadelphia group (Edgar, 1970; Edgar, Ball, McIntyre, & Shotwell, 1969). Second, the almost evangelical nature of those practicing the program clearly evidenced the serious desire of many educators, therapists, and parents to modify the recalcitrant nervous system by quick and magical methods rather than by the gradual and developmentally sound approaches presently available (Bobath & Bobath, 1972).

What was simple sold well. Reduce a therapy to a few basics, and accompany it with a primer on the nervous system and brain which the average person can understand, and widespread acceptance will be yours. Others may learn from the example of Delacato and the Doman brothers.

In the late 1950s Jean Ayres, a student of Margaret Rood at the University of Southern California, began to publish research which reflected her interest in improving the motor functioning of brain-damaged children (Henderson, Llorens, Gilfoyle, Myers, & Prevel, 1974). Her doctoral work resulted in a test, which she gradually refined with continued factor-analytic work in the 1960s and 1970s. In 1972 both a text (Ayres, 1972a) as well as a research article (Ayres, 1972c) appeared. The former detailed a theory which explained how "sensory integration" might be improved through the practice of three kinds of tasks, while the latter described changes in academic improvement which came about because of exposure to her methods.

Her views have been widely read, and the practices and tests which she describes in her writings and workshops are practiced avidly by a large number of occupational therapists. Children and adolescents as well as adults evidencing a wide variety of learning and motor problems are currently being exposed to the program she recommends. The following three kinds of practices are commonly included: (a) motor experiences, primarily those experienced while prone on a scooter board, (b) tactual stimulation, administered much of the time by a circular, battery-operated brush, and (c) vestibular stimulation, extended to the patient by rocking motions elicited by positioning the patient within inner tubes, or cargo nets.

Some parents seeking to have their child's "problem" helped, armed with the tenets in Public Law 94-142, have been, and are, insisting that "sensory-integrative therapy" be offered in many school districts throughout the country. Administrators of hospitals, therapy services, as well as of school districts have been forced to come to grips with the staffing and financial requirements this type of therapy represents.

Ayres, in numerous articles extending over the past 11 years, reiterates that the higher brain structures, remaining functionally dependent upon the lower structures, may be positively changed if one exposes the child to basic sensory and motor activities which are purportedly mediated by these structures within the brain stem; and that improved "sensory integration" will be the result, a quality which seemingly permeates a number of basic as well as complicated tasks facing infants, children, and adults, including reading.

Initially, Ayres seemed to have taken her lead from her mentor, Margaret Rood, who included tactual stimulation as a portion of the recommended therapy for the improvement of *motor functioning*. Ayres, however, has expanded the objectives attributable to the stimulation of touch receptors, as well as receptors within the vestibular apparatus and the sensory-motor system, to include a wide variety of *learning tasks* found in special and "regular" schools (Ayres, 1968b, 1972c).

Prior to evaluating the program and theory, let us briefly review the metamorphosis of Ayres's thinking as reflected in her writings published from 1954 to the present. For example, in a 1954 publication (Ayres, 1954), she reviews the developmental stages within hand–eye coordination. Her scholarship is careful, and the insights she presents are typical of those espousing traditional developmental methods of therapy (Bobath & Bobath, 1972; Ayres, 1954).

In a 1958 article (Ayres, 1958), the first reference is made to the concept of "integration." She states that a child having a problem in integrating motor output with perceptual input may be having an "integration problem" rather than an inability to engage in motor planning per se, which would be manifest in apraxia.

An eclectic approach to understanding motor functioning seems to be reflected in a 1960 article (Ayres, 1960). In it, Ayres attributes failure to perform motor tasks well to conceptual problems, as well as to not following Skinnerian learning principles. John Dewey is quoted in the context of her suggestion that the best learning occurs in a problem-solving context. Thus her early writings reflect a broad theoretical orientation, ranging from Skinner, through Gesell, to cognitive theorists as represented by Dewey.

During her doctoral program, Ayres apparently became acquainted with factor-analytic techniques, and began to carry out studies of just how tests, purportedly reflecting sensory-motor dysfunctions, group themselves. In one of her first efforts (Ayres, 1965), she isolated what she termed "five syndromes." These five syndromes emerged from a study of 100 children who were "suspected" of having perceptual deficiencies. She labeled these apraxia, perceptual dysfunction, form and position in space, figure-ground, and tactile defensiveness. It is unclear (a) how or why these children were "suspect," and (b) why she used the term "syndrome" to indicate each of these areas, rather than suggesting that the total made up a *single syndrome,* composed of five *symptoms* or factors.

In an address given to the 3rd International Congress of the World Federation of Occupational Therapists (Ayres, 1963), Ayres revealed that she, like Delacato, believed in what was previously termed a recapitulation theory. In this address Ayres, like Delacato (1964), quoted the neurologist Temple Fay, in substantiating the axiom that ontogeny parallels phylogeny and that, further, the principle has relevance to developmental motor therapy. Subsequent writings by Ayres also reflect an allegiance to this principle.

As her factor-analytic studies proliferated, more data appeared which purportedly substantiated her assumptions concerning the manner in which sensory and sensory-motor behaviors seem to divide themselves into discrete groups. Thus, the ways in which these groupings occur suggested the validity of her three types of methods. More and more, she postulated *causal* attachments between human qualities, for relationships which were not even very *predictive*. For example, upon finding a correlation of +48 between hyperactivity and tactile functions, she suggested that one need only stimulate tactile receptors in order to elicit a positive change in hyperactive behaviors (Ayres, 1964).

By the late 1960s, Ayres began to look for an expanded list of objectives for the therapy she recommended, while at the same time she seemed to constrict the kinds of remedial activities included in her program. Rather than simply improving "sensory integration" as reflected in motor functions, the term "learning disability" began to appear with frequency in her writings after 1968. For example, she stated that "several behavioral areas which are vulnerable to dysfunction resulting from poor integration is academic learning (Ayres, 1968a). This same article contains reference to the importance of what were termed "centrifugal influences" upon the reticular formation, which in turn controls and regulates arousal, attention, and perception.

During these years, the importance of vestibular stimulation via rotation of the child began to assert itself in Ayres's writings. The criteria for improvement of the vestibular centers of the brain were taken to include the shortening of postrotational nystagmus which occurred at the termination of this spinning action (Ayres, 1968a). Additional research, in which this component of the therapy is employed, is reviewed below.

The increased importance attached to tactile stimulation is also revealed in Ayres's writings of this time (Ayres, 1968a). In many articles, she stated that other sensory modalities may be improved through stimulating the tactile receptors (e.g., Ayres, 1968a).

At the conclusion of her important article (Ayres, 1968a), Ayres makes a point highly significant to those attempting to understand her approach. She points out that children *without* sensory-motor dysfunction are not likely to be aided by the "integrative activities" she suggests. Rather, the cognitive development of children free of motor problems may be aided in other ways. Whether she still holds to this principle is difficult to ascertain even now.

In this same (1968a) article, she is emphatic in stating that if a child *does* evidence "sensory-motor problems, *and* learning disabilities, the latter qualities will be improved only by changing the former." This principle is reflected in the manner in which she selected subjects in future research studies; it is, however, a principle not always recognized or accepted by some who wholeheartedly embrace "sensory-integrative therapy." For example, as this is written an occupational therapist a few miles away is industriously spinning Chicano children in cargo nets in order to facilitate their learning of English!

It is sometimes difficult to interpret Ayres's ideas. She writes, for example, that "conjecture as a basis for association between reading disability and apraxis helps build a working theory to guide treatment" (Ayres, 1968a). Some might feel that conjecture provides a somewhat sandy base for the establishment of viable models, rather than the cement suggested by Ayres.

In this same article (1968a), after suggesting that tactile receptors, when stimulated, improve other sensory modalities, Ayres states that olfactory stimulation in the blind influences tactile perception! Should one interpret this to mean that one must first stimulate olfaction in the blind to then aid tactile perception, which then leads to an improvement in a number of other qualities?

There are also marked contrasts between the tentative way in which Ayres presents her model, and the rather dogmatic and clear-cut remedial techniques she carefully outlines in her text and writings (Ayres, 1972a). For example, she concludes in a 1968 article (Ayres, 1968b) that

> these thoughts are presented as tentative and a part of a constantly evolving theory which will undergo many changes as knowledge unfolds. . . . *Meantime, its productiveness warrants its use and continued exploration.* (italics mine)

Inspection of Ayres's factor-analytic work might lead some of the more statistically tough-minded to question the outcomes and interpretations. For example, in her 1965 study, upon which her test is based (Ayres, 1965), numerous tests whose reliability have only been estimated have been used; while two critical tests in the battery evaluating "freedom from hyperactive and distractable behavior," and "freedom from tactile defensive behavior" are both reported as having "no estimate of reliability" of the rated scores. However, it is these two scores which Ayres consistently finds loading into a common factor, and which serve as a cornerstone for at least one-third of her therapeutic techniques—for example, tactile stimulation to aid "tactile defensiveness" (resistance to learning and to perceiving information).

Moreover, her factor-analytic studies indicate the specific nature of various subcomponents of perception and motion, rather than their close alignment. The results of these studies, in which from five to seven and eight factors have been identified, would seem to indicate that one ought to go directly to the symptom (factor) when devising remedial techniques, rather than confining oneself to the three strategies continually advocated by Ayres.

Most importantly, in numerous writings Ayres suggests that various academic tasks, including reading, are a reflection of the quality of a child's ability to engage in "sensory integration." However, in a 1972 study (Ayres, 1972b), it was found that "reading, with spelling and intelligence closely associated" formed a factor *separate* from the usual ones she had previously identified using her test of sensory integration. In another article (Ayres, 1972c), she states that her factoral work indicated that "auditory-language functions" fell into a factor *apart* from those reflecting "sensory integration."

Thus to many, including this writer, Ayres's own data suggest the validity of a "symptom specific" approach both to the remediation of language, auditory-perceptual, and reading difficulties, as well as to specific subcomponents of motor awkwardness. The model advocated by Ayres in which a broad transfer width from three types of remedial techniques to a broad range of learning and motor abilities seems less tenable.

In her often-cited 1972 study (Ayres, 1972c), techniques are used which further reveal subtleties in her rationale and in her research methodologies. She first selected 148 children to test. Upon administering a series of sensory-motor tests—her own battery—she identified for inclusion 68 subjects with apparent "sensory integration" problems, "to assure inclusion in the experiment only those children for whom the treatment was designed," and "in order to provide an adequate test of the method of intervention." This selection was carried out despite the fact that the school district had identified the original 148 as evidencing "learning disabilities."

Thus, upon reflection, it appears that those who administer Ayres's program in indiscriminate ways might be wasting their time as well as the time and resources of the children, the school system, and the parents involved. The statistical treatment of the data in this study (Ayres, 1972c) leaves much to be desired, as is also the case with subsequent studies of this nature (Ayres, 1976). Multiple t tests are used, together with numerous chi squares, when in reality multivariant techniques are called for.

Thus, the results of the 1972 study (Ayres, 1972c) are suspect, even though they are reported as positively supporting Ayres's theory. The results of the 1976 study were, according to the author, nonsignificant.

The rationale underlying the popular "sensory integration" theory of Ayres is clear, and the theory is understood and practiced by many. Stimulate portions of the brain stem with tactile, vestibular, and motor activities, and the higher centers will become "energized," and contribute positively to a variety of learning tasks, including reading. It is not entirely clear, however, if the practitioners of this therapy realize the limitations suggested by its instigator, and that it *may* "work" only if the child has a "sensory integrative" problem identified by the Ayres battery. Data supporting the premise that academic competencies will be radically modified are virtually lacking, despite the fact that some gains in motor competencies have been recorded recently using a few subjects in clinical settings. Evidence that the difficult task of reading is improved via "brain stem" stimulation is lacking (Bhatara, Clark, & Arnold, 1968; Kanter, Clark, Allen, & Chase, 1976).

Research activity since the publication of Ayres's (1972c) study has focused upon the manner in which sensory-integration therapy may act upon a variety of behaviors. The number of subjects is often few, while the controls employed and the statistical procedures of many of these studies are open to question. For example, Bhatara (Bhatara *et al.,* 1968) studied the effects of vestibular stimulation (spinning to produce accommodation to postrotational nystagmus), using a single "hyperkinetic" subject. They found that while the treatment invariably produced "nausea, pallor and sweating," there was a change in the measure of hyperactivity employed, although the subject still remained within the "hyperkinetic portion" of their scale. An interview, they claim, resulted in the finding that the subject improved in "organization, integration and sense of proportion," and showed a decrease in "errors of omission." They also report cheerily that the subject failed to vomit after each of the treatments administered.

Several studies have focused upon the possible improvement of movement capacities after exposure to "sensory integration" therapy. For example, Clark, Miller, Thomas, Kucherawy, & Azen (1978) compared the effects of operant-conditioning methods and sensory-integration techniques upon the development of profoundly retarded adults. Upon finding that improvement under the two methods (as well as a third which combined the two) was equal, they concluded that their findings lent credence to the viability of sensory-integrative techniques. The absence of a "Hawthorne Control" group, they acknowledged, made their findings less than conclusive. They reported only slight gains on seven of the numerous measures obtained.

Kanter (Kanter *et al.,* 1976) also looked at the effects of vestibular stimulation upon the motor performance of three developmentally delayed infants, and four children with Down's Syndrome. As is typical in studies of this nature, habituation was found when the subjects underwent vestibular stimulation, as reflected in the reduction of postrotational nystagmus. The motor-development scale in this study was not identified, although positive changes in the children were reported.

Ayres also studied possible changes in "choreoathetoid movements" using sensory-integrative therapy (Ayres, 1977a). Although finding no significant differences in the treatment group when contrasted to the controls, she did report that "some but not all" of the children were helped to reduce the appearance of extraneous movements as a result of her efforts. In this article she also states that "sensory integrative therapy is designed to enhance 'sensory integration' rather than neuro-muscular coordination."

In another extensive study (1976), Ayres investigated the effects of sensory-integrative therapy on a number of traits of "learning disabled" children. As in some of her previous work, she reported that the subjects were "specially selected." However, in this monograph the criteria for selection were not specified. No significant differences were reported at the conclusion of the study, in which 128 subjects took part. The subjects did accommodate, however, to the effects of vestibular stimulation, as reflected in measures of postrotational nystagmus.

Ayres (1977b) reported a "cluster analysis," in which findings similar to those of previous studies of this nature indicated that measures of language functions and auditory perception loaded in factors *separate* from those found in tests evaluating various components of "sensory integration."

Thus, in recent work verification of the manner in which "sensory-integrative therapy" may aid academic learning may not be found. And even improvement in motor functions has not been clearly demonstrated by the data of recent studies in which this type of therapy has been a dependent variable.

To make viable the role of sensory-integrative therapy in the reme-diation of learning disabilities, it would seem necessary to (a) identify just what portions of the program (tactile stimulation, motor activity, and/or vestibular stimulation) may be working to change what; (b) accompany the studies by proper controls, a significant number of subjects, and include a research design incorporating contemporary statistical techniques; (c) produce factor analyses, if possible, which indicate that various language and cognitive functions load in the *same* factors as do tests of "sensory integration;" (d) more clearly describe just why and how certain subjects are "selected" for inclusion in the studies undertaken; and (e) explore the possible emotional effects, both negative and positive, emanating from the (sometimes soothing) stroking and rocking techniques found within the program.

Dr. William Cruickshank has written a generally complimentary forward to a collection of Dr. Ayres's works (Henderson *et al.,* 1974). However, those who presently practice or who contemplate engaging in "sensory-integrative therapy," would do well to heed his words, in his opening remarks, as he states that "the teaching of children . . . is more than perceptual-motor training." Further on he reminds the readers that

"It would be a sad day if the depth and breadth of occupational therapy preparation and function gave way to an overemphasis of one thing, that is, perceptual-motor development."

6. Summary

It has been the intent in this chapter to present a contemporary view of some of the current models formulated by those proposing a sensory-motor or perceptual-motor approach to the enhancement of perception and the improvement of other attributes. The theories and operational objectives of Kephart, Getman, Ayres, and Doman-Delacato have been accorded special attention within the chapter.

Emphasis was placed upon surveying basic theoretical information which might help to clarify the rationales of these theories, as well as upon research which reflects whether or not the objectives stated by their proponents were, or are, being met.

In general it was argued that current research in child development renders somewhat questionable the assertion that movement is the basis of a number of attributes, including perception and cognition. In addition, data cited by Bower and others suggest that rudimentary cognitive and perceptual abilities appear at birth. At times, these processes appear to fuse when the child attempts various tasks, and at other times these processes seem independent of each other and of emerging movement capacities. Acceptance of this premise also leads one to question whether improving movement traits of both normal and atypical youngsters has a facilitating effect upon visual perception and other abilities, including academic learning.

The data cited indicated that the outcomes of exposing a child to a perceptual-motor-based program are predicated upon the specific content of the program; and that a large number of objectives, including the improvement of perceptual attributes, should not be expected from a program containing instructor-directed movement activities. It was suggested that the increased use of "motor free" tests of perception should help to clarify further the outcomes of the sensory-motor or perceptual-motor program.

The Doman–Delacato program as well as the Ayres "sensory-integrative therapy" were discussed, and grouped together as models which reflect approaches tied in with their proponents' concepts of developmental neurology. Both programs, upon surveying the quality of the data supporting the claims made by the authors of the theories, were questioned. The tenuous theoretical assumptions upon which both programs rest were also briefly examined.

Further research should include efforts to answer the following questions: (a) What is the relationship of components of the various perceptual-motor programs to the potential outcomes of these programs, including the improvement of movement attributes? (b) What possible intermediate variables may be operative when real changes *are* recorded as children and adults are exposed to these programs? These intermediate variables might consist of (1) improvement in the emotional tone and self-concept of the clients resulting from special attention; (2) the spacing in time of arduous primary tasks (e.g., reading) resulting from the insertion of less arduous movement programs; (3) the possible calming and emotionally satisfying effects of program components within the Ayres program—for example, rocking and stroking a child; and (4) the prolongation of attention in motor tasks to which the child must pay strict attention, for example, walking a balance beam.

The instigation and popularization of these sensory-motor and perceptual-motor programs, as well as those which are "neurologically based," during the past 30 years, have been beneficial insofar as they have helped to focus attention upon a rather obvious and often deficient component of children's behavior—their movement capacities. However, the credence such programs will continue to have within both the educational and university-based scientific communities will depend upon the quality of future research, which should investigate in penetrating ways the subtleties of the programs' contents, aims, and rationales.

7. References

Ayres, A.J. Ontogenetic principles in the development of arm and hand functions. *American Journal of Occupational Therapy,* 1954, *8,* 12–18.

Ayres, A.J. The visual-motor function. *American Journal of Occupational Therapy,* 1958, *12,* 176–182.

Ayres, A.J. Occupational therapy for motor disorders resulting from impairment of the central nervous system. *Rehabilitation Literature,* 1960, *21,* 302–310.

Ayres, A.J. *Integration of Information.* 1962 Study Course IV, Third International Congress, World Federation of Occupational Therapists.

Ayres, A.J. *The development of perceptual-motor abilities: A theoretical basis for treatment of dysfunction.* The Eleanor Clark Slagle Lecture, presented at the 1963 Conference of the American Occupational Therapy Association, St. Louis, Missouri, June 1963.

Ayres, A.J. Tactile functions: Their relation to hyperactive and perceptual motor behavior. *American Journal of Occupational Therapy,* 1964, *13.*

Ayres, A.J. Patterns of perceptual-motor dysfunction in children: A factor analytic study. *Perceptual and Motor Skills,* 1965, Monograph Suppl. I, *20,* 335–368.

Ayres, A.J. Sensory integrative processes and neuropsychological learning disability. *Learning Disorders,* 1968, *3,* 41–58. (a)

Ayres, A.J. *Reading—a product of sensory integrative processes.* Perception and Reading, *Proceedings of the 12th Annual Convention* 1968, *12,* part 4, 271–275. (b)

Ayres, A.J. The challenge of the brain. *Proceedings of the Perceptual motor conference,* Sparks, Nevada, May 1971.

Ayres, A.J. *Sensory integration and learning disorders.* Los Angeles: Western Psychological Services, 1972. (a)

Ayres, A.J. Types of sensory integrative dysfunction among disabled learners. *American Journal of Occupational Therapy,* 1972, *26,* 13–18. (b)

Ayres, A.J. Improving academic scores through sensory integration. *Journal of Learning Disabilities,* 1972, *5,* 338–342. (c)

Ayres, A.J. Sensorimotor foundations of academic ability. In W. Cruickshank & D. Hallahan (Eds.), *Perceptual and learning disabilities in children. Vol. 2. Syracuse: Syracuse University Press, 1975, pp. 300–358.*

Ayres, A.J. *The effect of sensory integrative therapy on learning disabled children.* Unpublished monograph, University of Southern California, 1976.

Ayres, A.J. Effect of sensory integrative therapy on the coordination of children with choreoathetoid movements. *American Journal of Occupational Therapy,* 1977, *31,* 291–293. (a)

Ayres, A.J. Cluster analyses of measures of sensory integration. *American Journal of Occupational Therapy,* 1977, *31,* 362–366. (b)

Ayres, A.J. Dichotic listening performance in learning disabled children. *American Journal of Occupational Therapy,* 1977, *31,* 441–446. (c)

Barsch, R.H. *Achieving perceptual motor efficiency: A space oriented approach to learning.* Vol. 1. Seattle: Special Child Publications, 1967.

Beck, R., & Talkington, L. Frostig training with headstart children. *Perceptual and Motor Skills,* 1970, *30,* 521–522.

Bhatara, V., Clark, D.L., & Arnold, L.E. Behavioral and nystagmus response of a hyperkinetic child to vestibular stimulation. *American Journal of Occupational Therapy,* 1978, *32,* 311–316.

Bobath, K., & Bobath, R. Cerebral palsy diagnosis and assessment and neurodevelopmental approach to treatment. In P.H. Pearson & C.E. Williams (Eds.), *Physical therapy services in the developmental disabilities.* Springfield, Illinois: Charles C. Thomas, 1972.

Bower, T.G.R. *Development in infancy.* San Francisco: W.H. Freeman, 1974.

Bower, T.G.R., & Paterson, J.G. Stages in the development of the object concept. *Cognition,* 1972, *1* (1), 47–55.

Bower, T.G.R., Broughton, J.M., & Moore, M.K. The coordination of vision and touch in infancy. *Perception and Psychophysics,* 1970, *8,* 51–53.

Bower, T.G.R., Broughton, J.M., & Moore, M.K. The development of the object concept as manifested by changes in the tracking behavior of infants between 7 and 20 weeks of age. *Journal of Experimental Child Psychology,* 1971, *11* (2), 182–193.

Brekke, B., Burke, J., Landry, R., & Schaney, Z. Effects of perceptual-motor training program on kindergarten children. *Perceptual and Motor Skills,* 1976, *43,* 428–430.

Bruner, J. Heinz Werner Lectures in Developmental Psychology. Clark University, Worcester, Massachusetts, May 1968.

Clark, F.A., Miller, L.R., Thomas, J.A., Kucherawy, D.A., & Azen, S.P. A comparison of operant and sensory integrative methods on developmental parameters in profoundly retarded adults. *American Journal of Occupational Therapy,* 1978, *32,* 86–92.

Cohen, L.A. Manipulation of cortical motor responses by peripheral sensory stimulation. *Arch, Physical Medicine and Rehabilitation,* 1969, *50,* 495–505.

Colarusso, R., & Hammill, D. The motor free visual perceptual test. San Rafael, California: Academic Therapy Publication, 1972.

Cratty, B.J. *Physical expressions of intelligence.* Englewood Cliffs, New Jersey: Prentice-Hall, 1973.

Cratty, B.J. *Perceptual and motor development of infants and children.* 2nd Ed. Englewood Cliffs, New Jersey: Prentice-Hall, pp. 29–47.

Cratty, B.J., Ikeda, N., Martin, M., Jennett, C., & Morris, M. *Movement activities, motor ability and the education of children.* Springfield, Illinois: Charles C. Thomas, 1970.

Cratty, B.J., Apitzsch, E., & Bergel, R. *Dynamic visual acuity: A developmental study.* Unpublished monograph, Perceptual-Motor Learning Laboratory, University of California at Los Angeles, 1973.

Delacato, C.H. *The diagnosis and treatment of speech and reading problems.* Springfield, Illinois: Charles C. Thomas, 1964.

Edgar, C.L. The adaptation of perceptual-motor training techniques to the profoundly retarded. In B.J. Cratty (Ed.), *Some educational implications of movement.* Seattle: Special Child Publications, 1970.

Edgar, C.L., Ball, T., McIntyre, R.B., & Shotwell, A.M. Effects of sensory-motor training on adaptive behavior. *American Journal of Mental Deficiency,* 1969, *73,* 713–720.

Fishkin, S.M. Passive vs. active exposure to lateral displacement. *Perceptual and Motor Skills,* 1969, *29,* 291–297.

Fleishman, E.W. *The structure and measurement of physical fitness.* Englewood Cliffs, N.J.: Prentice-Hall, 1964.

Friedrich, D., Fuller, G., & Hawkins, W. Relationship between perception (input) and execution (output). *Perceptual and Motor Skills,* 1969, *29,* 923–934.

Frostig, M. *Developmental test of visual perception.* Palo Alto, Calif.: Consulting Psychologists Press, 1964.

Frostig, M., & Horne, D. *Teachers' guide: The Frostig Program for the Development of Visual Perception.* Chicago: Follett Educational Corporation, 1964.

Getman, G.N. *How to develop your child's intelligence: A research publication.* Luverne, Minnesota: G.N. Getman, 1952.

Gibson, E.J., & Levine, H. *The psychology of reading.* Cambridge, Mass.: MIT Press, 1975.

Glass, G.V. *A critique of experiments on the role of neurological organization in reading performance.* Monograph, Center for Instructional Research and Curriculum Evaluation, University of Illinois, Champaign, Illinois, 1967.

Goodman, L., & Hammill, D. The effectiveness of the Kephart-Getman activities in developing perceptual-motor and cognitive skills. *Focus: Exceptional Children,* 1973, *4,* 121–126.

Hammill, D. Training visual perceptual processes. *Journal of Learning Disabilities,* 1972, *5,* 552–559.

Hebbelinck, M. *A multidisciplinary longitudinal growth study: Introduction of the Project LLEGS.* 21st World Congress of Sports Medicine, Brasilia, Brazil, September 1978.

Held, R., & Freedman, S.J. Plasticity in human sensorimotor control. *Science,* 1962, *142,* 455–462.

Henderson, A., Llorens, L., Gilfoyle, E., Myers, C., & Prevel, S. (Eds.), *The development of sensory integrative theory and practice.* Dubuque, Iowa: Kendall Hunt, 1974.

Johnson, D.L., Brekke, B., & Harlow, S.D. Appropriateness of the motor-free visual perception test when used with the mentally retarded. *Education and Training of the Retarded,* 1977, *3,* 312–315.

Hammill, D., & Weiderholt, J.L. Review of the Frostig Visual Perception Test and the related training program. In L. Mann & D. Sabatino (Eds.), *The first review of special education.* Philadelphia: Lea & Febiger, 1972.

Kanter, R.M., Clark, D.L., Allen, L.C., & Chase, M.F. Effects of vestibular stimulation on nystagmus response and motor performance in the developmentally delayed infant. *Physical Therapy,* 1976, *56,* 414–421.

Keogh, B., & Smith, C.E. Changes in copying ability of young children. *Perceptual and Motor Skills,* 1967, *26,* 773–774.

Kephart, N. *The slow learner in the classroom.* Columbia, Ohio: Charles E. Merrill, 1960.

Kilpatrick, F.P. Two processes in perceptual learning. *Journal of Experimental Psychology,* 1946, *36,* 187–211.

Koppitz, E.M. *The Bender-Gestalt for young children: Research and application 1963–73.* Vol. 2. New York: Grune & Stratton, 1965.

Larson, S.C., & Hammill, D.B. *The relationship of selected visual perceptual abilities to school learning.* Unpublished paper, Department of Psychology, University of Texas, 1964.

Licht, S. Chapter 13: History. In S. Licht (Ed.), *Therapeutic exercise.* 2nd Ed. Baltimore: Waring Press, 1965, pp. 426–471.

Lipsitt, L.P., & Kay, H. Conditioned sucking in the human newborn. *Psychological Sciences,* 1964, *1,* 29–30.

Mann, L. Perceptual training, misdirections and redirections. *American Journal of Orthopsychiatry,* 1970, *40,* 18–23.

McGraw, M.B. *Growth: A study of Johnny and Jimmy.* New York: Hafner, 1966.

Montessori, M. *Montessori's own handbook.* New York: Frederick A. Strokes, 1914.

Mosston, M. *Teaching: From command to discovery.* Belmont, Wadsworth, 1972.

Neman, R. A reply to Zigler and Seitz. *American Journal of Mental Deficiency,* 1975, *79,* 493–505.

Neman, R., Ross, P., McCann, B.M. Menolascino, A., & Heal, L.W. Experimental evaluation of sensorimotor patterning used with mentally retarded children. *American Journal of Mental Deficiency,* 1974, *79,* 372–384.

Newcomer, P., & Hammill, D. Visual perception test for motorically impaired children. *Rehabilitation Literature,* 1973, *34,* 45–46.

Official Statement. The Doman–Delacato treatment of neurologically handicapped children. *Arch, Physical Medicine and Rehabilitation,* 1968, *49,* 183–186.

Piaget, J. *The early growth of logic in the child.* New York: Harper and Row, 1964.

Rarick, G.L., & Dobbins, D.A. Basic components in the motor performance of children from six to nine years of age. *Medicine and Science in Sports,* 1975, *7,* 105–110.

Robbins, M.P., & Glass, G.V. The Doman–Delacato rationale: A critical analysis. In J. Hellmuth (Ed.), *Educational therapy.* Vol. 2. Seattle: Special Child Publications, 1968.

Seefeldt, V. Perceptual-motor programs. In J. Wilmore (Ed.), *Exercise and sport sciences reviews.* Vol. 2. New York: Academic Press, 1974, pp. 265–288.

Siqueland, E.R. Continued sucking and visual reinforcers with human infants. Unpublished paper, Brown University, 1970.

Smith, K.U. Feedback mechanisms of athletic skills and learning. In L.E. Smith (Ed.), *Psychology of motor learning.* Chicago: Athletic Institute, 1970.

Smith, O.W., & Smith, P.C. Developmental studies of spatial judgements by children and adults. *Perceptual and Motor Skills,* 1966, Monograph suppl. *22* (12), 3–73.

Taylor, E.A. Eye movements in reading: Facts and fallacies. *American Educational Research Journal,* 1965, *2,* 187–201.

Tinker, M.A. Recent studies of eye movement in reading, *Psychological Bulletin,* 1958, *55,* 215–231.

Weiderholt, J.L., & Hammill, D. Use of the Frostig-Horne Visual Perceptual Program with kindergarten and first grade economically disadvantaged children. *Psychology in the Schools,* 1971, *8,* 268–274.

Werner, P. Education of selected movement patterns of preschool children. *Perceptual and Motor Skills,* 1974, *39,* 795–798.

White, B.L., & Held, R. Plasticity of sensorimotor development in the human infant. In H. Harlow & C. Woolsey (Eds.), *Biological and biochemical bases of behavior.* Madison: University of Wisconsin Press, 1958.

Whitsell, L.J. Delacato's "neurological organization": A medical appraisal. *California School Health,* 1970, *3,* 1–13.

Wilkinson, D., & Adrian, P. Visual-motor control loop: A linear system? *Journal of Experimental Psychology,* 1971, *89,* 250–257.

Zigler, E., & Seitz, V. On "An experimental evaluation of sensorimotor patterning": A critique. *American Journal of Mental Deficiency,* 1975, *79,* 483–492.

12

Individual Differences in the Interaction of Vision and Proprioception

JACQUELINE M.F. SAMUEL

1. Introduction

In this chapter, I should like to propose that experimental research on individual differences in perception can contribute to the study of perception in general. Investigators have always been concerned about individual differences, but mostly as a source of unwanted variation in their measurements which was beyond their control. However, rarely have personal perceptual habits been studied to learn about perception. I will try to show that this may be worth doing by describing research on the interaction of vision and proprioception. A few studies about audition will be included as well.

Individual differences in the interaction between vision and proprioception can be observed in tasks where both modalities are sources for the same spatial information. That is, the degree of reliance on one modality compared to the other differs from one person to the next. An example is keeping one's balance, a skill that involves both vision and proprioception. When standing on one leg, some people may depend more on their vision for balance than others do and thus fall over more readily after closing their eyes.

JACQUELINE M. F. SAMUEL • Department of Psychology, George Washington University, Washington, D.C. 20006.

This idea of modality preference is not a new one. In 1945, Lowenfeld developed a series of tests for visual and haptic aptitudes. He found that approximately half of his subjects were of the "visual type" and a quarter were of the "haptic type." He defined the extreme "visual type" as a person who relies completely on visual experiences in dealing with the world and who is lost in the dark. Individuals of the extreme "haptic type," however, depend on touch and kinesthesis as much as possible as "intermediaries for their sense impressions" (Lowenfeld, 1945, p. 100).

Even though today such perceptual typologies appear rather exaggerated, they have been given serious consideration in the field of education. For example, Sperry (1973) pointed out that people have different learning styles: proprioceptive, visual, or auditory. The only evidence he offers for such perceptual styles is observational. The assessment of the dominant modality, he suggested, could be achieved, for example, by having the subject relate a movie and then analyze whether motor, visual, or auditory aspects are stressed in the description. Sperry argued that the dominant learning modalities have to be identified in order to adjust the curriculum so that it is most advantageous for the individual.

Until recently, experimental psychologists have all but ignored such individual perceptual biases or preferences. Consequently, the experimental evidence is scarce, but what there is suggests that the individual-differences approach might be a way to study different perceptual strategies in a particular task. Thus, rather than the traditional approach of observing strategy changes following manipulation of a task characteristic, one could observe strategy differences among individuals in the unchanged task.

As was mentioned earlier, the experimental evidence for individual differences in the relationship of vision and proprioception is minimal. However, two experiments stand out as examples. The first experiment, by Warren and Platt (1974), showed that individual differences in aptitude in vision and proprioception affected visual and proprioceptive adaptation to prism-induced lateral shift. This finding suggested that a portion of what is normally considered error variance in research with prisms could be explained by differences in perceptual ability. Taking such ability effects into account might be of practical importance in experiments where the variation tends to be large. This experiment will be described in more detail later.

The second experiment, where vision was not compared to proprioception but to audition, exemplifies how the individual-differences approach could be of theoretical importance. Ingersoll and Di Vesta (1972) presented digits simultaneously aurally and visually. If, in this bisensory task, recall of visual stimuli exceeded recall of auditory stimuli, a subject was classified as a visual attender or someone who preferred vision over audition. Similarly, if auditory stimuli were recalled more often than visual stimuli, a subject was considered an aural attender or someone who showed a preference for the auditory modality.

In a second bisensory task, sets of five words were presented aurally and visually at the same time. Then four of the five words were repeated by the experimenter in a random order and the subject had to write down the missing word. The results showed that on the second task visual attenders recalled more words presented visually than aurally and aural attenders produced more missing words presented aurally than visually. The recall of words in the five positions of the word sequence differed between the two groups. The accuracy of the visual attenders was greatest when the stimulus word to be identified was originally presented at the beginning of the list. This primacy effect was stronger for the visually presented words than for the aurally presented words. Conversely, aural attenders were more accurate in remembering words toward the end of the sequence and this recency effect was stronger for the aurally than for the visually perceived words. The different recall patterns in the two groups indicate differences in information processing as a result of modality preferences. Ingersoll and Di Vesta suggested that "preferences serve as monitoring or filtering systems which control the flow of information within the processing system" (1972, p. 391).

I describe this experiment in some detail because it demonstrates clearly that the investigation of individual differences in intersensory relationships can contribute to the study of information-processing strategies. Similar work comparing visual and proprioceptive preferences has not, to my knowledge, been done.

Keeping in mind that the studies by Warren and Platt and by Ingersoll and Di Vesta represent the kind of approach needed in further research, I will now turn to evidence for individual differences in the interaction between vision and proprioception from a variety of areas in psychology. This evidence is frequently indirect in the sense that individual differences were not the focus of the research. The research comes from experiments in child development, perception of the blind, visual rearrangement, and perceptual style.

2. Developmental Changes in Modality Preference

Bruner's theory of cognitive development provided an explanation as to how modality preferences in adults might come about (Bruner, Olver, & Greenfield, 1966). He argued that cognitive style was characterized by sensory-modality preferences. Knowledge about the environment can be obtained in three major ways: through proprioception, leading to motoric thinking; through vision, leading to figural or spatial thinking; and through audition, leading to verbal thinking. Developmentally, according to Bruner, the preference shifts from proprioceptive to visual to linguistic interaction with the world. Bruner believed that in adults all three modes are used, but that individuals differ greatly in their reliance on one relative to another of these ways of sensory coding. Although Bruner's experimental evidence is meager, his developmental theory has been quite influential.

If the observed modality preferences in adults are related to development, as Bruner suggested, the age changes in intermodality organization may tell us more about how these individual differences originate. Of interest here is the shift from proprioceptive to visual dominance. The motoric involvement of young children in perceptual tasks is well known. Piaget's sensory schemata and the Russian motor-copy theory describe the importance of haptic manipulation of an observed object at an early age. The necessity for this motor activity diminishes with age and at the same time visual analysis improves. Several studies provide evidence for such a change.

Wolff (1972) gave a visual matching-to-sample task in which 4- to 7-year-olds learned to recognize nonsense forms. He observed that some subjects spontaneously traced the outline of the bloblike form with their hands whereas others did not. When hand manipulation was not allowed, several subjects made tracing movements with their heads. The hand and head explorers learned to recognize the standard in an array of similar forms faster than those who depended on vision alone. This haptic facilitation of visual recognition tended to decrease with age, whereas visual recognition significantly increased with age.

Wolff suggested that two visual processes are operating in young children. One involves information obtained from movement and the other does not. The former declines with age and the latter becomes more efficient. He related his results to Noton and Stark's (1971) feature-ring hypothesis, which stated that motoric scanning provides a structural framework within which the feature information has to be processed separately. Wolff indicated that whereas the visual-feature discrimination improves with age, dependence on the motor scan diminishes. It seems that the motor scan that provides a global impression of the object, or a gestalt, is sufficient at an early age but, as discrimination becomes more refined, reliance switches to the more detailed analysis of separate characteristics.

A spatial-localization experiment by Renshaw and Wherry (1931) also showed the decline of proprioceptive efficiency concurrent with a greater reliance on vision as the child grows older. Their subjects, ranging in age from 6 years to adulthood, localized a tactual stimulus on the forearm either by pointing (proprioceptive localization) or by naming the location on a grid imprinted on the stimulated skin area. The errors of visual localization—naming grid location—decreased with age but the pointing errors increased. Proprioceptive localization was superior to visual up to the twelfth year, and after the fourteenth year visual localization became more accurate. The authors talked about a shift in dominance from one modality to the other that occurs around age 13. The blind subjects kept improving in pointing accuracy. H.L. Pick (1974) suggested that these results meant that visual experience in fact interfered with the availability of the tactual information to proprioception.

Vision may interfere intermodally more with age, but it also enhances nonvisual perception. The increased importance of vision for other modalities is apparent in an experiment involving audition. Warren (1970) reported the phenomenon of visual facilitation of auditory localization. When adults had to point to the position of a sound source, accuracy was greater when the subjects kept their eyes open than when their eyes were closed, even though visual information about the auditory-target location was not available. Second and third graders failed to show such a visual facilitation effect. Presumably, a structured visual field provides a spatial reference system for adults that can be used by audition. Thus, developmentally, there appears to be an increase in visual involvement in auditory localization.

Using a perceptual-conflict paradigm, Warren and H.L. Pick (1970) obtained evidence for a decrease with age in reliance on proprioception for spatial localization. They investigated dominance relationships among vision, audition, and proprioception by presenting competing information from two modalities at the same time. Apparently in order to obtain greater intermodal congruency, one modality usually biases perception in the other and vice versa. Conflict with audition was induced by pseudophone displacement of the sound source. Prisms that shifted the visual field laterally produced conflict with vision. Localization responses—hand pointing—indicated where the seen, heard, or felt target was.

Whereas Warren and H.L. Pick were not able to report age changes in visual bias of proprioception (visual capture) or proprioceptive bias of vision, other dominance relationships did shift. The proprioceptive bias of audition decreased with age, and audition biased proprioception more in adults than in second graders. Both these findings indicate a reduced involvement of proprioception. The finding that auditory bias of vision decreased with age supported Warren (1970). This experiment again showed the growing importance of vision in processing spatial information.

H.L. Pick (1974) used the last three studies as supportive evidence for his visual-encoding hypothesis. He suggested that each modality is optimally fit to encode a certain type of information. And for spatial information, vision is the most relevant modality. He speculated that spatial information is visually coded no matter which modality obtained the information. Pick's hypothesis implies that, developmentally, spatial information from other modalities becomes more available to vision, which develops into the spatial coder par excellence, whereas proprioception may specialize in other types of information that are more conducive to the proprioceptive coding characteristics.

Finally, two perceptual illusions, the size–weight and the Ponzo illusions, provided further evidence for a shift away from reliance on proprioception toward greater dependence on vision with age. Warren (1979) cited reports on the size–weight illusion. The visual size information influenced the older subjects more in their weight judgments than the younger ones. This could mean that children are less dependent on vision than adults, but also that they do not have sufficient experience in correlating seen size and felt weight to have built an expectancy of weight on the basis of size. An illusion that occurs both visually and haptically is the Ponzo illusion—the railroad tracks. The magnitude of the visual illusion increased with age until 11 years, after which it remained the same (Crall, 1973). In the tactual version, the effect was well established by age 9 but by age 12 it had totally disappeared.

In both illusions, a greater reliance on vision as the subject gets older partly explains the findings. As vision becomes more important, its capacity to influence perception in other modalities becomes greater. How a decrease in reliance on proprioception results in the disappearance of the tactual Ponzo is not clear. Crall found that in blind subjects the illusion remained in full strength. Again, as in Renshaw and Wherry's experiment of localizing a stimulated skin area, visual experience appears to interfere with haptic processing. Following Pick's hypothesis, it could be that in the sighted subjects, the haptic information on the Ponzo is coded visually increasingly with age and that somehow, in the translation, the illusory effect is lost. In younger children and in the congenitally blind, proprioception can code the Ponzo information directly, and the illusion occurs.

This series of investigations illustrated the developmental change in importance from proprioception to vision. The shift occurred any time from 6 years to 13 years depending on the task. It is quite probable that the shift could also occur earlier or later than this age period with other types of visual-proprioceptive interactions. According to Bruner's position, for some people proprioception remains more important than for others. Thus these individuals, when adult, may rely relatively less on vision compared to proprioception than those who shifted more toward visual dominance. Whether the amount of change depends on specific sensory experience and/or abilities cannot be ascertained from this developmental work. In view of research that will be described later, it is likely that this is the case.

3. Research with the Blind

Comparison of the congenitally blind with the late blind and with sighted individuals is of interest because it shows the effect of visual experience on proprioceptive performance. Experiments mentioned in the previous section indicated that visual experience could enhance perception in another modality (Warren, 1970), but could also impair it (Crall, 1973; Renshaw & Wherry, 1931). Similar effects are reported in the research on perception in the blind. The lack of vision experience in the congenitally blind can lead to either better or worse proprioceptive performance than the sighted. Even though many problems are involved in using congenitally blind as controls when assessing the effects of visual experience (see Warren, 1979), several experiments are worth mentioning in this context. In the tasks in which the blind perform better than the blindfolded sighted, it is either the visual interference that is lacking in the blind or the greater proprioceptive experience that gives the blind an advantage. In other situations the sighted perform better; this is thought to be related to the availability of a visual mental representation that guides proprioceptive behavior. These two types of effects have been observed in both form and spatial perception.

3.1. Form Perception

In simple-form perception, the blind have shown superiority in several skills. Haptic sensitivity to a feature such as curvature was greater in blind than in sighted subjects (Davidson, 1972; A.D. Pick & H.L. Pick, 1966). Again, visual experience seemed to interfere with this type of discrimination, because blind subjects with some visual experience performed more like the sighted subjects. Discrimination of simple dot patterns in a matrix was easier for blind than for sighted subjects (Foulke & Warm, 1967). When the size of the matrix increased, performance of the sighted subjects when blindfolded became superior. The authors felt that the greater proprioceptive experience in the blind aided simple-pattern discrimination, but with increased complexity the ability to visualize the haptic pattern resulted in the better performance of the sighted subjects. Witkin, Oltman, Chase, and Friedman (1971) found blind subjects to be able to tactually extract embedded figures better than blindfolded sighted subjects.

Superior performance was often explained in terms of experience. Familiarity with haptic stimuli leads to improvement in localizing distinctive tactual characteristics. The sighted may never need to develop such skill; or possibly it deteriorates at later stages in development because vision becomes dominant with age and reliance on proprioception diminishes.

Shagan and Goodnow (1973) drew attention to the effect of experience in the proprioceptive modality when it was compared to vision in memory tasks. Posner (1967) had reported that recall of distance information was better when gained by hand than when gained by eye after an intervening classification task. The task required reproducing a distance covered by a moving lever. Posner suggested that this effect was due to coding characteristics that were modality-specific. Shagan and Goodnow believed that experience might provide an alternative explanation. They compared congenitally blind and sighted subjects on Posner's task. The intervening classification task affected the recall of the blind sample more than the sighted, so that the haptic performance of the blind, proprioceptively experienced subjects approached the visual performance of Posner's sighted subjects. The authors concluded that the modality differences should perhaps not be attributed to coding differences between vision and proprioception, but should be ascribed to differences in the experience of judging distance that affect an amodal type of distance coding.

In three-dimensional-form perception, such an experience effect was demonstrated by Davidson, Barnes, and Mullen (1974). They used smooth solid shapes in a matching task where the standard had to be compared to three or to five forms. Blind and blindfolded sighted subjects performed similarly with the three-stimuli comparison array. Thus, haptic experience appeared to have no effect. But when the memory load was greater, in the five-stimuli array, blind subjects showed better retention than the sighted. (Here, as opposed to the complex dot patterns in Foulke and Warm's experiment, the haptic information may not have been as conducive to visual coding.) The authors observed more efficient scanning strategies in the blind than in the sighted subjects. They noted a systematic search by the blind for distinctive features of the shapes and the relationships among them. The sighted subjects mostly used a less advantageous, holistic approach. Comparison of information-gathering techniques seems especially useful because it shows whether the subject uses the optimal strategies for a particular modality or not. It could be that the sighted subjects used a strategy that is more appropriate for vision.

3.2. Spatial Perception

In spatial tasks, performance by the blind depends on whether the body or a body part gives sufficient proprioceptive spatial information or whether a spatial reference system outside the body is involved. In the former type of task, the greater proprioceptive experience of the blind has been shown to be advantageous. Such experience appears to provide a spatial reference system that is based on body dimensions. In the latter type of task, the visual imagery in the sighted seems to assist performance.

Experiments on locomotion with blind and sighted subjects suggest use of a spatial framework based on body experience or visual experience, depending on the required activity (Cratty, 1971). A blindfolded individual who is asked to walk in a straight line tends to veer to one side. This veering tendency was less in the blind, and also less the longer the subject had been blind. The floor's incline or decline was also more easily detected by the blind than by the blindfolded sighted. Cratty believed that sensitivity to such directional changes was related to a spatial framework derived from the body. However, blind subjects who had walked along the perpendicular sides of a right-angle triangle had more difficulty returning to the starting point along the hypotenuse than blindfolded sighted subjects. The external geometric shape was more difficult to negotiate for the congenitally blind than for the late blind and the sighted. Supposedly, this was so because they were not able to visualize the triangle.

A similar effect of body vs. external frame of reference was found in spatial localization. Renshaw and Wherry's (1931) experiment, described earlier, also used blind subjects. Subjects of different ages were asked to point at a previously touched location on a grid printed on the subject's forearm. Blind subjects improved in accuracy with age on this proprioceptive response, whereas blindfolded sighted subjects performed progressively worse. On the other hand, an experiment in which the target area was not on the skin showed different results. A maze-learning task which involved learning the relationships between maze location points was more difficult for blind than for sighted subjects (Koch & Ufkess, 1926). Since longer visual experience before onset of blindness diminished the handicap on the task, the authors concluded that visual imagery helped maze learning.

Visual-imagery involvement in spatial tasks may not be as necessary as is generally believed. Recent evidence indicates that proprioception is capable of providing, even in the sighted, a spatial framework that assists spatial mental manipulations. Possibly, such a framework is used by young children before vision becomes more dominant.

Two experiments have compared mental rotation in the visually handicapped and the sighted (Carpenter & Eisenberg, 1978; Marmor & Zaback, 1976). Mental rotation is measured in terms of the time it takes to compare a rotated, felt form or letter to an upright standard. The response time increases with the stimulus orientation's departure from the upright. The investigators assumed that the response-time change indicated a mental-rotation process. When congenitally blind subjects performed such a task, they were slower than the adventitiously blind, who were in turn slower than the blindfolded sighted subjects. But all subjects showed the same relative increase of response time with greater rotation. The results suggested the use of some spatial representation in mental rotation in the blind (Marmor & Zaback, 1976). Carpenter and Eisenberg corroborated these results. In addition, they demonstrated that sighted subjects did not necessarily code spatial information of the stimulus orientation visually. When the angle of the arm that explored the rotated forms was changed, the response latencies changed. Thus, even the sighted used their body as a reference.

Of course it is possible that an internal spatial reference system develops as a result of spatial experience regardless of the modality through which the information is obtained. Such an amodal representation would be in accordance with E.J. Gibson's theory (1969). On the other hand, such a spatial system may be more or less visually or haptically coded depending on the most experienced modality. According to Pick's hypothesis, visual coding of spatial information is generally the most efficient. This fact explains the faster response time for the sighted subjects in mental rotation. However, the fact that arm position influenced performance indicated that orientation relative to body position is not totally irrelevant in the sighted.

In summary, research with the blind shows two kinds of influence of vision on proprioception: Visual experience either interferes with or assists in proprioceptive performance. The interference seems to stem from the developmental change in the sighted toward visual dominance so that proprioceptive strategies for processing spatial information cease to develop further and may even deteriorate with age. This does not occur in the blind who, consequently, perform better than the sighted on tasks where proprioceptive information-gathering techniques result in more efficient spatial coding (Davidson et al., 1974), or where a spatial reference system derived from the body mediates spatial-information processing (Cratty, 1971; Renshaw & Wherry, 1931). Visual experience appears to assist proprioceptive performance in tasks where the stimuli are so complex that a visual mental image of them is advantageous

(Foulke & Warm, 1967), or where a spatial reference system external to the body can guide proprioceptive functioning (Crall, 1973; Koch & Ufkess, 1926).

4. Prism Adaptation and Visual Capture

The intermodal conflict resulting from exposure to wedge prisms has been used frequently to investigate visual-proprioceptive relationships. The subject compensates for such visual rearrangement by adapting either proprioceptively or visually. The former type of adaptation refers to a change in the position sense of the limb that was viewed through the prisms, and the latter to a change in eye or head position. Often a combination of the two occurs. Investigators have shown that the kind of perceptual experience during exposure to the visual shift determines which modality adapts most. However, some recent evidence indicates that the location of adaptation also depends on the individual's sensory abilities.

Three experiments showed differences among individuals in the adaptability of the sensory components of adaptation to visual rearrangement. Kahane and Auerbach (1973) found a greater prism-induced shift in the felt location of body parts—proprioceptive adaptation—in non-dancers than in dancers. They concluded that the dancers' greater awareness of the location of body parts in relation to one another counteracted proprioceptive adaptation. The dancers were believed to be more sensitive to the intersensory conflict than the nondancers, and resisted assimilation by not adapting as much.

Warren and Platt (1974) pointed out the large between-subjects variation in prism-adaptation work. They suggested that considerable individual differences exist in the use of visual and proprioceptive information. Consequently, they argued, such differences should not be dismissed as error variance. In their first experiment, they found that subjects with good control of eye movements and fixations (as measured by eye-proficiency tests) adapted most in the felt position of the exposed limb, whereas subjects with good control of their body movements and dexterity (as measured by hand- and body-movement tests) tended to adapt more visually. In their next experiment, Warren and Platt (1975) again gave eye- and hand-proficiency tests as well as two different prism-exposure conditions: terminal exposure, where the subject sees his pointing finger only at the end of the pointing movement near the target, and continuous exposure, where he sees the movement throughout. Normally, the former leads to visual adaptation and the latter to proprioceptive adaptation. The results for the terminal-exposure condition showed that the subjects with good eye ability adapted less visually than was expected, whereas subjects proficient in hand ability adapted more. For the continuous exposure, the opposite was the case. The visually proficient subjects adapted more in the felt position of the pointing arm than the proprioceptive subjects. The authors concluded that these differences in adaptation were due to the differences in the sensory abilities.

This research suggests that adaptation takes place in the modality of the least experience or ability. Canon's attention hypothesis (1970, 1971) is particularly relevant to these findings. According to this hypothesis, adaptation occurs in the modality that receives the least attention. Canon examined the effects of allocation of attention on adaptation when information from vision and audition conflicted. The auditory location of a sound source did not coincide with its visual location, but was instead shifted sideways. Subjects who were instructed to attend to the visual location during exposure to the conflicting stimuli showed a greater shift in where the sound was heard (auditory adaptation) than in where it was seen (visual adaptation). Subjects who were instructed to attend to the auditory location showed the opposite effect. They adapted more visually than auditorily.

Kelso, Cook, Olson, and Epstein (1975) tested Canon's hypothesis using prism-induced conflict between vision and proprioception. During the conflict-exposure period, the subjects performed a task that directed their attention toward the visual or toward the proprioceptive modality. The visual-attention condition yielded proprioceptive adaptation, and the proprioceptive-attention condition resulted in visual adaptation. Whereas Canon still found some adaptation in the unattended modality, Kelso *et al.* did not report any. The authors concluded that, in general, the adaptive shift will not take place in the modality that the subject spontaneously selects for his attention, thus making that modality the standard for recalibration of the other modalities.

When these two attention experiments are compared to the Kahane and Auerbach (1973) and the Warren and Platt (1974, 1975) studies, it seems that the modalities with the greatest experience or abilities also receive the most attention. Thus, an individual would attend to a preferred modality in a situation where more than one modality can provide the same information.

4.1. Visual Capture

The use of one modality as the standard for recalibration of another one in a sensory-conflict situation also occurs in the visual-capture phenomenon (Hay, H.L. Pick, & Ikeda, 1965; Tastevin, 1937). *Visual capture* refers to the dominance of vision over proprioception in a prism-induced rearrangement of the visual field. For example, when one looks

at one's hand through a wedge prism, the hand feels to be at the same location as where it is seen. Thus, it is as if the observer considers vision to be more veridical than proprioception and therefore ignores proprioceptive feedback.

However, as opposed to what was previously believed, information from the nondominant modality is not ignored at all. Several experiments (H.L. Pick, Warren, & Hay, 1969; Warren & H.L. Pick, 1970) indicated convincingly that visual capture of the position sense differs in degree depending on the task, and that proprioception biases vision. The visual-proprioceptive conflict does not appear to be resolved in terms of a total dominance of one modality over the other; rather a compromise is made in the reliance on the two sources of information.

This compromise is not unalterable. It depends on task demands and attentional factors. Warren and Cleaves (1971) established that the amount of dominance varies according to the response modality. When they used a visual response, visual capture was greater than when a proprioceptive response was required. The opposite effect resulted for proprioceptive capture of vision. Warren and Schmitt (1978) investigated this plasticity of the dominance relationship further. They developed a procedure whereby exposure to conflicting information was interrupted by either visual or proprioceptive responses in nonconflicting situations. These responses were intended to gear the subject's concentration to one of the two modalities. The result was that the subjects who were exposed to the visual-context training showed a visual bias of proprioception of 67% and a proprioceptive bias of vision of 18%. The proprioceptive-context training had the same effect in the opposite direction, with a proprioceptive bias of vision of 63% and a visual bias of proprioception of 38%. Thus, this experiment demonstrated how, by manipulating the perceptual context, "shifts in weighting of the proprioceptive and visual information available" (Warren & Schmitt, 1978, p. 309) occurred.

These findings support Kelso's (Kelso et al., 1975) contention that the dominance relationships between modalities often depend on allocation of attention. Therefore, like prism adaptation, the capture phenomenon also follows Canon's attention hypothesis. Even though, to my knowledge, no individual differences in the degree of capture have been reported, the attentional effects indicate that there may be some.

5. Rod-and-Frame Experiments

The best-known work on perceptual abilities and individual differences was initiated by Witkin (Witkin, Lewis, Herzman, Machover, Meissner, & Wapner, 1954), who postulated that personality could be

studied through perception. He investigated the role of visual factors in the maintenance of balance and the upright posture, and found that the more the visual field was tilted, the more the body swayed. He developed the rod-and-frame test, a test that involves setting a tilted rod within a tilted frame to the gravitational vertical, which allowed him to measure dependence on the visual field (the tilted frame) and reliance on internal proprioceptive cues. Persons who were greatly influenced by the tilted frame and therefore made errors in their judgments of the vertical were labeled field dependent. Those who could separate the rod position from the frame position were field independent.

Even though the rod-and-frame test is mostly used now as an indicator of personality characteristics, such as a person's cognitive style, body concept, or social skills, experiments involving perceptual skills are of interest here. Thus the term *field independence* refers in this chapter to the ability to make use of visual and/or proprioceptive information.

5.1. Visual Skills

Several experiments have correlated field independence with visual skills. Eye movements were used as a measure of attentional strategies in the rod-and-frame test. (They indicated how characteristics are sampled from the environment.) Process schizophrenics obtained low error scores, but they did not show any of the other analytical skills of field independence (Silverman, 1968). Silverman noted that this unexpected result was possible because these subjects scan minimally. They focused on the rod and simply did not look at the frame. In normal subjects, lower rod-and-frame-test error was associated with more eye movements and with more time fixating on the rod (Boersma, Muir, Walton, & Barham, 1969). Thus, blocking out the frame, involuntarily or voluntarily, and scanning the rod appears to be a successful strategy.

Larger and higher rates of eye movement also led to better performance, but only for field dependents (Blowers & O'Connor, 1978). The investigators argued that faster eye movements prevented time for distraction to register between scans. The finding that for the dependents size and rate of eye movement were unrelated to performance indicated that this group was inefficient in its selective-attention strategies.

Other visual-perception measures that were related to rod-and-frame-test performance included sensitivity to the retinal image and disembedding hidden figures. Subjects who performed well on a size-constancy task, which required them to compare the retinal images of varying circles at different distances—they had to disregard constancy—showed competence in setting the rod to the upright (Gardner, Jackson,

& Messick, 1960). The visual, embedded-figures tests and the rod-and-frame test are highly correlated (Oltman, 1968).

Visual factors that are beyond the subject's control or that are less cognitive also affected the rod-and-frame test. Immergluck (1966) measured a visual afterimage that was longer lasting in field independents than in field dependents. Greenberger (1973) used this finding on differential latencies to explain the Pulfrich effect.

The Pulfrich effect is an illusion that occurs when a pendulum is swinging in a plane perpendicular to the subject's line of sight and is viewed with a filter over one eye. The pendulum appears to be swinging in an elliptical path. Greenberger's field-independent subjects saw a longer vertical axis of the ellipse than the field- dependent subjects. Greenberger proposed that the illusion arises from interference of the afterimage with the present stimulus and, consequently, different afterimage latencies result in different magnitudes of the effect. He concluded that field independence–related differences should be seen as residing in the central nervous system. Similarly, Fine (1973), who found field independents to be more accurate in color and weight discrimination, attributed his results to a general greater sensitivity in the nervous system. Thus, both higher-order visual functioning and simpler-level perceptual processes influenced sensitivity to the gravitational vertical.

5.2. Body Skills

Physical activity and sensitivity to body cues affected perception of the vertical. In a study on physical activity and cognitive functioning, Svinicki, Bundgaard, Schwensohn, and Westgor (1974) classified subjects as active or inactive. Subjects in the former group had a minimum of 5 hr of strenuous physical activity a week, classified themselves as active, and had a history of physical activity. In the latter group, subjects had less than 1 hr of strenuous activity a week, and saw themselves as inactive. The active subjects performed better on the rod-and-frame test than the inactive ones. Perhaps this is related to the finding that high-school women who rated highly in six sports were more field independent than less competent students (Meek & Skubic, 1971), assuming that greater physical activity is associated with better physical skill.

These results are interesting in view of Fine's hypothesis, which stated that general sensitivity of the nervous system could explain field independence. Whether activity leads to sensitivity of the nervous system, or whether sensitivity leads to greater activity, is difficult to say. Perceptual learning and, consequently, discrimination ability depend on activity. At the same time, a well-developed nervous system may seek more stimulation. Thus both explanations may be valid.

Sensitivity to internal body sensations has been correlated with the rod-and-frame test in three experiments. Jacobson (1966) administered the rod-and-frame test before and after 1 hr of sensory deprivation. The deprived subjects showed a lower error score after the procedure, whereas a control group did not. Jacobson concluded that the lack of external stimulation increased the awareness of internal body sensations and thereby their availability for use in orientation tasks. Klepper (1969) reported similar results.

Kurie and Mordkoff (1970) compared the effects of sensory deprivation and somatic concentration on field independence. One hr of concentration on somatic cues, in whatever manner the subject wanted to do this (movement was allowed), improved performance on the rod-and-frame test most. Subjects with 1 hr of sensory deprivation were next, and a control group showed no improvement.

Apparently, sensory deprivation and somatic concentration focus attention on proprioceptive sensation in general. And this increased attention heightens sensitivity to the direction of gravity. The assumption that the effect was confined to the proprioceptive modality is supported by the finding that performance on the visual, embedded-figures test was not affected by the two conditions (Kurie & Mordkoff, 1970).

5.3. Individual Differences and Sports

The research in the previous section related general proprioceptive sensitivity to field independence. This idea appears to be oversimplified, because performance on the rod-and-frame test changes considerably from one branch of sport to another. Barrell and Trippe (1975) compared team sports as well as nongame athletic proficiency. Track-and-field athletes (athletes in hurdle events, running, horizontal and vertical jumping, discus, hammer, and javelin throwing) were more field independent than controls. Next were cricket and soccer players and ballet dancers, and most field dependent were the tennis players, the highly skilled more so than those of medium ability. Pargman, who used an embedded-figures test, obtained similar results (Pargman, 1977; Pargman, Schreiber, & Stein, 1974).

What seems to occur is that athletes, such as tennis players and most team athletes, who have to react to a fast-changing visual situation, with the change caused by movement of other players or objects—ball, racquet, etc.—tend to be field dependent. Athletes such as runners, jumpers, and swimmers, who deal with a stable visual situation where visual change is mostly contingent upon their own movement, and thus predictable, tend to be field independent. In the sports literature, this dichotomy is characterized by the terms "reactive" versus "self-paced" sports.

These results could be explained in terms of focus of attention. For example, the track athlete can concentrate a great deal more on his body than the tennis player, who must focus intensely on subtle visual changes. Thus, the two types of athletes have to rely on a different modality for maximal performance, so that even within the field of sports, different sensory abilities may influence perception and, therefore, achievement.

According to this argument, self-paced athletes are more sensitive to the upright than reactive athletes because they are relatively more sensitive to their body cues and visually less easily distracted. This hypothesis was tested in the research that will be described next.

6. Artists and Athletes

In my own preliminary research on the subject of individual differences, I was interested in the effects of perceptual experience. Warren and Platt (1974, 1975) established that eye and hand ability were related to visual and proprioceptive adaptation to prisms; Kelso et al. (1975) demonstrated the role of attention in adaptation; and many experiments showed that field independence varies with perceptual history or abilities. On this basis I hypothesized that the differences in perceptual experience of artists in the visual arts and athletes should result in differences in performance on tasks where vision and proprioception interact, because the dominance relationship between the two modalities should not be the same in the two groups.

The first of two experiments measured adaptation to prisms and performance on an embedded-figures test in undergraduate students. Before the testing, the subjects rated themselves on a questionnaire assessing their ability and active participation in the visual arts and in sports or dance. The subjects were divided according to their score, above or below average, on both variables. Prism exposure consisted of 4 min of walking in a hallway while wearing base-left prisms. To measure the prisms' effect, the subject marked a visual target with the hand out of view, a procedure that does not distinguish between the visual and proprioceptive components of adaptation. Twelve Gottschaldt figures made up the embedded-figures test. Time for completion with 30 sec added for each error determined the score.

The above-average-athletic subjects adapted less and took longer on the embedded-figures test than those below average. The subjects with above-average experience in the visual arts showed a tendency toward more prism adaptation and were faster in tracing the embedded figures than those who said they were less artistic. Prism adaptation and the embedded-figures test were negatively correlated. This meant that the better the identification of the hidden shapes, the larger the prism adaptation.

It was important to know what type of adaptation had occurred. According to Hay and H.L. Pick's (1966) research, adaptation must have been largely proprioceptive; 4 min of free ambulation was not long enough to elicit much visual adaptation. If most of the adaptation was indeed proprioceptive, and if the questionnaire scores were an indication of visual and proprioceptive abilities, then the results agreed with the findings of Warren and Platt, who found more proprioceptive adaptation in visually apt subjects than in subjects with good proprioceptive skills.

The second experiment showed that the problem was not that simple. The rod-and-frame research indicated that field independence differed considerably among sports. The reactive vs. self-paced dichotomy suggested that when an athlete has to react to a fast-changing visual field, as in team sports and tennis, he tends to be field dependent, whereas visual change contingent on self-initiated body movement, as in the self-paced sports, leads to field independence. The reason appeared to be that reactive athletes pay more attention to vision, whereas self-paced athletes attend more to body cues. This argument led to the expectations that, compared to artists, swimmers (self-paced athletes) would show: (1) less proprioceptive, and (2) more visual adaptation to lateral prismatic shift, and they would be (3) less field independent on the embedded-figures test, because proprioception is not involved, but (4) as field independent on the rod-and-frame test (Oltman's portable apparatus), because of their proprioceptive sensitivity.

The results were disappointing. Performance of the two experimental groups did not differ significantly; the swimmers showed as much visual skill as the artists. This placed in doubt the assumption that self-paced athletes are less visual, because they attend more to their body cues, than reactive athletes. However, an effect of perceptual experience was observed when the artists were compared to a control group. The artists showed greater reliance on vision: they adapted less visually, and they performed better on both field-independence tests.

The prism adaptation in the two experiments and the rod-and-frame scores in the second study confirmed what other investigators found. Sensory interaction is partly dependent upon an individual's perceptual history or ability. In comparing standard deviations of the experimental groups with controls, there was a trend toward less variation among the experimental subjects. This finding supports Warren and Platt's opinion that not all between-subjects variation can be dismissed as error variance, and that in some perceptual research the subject's perceptual background should perhaps be considered.

Two findings in the second experiment indicated that there were qualitative individual differences in perceptual processing. First, in addition to the tasks already mentioned, the subjects also took a balancing test. It consisted of balancing on a stabilometer, both with their eyes open and blindfolded. The blindfolded condition gave a measure of the proprioceptive component in balancing. The difference between eyes-open and blindfolded balancing measured the visual contribution to balancing.

The results showed that the artists relied significantly less on vision in balancing than the control group, whereas in prism adaptation they depended significantly more on the visual modality. The explanation of this apparently paradoxical finding seems to lie in the hypothesis proposed by Trevarthen (1968) concerning two visual systems, ambient and focal vision. Ambient vision involves visual information necessary for orientation of the body in the environment. Focal vision refers to visual information necessary for analyzing pattern structures and activities requiring close eye–hand coordination. Ambient vision is important in the balancing task, whereas focal vision appears to be critical in prism adaptation (eye–hand coordination) and the field-independence tasks. Thus the visual experience of artists seems only to be advantageous in tasks that require focal visual processing, the mode in which the artists normally operate in their work. The fact that the artists relied less on vision than the controls in balancing suggests that the activities that develop focal processing may prevent or interfere with the development of the ambient mode.

The second finding was an informal observation. It appeared that there were two different approaches to the rod-and-frame test. After the testing, I asked 25 subjects how they came to their decision on verticality of the rod. Twenty-one of the answers were easily categorized in visual or proprioceptive strategies. The visual strategies involved visual landmarks as reference points and scanning strategies, such as focusing on the top and bottom edges of the rod, not looking at the frame but focusing on the rod, and using specks of dust inside the apparatus. The proprioceptive strategies were those where body parts were used as reference points: pointing the rod at the feet or perpendicular to the table top that was felt with the arm, alignment with the nose or with the perpendicular plane between the eyes. It seemed that the use of visual strategy led to greater accuracy than a proprioceptive approach, even though this difference did not reach statistical significance. The 11 subjects who used visual reference points obtained an average rod-and-frame score of 9°, whereas the 10 subjects who referred to body parts had an average score of 16°. The visual strategy tended to be more prevalent in the experimental groups than in the control group.

The two strategies showed the characteristics of what Lee (1978) called the exteroceptive and the exproprioceptive modes. The first term, which originated with J.J. Gibson (1966), refers to obtaining information on the layout of the environment. The second refers to relating information about position and movement of the body, or its parts, to the environment.

These two findings with the artists and the swimmers suggest that there might be individual differences in the perceptual modes of processing information, using "modes" in the sense that was recently introduced by H.L. Pick and Saltzman (1978). Perceptual modes are inferred when a single pattern of stimulation can be the source for different types of information, depending on what function that information has for the subject. Modes are ways of processing information that cut across modalities. The types of sensory processing proposed by Trevarthen and by Lee are examples of such modes. Perhaps, rather than looking at preference for one modality compared to another, it might also be useful to look at preference for one mode compared to another. This might tell us more about individual information-processing strategies than would considering each modality separately.

7. Conclusion

The experiments described in this chapter show that individuals differ in their reliance on vision and proprioception in tasks where both modalities are used. The purpose in presenting these studies was to show that knowledge about such perceptual habits can contribute to the study of intermodal relationships in general. Unfortunately, most of the research investigated quantitative differences. In order for the individual-differences approach to relate to studying sensory interaction, qualitative differences in coding and processing information should be examined as well. A beginning has been made by those few studies in which differences in perceptual strategies were observed. Future experiments should focus on identifying a person's perceptual approach to a task. The notion of perceptual modes could provide a useful framework for this purpose.

8. References

Barrell, G.V., & Trippe, H.R. Field dependence and physical ability. *Perceptual and Motor Skills*, 1975, *41*, 216–218.

Blowers, G.H., & O'Connor, K.P. Relation of eye movements to error on the rod-and-frame test. *Perceptual and Motor Skills*, 1978, *46*, 719–725.

Boersma, F.J., Muir, W., Walton, K., & Barham, R. Eye movements during embedded-figures tests. *Perceptual and Motor Skills,* 1969, *28,* 271–274.

Bruner, J.S., Olver, P.R., & Greenfield, P.M. *Studies in cognitive growth.* New York: Wiley, 1966.

Canon, L.K. Directed attention and maladaptive "adaptation" to displacement of the visual field. *Journal of Experimental Psychology,* 1970, *88,* 403–408.

Canon, L.K. Intermodality inconsistency of input and directed attention as determinants of the nature of adaptation. *Journal of Experimental Psychology,* 1971, *84,* 141–147.

Carpenter, P.A., & Eisenberg, P. Mental rotation and the frame of reference in blind and sighted individuals. *Perception and Psychophysics,* 1978, *23,* 117–124.

Crall, A.M. The magnitude of the haptic Ponzo illusion in congenitally blind and sighted subjects as a function of age. *Dissertation Abstracts International,* 1973, *33* (9-B), 5010.

Cratty, B.J. *Movement and spatial awareness in blind children and youth.* Springfield, Illinois: Charles C. Thomas, 1971.

Davidson, P.W. Haptic judgments of curvature by blind and sighted humans. *Journal of Experimental Psychology,* 1972, *93,* 43–55.

Davidson, P.W., Barnes, J.K., & Mullen, G. Differential effects of task memory demand on haptic matching of shape by blind and sighted humans. *Neuropsychologia,* 1974, *12,* 395–397.

Fine, B.J. Field dependence–independence as "sensitivity" of the nervous system: Supportive evidence with color and weight discrimination. *Perceptual and Motor Skills,* 1973, *37,* 287.

Foulke, E., & Warm, J. Effects of complexity and redundancy on the tactual recognition of metric figures. *Perceptual and Motor Skills,* 1967, *25,* 177–187.

Gardner, R., Jackson, D., & Messick, S. Personality organization in cognitive controls and intellectual ability. *Psychological Issues,* 1960, *2,* 8.

Gibson, E.J. *Principles of perceptual learning and development.* New York: Appleton, Century, Crofts, 1969.

Gibson, J.J. *The senses considered as perceptual systems.* Boston: Houghton Mifflin, 1966.

Greenberger, M.D. Individual differences and field dependence in the Pulfrich effect: A re-examination. *Perceptual and Motor Skills,* 1973, *36,* 713–714.

Hay, J.C., & Pick, H.L., Jr. Visual and proprioceptive adaptation to optical displacement of the stimulus. *Journal of Experimental Psychology,* 1966, *71,* 150–158.

Hay, J.C., Pick, H.L., Jr., & Ikeda, K. Visual capture produced by prism spectacles. *Psychonomic Science,* 1965, *2,* 215–217.

Immergluck, L. Figural aftereffects, rate of figure-ground reversal and field dependence. *Psychonomic Science,* 1966, *6,* 45–46.

Ingersoll, G.M., & Di Vesta, F.J. Effects of modality preferences on performance on a bisensory, missing units task. *Journal of Experimental Psychology,* 1972, *93,* 386–391.

Jacobson, G.R. Effect of brief sensory deprivation on field dependence. *Journal of Abnormal Psychology,* 1966, *71,* 115–118.

Kahane, J., & Auerbach, C. Effect of prior body experience on adaptation to visual displacement. *Perception and Psychophysics,* 1973, *13,* 461–466.

Kelso, S.J.A., Cook, E., Olson, M.E., & Epstein, W. Allocation of attention and the locus of adaptation to displaced vision. *Journal of Experimental Psychology: Human Perception and Performance,* 1975, *1,* 237–245.

Klepper, I.L. Induction of field dependence changes by attention procedures. *Perceptual and Motor Skills,* 1969, *29,* 139–145.

Koch, H.L., & Ufkess, J. A comparative study of stylus maze learning by blind and seeing subjects. *Journal of Experimental Psychology,* 1926, *9,* 118–131.

Kurie, G.D., & Mordkoff, A.M. Effects of brief sensory deprivation and somatic concentration on two measures of field dependence. *Perceptual and Motor Skills*, 1970, *31*, 683–687.

Lee, D.N. The functions of vision. In H.L. Pick, Jr., & E. Saltzman (Eds.), *Modes of perceiving and processing information*. New York: Wiley, 1978.

Lowenfeld, V. Tests of visual and haptic aptitudes. *American Journal of Psychology*, 1945, *58*, 100–111.

Marmor, G.S., & Zaback, L.A. Mental rotation by the blind: Does mental rotation depend on visual imagery? *Journal of Experimental Psychology: Human Perception and Performance*, 1976, *2*, 515–521.

Meek, F., & Skubic, V. Spatial perception of highly skilled and poorly skilled females. *Perceptual and Motor Skills*, 1971, *33*, 1309–1310.

Noton, D., & Stark, L. Eye movements and visual perception. *Scientific American*, 1971, *224*, 34–43.

Oltman, P.K. A portable rod-and-frame apparatus. *Perceptual and Motor Skills*, 1968, *26*, 503–506.

Pargman, D. Perceptual cognitive ability as a function of race, sex and academic achievement in college athletes. *International Journal of Sport Psychology*, 1977, *8*, 79–91.

Pargman, D., Schreiber, L.E., & Stein, F. Field dependence of selected athletic groups. *Medicine in Science and Sports*, 1974, *6*, 283–286.

Pick, A.D., & Pick, H.L., Jr. A developmental study of tactual discrimination in blind and sighted children and adults. *Psychonomic Science*, 1966, *6*, 367–368.

Pick, H.L., Jr. Visual coding of non-visual spatial information. In R.B. MacLeod & H.L. Pick, Jr. (Eds.), *Perception: Essays in honor of James J. Gibson*. Ithaca: Cornell University Press, 1974.

Pick, H.L., Jr., & Saltzman, E. *Modes of perceiving and processing information*. New York: Wiley, 1978.

Pick, H.L., Jr., Warren, D.H., & Hay, J.C. Sensory conflict in judgments of spatial direction. *Perception and Psychophysics*, 1969, *6*, 203–205.

Posner, M. Characteristics of visual and kinesthetic memory codes. *Journal of Experimental Psychology*, 1967, *75*, 103–107.

Renshaw, S., & Wherry, R.J. The age of onset of ocular dominance. *Journal of Genetic Psychology*, 1931, *39*, 493–496.

Shagan, J., & Goodnow, J. Recall of haptic information by blind and sighted individuals. *Journal of Experimental Psychology*, 1973, *101*, 221–226.

Silverman, J. Towards a more complex formulation of rod-and-frame performance in the schizophrenics. *Perceptual and Motor Skills*, 1968, *27*, 1111–1114.

Sperry, L. Counsellors and learning styles. *Personnel and Guidance Journal*, 1973, *51*, 478–483.

Svinicki, J.G., Bundgaard, C.J., Schwensohn, C.H., & Westgor, D.J. Physical activity and visual field dependency. *Perceptual and Motor Skills*, 1974, *39*, 1237–1238.

Tastevin, J. En partant de l'experience d'Aristote. *L'encephale*, 1937, *1*, 57–84, 140–158.

Trevarthen, C.B. Two mechanisms of vision in primates. *Psychologische Forschung*, 1968, *31*, 299–337.

Warren, D.H. Intermodality interactions in spatial localization. *Cognitive Psychology*, 1970, *1*, 114–133.

Warren, D.H. Perception by the blind. In E.C. Carterette & M.P. Friedman (Eds.), *Handbook of perception*. Vol. 10. New York: Academic Press, 1979.

Warren, D.H., & Cleaves, W.T. Visual proprioceptive interaction under large amounts of conflict. *Journal of Experimental Psychology*, 1971, *90*, 206–214.

Warren, D.H., & Pick, H.L., Jr. Intermodality relations in localization in blind and sighted people. *Perception and Psychophysics*, 1970, *8*, 430–432.

Warren, D.H., & Platt, B.B. The subject: A neglected factor in recombination research. *Perception,* 1974, *3,* 421–438.

Warren, D.H., & Platt, B.B. Understanding prism adaptation: An individual difference approach. *Perception and Psychophysics,* 1975, *17,* 337–345.

Warren, D.H., & Schmitt, T.L. On the plasticity of visual-proprioceptive bias effects. *Journal of Experimental Psychology: Human Perception and Performance,* 1978, *4,* 302–310.

Witkin, H.A., Lewis, H.B., Herzman, M., Machover, K., Meissner P., & Wapner, S. *Personality through perception.* New York: Harper, 1954.

Witkin, H.A., Oltman, P.K., Chase, J.B., & Friedman, F. Cognitive patterning in the blind. In J. Helmuth (Ed.), *Cognitive studies.* New York: Brunner-Mazel, 1971.

Wolff, P. The role of stimulus-correlated activity in children's recognition of nonsense-forms. *Journal of Experimental Child Psychology,* 1972, *14,* 427–441.

Author Index

Subject Index